# STORIES ABOUT STORYTELLERS

*Publishing*
Alice Munro, Robertson Davies,
Alistair MacLeod, Pierre Trudeau, and Others

*by* Douglas Gibson

*with illustrations by* Anthony Jenkins

ECW Press

Published by ECW Press
2120 Queen Street East, Suite 200, Toronto, Ontario, Canada M4E 1E2
416-694-3348 / info@ecwpress.com

Library and Archives Canada Cataloguing in Publication

Gibson, Douglas
Stories about storytellers : publishing Alice Munro, Robertson Davies, Alistair MacLeod, Pierre Trudeau, and others / Douglas Gibson.

ISBN 978-1-77041-068-8
Also issued in electronic formats
978-1-77090-049-3 (EPUB); 978-1-77090-050-9 (PDF)

1. Gibson, Douglas. 2. McClelland and Stewart Limited — History. 3. Publishers and publishing — Canada — Biography. I. Title.

Z483.G53A3 2011          070.92          C2011-902828-x

Editor for the press: Jennifer Knoch
Cover design: David Gee
Text design: Tania Craan
Typesetting: Mary Bowness
Printing: Friesens  1  2  3  4  5

The publication of *Stories About Storytellers* has been generously supported by the Canada Council for the Arts which last year invested $20.1 million in writing and publishing throughout Canada, and by the Ontario Arts Council, an agency of the Government of Ontario. We also acknowledge the financial support of the Government of Canada through the Canada Book Fund for our publishing activities, and the contribution of the Government of Ontario through the Ontario Book Publishing Tax Credit. The marketing of this book was made possible with the support of the Ontario Media Development Corporation.

Canada Council   Conseil des Arts
for the Arts      du Canada

Canadä

ONTARIO ARTS COUNCIL
CONSEIL DES ARTS DE L'ONTARIO

Printed and bound in Canada

MIX
Paper from
responsible sources
FSC® C016245

To four Gibson Girls —

Jane, Jenny, Meg, and Katie

# TABLE OF CONTENTS

# *by* Alice Munro

One of my favourite things to read is a tightly packed and punchy piece of biography, or, as you might call it, biographical observation. Finding out about people who seem to have become somewhat special — it's addictive. Maybe we think it will become instructive. I don't know. I do enjoy it.

Some are famous, it seems, because they always knew they would be. Others won't admit they are famous at all. (These are mostly Canadians, and over 50.) And there are rare people who just don't notice, because they are busy all the time doing something more worthy and exciting.

Doug Gibson has met a number of these people, and tells about it in this book. He is their editor and their publisher. He tells us something about what they're like, catching them in dire, or proud, or funny moments, when they are preparing for, enduring, enjoying, or living down whatever limelight falls on them. He's the man who helped them to get there.

He sees them in less fateful moments, too, if they have any. He deals with them, on these pages, with lots of good humour and observes them in ways that are acute, but mostly understanding. He is not easily dismayed.

People in this book have latched onto their fame in various ways, but it's the writers — fiction writers — that I go after. I don't care (much) who they might be having an affair with, or who they're not speaking to, and that's a good thing, because in this book I'm not going to find out. What I want to know is how they manage the separation — or the lack of it — between writing and life. What about their behaviour when they're recognized in public? The dismay when they're not? Do public readings throw them? Or buoy them up? Or both? Do they ever feel like a fraud? Is writing competing with real life or could they not tell the two things apart? Did all of them have wonderful wives? (Yes. Yes.)

And here is a digression. I am noting that nearly all of them are of the gender that has wives, and the very stroke of my pen could get grumpy, but I have to tell you this was never Mr. Gibson's fault. He was as determined to spot, harass, encourage, and publish a female writer as anybody could possibly be. There just weren't many of us around.

Do I discover what I'm looking for about writers, do I get some idea of the everyday, unique person? Oh, yes. Some are bare-boned organizers, while some are ready to dance on tables, often showing that strange mix of humiliation and self-exposure that makes for a bumpy life and fine fiction.

There are the writers, of course, who go around marvellously disguised as perfectly normal human beings and are not much fun. There's another type of storyteller, too. They don't invent much. They pick up yarns and tales and pass them along as they go. Doug has some of them in his pocket as well. He has paid attention to the stories, the ways of life, belonging to those whose lives have meant a lot more to them than literature of any sort, who just like to tell you about something, then let it fall by the way.

A remarkable mix, this book.

And because of that, I have to break off from fiction, even though I believe it's in every breath we draw. Even in the story sworn as true, and provided with names, about the Mean-Daughter-In-Law that I heard in Tim Hortons the other day.

We have to bow to all the non-fiction writers here as well, prime ministers and others, and to all the accounts of events that really happened and maybe even changed the world forever. And make another bow to the once-living (or still-living) amazing characters, often beyond anything you'd get away within a mere story, faithfully produced in this book. As a former bookseller I know that here's what your father, your grandfather, or any other fiction-snooting fellow wants as a gift on important occasions. I have to say that the stories are interesting, sometimes compelling. Doug feels a powerful interest, and so will you. So do I.

Here I am, giving this book its due, and reading it with appetite and pleasure. How else would I ever know what the suave and delightful Charles Ritchie said to the thoroughly unpleasant Edward Heath?

So here is my prize read for people who are interested in books, writers, Canada, life, and all that kind of thing.

Thanks, Doug.

CHAPTER 1                                               1869–1944

# STEPHEN
# LEACOCK

Professor, Humorist, and Immigration Agent

It was Stephen Leacock who brought me to Canada. Not literally, of course, for he died in March 1944, when I was only three months old — which, I suppose, in a way makes us contemporaries. But his books set me giggling and snorting as a kid in Scotland spending the lunch hour sheltering from the Glasgow rain in our high school's library. There his *Nonsense Novels* and *Literary Lapses* were my favourite reading. I chortled — Lewis Carroll's invented word for "chuckle and snort" is exactly right — over people riding off madly in all directions, and at immortal lines like "'John!' pleaded Anna, 'leave alone the buttermilk. It only maddens you. No good ever came of that.'"

I knew that Leacock was Canadian, but recognized that he had a shrewd take on Scots and Scotland, and on the attitude that had long ago produced my favourite line of old Scottish poetry, "The English, for once, by guile won the day." For instance, in "Hannah of the Highlands," Leacock's opening lines describe a typical heathery landscape where various Scottish heroes had rested (in one especially heroic case, pausing to change his breeches) while escaping or hiding from the English. In the course of this story Hannah's father shows his Scottish pride when he learns that she has accepted a silver coin from a member of a rival clan with which he is feuding.

"Siller!" shrieked the Highlander. "Siller from a McWhinus!"

Hannah handed him the sixpence. Oyster McOyster dashed it fiercely on the ground, then picking it up he dashed it with full force against the wall of the cottage. Then, seizing it again he dashed it angrily into the pocket of his kilt.

Later, in Winnipeg in 1982, I was to see a real-life example of such pride. Ed Schreyer had used his vice-regal position to steer the Governor General's Awards ceremonies to his hometown, and I was there at the Fort Garry Hotel auditorium to receive the Governor

General's Award for Fiction (English) on behalf of Mavis Gallant, who was stuck in Paris with a broken ankle.

These were difficult days for federal supporters in Quebec, and the person accepting the French-language fiction award was clearly not among them. From the stage he made a fiery separatist speech, entirely in French, denouncing the event, Canada, English-speaking Canadians in general and the Governor General and the audience in particular, then showed his utter contempt for the award by taking the winner's cheque and dashing it angrily into his pocket.

The unilingual audience of polite Winnipeggers applauded him warmly.

As the next speaker, I tried to rise to the occasion. I gave the first half of Mavis's acceptance speech (for, as luck would have it, a book entitled *Home Truths*) in my harsh French. This, I like to think, was painful to my separatist predecessor's ears. Certainly, my *savoir faire* seemed to impress the Winnipeg audience. Polite applause again.

Leacock, of course, knew Winnipeg well. It was for that city that his father set off from the Old Homestead near Lake Simcoe with his fast-talking brother, E.P., to make their fortunes as land agents, only to return to Ontario flat broke. Many years later, after his own much more profitable visits as a speech-giving celebrity, Leacock produced his famous line about Winnipeg's challenging winter climate. He noted that when a man stands in winter at the corner of Portage and Main with a north wind blowing "he knows which side of him is which."

A twenty-minute walk from the Fort Garry Hotel, if you go via Portage and Main, lies the University of Winnipeg, where my friend Ian McDougall spent his career teaching Classics. It was Ian who, back in that Glasgow Academy library, hired me (at zero salary) to be an official lunch-hour librarian — thus, arguably, setting me stumbling towards a literary career.

I was not a good librarian. I kept sloppy records, and even resetting the date stamp remained an inky mystery to me, but I did read lots of Leacock. (And over the years, I should note, that school library has nourished authors all the way from George MacDonald Fraser — of Flashman and McAuslan fame — to historians Norman Stone, Walter Reid, and Niall Ferguson.) And in due course, like my friend Ian, I went on to attend the University of St. Andrews, for four happy years.

There Leacock crossed my path again. Not only because of his witty remarks about golf, which were much-quoted in that Royal and Ancient town, "the home of golf." After a tour of Scotland (where he claimed that during two or three pleasant weeks spent lecturing there, he "never on any occasion saw whisky made use of *as a beverage.* I have seen people take it, of course, as a medicine, or as a precaution, or as a wise offset against a rather treacherous climate; but as a beverage, never") he noted that even in Sabbath-respecting Scotland, rules against Sunday sports did not apply to golf, since golf was not, strictly speaking, a sport, but rather "a form of moral effort." St. Andrews people agreed without question, especially after missing a short putt.

Another acceptable Sunday activity in St. Andrews was to attend the Film Society, which brought what we would now call "art house films" to the little university town, extending our education to include people like Antonioni, Kurosawa, and Eisenstein. Ingmar Bergman's films were a regular feature, often set beside the same sort of chilly seas that washed against our local beaches. Later these cold sands were to gain movie immortality as the barefoot runners at the start of *Chariots of Fire* splashed across them.

To lighten this solemn highbrow fare ("The horses are slipping on the ice!" one famous subtitle ran, while another had a sad Swedish woman confiding to another, "I hate the smell of semen"), the program always included short films. And the greatest of these was Stephen Leacock's *My Financial Career.* From the opening line, "When I go into a bank I get rattled," this was a faithful, deadpan rendering of Leacock's classic story, which I knew almost by heart. I watched it with delight — and with amazement, when I saw that this witty cartoon had been produced by the National Film Board of Canada.

It struck me then that any country that spent public money producing fine pieces of comedy based on a local writer's work must be something special. As a subtle piece of advertising for a country's culture, it worked on me then, and it still does. I began to think seriously about heading off to Canada after graduation, to see this place for myself.

For a Scot, moving to Canada was hardly a stretch. My grandmother's sister had left Ayrshire in 1903 to homestead with her new husband on the open prairie northwest of Saskatoon, a couple of years before Saskatchewan became a province. As a result, my father's cousins were spread across the West, so that Arelee, Lethbridge, and Fairview rivalled Montreal, Toronto, and Vancouver in importance in our mailbox. One cousin, Ian Robertson, spent his RCAF leaves at my parents' house in Dunlop, until a bombing run over Germany swallowed him up.

Now, courtesy of Stephen Leacock, Canada was in my sights.

A graduate scholarship to Yale in September 1966 brought me within striking distance. Towards the end of the year that earned me an M.A., some of my Yale friends returned to Connecticut wide-eyed from a spring visit to Expo in Montreal, confirming the wisdom of my plan. So I left New Haven and set off across the continent in a great clockwise loop that would take me to Canada's west coast. For almost ninety-nine days I used my ninety-nine-dollar Greyhound bus pass, learning tricks like the best seat in the bus to sleep free from oncoming headlights, how to find a good café near a bus station, and the best way to stow a battered suitcase and a smelly rucksack.

This was the summer that American inner cities burned, but much more important to me, it was also the Summer of Love. So instead of Stephen Leacock my inspiration came from Bob Dylan and Joan Baez as I drifted hopefully around Haight-Ashbury and the Golden Gate Park in my very hip black cord jacket (later to be worn, ironically, to their Toronto high school by my disrespectful daughters). Eventually I arrived in Victoria in my role as a Scottish immigrant with a very poor sense of direction. I was the only passenger on the ferry from Seattle who planned to immigrate — people stared when I spoke up and was led away — and it turned out that I was very unprepared, lacking medical papers and other prudent evidence of sensible planning for such a big step.

But my immigration officer was wonderfully reassuring. Leacock, you recall, once wrote that a person gains an Oxford education by sitting with his or her tutor and being "smoked at" by the tutor puffing on his pipe. I gained admittance to Canada amid a tableful of teacups, being "drunk at" by a kindly immigration man in his shirtsleeves who helped me to fill in the unconsidered forms. And I mean helped. "It doesn't matter if you don't have an address in Fairview . . . it's a small enough place we don't need it." At one point he asked me about what sort of career I had in mind. I realized that with a couple of degrees, my summer jobs stacking bales of hay, rowing boats, and shovelling wet cement were not really worth mentioning, and hesitantly suggested that I was interested in working in journalism, maybe, um, even in book publishing. He grunted, encouragingly, and wrote something down. He was, as I say, a kind man.

The only crisis arose when he looked at his watch in alarm and said, "Hey, if you're heading on to Vancouver, there's a bus going in fifteen minutes. Let me just show you the way to the bus station. It's very close."

And so it was, and I caught the bus, missing the chance to roam around Victoria, where I would probably have found Munro's Books, with a good chance that a young, still-unpublished writer named Alice might have been behind the counter. It took a few years for us to meet, but in the end we got together. We've now worked with each other on twelve books, and counting.

The story leaps across half a continent, where about thirty hours east of Winnipeg I noticed that the endless lakes and rocks and pines outside the Greyhound bus window were giving way to fields and farms and maple trees, and soon we were approaching a sunny little town of orange brick named, according to the signs . . . Orillia. I wasn't at my most alert. Wait a minute! Surely this was the place that Leacock had . . . and of course it was, and in a sense I had arrived at the Canada I was seeking, even though we spent only a few minutes there, loading the bus for the remaining stages to Barrie and Toronto. But we got to stretch our legs, and the sun was shining, and the little town did indeed look like a scene "of deep and unbroken peace" — although I knew that, in reality, the place was "a perfect hive of activity."

In Toronto I spent a fair number of weeks in a sleeping bag on friends' floors, looking for work that would give me the essential "Canadian experience." I found my first job in Hamilton, working in the McMaster University administration for the registrar, Jack Evans. (McMaster was so good to me that I was glad to donate my publishing papers to Archivist Carl Spadoni when the time came, forty years later.) Then in March 1968, after replying to a *Globe and*

*Mail* want ad for a "Trainee Editor," I started work in downtown Toronto at Doubleday Canada — and very soon found myself at work on my first non-fiction book already under contract. It was, of course, a biography of Stephen Leacock.

The author was David M. Legate, a legendary figure in the Canadian book world as the literary editor at the *Montreal Star*, at that time a major newspaper in a city with two thriving English daily rivals. He had signed a two-book contract with the man who had hired me, the amiable and energetic David Manuel, and had gained the contract on the strength of three things: his reputation, his fund of fine tales of the book world and its denizens, and his long association with Leacock, which began in 1923, when young Legate signed up for Professor Leacock's course in Political Economy at McGill.

David Legate was born in Australia, as the title of his first book of memoirs, *Fair Dinkum* (which might be translated as "the real stuff") indicates. But I know that my boss was disappointed that Legate had chosen to hold back some of his best literary stories from that first, only fairly dinkum volume, in order to bolster a second volume. The fact that no second volume ever appeared is a lesson for all those who write their memoirs.

One story that never appeared — though Legate, a good, cackling raconteur, delighted me with his verbal account — described the time when as an undergraduate he managed to get the perfect summer job for a *McGill Daily* writer with literary aspirations. He was hired by a major Montreal newspaper to assist in the book review section that was run with an iron hand by a Great Canadian Literary Authority. After a few weeks of learning the ropes, young Legate was allowed to take over the section, inserting the reviews written by the G.C.L.A. as required, while the Great Man went on vacation.

The Monday after a major review ran in the paper, an indignant lady showed up at the newspaper office, demanding to see the Great Man. Young Legate received her in his absence and was appalled when she produced the Great Man's recent signed book review, and also a review by another hand from a London magazine some months earlier, which matched the Montreal book review word for word.

Legate was flabbergasted. He lost sleep over how on earth to handle this undeniable case of plagiarism (almost a capital offence in the newspaper world, then as now) by his legendary boss. Finally, the day of reckoning arrived, the day a great and honoured career would perhaps collapse in . . . who knew?

"Anything happen while I was away?" asked the tanned Great Man, settling into his office chair.

"Well . . . this," squeaked Legate, pushing the two dated reviews across his desk.

The Great Man looked at them. His brow darkened. He rose, smashed a fist on the desktop and bellowed. "Why wasn't I informed about this?"

Then he stormed out of the office, leaving Legate agape.

Later, when it became clear that nothing further was to be said or done about the incident, Legate absorbed a valuable life lesson, that attack is often the best form of defence.

Not that Legate really needed instruction in this matter. The last lines of his preface to the 1970 book, *Stephen Leacock: A Biography*, catch the man's combative side. "A final note. This book was written without any assistance from the Canada Council, which refused my application for a grant-in-aid."

Earlier, the preface speaks of his youthful fascination with Leacock, thanks to his father, a Presbyterian minister in New Brunswick. Since his old man was so clearly delighted by Leacock's work, Legate

quickly developed the habit of visiting the local public library every Saturday morning to borrow a Leacock volume. My judgment of my father's judgment was soon confirmed. Here was sparkling fun. But along came a black Saturday. As usual, I had blindly pulled off the shelf a Leacock title and taken it home. What I read dismayed me. It was deadly dull. Leacock had lost his touch. I informed my father, who hastened to point to the title, *Elements of Political Science*.

It was Stephen Leacock who brought him to McGill University (and who later enjoyed hearing the story of young Legate's textbook case of reader's disappointment). *Fair Dinkum* records that making an application to this university in distant Montreal, "where the teaching staff included a person I devoutly wanted to meet in person, Stephen Leacock," was not easy. "Since I had not sat for my matriculation (Principal Miles of the Saint John High School dismissed the idea, noting that he didn't want the name of the school 'dragged in the mud') some sort of ingenuity was required in filing the application." So with what he described as "untamed superciliousness," he wrote to McGill's registrar stating that he had looked over the 1923 freshman year curriculum and decided that he really deserved to be *admitted to the sophomore year* in Arts.

Incredibly, acceptance followed. Only later did he learn that the letter so outraged the McGill authorities that they decided to make an example of him, with the principal himself, Sir Arthur Currie, roaring, in his best military style, "Admit him and pluck him."

Somehow, David Legate survived, going on to become the editor of *The McGill Daily*, and a Big Man on Campus. Even better, he met an interesting classmate named Marjorie, and their marriage lasted all their lives. And he did spend a great deal of time studying under — and studying — Stephen Leacock, who revelled in the academic life, tattered gown and all. The long vacations were especially appealing to Leacock: "I thus have what a businessman can never enjoy, an ability to think, and, what is still better, to stop thinking altogether for months at a time."

Young Legate revealed his uncanny ability to be part of the most interesting action when he was present at the Punch Felt Around the World. The famous magician Harry Houdini was in Montreal, and was boasting to Legate and a group of student friends that his stomach muscles were so strong that they could take any punch. They were invited to try (we can imagine the assurances, "Go on, as hard as you like!"). A McGill pal of Legate's, a heavyweight boxer, stepped forward and obediently threw a punch. It ultimately killed Houdini, who died in the U.S. a few days later. For a brief period of fame newsmen researching the incident reported that Legate was the man with the deadly punch.

Fisticuffs were involved in ending his academic career. Graduate students, past and present, right across the land will be impressed to hear that Legate's time as a grad student at McGill's English department ended when he got into a physical fight, in the corridor, with the dean of arts, Cyrus MacMillan. Having struck out, in every sense, he marched down to St. James Street to join the *Montreal Star* as a journalist, as nature surely intended.

His career was interrupted by the Second World War, where he served with the Royal Canadian Army Medical Corps in London during the Blitz, then switched to become assistant overseas commissioner of the Canadian Red Cross. And from these days one literary story did slip through his self-imposed barriers. On an introductory tour to meet the Red Cross staff in the London office, he came across four mature lady volunteers sitting at a table armed with scissors, glue, and strips of linoleum. They were gallantly pasting the linoleum on to paperback book covers, to provide sturdy reading for patients in Canadian hospitals. *Fair Dinkum* records what happened next:

"Trying to think of something to say, I patted one lady on the back and allowed as how, who knows, she might be an author herself one day."

His tour guide reacted strangely, and back in his office was clearly in the grip of some deep emotion as he asked, "Do you know who you were speaking to?"

"'No. Who?'

'Agatha Christie.'"

As we worked together on his Leacock biography, this was the man who kindly made it his business to show me Montreal. Later, when I published William Weintraub's marvellous look at Montreal in the forties and fifties, *City Unique*, with its accounts (second-hand, of course) of brothels and gambling dens and cops looking away, I realized that Legate had given me, a beardless boy, a censored version of his city.

He was a founding member and a regular attendee — even after his pancreas took him off the booze — at the Montreal Men's Press Club. The name is significant, and reminds us that Mavis Gallant had left her successful Montreal newspaper column in 1950 to move to Paris at least partly because she realized that in Montreal she could never be "one of the boys." David Legate kindly took me there, and the bar area was full of amiable legends with names like Dink and Red (and indeed I later published Red Fisher's hockey-beat memoirs). Great journalism war stories were paraded, not always for the first time, including the tale of How Legate Scooped the World.

The Westminster Abbey coronation of Queen Elizabeth in 1953 included several hundred reporters from across the world, and they were kept on the premises, in a metaphorical lock up, until the ceremony had ended. David Legate, however, "fainted" and was carried out, ignoring offers of brandy and gasping for "fresh air." Once free of the Abbey, he scampered off through the fine fresh air and filed his "I was there" story first in all the world. I politely pretended to be more impressed than I was, since watching it at home on black-and-white TV, I had been "there," too, but in the scoop-crazy Press Club that was clearly a minority opinion.

Like the legendary Normandy Room, ideal for special dates and fine dining, the Press Club was then located in the Mount Royal Hotel (now deceased, transformed into a shopping mall). I stayed at this fine central hostelry for every Montreal visit. So did another Doubleday Canada employee, a salesman named Bruce. Now Bruce, I must insist, was a man of great probity and a controlled imagination, and yet he had almost incredible adventures at this hotel unique. Once, retiring to bed in his sober Toronto pajamas, he happened to pause at the window looking out across the hotel's interior well. A woman at a window opposite noticed him and proceeded to stage a striptease that may have been impromptu, but was impassioned, and slow, and very impressively complete. On another occasion Bruce was wakened by a midnight thud at his hotel room door. Opening it, he found a man and a woman wrestling, naked, on the corridor carpet outside. Since they seemed evenly matched (although one must have had a sore heel from banging it against his door, in mid-tumble), he thought it best to leave them to it.

Ah, Montreal.

It was then, of course, indisputably Canada's greatest city, and St. James Street, where David Legate's office lay, still represented Canada's financial centre, and had not yet become Rue St. Jacques. Those immediate post-Expo years were exciting ones, with an unconventional Montreal intellectual in Ottawa as prime minister, and a future one working his way up from Baie Comeau through a downtown Montreal law firm in Place Ville Marie itself, the sky-scraper at the heart of the smart new city. The October Revolution and the murder of Pierre Laporte were still to come.

Montreal was Leacock's home for forty years, and among his sixty or so books was one about the city. Legate directed me to areas that Leacock would have recognized easily, despite the twenty-five years that had passed since his death. The McGill campus would have been especially interesting to him, now that the main building at the top of the avenue off Sherbrooke was named after him. And west and north of McGill, despite the invasion of new apartment buildings, he would have recognized the surviving grand old mansions of the former "Square Mile," many of them family homes of the "idle rich" that he had enjoyed mixing with, and drinking with, because, as he said . . . "I like the drinks they mix."

As we put the book together, I was pleased to be escorted into Leacock's old haunt, the University Club (not an exact copy of his Mausoleum Club), where he was a founding member, and his portrait by Richard Jack could be seen hanging in a place of honour above the fireplace. Club fireplaces, I learned, are especially important in Montreal. Apparently another club saw the dictatorial Premier Maurice Duplessis stride in (uninvited), unzip his pants (also uninvited), and urinate into the fireplace to demonstrate his contempt for the institution and its members. Some might dismiss it as just letting off steam, but others understood the serious message. And they also understood how essential Jean Lesage's Quiet Revolution was if Quebec was to catch up to the modern world.

Over the years in publishing, I learned that portraits, either by photographers or painters, are important, since they show the face the subject wishes to present to the world when they are allowed to pose — a significant word. That Leacock painting by Richard Jack was what we chose to put on the front cover. It was exactly right for the book, showing a tweedy, rumpled Leacock sitting there, his tie askew, fresh from marking student essays with the red pencil in his hand. And on his squarely handsome, grizzled face he has the "old-boyish" grin we all know, the one that perfectly represents the chuckling humorist every reader imagines him to be.

And I fear that it was misleading.

In my experience, every humorous writer finds that his or her public confidently expects them to be a happy person, facing life with a wry chuckle, and perhaps a slow, smiling shake of the head. To his great credit, Leacock tried to shoot down this view. He wrote: "If a man has a genuine sense of humour he is apt to take a somewhat melancholy, or at least a disillusioned view of life. Humour and disillusionment are twin sisters."

Robertson Davies (who knew more than most people about the expectations placed on successful authors in their private lives) wrote in his 1981 introduction to *The Penguin Stephen Leacock*, "I have written a good deal about Leacock, and I believe that I was the first to press the point that he was not necessarily a man of continuously sunny, carefree temperament. . . . He had, in fact, the temperament of a humorist, and they are by no means unfailingly sunny people."

Leacock's life was not short of events that would have disillusioned anyone. His family (of, eventually, eleven children) came from England to rural Ontario and a life of genteel poverty (the boys were not allowed to go barefoot in the summer, like the other local kids; a matter, Leacock later said, "of caste and thistles"). The father, Peter, was a Catholic whose runaway marriage was never accepted by his wife's Anglican family (and to make matters worse the bride was older, and may have been pregnant). Peter was excellent at provoking pregnancies, but less productive with his work on the farm near Sutton, just south of Lake Simcoe. He is politely described by the notable Leacock scholar David Staines as "a man of sluggish character." In fact, he was so bad that Stephen and his brothers threw him out of the house (one version involves that Victorian staple, a horsewhip, and there were rumours of drunken violence in the marriage), telling him to stay away, which he did. Lack of money forced young Stephen to drop out of university for a year. For ten years he laboured as a schoolmaster, and, in the words of Robertson Davies "disliked the work heartily."

Although he went on to enjoy great professional success and prosperity, in his marriage he lost his wife to cancer when she was forty-five, and never remarried. His beloved only son, "Little Stevie," remained miniature, so tiny that he barely attained a height of five feet, and became an embittered drunk, his escapades hushed up by the local community. Even the teaching life Leacock loved, where in his tattered gown he could put on an Eccentric Old Professor show for his students, was taken from him when McGill briskly removed him from the faculty when he reached sixty-five — a crushing blow: "I was then retired, much against my will, on grounds of senility, having passed the age of sixty-five." It should not have been a surprise, of course, since he had voted, many years earlier, for precisely that retirement provision.

And what a perfect Leacock funny story that would be: a middle-aged professor, certain that old age will never come to him, votes for compulsory retirement at sixty-five, then reacts with outrage when it is applied to him. Leacock's coolly classical view of human nature, in which people routinely fall prey to false hopes and small hypocrisies, believing that they are exceptions to the follies of human nature, provided him with his profitable living as a humorist. But it did not protect him here, in his own life. He did not die a happy man.

So what remains? In Montreal there is, of course, the Leacock Building at McGill, and the portrait in the University Club. Margaret MacMillan's excellent 2009 short biography (*Stephen Leacock*, in Penguin's Extraordinary Canadians series) notes that in Toronto there is a Scarborough high school named after him, which was attended by young people arrested as accused Islamic terrorists in 2006: a stranger-than-fiction example of how the old Victorian imperialist's conservative Canada has changed.

By way of contrast, there is the Stephen Leacock Museum at Old Brewery Bay in Orillia. Built in 1927 from his book royalties as the world's most popular humorist, it is a fine example of a rich Canadian's lakeside cottage. It was Leacock's base for fishing and sailing and other summer pursuits, which included paying proper respect to the site's convivial name. But it was also a research base, though his excursions into Orillia as a famous but unaffected local writer did not have the desired effect. The town barber once complained about the summer visitor's shameless use of hot local gossip as material for his writing. The complaint predictably ran along the lines of "How the hell was I to know that he was going to take that stuff and . . ."

Time has healed these wounds, and the Leacock Museum has become a tourist asset. Despite the spread of nearby houses (a scandal worth a Leacock story), the house itself is protected by its site on a point on Lake Couchiching, in tree-shaded grounds. The building is preserved as an old-fashioned cottage, with dark wood panelling throughout its interior, and comes complete with a library, straw hats on pegs, and ancient tennis racquets apparently ready for service. As you tiptoe through the two-storey house, upstairs and downstairs, peering at book titles, or at the papers on the desk in the study, or at the dishes in the kitchen, it's hard to avoid the Goldilocks sense that the owners will return at any moment.

One missing component is Leacock's flourishing garden, which inspired the famous beaming-farmer-in-straw-hat Karsh photograph, still on display in the lobby of Ottawa's Château Laurier hotel. It also produced the story, recounted by a niece, of the late-summer family dinner that was interrupted by the grumpy host's complaints about the soup. The surprised guests were then hounded from the table to pick fresh tomatoes in the garden, which were to be delivered to the kitchen and turned into a (very) fresh batch of soup. It could be called the Hundred-Yard Diet.

And the final biography? Legate's book was well researched, inspired by direct knowledge of the subject, and well written, and it was respectably reviewed, but is now sadly out of print. Even Robertson Davies' thoughtful selection, *Feast of Stephen*, is no longer available. (I should note that my wise old friend, who as the author of *Fifth Business* and much else, knew about writing novels, once told me in passing that Leacock could have been a fine serious novelist.) Sadly, too, David Legate is long gone. I heard of his death and asked for details at his old Press Club. The French-Canadian barman, who liked him, told me that "To the en', he fought like a ti-gerr!" There are worse obituaries.

To be selfish, Legate's ambitious book taught me a lot, since I was working on a biography with all the trimmings — a photo section, captions, an index, and so on. In editorial terms, when David Legate and I disagreed he would refer the matter to a mysterious authority, another McGill grad who knew Leacock, he said. It took me a shamefully long time — perhaps after too many hours in the Montreal Men's Press Club — to realize that this authority figure was his wife, Marjorie.

I even learned a technical lesson about book making. The unvarnished truth, you might say. Soon after the books appeared in the shops, complaints flooded in that the attractive scarlet colour on the cover was rubbing off, to reveal the yellow below. This was serious, and evidence of a problem with the printer's varnish. In his office my boss and I had a tense meeting with the printer and his salesman. The young salesman set out to prove that there was no problem. "See," he began confidently, "when I take this pencil with the eraser at the end and start to rub at the red cover, there's no . . ."

He faltered, as streaks of yellow began to appear.

"Bob, why don't you go and wait in the car?" his boss said, not unkindly. We soon reached an agreement with him.

And Leacock's reputation? Leacock, born in 1869, was literally a nineteenth-century figure. As a young boy in England he knew an old sailor who spoke of his service in "The Great War" — the Napoleonic war. And Leacock was both Conservative and conservative. Much of what he wrote (and with sixty books he wrote too much, and much too fast) makes jarring reading today, especially when he deals with women and with people from other cultures. For instance, his innocent mention of "smiling negroes" glimpsed in a glamorous passing train produces unease, even if his point is just to establish that this train has a grand dining car, with waiters.

Yet for all that, and for all his "disillusionment," his best work is still very funny, and not just to those traditionalists familiar with the term "Upper Canada." (So funny, in fact, that Robertson Davies records that at Leacock's readings, people in their seats laughed so hard that "small but significant personal misfortunes befell them.")

It's interesting to note that, as Legate discovered, "How We Kept Mother's Day" (a satire on selfish male domestic blindness) was taught in Soviet Russia to millions of student readers. Leacock dealt well with universally understood themes like hypocrisy — for instance when five men who talk a great game about the joys of early morning fishing never actually make it onto the lake in the chill of dawn. Or when the suicidal hero Peter Pupkin tries to throw himself in front of a train (surely an interesting literary theme for those Russian students), but finds that "he was never able to pick out a pair of wheels that suited him."

Peter Pupkin, of course, features in *Sunshine Sketches of a Little Town*, where we find him screwing up his courage to "do a thing seldom if ever done in Mariposa. He would propose to Zena Pepperleigh." Critics disagree about just how "gentle" Leacock's humour was; Robertson Davies makes the point that the town contains — by contrast with the novels of Dickens — not a single character that we would like to associate with in real life. Yet most, including Davies, seem to agree that *Sunshine Sketches* shows Leacock at his best, giving us glimpses of the town, with its "buildings of extraordinary importance" on Main Street.

Vancouver Island's Jack Hodgins, who knows about small towns with large portions of self-regard, has written a thoughtful afterword to the classic New Canadian Library edition of the book (published, I'm proud to say, under my aegis at McClelland & Stewart). There Hodgins claims that among the few scenes in Western literature worthy of catching the wide public imagination is the sinking of the *Mariposa Belle*, in six feet of water, something that even non-literary types recall with relish. It's worth recalling, too, that the first time the steamboat is mentioned, in the book's first hundred words, it is "tied to the wharf with two ropes of about the same size as they use on the *Lusitania*." Leacock was good at seeing the world through the excited eyes and exaggerated speech of a young boy, a Tom Sawyer, if you like. The title of his posthumous memoir, *The Boy I Left Behind Me*, may set us whistling, but it may not be true that the boy was ever really left behind.

Then Jack Hodgins raises the puzzling final story of the book, "The Train to Mariposa," where Leacock's ironic outsider's tone changes. Magically, we are transported aboard a little train from the city, where we have all spent far too much time getting and spending, and forgetting the old hometown. Even more magically, as the train moves north, it changes, with the electric locomotive that took us out of the city now replaced by an "old wood engine hitched on in its place." The inside of the cars change, too, becoming older, and strangers start to chat. And most magically of all, we change, as well: "No, don't bother to look at the reflection of your face in the window-pane shadowed by the night outside. Nobody could tell you now after all these years. Your face has changed in these long years of money-getting in the city."

In the end, when we reach the bright lights of Mariposa station, we have reached what Robertson Davies might have called the Land of Lost Content. While some may find this last chapter puzzling, I find it moving, perhaps the most powerful of all his work, worth reading by anyone who now lives far — in time or space — from what they grew up calling home.

Another living part of Leacock's legacy is the Stephen Leacock Award for Humour, given annually to the best humorous Canadian book, as judged by a jury selected by the Orillia organizers. I have a weakness for publishing funny books, so I have been involved with many celebratory dinners down through the decades, featuring my friends Harry J. Boyle (who enjoyed being Mariposa's Honorary Mayor), Robert Thomas Allen (author of *Children, Wives, and Other Wildlife*, who was delighted but shy), Donald Jack (who played up to his multi-book character, Bartholomew Bandy, by dressing in a cocked hat), and W.O. Mitchell (who misbehaved, and got into a public spat with a cousin). In 2008 the winner was my pal Terry Fallis, who was such a good friend that he had never once asked me to "take a look at" his then-unpublished first novel, *The Best Laid Plans* (which later was declared the "essential novel of the decade" by the 2011 Canada Reads panel). When he published it himself, and then went on to win the prestigious Leacock Award, that opened the door to my reading it, and publishing it with pride . . . as I did the follow-up volume, *The High Road*, in 2010. His win was astonishingly appropriate; Leacock's own success began with a self-published book, which he placed in outlets like railway stations. By a happy fluke, a British publisher, John Lane, was travelling in Canada and happened to pick up a copy of *Literary Lapses* to read on the ocean voyage home. The rest is publishing history, with Lane's firm, the Bodley Head, taking on the new author, to great worldwide effect.

Finally, two other examples of how Leacock continued to run my life. One of the most interesting books I ever published came from little Orillia, specifically out of the editorial office of the *Orillia Packet & Times* — which is not, by the way, a fictional Leacock title. The peaceful little inland town was a most unlikely source for *The Corvette Navy*, a personal account of the war waged on the wide Atlantic between German U-boats and corvettes manned by amateur Canadian sailors. As the editorial director at Macmillan of Canada in 1977, I was proud to publish this classic war story by James B. Lamb, and several other books from his pen. Later, Jim Lamb paid me the compliment of including a fictional character based on me — "Gib Douglas" is hard to dispute — in a spy novel he wrote, *The Man from the Sea*. I was, at least in the novel, a source of level-headed advice.

"Level-headed" does not apply to any aspect of the next story. In the summer of 2001 I travelled to Geneva Park, near Orillia, to give a speech to those assembled at the annual Couchiching Conference on globalization and publishing, or something equally grand. At the conference was a member of the board named Jane Bartram, who was to my smitten eyes clearly The Most Fascinating Woman in the World. Our first date was a canoe ride together on Lake Couchiching, where we did not quite reach Leacock's Old Brewery Bay on the opposite shore. But having brought me to Canada he was still obviously running my life. Jane and I were married within the year.

Keep up the good work, Professor Leacock.

CHAPTER 2                                                    1907–1990

# HUGH
# MacLENNAN

Teacher, Novelist, Essayist, and Cottager

Unlike my relationship with Stephen Leacock, I knew Hugh MacLennan. Knew him as a friend for over twenty years. Knew him as a friend, in fact, long before I worked with him, as his editor, his publisher, and, later, as his anthologist, putting together the selection *Hugh MacLennan's Best* in 1991.

The key lies in North Hatley, an idyllic spot in the Eastern Townships, ninety minutes east of Montreal. Set beside Lake Massawippi, North Hatley — or, increasingly, Nord Hatley — was a summer resort for generations of Anglo-Montrealers like the MacLennans, and for East Coast Americans like my first in-laws, the Satterthwaites.

I had met Frank Satterthwaite early in my time at Yale, when he shared tickets to the "Yale Whale," the elegant rink designed by the Finnish architect Eero Saarinen, where I saw my first game of hockey. We hit it off, he took me home to Manhattan, and there was this interesting younger sister hanging around, when she was not attending Vassar, or off winning tennis tournaments. You can imagine the rest, including a visit from Toronto to "Willow Wood," the lakeside cottage in North Hatley. Eventually we got engaged at Hovey Manor, the ancient inn just up the lake.

In due course Sally and I were married. After a grand New York wedding (which involved hiring a red London double-decker bus from a tour group to transport the wedding party down Park Avenue to the Colony Club reception) we had our honeymoon in North Hatley.

And the first couple-to-couple dinner of our married life was there, as guests of Tota and Hugh MacLennan.

Let me step aside, however, to tell two stories that spring from that wedding reception. The photograph of Sally and me smiling and waving from the bus deck appeared in the next day's *New York Times*. Weeks later a Yale friend visiting London came on the relevant page covering his American host's kitchen floor, and launched into a fierce rant about the shameless excesses of "the idle rich." When he happened to stoop closer to the floor, he recoiled, swearing mightily, along the lines of "Christ, it's Gibson!" It ruined his day.

It's important for readers of this opinionated book who want to try to understand where this particular "unreliable narrator" is coming from (literally) to know that the Gibsons in Scotland were anything but "idle rich." No and no. My father's role at the wedding reception was revealing. During the speeches he was standing chatting quietly with the bandleader, who whispered that he attended dozens of similar events every year, but that this was the very best speech he had ever heard at such an occasion. My father modestly allowed that with my experience as president of the Students' Union at St. Andrews, I was used to speaking in public. "No, no, *not the groom!*" hissed the band leader, "his brother, the best man." This became a very popular story in the Gibson family, especially with my brother, Peter, who had assured the alarmed company that the Satterthwaite parents were opposed to the marriage until they came to see that the match involved not losing a daughter, but "gaining a son-in-law's brother!"

The main point in the story is that Dad was happily chatting, not with any of the glittering guests, but with the bandleader, who might have been dismissed by some as just hired help. Not by my father. I never knew a more determined anti-snob, at ease everywhere. In his job as the timber department manager of the local employer, Howie of Dunlop, he spent his mornings dispatching tough truck drivers across the country to deliver loads of pit props to coal mines or to pick up felled trees from logging sites across the West of Scotland for sawmilling. He himself was a hardy fellow, once the captain of the local Kilmarnock rugby team, and I heard a tale (from one of the work crew, not from him) from his hot-blooded youth when he invited a surly driver to step aside and settle a dispute with his fists. Cooler heads prevailed.

By contrast, his afternoons might be spent sipping sherry with the Duke of This or That while they discussed the best way of thinning trees on the ducal estate. One such noble figure met me on a forestry excursion (steel yourself before shaking hands with foresters, where a good hand has three fingers) and asked me, keenly, if I was "a debater like your father." The words "outspoken troublemaker" were not actually used. If the duke or landowner was not present for sherry or Scotch, the negotiations might well be with a "factor," a term for manager that is restricted to Scotland and Canada, where it was inherited from the Scots who ran the Hudson's Bay Company, in places like, say, Moose Factory.

The most painful question I ever asked my father was about a four-letter word that I had heard when I was seven or eight. What, I wanted to know, was a snob? My father was in anguish, confronted by having to explain the class system he abhorred; any other four-letter word would have been much easier. He did his best, talking about how stupid people might want me to stop playing with my friend Billy because his father was "just a joiner," making it clear that to be called a snob was the worst possible insult, and that I should govern myself accordingly. To this day I find it hard to pass someone digging a hole in the road without enquiring about his progress. To walk by without a word is to risk seeming snobbish.

How important is this? When Rhona Martin, a friend from my home Scottish village, won the Olympic Gold Medal for curling in 2002, the English reporter (and Scots would see his nationality as important) for the *Times* described the fit young women curlers on her team as looking like "the wives of electricians." My Canadian friends, to their great credit, simply did not understand this comment. My father would have exploded in rage to hear it.

To sum up: my background training in this area has been immensely useful in my role as editor and publisher happily dealing with Canadians from all walks of life. Hugh MacLennan wrote about fatherhood in *Each Man's Son*. I am my father's son.

One of the things I liked best about Hugh MacLennan — and there were many things to like — was his easy democratic touch. He loved to tell the story from his earliest days about his household in Cape Breton being wakened by a crowd of men fresh from an altercation. When his doctor father threw up the window to make enquiries, a voice floated up. "We're sorry to disturb you, Doctor, but the gentleman I was fighting with has bitten off my nose!" (I once told that story in Alistair MacLeod's presence, and Alistair — a proud son of Cape Breton — was not pleased. I hope he'll forgive this repetition, with its marvellous use of the courteous "gentleman," which Robert Louis Stevenson's Alan Breck would have understood completely, and which Hugh relished.)

He liked and respected real, live ordinary people, disliking, by contrast, the "red tabs and red officer faces" he mentions in *Two Solitudes*. In his essay "An Orange from Portugal," he writes affectionately about Halifax in his youth. "In the old days in Halifax we never thought about the meaning of the word democracy: we were all mixed up together in a general deplorability."

The essay "Einstein and the Bootleggers" gives us an intriguing look at Hugh and that "general deplorability." Any Princeton graduate student with half a brain would have eagerly collected stories about Einstein on the campus — but how many of them would have hung around with bootleggers? "In those days," Hugh says, "some of my best friends were ex-bootleggers," and we learn that these were real, very tough characters who had used baseball bats for other than sporting purposes and had done time in jail. They send an intruding truck driver on his way with threats because he was rash enough to sneer at Einstein, who was, after all, *their* genius.

But let's go back to the basic facts about Hugh MacLennan. He was born in 1907 in Glace Bay, a mining town in Cape Breton, Nova Scotia, and his family soon moved to the province's capital, Halifax. He studied Classics at Dalhousie and went on to win a Rhodes Scholarship to Oxford. His father, a hard-working doctor, made sure that he was indoctrinated with Calvinist Scottish values, greeting the scholarship news (which might have led to unseemly celebration in the snow) with the words, "Go and shovel the walk, Hugh. It badly needs it." Doctor Sam, by the way, had earlier gained fame in the local paper by provoking the headline "Doctor Hunts Gas Leak With Burning Match — Finds It!"

After Oxford, Hugh got his Ph.D. at Princeton, where he once came across Albert Einstein gazing at a snowball in his hands with total fascination, and once (as I've just mentioned) found him blundering into a bootlegger's café, to be protectively treated there.

Hugh came back to Canada in 1935, at the height of the Depression. Unable to get a university job, he took one at the private boys' school, Lower Canada College, in Montreal. There he was a notable teacher. One boy, later a distinguished MP, told me that he was summoned to the headmaster's study and briskly informed that his mother had just died. Released into the school corridor, he stood there blinking in shock, until one of his teachers, Hugh MacLennan, came up, threw his arms around him, and held him fast, while the macho crowds flowed around them, gaping.

In 1951, by then an acclaimed author, he accepted a position in the Department of English at McGill University. The salary was so low that, in the telling phrase of his biographer, Elspeth Cameron, "Even his publishers were horrified."

Money *was* a problem. His first wife, Dorothy Duncan, was stricken by a series of embolisms, and in those days medical care in Canada was ruinously expensive. So Hugh not only taught and wrote books, he took on regular magazine writing assignments, amassing more than 400 essays over the years, and winning two Governor General's Awards for his essay collections, in addition to his three fiction prizes. After three decades, he left McGill, the university botching his departure so badly that alumni were enraged. Hugh, of course, refused to make a fuss, despite my urging, and moved out of his urgently required McGill office. Thanks to the intervention of Graham Fraser, the son of a North Hatley friend, a rival university, Concordia, was able to supply him with an office, but his heart wasn't in it.

He lived quietly at home with his second wife, Tota, spending their summers in North Hatley. He died in 1990. I was informed of his death by the wonderful Doris Giller — after whom the famous literary prize is named. She was at the time a journalist, on deadline, phoning for the *Toronto Star*, but was so aware of my affection for Hugh that she offered to give me half an hour to compose myself for the necessary interview about Hugh's career. As for that career, the five Governor General's Awards speak for themselves, as do the nineteen honorary degrees he earned during his lifetime. As an article in the *National Post* put it in 2009, he was Canada's "first world-class writer."

North Hatley, of course, is where I first met him. It is only vaguely disguised as Ste. Elizabeth ("for the purpose of non-identification") in Hugh's essay "Everyone Knows the Rules." There he summed it up as "a place where everyone loves everyone else. We play tennis and sail together and sit on verandas and are wise about the affairs of the world." It is also the setting of one of Hugh's best essays, "Confessions of a Wood-Chopping Man," which, with its obvious love of the Eastern Townships landscape, is still infectiously good reading. At the cottage Hugh was at his relaxed best, and I got to know him in the round of cocktail parties and visits for drinks and/or dinner that mark the end of a well-spent August day.

I can report that he was a charming guest — in a brief encounter he looked like a gentler version of the British actor Trevor Howard — and was interested in everyone, courteous in a slightly formal way, and always willing to discuss any point raised, whether it was the fortunes of the Athenians, the Jacobites, the local tennis champion, the Liberals in Ottawa, the Vietnamese, the Book of the Month Club, or the Montreal Canadiens. In his elder-statesman role he was willing to hold the conversational floor and become the centre of attention if that was appropriate. But — and here he differs noticeably from some other authors I have known — he was quite happy to lapse back into the audience while someone else held centre stage.

He was a courteous host — although one not totally at ease with infants and small children, who were the realm of his wife, Tota — and adult encounters worked better at his cottage than those where crayons were involved. But at that first honeymoon dinner party chez MacLennan and over the years, at lunches or dinners or other events in North Hatley, Montreal, or Toronto, I always found him to be very good company and enjoyed his Halifax-Oxford drawl, his mischievous smiles, and his emphatic bursts of laughter.

He was regarded with affection and pride in North Hatley, which was a place of more than average literary accomplishment. People like Frank Scott, Blair Fraser — and now Graham Fraser and the elegant columnist Norman Webster — were to be found there in the summer. (Four-year-old Graham Fraser was so impressed by the tall legal scholar/poet Frank Scott falling splashingly out of a canoe at the dock that he clamoured admiringly, "Do it again, Mr. Scott, do it again!") Ralph Gustafson, Ronald Sutherland, Douglas Jones, Alison Pick, and other literati have also graced the little town.

Local legend has it that Hugh was a highly competitive tennis player (he won the Nova Scotia doubles title in his youth) but one constantly afflicted — sometimes to a slightly amusing extent — by aches and pains that prevented his game from ever quite reaching its zenith. And certainly in his later years, friends found that enquiries about the state of his health were not to be casually made.

He was a kind and caring man, of course. I once saw him break into a run — in his late sixties — as he rushed off to give assistance on hearing that an elderly friend had just suffered a heart attack at the tennis court. I have mentioned, too, the incident from his days as a teacher at Lower Canada College when his instinctive kindness helped a boy in trouble. The reader will not be surprised to learn that that particular boy grew up to keep a watchful and helpful eye on Hugh and his wife in their last difficult days.

They *were* difficult days, too, since our society is not good at looking after an old, very proud couple like the MacLennans. In the last few years of his life, Hugh's activities were severely circumscribed by the fact that his beloved wife was almost bedridden. Hugh faithfully — though somewhat inexpertly, since he was a man of his generation — looked after her and ran the household, doing the shopping and the cooking, which took up most of his day and caused friends to be concerned about their diet.

In the summer of 1990, just before what proved to be my last visit to their apartment on Summerhill Avenue, a pleasant walk from the McGill campus, I stressed on the phone from Toronto that I wanted to take them out for a really fine dinner. Yet when I reached the apartment and indicated that all of Montreal was our oyster — the Ritz, perhaps, or somewhere in Old Montreal? — discussion revealed that the place they really preferred for dinner, the culinary pinnacle, as it were, was Ben's Delicatessen, "Home of the Best Montreal Smoked Meats." Yes, Ben's brightly lit café on De Maisonneuve, which famously had fed lines of hungry men each day during the ten lost years of the Depression. So to Ben's we went. But not before I had been forced to stop Hugh, who was then very frail, from courteously hastening off to hail us a cab on Côte-des-Neiges. I finally managed to persuade him that I *needed the walk* — and at that point honour was satisfied, and I was permitted to go out and get the cab.

He was a great gentleman, a dignified man for whom the word "courtly" might have been invented, yet he was far from stuffy. His conversation was frequently uproariously funny, sometimes bawdily so. That earthy humour rarely finds its way into his writing, although I proudly included in the anthology *Hugh MacLennan's Best* the story of the buxom Cape Breton lady teacher unwise enough to ask a small boy trying to define "quadruped," "What have I got two of that a cow has four of?" The plainspoken boy obviously came from a dairy farming background. We can imagine the nickname young Neilly bore to the end of his Cape Breton days.

But MacLennan's gift in conversation was genuine wit — pointed, clever, perfect. Three examples. In the sixties his student, then friend, young Leonard Cohen explained to Hugh the importance that he and his generation ascribed to enjoying every possible sexual opportunity that offered itself. "Leonard," said Hugh, "you're no different from a girl back home in Nova Scotia. She was called 'Anytime Annie.'" Leonard, of course, did not take Hugh's abstemious advice, to the relief of many ladies, going down though the years.

Once, in a discussion about the latest tragic outbreak of violence in Northern Ireland, he said to me, "Of course you must understand, Douglas, that the trouble there is caused by the fact that the population of Ulster is split between two religions — [long pause] — anti-Protestantism and anti-Catholicism."

And let me quote another flash of wit, not his, but retold by him with what I might call adoptive delight. The not altogether popular principal of McGill, Cyril James, once happened upon a group of four deans lunching at the Faculty Club. "Aha," he said, "the proper collective noun for such a group would perhaps be 'a dread of deans.'"

"And for you, I suppose," shot back a dean, "it would be 'a lack of principals.'"

His stories — and he was full of stories — revolved around characters he had known. He loved unusual characters and enjoyed meeting and chatting with them. He made slow progress along the street at North Hatley towards the post office, or along Sherbrooke on his way to and from McGill, as he encountered acquaintances of all sorts, and of all collar colours, and stopped to chat with them.

I never knew him as a teacher, but I know the type of teacher he must have been. The same well-stocked, allusive mind that saw connections everywhere and made him a great essayist — from Captain Bligh to Albert Schweitzer in two easy moves — must have made him a good, challenging, and thought-provoking teacher for bright kids. It must also have made him the despair of lesser lights, who expected the course to follow the outline, for God's sake, and failed to see what on earth the Mafia in Montreal could possibly have to do with Robert Browning. And Leonard Cohen, a great admirer, once told me of Hugh becoming so moved as he tried to describe the depth of James Joyce's loneliness in exile that he stood lost in tears, while the awestruck class filed silently out of the room.

It is important to note the extent to which this kind, decent man was an inspiration to so many other writers, both directly (in his encouraging correspondence, and in person) and indirectly by way of example. He was a trailblazer. It was 1941 in October, in the darkest days of the Second World War, that *Barometer Rising*, his first book, came out. At the time it was regarded as almost foolhardy to set a novel in Canada, and the book's opening words show what a mountain he had to climb: "It seems necessary to offer more than a conventional statement about the names of characters in this book, since it is one of the first ever written to use Halifax, Nova Scotia, for its sole background. Because there is as yet no tradition of Canadian literature, Canadians are apt to suspect that a novel referring to one of their cities must likewise refer to specific individuals among its characters." He emphasizes that these are made-up characters, going on to regret that "there is no great variety in Scottish given names" and then, sure enough, we find ourselves pursuing Neil Macrae, in search of Big Alec MacKenzie, later aided by Angus Murray, going on a virtual street by street tour of the city.

And then, something much more significant, perhaps one of the most important paragraphs in the history of Canadian writing:

He stopped at a corner to wait for a tram, and his eyes reached above the roofs to the sky. Stars were visible, and a quarter moon. The sun had rolled on beyond Nova Scotia and into the west. Now it was setting over Montreal and sending the shadow of the mountain deep into the valleys of Sherbrooke Street and Peel; it was turning the frozen St. Lawrence crimson and lining it with the blue shadows of the trees and buildings along its banks, while all the time the deep water poured seaward under the ice, draining off the Great Lakes into the Atlantic. Now the Prairies were endless plains of glittering, bluish snow over which the wind passed in a firm and continuous flux, packing the drifts down hard over the wheat seeds frozen into the alluvial earth. Now in the Rockies the peaks were gleaming obelisks in the mid-afternoon. The railway line, that tenuous thread which bound Canada to both the great oceans and made her a nation, lay with one end in the darkness of Nova Scotia and the other in the flush of a British Columbian noon.

Think of that! A deliberately, even defiantly, pan-Canadian book — about Canada, coast to coast, and what it is to be Canadian. It seemed important to the thousands of Canadians who passed dog-eared copies of the book around barrack rooms in Britain or among the hammocks in corvettes bouncing in mid-Atlantic storms, or grabbed them from bookstore shelves . . . and it still seems damned important to the Canadian writers who follow in his footsteps seventy years on, and to their publishers — which brings me to my encounter with Hugh MacLennan as an editor and publisher.

When I joined Macmillan of Canada as editorial director in 1974, I inherited a galaxy of major Canadian authors, my North Hatley friend Hugh among them. Like so many of these stars, he was there because of John Gray, the legendary publisher at Macmillan who was perhaps Hugh's best friend. I was lucky enough to get to know John Gray fairly well, acting as editor for his memoirs, *Fun Tomorrow*, and I can see why the two men were close. Their relationship was a model for contacts between author and publisher — respectful, friendly, and encouraging, with tact and frankness blended to a nicety. It was John Gray who went out on a limb and printed ten times the usual print run for 1959's *The Watch That Ends the Night* — ordering 25,000 copies for Canada — while all the publishing world wondered, and his colleagues thought him mad. Yet he was right. It proved to be Hugh's best — and his most successful — book.

This leads to a confession. When I read all of Hugh's work to produce *Hugh MacLennan's Best*, I suffered from the anthologist's secret disease: I hoped to discover a hidden jewel, unjustly overlooked. I was disappointed to find that his most famous novel, published in 1959, is in fact his best. Hugh's own years, from 1947 to 1957, spent watching over his sick wife "knowing," in the words of the novel's narrator, "that at any hour of any day she might die," informs this novel, told by George Stewart, a man who teaches at McGill. There is one striking difference between Stewart and the author: after years of happy marriage to a widow named Katherine, at the end of the first chapter Stewart receives the most dramatic phone call in Canadian literature, from his wife's long-dead first husband, who in fact has survived both Nazi and Soviet death camps.

*The Watch That Ends the Night* sold like wildfire around the world, even, to the author's shy amazement, dominating bookstore windows on Fifth Avenue in New York. It still provides fine reading.

In 1974 Macmillan was about to publish Hugh MacLennan's so-called coffee-table book *Rivers of Canada*. My role on that book was a minor one, restricted mainly to writing the flap copy summarizing the book. (Editors, you should know, tend to be unreasonably proud of their flap copy, the writing on the book's cover: I note now that I described the book as "bringing a new standard of excellence to those rare and wonderful books that succeed in pleasing both the eye and the mind," and I've happily used variants of that phrasing several times since.)

But the process of publishing *Rivers of Canada* involved running excerpts in *Maclean's* magazine, and I recall Hugh arriving from Montreal for a meeting in the *Maclean's* boardroom at 481 University Avenue with Peter C. Newman (then the magazine's editor) and some of his senior staff. In those days Peter Newman shrewdly used Hugh as an occasional columnist/essayist, producing pieces such as the extraordinary 1972 essay on Trudeau and Nixon, "Trudeau Unveiled: Facing Up to the Public." And even though the occasion was to discuss excerpting *Rivers of Canada*, the *Maclean's* meeting turned into a fascinating, wide-ranging seminar on politics, economics, history, and life, as Newman and his colleagues drew Hugh out, and either literally or metaphorically took notes as he talked.

Hugh, always a "writer engagé," contributing to public debate, had an extraordinary record in anticipating the political themes that were to convulse Canadian society. One of the themes of *Barometer Rising* is Canada's switch from its position in what he called "the butler's pantry of the British Empire." By the time of *The Precipice* (1948) he was warning us about the dangers of becoming a branch plant of the United States — a theme he returned to again and again, most directly in 1960 in the essay "It's the U.S. or Us." That essay, some say, helped to create a groundswell of opinion that led to the creation of a Royal Commission to study the Americanization of our media, which, it can be argued, led in turn to the creation of the CRTC, and much else.

Back in 1945, of course, in *Two Solitudes* he tackled the grand theme of friction between English- and French-speaking Canadians, and in doing so changed at the very least the language of political debate in this country. He returned to the theme in *The Return of the Sphinx*. That now-forgotten book was published in 1967, the glorious year of Canada's Centennial, and the novel's predictions of precisely the sort of revolutionary violence that the FLQ was to produce just three years later were not warmly received in the midst of all the celebrations.

Let me add some further points about that 1972 *Maclean's* piece on Trudeau. In that essay he actually called Trudeau "a genius," going on to define the term: "My idea of a genius is a person who can reach a destination without having travelled there, which is pretty well what Trudeau did when he reached No. 24 Sussex Drive." (Max and Monique Nemni's recent research on Trudeau's preparation for office, detailed in *Young Trudeau*, and in *Trudeau Transformed*, has now cast doubt on Hugh's interpretation.) There is no doubt that Hugh sympathized with Trudeau's dream — one that, sadly, is now seen as an impractical, hopelessly idealistic one — of a bilingual Canada where the two solitudes would indeed touch and greet and protect each other. In his last years Hugh was deeply saddened by the path we seemed to be taking, and he saved his most savage invective — much of it unprintable, especially when he phoned at night after a drink or two — for our then–prime minister, whom he insisted on calling Muldoon. It was not an affectionate nickname, and since I had not then worked with Mulroney, I had no defence to offer.

The friendship with Trudeau was returned, and the admiration was mutual. The ex–prime minister joined us at the small celebratory reception in Montreal's Racquet Club to mark Hugh's eightieth birthday, slipping in quietly while the dinner was under way. Later, in correspondence with me following Hugh's death, he said how sorry he was to be abroad and thus unable to attend the memorial service at McGill for "that great human being."

The *Maclean's* essay is important, I believe, because it suggests an answer to why Hugh was such a shrewd predictor of future trends. Simply put, his education allowed him to take the long view. In fact, Hugh MacLennan was the sort of person who gives education a good name. In theory, if you give people the best education three countries can provide — Dalhousie, then Oxford, then Princeton — and after that expose them through wide travel to many different cultures and imbue them with a keen and continuing interest in people and human affairs in all their variety — then, the theory goes, you will produce wise men and women who will be able to fit current events into a wider pattern.

Well, we all know how rarely this happens. But in Hugh MacLennan's case, it seems to me, the system worked. At the time of the Vietnam War many commentators wrote comparing the American Empire to the Roman Empire. Yet how many were able to compare the Vietnam adventure to the expedition into Germany of Quintilius Varus? That sort of precise comparison speaks for itself about the range of his accumulated knowledge.

With its links to events two thousand years ago, that essay displays, yet again, the same uncanny ability to predict the themes of the future debates. How many other 1972 essays on politics can we find that include the words "ecology" and "non-renewable resources"? How many of us could even define the word "ecology" in 1972?

Reviewing *Hugh MacLennan's Best*, Robert Harlow, the West Coast novelist and teacher, said simply, "The man was prescient to the point of clairvoyance." I'd like to give one example where the word clairvoyance is amazingly apt. In *Two Solitudes*, Huntly McQueen, the St. James Street tycoon, reminded many readers of Prime Minster Mackenzie King. This passage is about McQueen and the office where his mother's portrait hangs: "Except when he was alone in the room McQueen never even glanced at the portrait, but whenever he had a decision to make he shut everyone out and communed with the picture, and after he had looked at it long enough he was usually able to feel that his mother was silently advising him what to do. It was the most closely guarded of all his secrets."

That was written in 1945. The full extent of Mackenzie King's reliance on his dead mother for advice, and the role played by her portrait in his decisions, was one of the prime minister's most closely guarded secrets. It only emerged *thirty years later* when his private diaries were released and were then used, not kindly, by C.P. Stacey in his book *A Very Double Life* (1976), published by Macmillan and launched by us, impudently, at the ancestral Mackenzie House in Toronto. So how do we explain MacLennan's passage? Clairvoyance? Or the flash of insight that strikes an imaginative artist and qualifies as genius? I don't know. But I do know that we must all desperately hope that his predictions in *Voices in Time* (1980) of "The Destruction" leading in time to "The Bureaucracy," which enforces ever greater conformity on citizens, are less accurate than his earlier ones have proved to be.

My role as editor and publisher in 1978 involved working with Elspeth Cameron on her excellent selection of essays *The Other Side of Hugh MacLennan*. In the creation of that book, Hugh was a model of co-operation, especially in the vital business of selection, where he gave Elspeth a free hand. And here a word of tribute to Elspeth is in order. In compiling the anthology I found her very professional biography, *Hugh MacLennan: A Writer's Life* (1981) to be invaluable; all MacLennan admirers are in her debt. And I remember fondly the unprofessional tears she shed at Hugh's funeral reception.

Hugh's sense of democracy — of liking and respecting ordinary people — comes through to me most strongly in *Each Man's Son* (which I found the most moving of his books, perhaps best read to the sound of distant bagpipes). There he writes with affection about the poor doomed men who will live confined, crippled lives underground in the mines until a lung disease or an accident at the coal face gets them. In the same book, you find Dr. Ainslie expressing that same sort of respect for unlettered Newfoundlanders who can somehow navigate their dories "like seals" through the fog. And of course you see it in the essay "A Disquisition on Elmer" — which takes us into sixteenth-century religious politics by way of Hugh's real-life encounter with Mr. Elmer Z. Stebbins, the trigger-happy barfly in Arizona who once shot a man "through the ass — sideways" in a fashion that, as Mr. Stebbins put it, "kind of stung him up a bit." It's obvious that Hugh — the product of the most patrician of educations in those days of greater social stratification — cared about and enjoyed these people.

In planning the publication of *The Other Side* it became clear to us that we had to fight a general perception of Hugh MacLennan as a writer of what his Oriel College predecessor, Mathew Arnold, would have called "high seriousness," and nothing but. His novels had suffered the fate of being taught in high schools and universities with the usual diligence, so it was a challenge to plant in the public's mind the idea of reading this serious, sober, even sombre purveyor of important themes for fun and entertainment. We worked at it by creating a carefully different title — *The Other Side of Hugh MacLennan* — and by running an unexpectedly relaxed image on the cover. Hugh happily went along with this, dressing casually and perching somewhat uncomfortably on a stool in Peter Paterson's photographic studio until I, crouching beneath the lights, coaxed a smile to his face by recounting, I believe, a string of true poaching stories from the Scottish Highlands, the setting of one of his finest essays, "Scotchman's Return." (That wonderful 1958 piece, by the way, ends with a real-life version of his imagined bird's eye view of Canada coast to coast in *Barometer Rising*: as his trans-Atlantic plane descended through the clouds, "I saw beside the Bras d'Or lake the tiny speck which was the house where my mother and sister at that very moment lay asleep.")

The 1978 selection of essays succeeded in restoring a balanced view of Hugh MacLennan as a writer, with William French in the *Globe and Mail*, for example, noting: "MacLennan's work as an essayist has been overshadowed by his reputation as a novelist, but that's an injustice that should be corrected by *The Other Side of Hugh MacLennan*." The book met with general critical acclaim, not least from David Helwig who was moved to review it in the following terms: "MacLennan is one of those writers whose personal goodness and decency shine through all his works. His generosity of spirit is such that after a couple hours spent with one of his books, the world seems a better place."

The reviewers' response to *Voices in Time*, his last novel, was less unanimous. I edited the book, so am perhaps too close to it to be properly objective. But I remember being delighted when Elspeth Cameron, in a quote for the jacket, hailed it as "Hugh MacLennan's greatest novel." My own line on the jacket, that the book is, "in every sense, the work of a lifetime," was undeniably true. Working on the anthology revealed to me how right from the start — from his Princeton Ph.D. thesis about the decline of the Roman Empire as seen in one small Egyptian outpost — Hugh was fascinated, perhaps obsessed, by what I call "the descent into barbarism." He was keenly conscious at all times of the skull beneath the skin of civilization.

How could European civilization produce the Passchendaele of his impressionable boyhood? (Note the bitter line in *Two Solitudes* about the returning soldiers parading through Montreal: "Some had stood up to their necks in cold water stained with blood and human excrement while they waited for hours to crawl a few yards closer to Passchendaele.") How could it produce the masses of aimless, shoeless, shuffling Kulaks he saw with his own eyes on a visit to Russia in the thirties, and described in *The Watch That Ends the Night*? How could it produce the total economic breakdown of the Depression that left his generation unwanted and mostly unemployable, lining up for handouts at Ben's? And above all how could German civilization — the civilization of his beloved Haydn, and Beethoven, and Goethe, and so many others — produce Hitler and his gang? Clearly there lies the most striking example of the descent into barbarism of our time, and so it is natural that he chose to examine the issue from the point of view of the "good German," Conrad Dehmel, while looking at our society's descent into an Orwellian future as a parallel. Let us hope that he was wrong.

The creation of *Voices in Time* took thirteen long years. During the last part of that period my role was to encourage him and to assure him that there was still an eager audience out there for his work. Like all the first-class writers of my professional acquaintance he was unsure of the current book's quality as he worked on it. He was also aware that in the Canadian literary firmament his star was waning as newer planets soared into view. There was even a technical problem, related in Harry Bruce's *Page Fright: Foibles and Fetishes of Famous Writers* (2009):

> When Hugh MacLennan was in his seventies and completing his last novel, *Voices in Time*, his elderly Underwood died of old age and overwork. With that black, noisy, anachronistic typewriting contraption — whose shape was as familiar to the elderly as Model T Fords had once been — MacLennan had earned his reputation as Canada's first

internationally acclaimed novelist and had written no fewer than five winners of Governor General's Awards. Now, the machine was just a mess of keys, spools, wheels, and other useless parts. It was too old to repair or replace, and he was too old to switch to another brand. How could he possibly finish *Voices in Time*?

His alarmed publisher, Douglas Gibson, asked Peter Gzowski, the host of CBC Radio's *This Country in the Morning* to appeal to his listeners for old Underwoods in working order. Gzowski was the most popular on-air personality in the country. He was "Mr. Canada," and to enable a pioneer of modern Canadian literature to finish his last novel, dozens of Gzowski fans now rummaged through their attics for dusty Underwoods of a certain age. MacLennan accepted the machine that best suited him and, sure enough, *Voices in Time* reached bookstores in 1980. . . . Without Gibson, Gzowski, and the Canadians who answered their request, this story could never have had a satisfying ending. They recognized the breakdown of a certain old man's certain old typewriter as a national emergency.

In the teeth of considerable domestic difficulties and health problems, Hugh worked away at the novel, until when he delivered it to me — complete — he said, "My brain is tired."

That wintry Montreal day when he walked through the snow in his overcoat and beret, an old man delivering his last manuscript, I was at the Château Versailles. About a dozen prominent Canadian authors making up the executive committee of the Writers' Union — people like June Callwood, Rudy Wiebe, and Jack Hodgins — were meeting there, and I was on hand to give a publisher's advice. I persuaded Hugh that he should go in and say hello. Being Hugh, he was reluctant to intrude, but I insisted, and he went in with me, very shyly. And everyone in the room stood up and applauded. They knew what Hugh MacLennan the pioneer had done for Canadian writing, blazing the trail for the writers who followed.

On the train back from Montreal I read the novel, which, I must record, was not especially well typed. But I read it with mounting excitement and called him right away to tell him how much I liked the work. My editorial role was minor, involving few major strategic shifts. My chief contribution, in fact, was to suggest that the line "voices in time" leapt out from page thirty-six as an ideal book title.

On the tactical side, when I went through line by line suggesting, as editors do, that an extra adjective here would make this clearer, or perhaps the paragraph should be split there, he was the consummate professional. I should note that the rule is unvarying: the less experienced writers are the most defensive in the editorial process, insisting that not a hair of their baby's head, not a comma, be touched.

With the editing process neatly accomplished, the book came out in the fall of 1980. The author's promotional tour produced a chorus of delighted responses from all our sales and publicity people who had to look after him, in Ottawa or Winnipeg or wherever: "What a wonderful man." The response is not always so enthusiastic when major figures have to be shepherded through a harrowing day of interviews, but Hugh was invariably pleasant and polite to those he encountered in the mad circus of a publicity tour.

When I left my role as Macmillan's publisher at the beginning of 1986 to set up my own editorial imprint at McClelland & Stewart, Hugh was one of the first authors to volunteer to come with me. He had a highly developed sense of loyalty that was central to his character. To my deep gratitude he signed up with me on my new venture, undertaking to write his memoirs for me, continuing to introduce me to his friends as simply "my publisher," and asking me to go to Vancouver in 1986 to accept his award from the Canadian Booksellers Association in recognition of his lifetime contribution to Canadian readers.

He never completed the memoirs. I'm certain that they would have been a marvellous piece of work if they had married his novelist's skills with his touch as an essayist and brought his historian's perspective (what I've called "the long view") to a life that spanned every decade in the turbulent twentieth century.

And so — *faute de mieux* — by arrangement with Shirley Woods, his literary executor, I became his anthologist, putting together the book called *Hugh MacLennan's Best*.

Here I put on the anthologist's hat. They say that no man is a hero to his valet. The literary equivalent must surely be that no author is a hero to his anthologist. Perhaps a professor never feels quite the same about an admired author once he or she starts to teach that author's work. But having read all of Hugh MacLennan's work

I found myself forced to select from an embarrassment of riches. In fact, I can reveal here that the original galley proof selection was a full one hundred pages longer than the final book, requiring further painful cutting. And at the end of the process I was an even greater admirer of his skills as a writer.

When I read his work start to finish, some themes emerged. The obsession with the descent into barbarism is one that I've discussed. His constant concern as a "writer engagé" with politics and the big issues, and his ability to take the long view of them, is another, as is his genuine interest in ordinary people.

Another theme worth investigating is how deeply war shaped MacLennan and how so much of his best writing deals with physical conflict. I'm speaking here of war scenes such as the Halifax explosion in *Barometer Rising* (in historical reality, the largest man-made explosion till Hiroshima, so massive that it not only shook young Hugh in Halifax, it broke windows in Truro almost one hundred kilometers away, and, as Alistair MacLeod reports, could be heard hundreds of miles away in Cape Breton). Then we have the naval engagements witnessed by Matt McCunn in *The Precipice*, Jerome Martell's account of his horrible deeds with a bayonet and the high drama inside Alan Ainslie's crippled bomber in *The Return of the Sphinx*, followed by the unforgettable screams on the ground below, *"Neunzig Kinder hier getötet. Neunzig Kinder."* ("Ninety children killed here.")

But there are other, more intimate scenes of combat outside war zones. Consider, for example, Young Tallard's back-street scuffle with the soldier, or the famous essay about hockey, "Fury on Ice," or, especially, in *Each Man's Son*, the heroic Archie McNeil's last fight in the sweltering New Jersey arena. All of them demonstrate what a fine, exciting writer MacLennan is when dealing with scenes of physical action, which he no doubt saw as Homeric combat. The critic Elizabeth Waterston, in *Rapt in Plaid*, has drawn interesting parallels between the outbreaks of fierce physical violence in Hugh's novels and those of John Buchan. It's conceivable that his old athletic skills are put to good use here, perhaps allowing him to write from what in kinetics they call "muscle memory." Certainly he can write about boxing or tennis or wood chopping with an enviable physicality that is convincing and infectious — at least to an old boxer and tennis player and even wood-chopping man like me.

I was struck once again by what a good writer he is about place. An American reviewer of the anthology in the *Princeton Alumni Weekly* wrote that "his sense of place is so strong the reader is tempted to pull out an atlas and follow the character's progress on a map." And from that magical opening of *Two Solitudes* where you'll recall he follows the St. Lawrence, the sword wrenched from the stone, down to the sea, his work impressed me again and again with his almost unmatched ability as an essayist to make, in John Oughton's words, "history and geography come dramatically alive." That is why so much of *Rivers of Canada* is to be found in the anthology, along with excerpts from his pen sketches in *The Colour of Canada*, because no one else, in my experience, can do it better. The voyageurs whose history puts grade five kids to sleep every year across the country are very different from the flesh and blood heroes that Hugh MacLennan creates with such impressive effect, as they bind the country together with birchbark, spruce gum, and sweat.

Another constant that struck me is the effectiveness of his humour. We see it in his fiction, with Aunt Maria in *Barometer Rising* disapproving of Mrs. Taylor. ("She's dreadful. People like that shouldn't be allowed to take part in the war.") Or in Jumping Rorie Macnair in *Each Man's Son* being scared out of his wits by old Doctor Mackenzie threatening him with a roomful of poisons, or in George Stewart's crossbow-inventing father in *The Watch That Ends the Night*. And we find it in his essays, where he takes pleasure in eccentric Oxford dons, like the one whose opening conversational gambit with strangers was "Whenever I see a naked woman I faint. Do you?"

Near the end of his life, speaking to the Writers' Union of Canada in Kingston, giving the lecture named after his old friend Margaret Laurence, I recall he reported with delight a recent encounter with a boy who said, "You're eighty years old and that's an awful thing. What does it feel like to know that you'll soon be dead?"

Finally, I was struck as an anthologist by the consistency of his tone. All of his books — fiction and non-fiction — are written by the same civilized, widely educated, informed, tolerant mind. I believe David Helwig was right when he noted that MacLennan's personal goodness and decency shine though all his works.

I tried to make the anthology a tribute, because I believe that the selections demonstrate that Hugh MacLennan was an excellent writer with an astonishing range. I see him as a heavyweight novelist and an equally fine essayist who could write, apparently, with ease and grace about everything under the sun. He can take us to the torture chambers of the Gestapo, the sunny courts of Wimbledon, or to a New Brunswick lumber camp with a murderer on the loose in the dark. He can make us see the yellow foam above the Fraser in flood at Hell's Gate, hear the wee pipers in Hudson's Bay Governor Simpson's canoe "blowing his ears off," feel the impact of Jerome Martell's bayonet in the German soldier's throat, or smell the scent of new-mown hay in St. Marc in *Two Solitudes.*

The anthology is also intended to entice readers into Hugh MacLennan's world, where I hope they will find they want to stay and roam. Because I believe the writing is strong, and will survive. In fact, I see Hugh MacLennan as a major writer in a long and honourable tradition whose work has been underestimated in recent years for simple generational reasons. It was time, as the world works, for the old order to change, for the council of elders to be replaced. But "decency," the consistent tone in his novels and his essays, "generosity of spirit," and the ability to make the world seem a better place are qualities with lasting appeal. And there's something more here. An artist. Not for nothing did Robert Kroetsch call Hugh MacLennan "the cartographer of our dreams."

A final note. Hugh's funeral was held at the McGill Chapel. I had the honour to be one of the four speakers who paid tribute to his life. One of the others, a nice but disorganized man, cast his voluminous notes aside, and spoke as the spirit moved him. He caught sight of Mordecai Richler, sitting quietly in the middle of the church, there to pay his respects to another senior writer. Mordecai, a shy man, found himself enthusiastically singled out for unwelcome attention, his moment in the spotlight ending with the words, "Keep up the good work, Mordecai!"

After we filed out of the chapel that day, I, as a non-Montrealer, found myself standing alone in the foyer, thinking sadly about Hugh. I was glad to be approached by a fine man who told me that he had come to the funeral in the hope of hearing a talk like mine, which had summarized Hugh's career brilliantly and paid eloquent tribute to his special qualities. I was delighted to hear this objective assessment by a well spoken and clearly intelligent stranger, and I shuffled modestly and looked at my shoes, and said that Hugh had meant a lot to me.

There was a two-beat pause, then my new friend cleared his throat and said, "Ah, I've just completed a novel, and I wonder if I could send it along to you at McClelland & Stewart for your consideration."

I was so startled that I agreed to have him submit it. I'm not sorry to say that it went nowhere.

But I know that Hugh would have loved that story.

# CHAPTER 3

# R.D. SYMONS

Cowboy, Writer, Artist, and Conservationist

Robert David (Bob) Symons was born in England in 1898, the son of artist William Christian Symons and pianist Cecilia Constance Davenport. He was educated at home ("I never saw the inside of a school") in a rural Sussex household. There, visitors like artist John Singer Sargent (his father's friends also included Whistler and Monet) and Rudyard Kipling made the wider world of the British Empire seem ripe for exploring. His father died in 1911, and with six brothers and two sisters Bob knew that the family, while rich in many things, could not afford to keep him indefinitely. At the age of sixteen his sense of adventure took him to the Canadian West, determined to be a cowboy.

After a sea voyage to New York, and a lot of Pullman car advice to steer clear of Canada, he reached Maple Creek, Saskatchewan, by train and hung around the livery stables in his smart tweed jacket and his New York–purchased knee-high laced "surveyor boots." How a local rancher, Scotty Gow, decided to take a chance on this five-foot-five-inch slim English lad is the start of his classic 1973 book, *Where the Wagon Led: One Man's Memories of the Cowboy's Life in the Old West.* It tells how the eager "green hand" learned the trade of mending fences, branding and driving cattle, breaking horses, and dealing with harsh winters, droughts, and long days in the saddle "with a tight belt for lunch." Not only is the book filled with anecdotes about memorable characters, including horse thieves and poetry-quoting Mounties, it is enlivened with seventy sketches, which even illustrate details of saddle and stirrup types, showing his intimate knowledge of that now-distant world.

After his years as a ranch hand, he joined up to do his duty in the First World War, his arrival delayed by height requirements. He saw action in France, but typically wrote more about the horses he knew there than his own deeds. After the war Symons (he insisted on the Cornish pronunciation, like "Timmins") was a rancher. But times were hard, and in one of his later books, *Grandfather Symons' Homestead Book*, intended for children, he thanks a country store-owner named Taylor with these words:

"He had many customers among the new settlers and did pretty well until the droughts and low prices of the 1920s, which were worse in the 1930s. Yet I must tell you that I never knew a customer to leave that store without some groceries, whether he had money or not. I ought to know, for I was one who sometimes had not. But he never told anyone, which is why I tell it now."

He then moved to a role as a Saskatchewan game warden, in the Battlefords, then the Pasquia Hills, then around the Cypress Hills, and finally, in 1942, in British Columbia. His respect for the native people he encountered, and his mastery of a number of their tongues (he loved to demonstrate the liquid sound of spoken Cree) helped him to be fair while still vigorously doing his job, bringing the laws on hunting into lonely places, to offenders who were all armed, and often hungry. He may have been small in stature, never more than 125 pounds, and his close-set eyes may not have been strictly parallel, but his bright keenness made him an unforgettable force of nature.

He was by birth a nineteenth-century man, and in practice such a keen student of ranching and conservation issues that he found a way to read Hansard on parliamentary debates, regularly, and to write many letters and articles on issues that engaged him. In 1945 he decided to change his life by reliving a Victorian dream. Although by now in his late forties he rode into unsettled country far beyond Fort St. John in northern B.C. He surveyed the land on horseback, staked a claim, and was soon felling the trees on the site to build a homestead cabin that became a successful cattle ranch. The traditional story — and it is told in a deliberately old-fashioned style, with the Black Wolf watching the Man and the Woman coming into his domain, and setting up the ranch — is told in *The Broken Snare: The Story of a Frontier Family*.

And here I step into the picture. If we never forget a first love, an editor never forgets the first manuscript — found, read, edited, and published. *The Broken Snare*, published in 1970, was my first book as an editor, the first of hundreds, but I remember it and Bob Symons well. There was no reference to his previous books in the letter accompanying the submitted manuscript to make it stand out from the others in what we disgracefully called "the slush pile." The manuscript simply stood out through its epic simplicity, and its knowledge of an excitingly remote ranching world, where an imported Highland bull could break the back of a bear attacking his herd. To my delight, I was able to persuade my bosses at Doubleday that we should publish it, and it became my first signed-up book.

This old-style ranching was heady stuff, of course, especially for a young guy fresh to Canada, and now living among the fancy new high-rises of hip St. James Town in the centre of Toronto. These chapters about rustlers, or the Moose being stalked through the willows by the Wolf, or the Man slowly building up his ranch, even carving out a new road to the nearest settlement, might have come from 1898, not 1968 — although it was, of course, back in 1945 when Bob started this great traditional adventure, along with his brave and determined wife, Hope.

Like most boys within the reach of Hollywood (and Hopalong Cassidy and Roy Rogers and "Shane") I had grown up wanting to be a cowboy, although I secretly knew that no such world still existed. *And now this!* A wonderfully romantic, true story! My own experiences growing up in a farming community in Scotland gave me something in common with Bob, since one summer I had been, literally, a cow-boy, helping with the milking, and so on. Working on a local farm that summer meant that I knew all about handling a pitchfork when bringing in the hay that would feed the stock in winter, as he had done on the ranch. I even knew something about horses, since as an awestruck small boy I had watched the giant Clydesdales being shod at Mr. Mabon's "smiddy" on Dunlop's main street. (I still catch a whiff of burning hoof occasionally in the dentist's chair, but there is no hiss as red-hot horseshoes are dropped into a pail of water.) I had even seen horses at work in the hayfields where I laboured; the old grandfather — who spoke pure Robert Burns — would follow along with his horse-drawn rake, suspicious of wasteful modern baling machines.

As for riding horses, I didn't have Bob's advantage of having grown up with them, but I had ridden in California's Sierra Mountains with only one stirrup (fun riding down a steep slope). And there was the incident in the historical procession in St. Andrews when, in the

Cavalier costume (wrong but romantic) of the Duke of Montrose, I spurred my horse into a runaway ride that scarred a centuries-old lawn.

In my travels east by bus from Victoria I had seen lots of cowboy country. In Lethbridge I had met my second cousin, Butch Barber, a guy of my age who played pro hockey in winter and worked the rodeo as a bull-wrestler in summer. And passing through Regina I had stayed overnight at a cheap hotel with old cowboys — no doubt friends of Bob Symons — crowding the lobby.

Bob and I worked happily together, by correspondence, and the letters went just northwest of Regina to his home in Silton. Why Bob retired there is instructive. Near the end of *The Broken Snare* Bob realizes that his calves can't happily coexist with the Black Wolf's pack. And when he sets about destroying them, the Black Wolf breaks the snare — to Bob's secret relief — and leaves the valley. In the same way, Bob and his family are driven out when the "civilization" that he fled in the first place discovers oil nearby. Soon the boys from Texas are casually driving through his fences, paying compensation, sure, but causing him endless problems with his stock. In the end he decides to sell up. And his lawyer in Fort St. John, as Bob leaves the office, sensing the importance of the moment, tells his staff to "Stand up and say good-bye to the last of the free men!"

Bob never mentions it in the book, but there was a further reason for his decision to sell up, and move south to Silton. He was fighting leukemia. As he crammed a lifetime of writing into his last, defiant decade, we also worked together on *Where the Wagon Led* (now a recognized classic account of The Old Canadian West, as I hoped it would be, when I suggested it to Bob) and on *North by West* (two fictional stories of the West and the North). I had no hand in *Where the Wind Blows*, *Many Trails*, or *Grandfather Symons's Homestead Book*, his fine, heavily illustrated book for children. All of his books, of course, were enriched by the sketches that he drew with such ease.

As an artist he made his reputation with *Hours and the Birds* (published first here, then around the world, thanks to Oxford University Press) which established him in 1967 as a superb naturalist and painter of birds — one signed painting of a myrtle warbler, a wedding present, hangs proudly in my house. On a larger canvas, from 1951, in the winters away from the ranch, he painted dioramas in Regina's

Royal Saskatchewan Museum of Natural History. As described by a museum employee, Robert W. Nero, he initially seemed to be "a rather flamboyant cowpoke-artist. . . . unfailingly a silk scarf tucked into an open shirt, talking at a great rate while busy painting" vivid scenes against which native Indian life, or the appropriate birds and animals, were displayed. In time the sceptical Nero came to see that he knew his stuff and was "a really good man. I'm so glad to have known him."

Bob Nero played an important — literally, a life-saving — role in our man's life. In 1965 his friend Bob was deathly ill in Regina General Hospital, his leukemia complicated by pneumonia. He was kept in isolation, and his family was informed that he was likely to die that night. Around midnight Bob Nero managed to sneak into his room, where he found his friend pouring sweat, but grimly reading the last of the proofs of *Hours and the Birds*. Nero asked how he was, and Symons gasped that he had almost finished checking the proofs, and was determined to complete that final task because "I think I'm going to die tonight."

"Boy," said Nero, "that's what I call a deadline!"

They both laughed so hard that Bob's temperature dropped, his fever disappeared, and the baffled doctors (unaware of the Norman Cousins system of laughing your way back to health) were able to send him home a few days later. Bob, a deeply religious man, saw this as a chance that God had given him "to write the books I was meant to write," and I, and his readers, benefitted from the burst of creative energy that followed.

In 1970 he was awarded an honorary LL.D. by the University of Saskatchewan, and forty years later, in the winter of 2010, the university's Kenderdine Gallery staged an exhibition of his art and books entitled "The Symons Trail." It was co-curated by his old friend, Dr. Stuart Houston, with whom he used to stay when he was in town, and who was a notable amateur ornithologist.

As a bird-loving conservationist Bob earned the Saskatchewan Conservation Medal in 1965, and he is listed by Sharon and Peter Butala as one of Saskatchewan's Environmental Champions. His most lasting contribution in this area may be his book *Silton Seasons* (1975), a month-by-month account of what he found in the natural world outside his door in Silton, near Last Mountain Lake. I published that remarkable local and universal book, adding a sad editor's note that told of Bob's death in 1973.

He only came to Toronto once in my time, and I vividly remember the short, slim man in the white Stetson who lit up every room with his enthusiasm. I saw him being interviewed by the *Toronto Star*'s book man, Peter Sypnowich, and at the end heard Bob express his pleasure at meeting him by telling the surprised journalist, "I like the cut of your jib!"

He was a man from a different era. When he invited my brother to stay at Meadowlark Cottage in Silton on his way back from graduate work in California, he couched the invitation in language that included phrases like "Mark you, 'twill be no easy task." My brother Peter spent some time with Bob, working hard in the Silton vegetable garden, Voltaire-style, with the political and environmental ills of the world being solved between the two enthusiastic talkers.

Some time after his death I visited Hope at their trim Silton cottage, where pride of place went to Bob's old saddle, lovingly preserved. It seemed right. It also seemed right that one of the sons of this man out of time had moved down to South America, ranching in such hostile frontier territory that his letters home, as Bob quoted them to me, told of attacks on his household "with flaming arrows."

His influence lives on. On a recent birding trip near Silton, the marvellous award-winning nature writer Trevor Herriot told me that as a young man he once sought out the old tent circle hidden on the prairie where Bob had sat, imagining earlier generations of native hunters camped in that spot.

In that passage in *Silton Seasons* you get a sense of Bob's magic:

I think I can hear the thumping of hobbled horses — lean, fleet Indian mustangs. They crop the young grass, and pause and look intently now this way, now that, blowing softly, then they crop again — but their ears are not still, and flit back and forth, for they were foaled on these plains and know its hazards. Steadily they tear the squeaking grass, and their jaw muscles work back and forth over the bony structures below their liquid eyes.

*Squeaking grass.* All these years later, young Trevor was able to sit there on the silent grass, imagining Bob letting *his* imagination roam, and in turn finding inspiration for a writing career.

# HAROLD HORWOOD

Newfoundlander, Novelist, Naturalist, and Neglected Genius

"Cancel the lunch appointment at the Westbury, Carol. Mr. Horwood is not wearing shoes!"

That exact quote summarizes the famous incident when the old take-the-author-to-lunch-and-feed-him-steak-with-martinis publishing culture (represented by George Nelson, a predecessor of mine at Doubleday Canada) crashed rudely up against the counter-culture of the sixties (represented by the long-haired Harold Horwood, in sandals).

Born in St. John's in 1923, into a seafaring family that had been in Newfoundland for three centuries, Harold was in his forties when he came to the hippie world. But by then he had already packed several lives into his single allotted one. After quarrelling with his parents about his plans for a literary career he went, not to a university, but into a life of labouring jobs, starting as a longshoreman on the St. John's waterfront. In turn this led to a life as an organizer with the Canadian Congress of Labour, and then as a crusading journalist and editor heavily involved in the campaign to bring Newfoundland into Canada in 1949. In this he was a major ally of Joey Smallwood, whose biography, *Joey*, he was to write in 1989.

I encountered Joey, who revelled in the title "The Last Living Father of Confederation," when he was touring Toronto publishers in the early 1970s, tempting them with the prospect of publishing his memoirs. He was the only author I ever met who, in the confines of a small publishing office, rose to his feet and began to pace, thumbs in his lapels, addressing a gaping audience of two like a huge public meeting. As he strode up and down, orating, with full gestures, he struck me the same way as he did Harry Bruce, who described him as a small man with "a head like an otter." He was sleek in other ways, too, and like so many perennially successful politicians, was a lovable rogue. He was not offended, I'm sure, by the story of his election-eering tour of St. John's alongside his fellow Liberal, Lester Pearson, who was waving cheerfully to the crowds their car skirted. When they passed a cemetery, Pearson stopped waving — to be scolded by Joey that he was neglecting some of his most reliable voters.

Ah, Newfoundland.

Harold Horwood worked hard for two years as Joey's "left-hand man" on the campaign to bring Newfoundland into Canada — which, lest we forget, was a very close decision. Then he joined Smallwood's government in the House of Assembly from 1949 to 1951 as the Member for Labrador.

To most Canadians Labrador is just a name, a complete mystery, a place where nobody goes. I am one of the lucky few who have sailed out of Ungava Bay all the way around Cape Chidley, then southeast down the entire coast of Labrador, which stretches almost as far as the distance from New York to Florida. It is another world, split by magical fjords fringed with black mountains plunging 5,000 feet (1,500 metres) into the sea, and the word "rugged" doesn't begin to do it justice. Twenty years after his time representing the area, in *White Eskimo* (1972) Harold wrote about one part of Labrador:

> To port were the mountains of Aulatsivk Island, to starboard the southern extension of the Kiglapaites. We could see snow falling on their peaks, and shafts of sunlight through the clouds turning them from slate-gray to pure yellow. The lower slopes were red and brown, with icefalls cutting pale gray swaths down their sides. Naked blocks of black basalt rose through the snow, as though the rocks had crystallized ages ago into ice cubes bigger than cathedrals — as perhaps they had. It is awesome country — the most impressive bit of geography I have ever seen. Sailing through it is rather like sailing through a valley in the Rocky Mountains.

The author's biography in that novel pays tribute to Harold's hard-won knowledge of that hidden land, from his time representing the huge area in the Newfoundland legislature: "He has travelled there extensively on his own boat, by other small boats and ships, by bush plane, by dogteam, and by canoe (which he was taught to use by a Labrador Indian)."

Later, he refers to travelling "many of the inland waters described in this book, in company with a party of Eskimo hunters." He did this in 1968, assisted by a Canada Council grant, possibly the very one that might otherwise have gone to the resentful Leacock scholar, David Legate.

Long before then, of course, Harold's formal political career had ended (everyone of independent mind eventually broke with Smallwood) and he was busy with his own new life as a crusading journalist, a political columnist, and an editor, creating an influential literary magazine, *Protocol*, on what the *Globe and Mail*'s obituary called "a hand-set typepress in Harold Horwood's bedroom." After founding a labour newspaper, the *Examiner*, which ran for two years, he even travelled as a delegate to the founding convention of the NDP in Ottawa in 1962. Thanks to training by the famous ornithologist, L.M. Tuck, for whom he worked as a field assistant and editor, he became a skilful naturalist who went on expeditions with his great pal Farley Mowat, another man of immensely varied, yet wildly unpredictable, talents. Indecent exposure rarely features in formal *Globe and Mail* obituaries, but J.M. Sullivan broke the taboo. When Farley stayed with Harold at his place on Beachy Cove outside St. John's, "Mr. Mowat's penchant for parading around in nothing but boots had startled the local fishermen." Ah, yes, Farley.

I knew, and published, Farley in my time at McClelland & Stewart, visiting him at his retreat in the small lakeside town of Port Hope. (Earlier, when Port Hope had trouble with nuclear fuel there, it came to regret its motto "The Town That Radiates Happiness" — but someone who went along with giving a fine novel the time-limited title *White Eskimo* is in no position to sneer.) By then Farley was living happily with the sobering influence of his wife, Claire, but he was still small, fierce, bearded, outspoken, and proudly controversial. He used to claim that his feud with the United States — which saw him as a dangerous left-winger, possibly because he opposed the Vietnam War, but possibly because he also (gasp) had written an admiring book about Siberia and its Commie people — led him to discharge shotgun blasts at American planes flying overhead. Thousands of feet overhead.

Farley is a great storyteller, even to the extent of talking about his reluctance to "let the facts get in the way of the truth." Certainly stories *about* him are legion, many of them possibly even true. Two of my favourites are worth mentioning.

Once, in his drinking days, he was resentfully completing a coast-to-coast book signing tour for a new book. An expectant crowd at a Victoria bookstore was lined up around the store and into the street. What they could not see was the delivery lane at the back, where the panting local McClelland & Stewart sales rep was hauling, hands under the armpits, a small comatose body out of his car and into the back door of the store. With his feet trailing, Farley was dragged inside the storage room and plumped into a chair. "Farley, Farley!" helpful voices shouted at him, "Can you hear us?" They tried to thrust a pen into his hand, asking, "Farley, can you sign your name?" They may have tried pouring coffee into him, may even have tried gently slapping his face, but all that his pen produced looked like the final entry in a dying explorer's diary, along the lines of "tired . . . so tired . . . the pen slips from my fing . . ." ending in a sad vertical line. It wasn't going to work, and the scores of Mowat-lovers lined up in front of the store were growing restive — yes, even in Victoria.

It was time for a stroke of genius.

"Ladies and gentlemen, Mr. Mowat has arrived, and is in the building." (Mollified sounds from the crowd.) "Unfortunately, he has come down with what he fears may be a very infectious type of flu, and he's afraid of spreading it. So what we're going to do is have him sign copies of his new book in our back room, and you will all get your own signed copies."

And in the back room the M&S man rolled up his sleeves and began to sign, "Best wishes, Farley Mowat," over and over again.

The other story concerns a fundraising dinner for the Writers' Trust. To raise money for this worthy charity, well-known writers would allow themselves to be rented out, for a handsome fee, as guests at smart dinner parties that the other guests could talk about for years. Apparently Farley was the Guest of Honour at just such a party in an upper-crust home in Toronto's Rosedale district, where the table was laden with the finest in glasses, plates, napery, and wines. He behaved well, at least until the hostess proudly produced a large, creamy bowl of whipped dessert and placed it carefully at the far end of the table.

This was Farley's moment to give the guests their money's worth. Climbing onto the table in his kilt (as an occasional kilt-wearing man, I shrink from explaining the implications), he began to crawl vigorously down towards the distant bowl, sending all of the table's precious contents flying. Then, dog-like, he plunged his bearded face deep into the dessert bowl, and proceeded to eat from it, very loudly, and very messily.

The guests were scandalized/delighted. "That Farley Mowat, I was once at a dinner party with him, and you wouldn't believe . . ."

Harold Horwood — as I was saying when great stories about Farley interrupted me — went on several expeditions to wild natural places with Farley. It's interesting that Harold laughed off Farley's famous *Never Cry Wolf* moment of, supposedly, frying up and eating a pan-full of mice to test their nutritional value. "Oh, that's just Farley," said Harold, affectionately.

In time, Harold began to write his own books. Before my day at Doubleday Canada, in 1966 he wrote and published *Tomorrow Will Be Sunday*, a powerful, bleak novel of life in Newfoundland that deals with a devastating rape at a religious school (naturally, this was long before the horrors visited upon the boys at Mount Cashel were revealed). By way of contrast, he also wrote a delightful nature book (one that did not involve the author in eating mice), entitled *The Foxes of Beachy Cove*, in 1967. (Beachy Cove is surprisingly close to St. John's, near Portugal Cove, and hard by the ferry to Bell Island that, open to the Atlantic swells, reminds visitors like me that a great big sea surrounds Newfoundland. The landscape at its easternmost point, Cape Spear, reminds anyone from Scotland or Ireland that, thousands of miles to the east, the same rocks and vegetation climb out of the same grey sea, as if joined by an underwater chain.) Now he was on a roll, and wrote the *Newfoundland* volume in the Provinces of Canada series in 1969, and revised it a few years later. He was clearly becoming *the* Newfoundland writer, even if as Sullivan puts it, he was "outspoken, flamboyant, and dynamic . . . a man of large gestures and a substantially gruff manner. His singular, sometimes prickly personality infused his writing."

In this chapter's subtitle I have referred to Harold as a "neglected genius." Let me explain that phrase, since he was rewarded in 1980 for his literary career with an Order of Canada, not usually a mark of neglect. Right from the start Harold struck me as having a truly amazing intelligence, the type that comes from a world where

university degrees are less important than much reading, close con-
templation of the things around you, and hard thought. How many
writers would list their recreations as "music, mathematics, boating,
ornithology, gardening," while writing more than twenty books that
range from pirates to politics, from novels to folklore, and from
poetry to accurately observed science in the natural world? In yet
another arena, the Writers' Union of Canada found him to be an incisive chair, and at all times a swift and certain authority on procedures
and rules of order. I speak affectionately, as an honorary member of
the Writers' Union, when I say that the phrase "herding cats" springs
to mind, but not when the cats were under the bright spotlight of
Harold's shining intellect, and his crisp, slightly nasal, commands
from the wheelhouse.

What impressed me most, though, was his genius as a writer. I
could have an editorial discussion with him where I would — for the
first time — raise the possibility that it might be good to add an extra
paragraph here. "Ah, yes," Harold would say, "something like this."
And then he would reel off five or six polished sentences that made
the ideal paragraph. And I would say, "Er, yes — that's perfect."

I never knew another writer with such amazing fluency, and
such confidence — which could, of course, be misunderstood. Once
Harold made the mistake of using the word "genius" about himself
on TV in St. John's, and I certainly heard about it.

As for "neglected," consider how familiar you, dear reader, are
with his work, compared with the household names featured elsewhere in this book. I'm sorry now that I didn't manage to remain his
publisher throughout, setting him higher and higher goals.

I'm sorry, too, that I never saw him in action as a teacher of creative writing. He may well have been excellent. Alternatively, on the
principle that superb natural athletes make lousy coaches, because
they never really had to *learn* their skills, he might not have been
very good. But simply being in close contact with that blazing intelligence must have been a great education for the writers who studied
under him at Memorial, or later in Ontario at Western and Waterloo,
where he was a Writer-in-Residence.

When I first met him in Toronto, I was delighted by this energetic, long-haired Viking-ish character, who looked shrewdly at you

through rimless glasses and, with a long-toothed smile, burst into fox-like barks of laughter if he liked your jokes. He was of middle height, broad-chested, as was appropriate to his labouring past, and he always seemed very fit, although I never heard him speak of exercise — apart from vigorous tasks like taking flaming torches on long poles to burn out an infestation of tent caterpillars.

Unlike George Nelson, I was pleased by his dashiki and sandals (and by the news that for a year he ran a hippie school in St. John's called "Animal Farm" for high-school dropouts), and very pleased indeed by the car that he had driven all the way to Toronto from Newfoundland. When I peered into the back seat, it was indeed possible that the disorder contained a kitchen sink.

"Harold," I said, "it looks as if you have rabbits in there!" He was not offended. It may even at one time have been true.

Our first book together, *White Eskimo*, allowed Harold to make great use of his travels in Labrador. One section reads: "The Eskimos still talk of the morning the giant stranger came down out of the hills in the dead of winter, dressed in the skin of a white bear, driving a team of white dogs . . ." The plot follows the deeds of a heroic rebel named Gillingham (and Harold was such a scholar that I'm certain that the echoes of the ancient Gilgamesh epic were deliberate) who sets up a trading empire in Labrador in the twentieth century. In the process, his own journeys are epic, and they involve the Indian, Inuit, and white inhabitants of the stark land where sheer cliffs rise out of the Atlantic, and powerful spirits haunt the interior. What's notable, too, is Harold's unsympathetic treatment of the sainted medical missionary, Sir Wilfred Grenfell, whose mission he despises. His radical views — against the Grenfell Mission, the missionaries in general, and the big traders — come through loud and clear in this book by an author who was later to deal admiringly with pirates.

One of his greatest achievements, however, was very quiet, and that is the assistance he gave to Cassie Brown for her book, *Death on the Ice: The Great Newfoundland Sealing Disaster of 1914*, a great classic, known to every school child in Newfoundland down through the years since we brought it out in 1972.

Cassie was a Newfoundlander, born and bred, who rose to become a reporter and columnist for the *Daily News* in St. John's for seven years, as well a writer of stage and radio plays. Somewhere along the line, though, she decided to research and write a book about the historic sealing disaster, when confusion led to ships sailing around a stranded party on the ice, each believing that another ship had picked up the men, who in reality were freezing to death. She did so, and submitted it to me for publication.

Sadly, the manuscript she turned in was only about 30,000 words long (enough to make a book of, roughly, only 100 pages). The story she had to tell, I wrote back to say, was very powerful and deserved a full book, but to stretch her story to book length she'd have to research this, and this, and this, and write much more about this, and that, and the other. Harold, I should say, got involved very helpfully at this stage, suggesting themes to be developed, and, above all, encouraging Cassie with his enthusiasm. But what we were proposing, I knew, would take months, maybe even years, of work — and if events followed the usual pattern I would never hear from her again.

Never underestimate a determined woman from Newfoundland, especially one with the straight, regal bearing of white-haired Cassie Brown. In my talks to editors and writers I use her name as an inspiration. (Incredibly, I was able to give such a talk in 2009, on a ship that had sailed, just a few hours earlier, across the very spot on the ocean floor where the bones of some of the stranded men still lie.) Because, by God, back she came, many months later, with a greatly expanded book, more than double the size of her first version. She had not been discouraged by my horrifying demands, but had buckled down and produced a fine, publishable book.

But there was something missing. With Cassie's agreement, I asked my friend Harold — who knew Newfoundland history in *his* bones, and whose grandfather had skippered a sealing ship — to take a look at this version of the manuscript. Would he, I asked, be willing to write a foreword? And could he, I wondered, in an editorial role take a hand in refining the manuscript, perhaps even adding some vivid touches?

Harold replied yes to both invitations. His foreword concludes:

This is Cassie Brown's book, not mine. She did more than nine-tenths of all the work on it. My contribution was limited to editorial advice, mainly to cutting and trimming the narrative from a much longer one to its present length.

*Death on the Ice* is the most moving story I have ever read. I am proud to have had some small part in preparing it for publication.

This is very generous, but the way he restricts his own role is not entirely accurate; he also added some very useful touches. Here's what I'm sure is a Horwood paragraph, showing how vividly he wrote when he added such dramatic touches:

The eager seal hunters knew what they were heading for — a terrible voyage, living and working like dogs, their arms constantly caked in blood up to the shoulder, short of sleep, and with little time to do more than snatch a bite to eat, and working, constantly cold, on heaving, cracking sheets of ice that could give way under them or break off and float away with them into the icy darkness — they knew all this, but they cheerfully flocked into St. John's to volunteer, in fact to compete, for tickets to berths on the ships going "to the ice." This was their one chance to earn hard cash. And besides, what else was there for a fisherman to do in Newfoundland in March?

I published the book as "by Cassie Brown" (then, in smaller type) "with Harold Horwood," an accurate description. When on Harold's death in 2006, an obituary restricted his role in this great classic to merely writing the foreword, I wrote a detailed account, setting the record straight, in a letter to the St. John's paper.

I did so because the book's account of the courage of the men in the lost party — one of whom froze his lips biting off the eyelash icicles that were blinding his comrades, all of them shuffling endlessly in circles on the ice, since to sit or lie down was to die, as over seventy men did before rescue came — is so unforgettable that it is a huge, continuing success. Even the ongoing debate about the seal hunt has not destroyed the modern reader's respect for these threadbare men a century ago who went to the ice as part of their traditional struggle to keep starvation at bay.

Two footnotes: first, to produce the cover illustration I turned to a young, leather-aproned printmaker named David Blackwood, who had already produced art on the lost party. In no time, he produced a magnificent print specially for the cover, and at the end of it all, quietly presented me with his original print, as a gift. It hangs in my house, instantly recognizable as a work by the David Blackwood whose prints have become so famous in the world of art.

Second, when the book was offered to bookstores across Canada, from B.C. to Nova Scotia we ran into a chorus of rejections from booksellers who refused to stock more than a token number of copies of the book, because it was "just a Newfoundland book." Meanwhile, newspapers as far away as Australia were running excerpts from this amazing story. Sometimes the provincial barriers in our country are discouragingly high.

Time for a personal confession: I never met a Newfoundlander I didn't like. Newfoundlanders I have known include the hungover young fellow who sat beside me on one flight from Halifax to St. John's. From the moment we were in the air, he was pleading with the flight attendant for a can of beer, wheedling for an urgent hair of the dog. When she relented, he grabbed the can gratefully, then nudged me.

"Watch my buddy there."

Buddy, sprawled in the seat across the aisle, was more than hungover, he was unconscious. Yet when my pal, with the skill and timing of a great magician, held his beer can aloft, and gently pulled off the tab with a tiny "Pfftt," Buddy sprang to life, sitting bolt upright, eyes wide open, head sweeping wildly from side to side, while his pal nudged me again in delight.

I think of my friend Daniel Jones, the fiddler and folk singer from Cow Head, who — despite his yards of long red hair — can strut a mean Elvis routine, in costume. You had to be there, maybe — as I was on the cruise down Newfoundland's west coast with Daniel (not to mention Latonia Hartery, the singing anthropologist, who can jump ashore on any Labrador beach and find you a centuries-old dwelling site in twenty minutes), and my cabinmate Dennis Minty, nature photographer without peer. True Newfoundlanders, all of them, with "ranting and roaring" available only on demand. We stopped in to meet the folk who live in fine places like Woody Point and La Poile, a seabound port with no access by land, where I met a brave teacher whose school must be in trouble, since it has only six pupils. And among the crew of young writers from the Rock,

I know and like long, tall Michael Winter, and Michael Crummey, who comes up to about Winter's waist, but writes big, as they say.

I missed the chance to publish Joey Smallwood's memoirs, as you know, but in 1993, when John Crosbie retired from politics, Avie Bennett, the owner of M&S, and I thought that it would be worth persuading him to write a book. John is a very bright man, the winner of gold medals at university, and he and Geoffrey Stevens combined well to produce a fine book, which we published as *No Holds Barred*, with a fighting photo on the cover of John damning all the Liberals who ever lived.

I had two problems with the book. The first was persuading my colleagues that this podium-thumping politician, the man who had Punch-and-Judy verbal fun with Sheila Copps in and out of the House (ascribing her lateness to one event to "trouble with her broomstick"), in private was a very shy, reserved man who would sit quietly, rarely making eye contact with new people in a meeting around a table.

My other problem was that this former minister of finance in Brian Mulroney's government (and of frugal Scottish heritage) soon proved to be full of free-spending ideas for getting rid of M&S's money, in promoting and publicizing his book. I turned down expensive ideas from him by letter, by fax, and eventually even by phone.

Once the conversation went like this:

"John, I know that you have relatives in Fredericton, and I'm sure they'd be delighted to see you again, but Fredericton's a very small book market, and you've already been there once to promote your book, so, no, we just can't afford to send you there again."

There was a heavy sigh. Then the Right Honourable John C. Crosbie, more in sorrow than in anger, gave me the benefit of The Full Newfoundland Rebuke.

"You goddam poblishers. Yer so toight with a dollar . . . when you walk across a nickel on the soidwalk . . . yer arse starts snappin'!"

I was deeply shocked, of course. But when John's book won the Book of the Year Award from the nation's booksellers at the ceremony in Toronto's Roy Thomson Hall, I was able to repeat the story, word for word, from the stage, and the grey walls of the elegant symphony hall trembled only slightly.

How does a Newfoundlander survive outside Newfoundland? Harold decided to find out. In 1979, with his wife Corky, and Andrew (age five) and Leah (age two), he left the Rock that had been home to his family for three centuries and moved to Nova Scotia. Their chosen spot was Upper Clements, just south of Annapolis Royal, on the way to Digby. They were attracted by "the beauty of the land, the fruitfulness of the soil, the gentleness of the climate, the variety of plant and animal life, the closeness of great forests and clear waters, the presence of the sea without its storms."

The Annapolis Basin is a blessed place, just off the Bay of Fundy, but so sheltered that peach trees and melons grow there in the surprising micro-climate that resembles Connecticut, which lies much farther south. Champlain spotted its possibilities, and established his "Habitation" there in 1605, and it turned out to be, as Harold wrote in *Dancing on the Shore: A Celebration of Life at Annapolis Basin* (1987) "the best site for a colony in eastern Canada, indeed, the only place where an early colony succeeded without support from Europe."

The Horwood family literally pitched their tents right across the basin from Champlain's finely reproduced timber "Habitation" (and the Parks Canada site is well worth a visit), and set about building their home. It was a sprawling, interesting building of passive solar design, with lean-to greenhouses and many Horwoodian touches.

Equally exciting was what they did with the six hectares of land that sloped from the road all the way down to the shore, where the willets danced. What Harold did — planting trees, restoring meadows to attract wildlife from butterflies to martens, harvesting seaweed as fertilizer for their fruits and vegetables, and encouraging and savouring the great dance of nature — is brilliantly told in his book.

*Dancing on the Shore* is worth quoting in its entirety, whether Harold is describing blue herons fencing in a courtship battle, or discussing how worms "remember" to curl into a ball to preserve moisture, or writing about finches, shrimps, stars, seaweed, beech trees, ponds, garter snakes, or squirrels hiding cookies all over the unconventional house. But let me give you just a taste, as he begins the chapter entitled "Water of Life."

For most of its length — at least for that part of it that you can navigate in a boat — the Annapolis River is slow and tidal, snaking its way between banks of mud and grass through a long succession of farms that have been tilled for three and a half centuries. The streams that feed the river have quite a different character. Roaring cascades, they come down the slopes of South Mountain, tumbling over granite boulders, pausing in ponds and lakes whose currents swirl like the winds of cyclones, rushing through cool stands of spruce and pine and hemlock, shouting as they go — until they collapse suddenly into the flat valley, directly from mountain to river bottom, where they wind sedately through muddy creek beds, being tamed and controlled by the tides until they join the Annapolis River itself, sedate and middle-aged, all shouting and laughter left behind.

Those streams are my kind of river, useless for trade but leaping with trout and dragonfly and kingfisher, home to the eagle and the goshawk, land of the marten and the mink.

The setting is obviously far from the Prairies (especially when Harold looks down from his green canoe and sees "the red fronds of the seaweed reach upward toward the bottom of the boat, the round blue domes of the mussels climb the towers of the rocks, the coralline algae grow like the trees of some forest in a Celtic myth") but the spirit is clearly the same as in *Silton Seasons*, the book set on the dry Saskatchewan prairie by R.D. Symons that I published twenty-five years earlier.

When I started my Douglas Gibson Books editorial imprint at M&S in 1986, one of the major pleasures was that I could avoid the usual round of office meetings, and simply find authors I would like to work with, and then turn them loose on a great project. It's amazing how cutting out meetings leaves you lots of time to roam around.

My visits to Nova Scotia, for example, produced a haul of remarkable authors and books, including Silver Donald Cameron (*Sailing Away From Winter*), and Harry Bruce (*Page Fright*). It was my first visit to the little Eden that Harold had created down beside the Annapolis Basin that inspired me to challenge him to write a *Walden*-like book about it.

Obviously, I'm glad that I issued the challenge to write about his tiny, infinite universe, and that Harold rose to it. And I'm very glad that I added the ingredient of the wonderful, detailed woodcuts of nature by the Ontario artist G. Brender à Brandis. Harold was, too. In researching this book I found that in his clear, unhesitating hand he inscribed my copy with the words, "For Doug, who was the moving spirit behind the finest production I've ever had the pleasure to enjoy."

In the fall of 2005, I was on one of my Halifax raids when I heard that Harold was dying. It was time for another visit to the Annapolis Basin. I rented a car and set out on a drive that took me through a landscape of Canadian history that intertwined with my personal and my publishing memories.

First, I drove west towards Windsor. Further west in that direction would take me, in time, to Cumberland County, at the head of the Bay of Fundy. In *Stephen Harper — and the Future of Canada*, a biography with a shrewd subtitle that seemed rash when I published it in spring 2005, William Johnson had revealed that Harper's ancestor made a big mistake settling there in 1774. In the American Revolution, Cumberland County *took the American side*. As a loyal settler from Yorkshire (ironically on a government-sponsored plan to settle the confiscated Acadian lands) poor Christopher Harper was "much frightened" by midnight threats from his neighbours, and was eventually burned out, settling a little further west in New Brunswick and seeking government compensation.

New Brunswick set me thinking, as I drove through the fall sunlight, about my life as an Acadian. After a wedding visit to Sackville, I once spent a happy day at Shediac, on that province's north shore. It was Festival du Homard time, and I obediently ate lobster on the elegant outdoor patio of a grand Confederation-era hotel, while live Acadian fiddle music filled and overflowed the neighbouring park, setting even the trees dancing. That experience was enough to turn me into an Acadian, a process that was reinforced when I published Clive Doucet's infectious account of the joys of rediscovering his Acadian roots, *Notes from Exile*.

Across Northumberland Strait from Shediac, of course, lies Prince Edward Island, a reassuring place to any publisher, since its economy owes so much to an author. When the Gibson family toured the Maritimes a quarter of a century ago, my elder daughter, Meg, was in thrall to Lucy Maud Montgomery, and we had to visit Green Gables so that she could drift about in a ten-year-old's romantic mist, while her younger sister, Katie, now a lawyer, denounced her "soppy" behaviour. Similar behaviour every year brings in thousands of literary tourists from around the world with a yen to see the province.

Now my drive was taking me into the heart of the Annapolis Valley, through a string of pretty little towns. Noting how well maintained all the clapboard houses were, Allan Fotheringham once joked that he planned to live his life next time around as a paint salesman in the Annapolis Valley. To make things even better for me, in September the apple-picking season was at its height, and when I opened the car windows the car filled with the smell of apples, as if the back seat had been covered with them. That gave me an idea. I stopped at a roadside stand and asked for apples that I could never buy in Ontario. No problem. There was a choice, and I loaded up a basket, which I inhaled the rest of the way.

But first there was a stop near Wolfville, at the Grand Pré museum that remembers the Acadian deportation. During the family visit twenty-five years ago I became obsessively interested in the Acadian dyking systems that allowed these settlers from Northwest France to wall off waterlogged salty marshes beside the sea. Using a one-way valve system, they would drain the marsh, turning it into rich pasture land, literally for centuries.

My fascination with this system (shared by Harold, who described the creation of the dykes as "an awesome feat" that allowed the Acadian settlers "not just to wrest a living from their former salt marshes, but to flourish, to become prosperous, to raise large families, to increase from a few hundred immigrants to a population numbering tens of thousands") led me to drive my long-suffering family down a single-track road where you could park close to the Minas Basin dyke system. At the end of the road was a parked Volvo, with a middle-aged man leaning against it. We exchanged greetings, then moved off, so that Dad could survey the ancient dykes.

When we returned, the man was still there. Questions revealed that he was a professor at nearby Acadia University, and he was there with a carload of interesting artefacts to give an on-the-spot lecture about this part of the Bay of Fundy, which he knew very well. His audience was supposed to be a busload of major international scientists who were attending a conference in Halifax. But their bus had failed to show, leaving him high and dry on the dyke. "Yes," he lamented, "the bus hasn't arrived, and here I am with all of this stuff to show them."

"Well," I said, "*We're* here, and it would be great to hear your lecture."

So out of the Volvo he pulled exhibits like ancient oyster shells the size of coffee tables and pointed to half-submerged stumps that were unbelievably old, and held enthralled an audience of two visitors from Toronto, and their little girls aged ten and eight. And the bus full of VIPs never did arrive.

More than twenty years later I was in the Arctic, on the Adventure Canada cruise that followed in James Houston's wake, along the south coast of Baffin Island. The cruise rules meant that as a lecturer and ship's crew member, I was expected to host a table full of guests at dinner — presumably guests who had drawn the short straw when it came to dining at The Captain's Table. When we were all seated, I went around the table, learning my new companions' names, and encountered a nice, older man named Sherman.

"And where are you from, Sherman?"

"Wolfville, Nova Scotia. Do you know it?"

"Yes, I do," I said enthusiastically, and launched into the tale of my fascination with Acadian dykes. The table listened with polite interest as I told the story of the memorable encounter with this professor who gave his lecture to us instead of the Halifax scientists.

Sherman waited until I had finished.

"*That was me,*" he said. "I was the one who gave your family that lecture."

A hush fell over the table. If my tablemates had been politely interested before, now they were fascinated to be present at an unfolding coincidence like this, more than twenty years and many hundreds of miles away from the original encounter. It was, yes, eerie, and I could see that some people shuddered slightly. For me, it helped to put in context the conversations I used to have with Robertson Davies about the role of coincidence in fictional plots and in real life.

Now, after the drive south had taken me through the ancient streets of Annapolis Royal, it was time to get serious, and to steel myself for real life, in the form of the dying Harold. Just before I reached his place at Upper Clements, I passed the park building where we held the launch party for *Dancing on the Shore*. So many wild apples grew around the building then that it was possible to stand at the party, chatting while picking different apple varieties with your right and your left hand. It was, in short, a launch party, among Harold's friends and neighbours, that was a touch different from the usual fancy-pants Toronto book launch, where people you talk to are likely to be looking over your shoulder, scanning the room for bigger fish. Bigger apples, that's fine!

Harold's property looked beautiful as I drove in and breathed deeply: apples, sea, and flowers. The distinctive house was just as I remembered it, and we went upstairs to sprawl in comfortable chairs and chat, while Corky sat watchfully nearby.

Harold was not much changed, and made my visit easier by being pleased to see me, yet puzzled that I would take the trouble to drive all this way, just to see him. Ah, well, I explained, it was a drive through my past, too, and I had had a wonderful day.

The fact that my day had to end at a dinner party in Halifax gave him the excuse to speed me on my way, as I stumblingly tried to tell him how proud I was of having worked with him. I wasn't very good at saying it — I hope it comes through now — and he wasn't very good at receiving it. An interesting man: on the one hand, in the book's dedication to his daughter, he could refer to himself as "an Ancient Prophet." On the other, he would shrug off praise in person — especially if he had the excuse of hustling me back, for the dinner party, with a notably firm handshake.

I made it back in time, no longer dawdling through the Valley, and that evening we ate the apples I had brought, while I thought about Harold. He died the following spring, at eighty-two. His many lives had run out. But his spirit was still dancing on the shore.

# CHAPTER 5

# BARRY BROADFOOT

Newspaper Guy, and Oral Historian

"What the hell." If Barry Broadfoot hadn't specified that he wanted neither a funeral nor a tombstone, those are the words that should have been carved as his epitaph. The phrase came up all the time in his conversation and could be said to summarize a philosophy of life, one that led him to shrug and underplay his own importance as a man who changed the way Canadians saw their history.

He was the original hard-bitten "seen-it-all" newspaper guy. Before that, he was born and raised in Winnipeg, in what his auto-biography, *My Own Years*, describes as a "modest but loving" home. As a teenager he acquired "two prominent gold teeth thanks to a hockey puck I did not see" and bad eyes thanks to an unquenchable love of reading. But as a kid growing up in the Depression, those eyes noticed things going on around him. Here is one of the stories from his 1973 book, *Ten Lost Years, 1929–1939: Memories of Canadians Who Survived the Depression*:

> There was this family named Thompson across the street and the father died. They hung a black wreath on the front door and, well, that sure impressed the kids in the neighbourhood.
>
> The day of the funeral, in fact when nobody was at home because they were all at the funeral, some of us kids saw a man go up the walk of the Thompson house and stand there. He was pretending to ring the doorbell, I guess, and then we saw him slip that wreath under his coat and walk away. We followed him on our bikes, just kind of goofing along, and he went around the corner and over a couple of blocks and into a house and then he came out and hung the wreath on his own door. I told my dad and he checked and found out the man's wife had died the night before.

(That was one of two stories, among the hundreds in the book, that I happen to know were Barry's own.)

In 1943, with Canada's Depression over (courtesy of Adolf Hitler), he got his first job, working for the *Winnipeg Tribune*. As a general reporter and the low man on the totem pole, he soon drew "the casualty list." This meant visiting the houses of young men who had just been killed in the war, trying to get their shattered families to give him precious photographs of their dead son to enliven the *Tribune*'s pages. Sometimes when he arrived with his list in a taxi, walked up and knocked on the door, the mother would misunderstand. Joyful tears that their boy had been found alive after all would flow, and seventeen-year-old Barry would try to explain the situation, and try to get his photo.

Joining the army seemed an easier option.

He served as a "poor bloody infantryman" in Europe, mostly working on camp newspapers. Later, when we worked together on *Six War Years 1939–1945: Memories of Canadians at Home and Abroad*, he was more animated than I ever saw him (far from his usual relaxed, "what the hell" attitude) when he insisted that in promoting the book I stay far away from implying that his two years of army service, 1944–45, had been in any way heroic.

After the war, thanks to the Department of Veterans' Affairs, he went to the University of Manitoba. Those were the years when kids straight out of high school were rubbing shoulders in class with former bomber pilots, when professors were being put on the spot by questions from quiet men who had commanded ships off the D-Day beaches, and when getting into disputes in food lineups with little guys who had been commandos was strongly discouraged. Barry wrote about these times of generational change in *The Veteran's Years: Coming Home From the War* (1985), and himself benefitted from the veterans' effect on the University of Manitoba, where he became the editor of the student newspaper. That was his proudest memory of those college years — along with the column he ran, unchallenged, under the name "C.A. Daver." Not to mention the fact that while he was "informally engaged" to one girl, he was "on good speaking terms with two others." Sadly, they compared notes, and Barry was "labelled a pariah," and retreated to the bar.

All of this was excellent training for the newspaper world, of course, and on graduation he plunged into journalism in Vancouver with the *News-Herald*, before having cups of coffee with papers in Edmonton, Montreal, Toronto, Calgary, then finally, in Vancouver again, as nature surely intended.

To me he was always a Vancouver guy, even after he became a sort of "Mr. Canada," roaming the country, gathering ordinary people's tales on his portable tape recorder. Vancouver suited him, just as it suited the informality of the turtlenecks he always wore, along with grey slacks and a tweed jacket. That was the uniform for his trim body, and I don't believe I ever saw him in a collar and tie, which he obviously dismissed as a crazy form of eastern formality that he disliked, just as he disliked all formality ("what the hell"). Vancouver seemed to suit his family, too, and there he and his first wife raised their two kids, while Barry worked at the *Sun*, and, like a typical B.C. guy, went boating and fishing in what he called "the saltchuck." When I met him on my frequent editorial visits to Vancouver, he seemed happy in his role as the *Sun*'s books editor. When he said that some day he was going to quit all this and write a bestselling book, I made encouraging noises, as I always did in newsrooms.

A word about Vancouver. My first week in Canada was spent there, and I never quite got over it. Stepping off the plane and taking a taxi from the airport along Grant McConachie Way still sets me sniffing the salt air and wondering why I ever left. Good old Mr. McConachie was a reason I was able to travel there so often as a boy editor in the late sixties and early seventies. A nice man named Ron Keith was writing the biography of his now-deceased old pal Grant, who had turned his career as a wild, seat-of-the-pants bush pilot into one as the president of Canadian Pacific Airlines. Ron was high in the CPAir structure, and he took it as a personal affront that CPAir jets — with napkins and plates *and real knives and forks!* — were flying half-empty between Toronto and Vancouver, when his editor could have been using one of these seats to come out and work with him. It seemed churlish to discourage him.

Happily, Ron Keith's book, *Bush Pilot with a Briefcase* (1972), was a huge success. It recounted stories of barnstorming early days (including the Alberta wedding party when Grant's mechanic, the bridegroom, so enraged the bride by his accidental revelation that he had a wooden leg, that she, a circus professional known as Bitsy the Snake-Charmer, insisted on demonstrating her famous flying splits routine, which went wrong, leaving her locked in full splits position in the local hospital for her wedding night). All this, and Grant's later business deals to expand CPAirlines around the world, with General MacArthur in occupied Japan (a good deal), and with General Chiang Kai-shek in China (a bad deal) meant that the book deserved its huge sales. It was a typical rags-to-riches business success story, and there is always a keen market for such books.

But I learned that even the clunky title helped. Any Canadian book with "Bush Pilot" in the title will do well. An American publisher once joked that since books about Abraham Lincoln, about doctors, and about dogs all did well in the United States, the perfect American book title was *Lincoln's Doctor's Dog*. In Britain, the humorist Alan Coren did similar research and learned that sure-fire success awaited any book that dealt with Nazis, golf, and cats. His solution was a book named *Golfing for Cats*, with the flag on the hole that the golfing cat was putting towards neatly adorned by a swastika.

In Canada, I can report — after a lifetime's research — that similar success awaits any book with a title that deals with hockey, bush pilots, bears, wolves, and getting rich slowly. I pass this information on as a community service.

Vancouver, for me, was a second home, and always a place of amazing stories. Sometimes I didn't even have to leave the airport to come across them. On one occasion I was hanging around, waiting for my bags to arrive off the Toronto flight, when there was an explosion of rage on the other side of the carousel. A big, burly guy who looked like a biker was standing nose to nose with his female companion, bellowing threats and waving his arms really close to her face. She just stood there, eyes closed, taking it. It was the most violent piece of non-violence I had ever seen, and I walked over to the nearby Mountie station to alert them to what was going on.

"Don't worry, sir" was the reply. "We're already on it."

A small female Mountie appeared on the scene, backed up by a male Mountie, who played no part in what followed. The biker guy reacted unwisely, and very loudly, to the police approach. "You tryin' to tell me in this country a guy can't talk to his lady . . . *aagh!*" In seconds she had his arm up his back and was frog-marching him away. She was very small, compared to Mr. Biker, but very determined. Around the carousel people exchanged pleased smiles. The threatened woman just stood there, not reacting in any way. Barry Broadfoot, promising anonymity, would have got a great story out of her.

Try this one, the most unlikely story of my life: I was a young editor — let's say in my early thirties — and was on business in the city, contacting current authors like Ernie Perrault and Eric Nicol, looking for new authors, and promoting forthcoming books to book review editors like Barry, and I was staying at the Hotel Vancouver. One night at about 9 p.m. (midnight, Toronto time) I was strolling in the lobby, near the Kon Tiki Lounge Bar, when suddenly my arm was gripped and a desperate female voice was hissing through clenched teeth, "Just keep walking, they're following me, but don't turn around. Just keep walking. I need you to get me out of this!"

I kept walking. A glance to the side (*not* behind) showed a well-dressed woman about ten or fifteen years older than me, bravely staring straight ahead, clutching my upper arm as though we were a couple out on a date.

We strolled into the Kon Tiki, and confronted by its low-lit tables and couches she whispered, "Over to the far side, where we can sit and face the entrance."

We did that.

She scanned the room cautiously, moving her eyes, not her head. "I think we're safe," she whispered. Then, giving me her full attention, she said, "Thank you, thank you, thank you — you may have saved my life."

Every chivalrous fibre in my body was now standing at attention. I called a waiter over, and she ordered a large brandy. (My usual tomato juice didn't seem up to the occasion, and I should have specified "shaken, not stirred.") As she took her drink I tried to find out what was up, and to soothe her fears. She was safe with me.

It was the Mafia, she explained. The mob ran the downtown area, and tonight they had pursued her into the hotel. If only I knew how deeply they had their hooks into people like her friend X (and here she mentioned a well-known Vancouverite) and the family of . . . and here the pressure the poor woman was under began to tell. Her voice cracked, and she started to cry, quite loudly. Couples having quiet drinks at nearby tables stared.

When I stretched out a gallant hand to pat hers, reassuringly, things got worse. "You're no goddamn good!" she cried, shaking me off, with similar loud reproaches.

What the very interested room saw was a young man who had obviously mistreated this older lady who was his — what? — companion? Waves of disapproval washed over me from the nice people at the nearby tables, and those beyond.

I excused myself and went across the lobby to the front desk. When I asked if the house detective was around, within ten seconds an anonymous man appeared at my side, so anonymous that to this day I can't begin to describe him. I explained to him what had happened so far, and that the strange lady was getting stranger, and louder and louder.

"Just go back and join her, sir, and leave the rest to me."

I went back to my seat in the Kon Tiki. I had barely sat down when the detective was happily hailing my companion. "Hey, Annie, there you are!" In greeting her he put a friendly arm around her shoulders and started to lift. "The rest of us are just around the corner, and I said I'd go and find you and bring . . ." and by this time, as everyone around the room resumed their conversation, the arm around her shoulders was propelling her easily across the room and out of the lobby. At a discreet distance I followed this unsung genius as he took her out to the taxi entrance and put her — uncomplaining, I noted — in a cab.

"Wow!" I said, as the cab whisked her away. "You've done this before."

"No problem, sir," he said, smiled, and melted away.

The only problem for me was the cost of the brandy, but the story was worth it.

For me, Vancouver was bursting with such stories. If I went walking in Stanley Park — which I always did, of course, my father's son revelling in the trees — I might come off the cricket pitch near Brockton Oval to find myself on the equivalent of a *Braveheart* set, as archery club arrows flew whistling at nearby targets. Who knew that arrows in flight were so frighteningly loud? And when I met a prominent Indian publisher at a Vancouver publishing event downtown, why were there so many official Canadian security guards around him, talking into their sleeves? Who knew — in those innocent days before the Air India bombing — that Vancouver was a terrorist centre? Later, after I had commissioned Kim Bolan to write her brave book about the Air India mass murder trial (which she did, despite threats against her life and shots at her house), I sat with her one day in the specially secure courtroom, while the two accused smiled and waved at their families and did not seem to notice the members of the bereaved families sitting sadly nearby.

More innocently, early in my search for potential authors, I visited Jack Webster's radio show the day Pierre Laporte's body was found, and I got to know the man who had given his Scottish-born friend Jack the name "The Oatmeal Savage," one Allan Fotheringham, then a hard-working local newspaperman given to breaking big stories. I even wheeled barrowloads of soil aboard the flower-laden False Creek houseboat occupied by my friend Stanley Burke; anything to get books out of promising prospects before they were snapped up by my friends Jim Douglas and Scott McIntyre.

Once, I gave an interview to Rafe Mair, the popular B.C. radio host, on the general subject of books, and he surprised me by telling me that I was famous for my puns, and could I come up with one right now. I failed miserably, explaining that puns didn't work that way. During the commercial break, and thus off-air, I told Rafe that my favourite pun was Dorothy Parker's joke: "If all the girls at the Yale prom were laid end to end, I shouldn't be at all surprised."

My friend Rafe went back on the air saying, "I'm talking to the well-known publisher Doug Gibson, and we were just discussing puns. Unfortunately Doug's favourite pun is too dirty for us to use on the air, so we'll turn to the question of why Canadian authors . . ."

My favourite punster was Vancouver's own Eric Nicol, with whom I happily published four books, starting with *Vancouver* (1970), his urbane urban history of the city. Even better, in the 1980s I turned Eric loose on the idea of "finding" diaries or letters home from Charles Dickens' son Francis, from his unsuccessful days as a member of the North West Mounted Police. Since the story is almost unbelievable, let me quote Andreas Schroeder's entry in The *Encyclopedia of Literature in Canada.*

Always poised for mischief, Canadian humorist Eric Nicol (rumoured to have been aided and abetted by well-known editor-publisher Douglas Gibson) published *Dickens of the Mounted* (1989), the fake confessions of Francis Dickens, son of the writer Charles Dickens, who (history confirms) really had joined up with the North West Mounted Police in 1874, and who (history suggests) really had been an utterly inept policeman during his twelve years with the force. The hoax became a runaway best-seller, appearing on both fiction and non-fiction lists, apparently fooling a lot more people than either Nicol or the totally unrepentant Gibson expected — including the RCMP itself, which initially promoted the book as an excellent history of the force's early days.

I am happy to report that the person doing the promoting was none other than the RCMP's head man, Commissioner Norman Inkster. I will not forget the exploratory call from his office saying that they had heard rumours that this "history" the commissioner had been touring the country recommending was actually fiction. I was very happy to confirm that it was all made up by Eric Nicol, right from the very first line, "It was not the best of times, it was not the worst of times, it was Ottawa."

The response from the assistant at the other end was as muted as if I had announced the death of a dear friend. I suspect the commissioner did not take the news well.

"Totally unrepentant" sums up my feelings very well. I take special pride that I gave the book a cover featuring a real, historic photograph of Francis standing on parade in his pillbox hat in, as the caption says, "Fort Pitt, NWT, 1884." Under the title and subtitle "The astounding long-lost letters of Dickens of the Mounted" I had the designer write in Francis's hand, "What would Pa think of me now, standing in the Canadian mud!"

Even better, the endpapers inside the book covers are adorned by an accurate map showing "The Travels of Francis Dickens" and by four copperplate letters, copied from the book, created by a hired calligrapher. Even the photograph of Eric Nicol, "the editor of this book," shows him poised enthusiastically above old, hand-written archival pieces of paper. The caption reads "Eric Nicol enthralled with his discovery in the UBC library."

Eric received such help from the library that he nixed my plan to advise readers who wanted to see the original Dickens letters to be very persistent, since a dispute between UBC's English and History departments over the ownership of the papers would lead the library to deny that they had any such letters — at least initially, until they were worn down. Mischief should only go so far, I guess. Though I would love to have seen Commissioner Inkster banging a white-gloved fist on the library counter.

At the centre of the Vancouver excitement — appropriate to any big port city, with a huge, wild hinterland to serve — was the *Vancouver Sun*, no relation to the papers that arouse male readers elsewhere in the country with morning views of Sunshine Girls. There I met many larger-than-life characters, including Jack Wasserman. He was the *Sun*'s long-time man on the entertainment beat, and is remembered today by the downtown street named "Wasserman Way." He is also remembered for his roast. The story goes that his many friends laid on a well-attended roast, with speaker after speaker having great fun insulting their pal Jack, to the delight of the audience. The moment came when Jack rose to reply. Great applause. Before he started to speak, he pounded on the podium and disappeared behind it. Huge hilarity. What a joker!

Then there was an uneasy pause.

You can imagine the rest. "Is there a doctor in the house?" "Call an ambulance!" "It's too late, there's nothing we can do."

And the evening ended with everyone heading off home, thoughtfully.

To my romantic eye, the *Sun* newsroom, loud with the clack of type-writers, was straight out of *The Front Page*. And right at home there was this what-the-hell guy Barry Broadfoot, the book review page editor, with his feet on the desk and — probably — a bottle of rye in the drawer.

In those days every office had its drunk (not that Barry played that role at the *Sun*, where I'm sure there were several candidates). I've worked with a few people where you knew that nothing that old Bill said after lunch really counted. Often old Bill was an ex-serviceman, and everyone else covered for him as a matter of course. Being a drunk then was a little like having a bad cold today; colleagues made allowances and helped out.

Barry stood out as such a character there that the CBC's obituary notice stated that at the *Vancouver Sun* he was "a reporter, editor, and troublemaker" for seventeen years, starting in 1955. Certainly Allan Fotheringham remembers the legend of Barry the known troublemaker wandering into the little room where tickertapes brought in the latest news. He came out into the noisy newsroom and shouted, "Hey, President Kennedy has just been shot!"

There was a chorus of groans, dismissive downward waves, and shouts of "Oh, Broadfoot" and "Barry, get lost" (or the journalistic equivalent), and Barry shrugged, true to his what-the-hell code, and went back to his desk.

Ten minutes later, the phones started ringing.

I enjoyed my encounters with this book editor who had seen it all, as we talked about my forthcoming books, which I hoped he'd find space to review. We spent time together eating, and (in Barry's case) drinking. In case you think this is unfair, in his memoirs he described himself in those days as "a fun-loving, hard-drinking, and fairly talented character." And one constant theme was that, dammit, he was going to quit this job and go off and write a big important book. Some day. You wait. Some day.

The scene shifts to my office in Toronto. A phone call comes in from my old pal Barry Broadfoot.

"Barry! Where are you?"

"Hi, Doug," came the light, slightly nasal voice, "I'm in Toronto. Any chance we can have lunch?"

So we had lunch that very day, a Friday, in a dive on Dundas Square, and he amazed me with the news that he had quit the *Sun*, cold turkey. As he later put it to that paper's Denny Boyd, "I came in, hung up my coat, took the cover off my typewriter and looked out at the newsroom. Suddenly it looked like a Russian tractor factory.

"I said 'the hell with it.' I put seventeen years of inter-office memos into a shoebox, liberated the typewriter, and walked out. I felt they owed me that much."

So what was he doing now?

"I'm travelling across the country in a Volkswagen, with *this*." He hauled out a surprisingly small tape recorder, the size of a paperback book, when in those days tape recorders were at least the size of a fat briefcase. "And I meet up with people and I ask them, 'What happened to you in the Depression?' And, you know, Doug, people were so ashamed of what happened to them that they're grateful for a chance to talk about it now. You wouldn't believe the number of people — men as well as women — who break down and cry when they tell their stories, and say, 'You know, I've never told anyone this.'"

"What sort of stories are they telling you, Barry?"

He reached into his bag, the one that had held the fancy little tape recorder that was proving to be so successful at recording people without intimidating them. He pulled out fistfuls of manuscript and passed them over.

"These are just samples of the sort of stuff I'm getting. I'm taking them with me to see Jack McClelland on Monday for lunch."

Right there at the table I started to read. It was a Hollywood moment, the one that never happens in real life, when a young editor reads a few pages and knows — just *knows* — that he is looking at an amazing bestseller, a book that will change people's lives, change Canadian history.

"Barry, can you let me have this material for the rest of the weekend? If you give me your number in Toronto I'll make sure you get this material back in time for your meeting with Jack McClelland."

The meeting with Jack never happened. I dashed back to the Doubleday office after lunch, talked to the manager, David Nelson, about the stories, and encouraged him to read them and to show them to his father, George, a former publisher and a Depression survivor. By Monday morning I was able to make an offer to Barry to publish his book, which he accepted, and we were off on a fascinating journey together, rewriting the history of Canada from 1929 to 1939.

We were inventing a new type of book as we went along, one that allows me now to take intelligent readers backstage, to see, in detail, how an editor and author work together on a book when the editor's role is unusually active.

Recently, the Chicago writer, Studs Terkel, had written a successful book, *Working*, which had been based on taped interviews with ordinary people. But apart from showing that ordinary people talking about their lives can produce fascinating stories, Terkel's book — which devoted an entire chapter to one single, named speaker — was in no way a model for us.

The unique type of book that Barry and I invented worked like this. Barry collected stories on his tiny tape recorder, promising the speakers anonymity, and simply not bothering with names. As for getting "permission," it was all based on common sense. "I'm collecting stories about the Depression. If you care to talk about what happened to you, this little tape recorder here will pick up what you say, and you may find your story — or part of it — in my book. Okay?" (It always was okay — although one speaker later wrote to Barry to tell him that his story — much edited and condensed — was recognized by his boss, who was not especially pleased.)

Barry would then transcribe these interviews with his "liberated" typewriter, on paper so cheap that it could indeed have come from "a Russian tractor factory." He was a fast, inelegant typist, who resented conventions like using upper case letters at the start of sentences, and his typewriter sometimes made holes in the cheap paper, so the pages were arguably the ugliest ever submitted in the history of Canadian publishing. And there were so many pages, hundreds and hundreds of them, that they were shipped by Barry in apple carton boxes. The pages may have looked terrible, but they smelled wonderful. They stood, in a wobbly pile, about a metre high.

Together, we soon hit on some basic rules. The stories would all be anonymous (although we broke that rule, once, to acknowledge the story by James Gray, the author of *The Winter Years*). Each story would be given its own title (my job, with an assist from Barry, if he had a better idea). Barry's own voice would be heard — always in italics — only in his general introductions to the book and to the individual chapters, and in the very rare stage directions that occurred, such as (*"He breaks down and cries"*).

The rest of the book would consist of first-person stories told by the ordinary men and women he encountered, told in their own words. That was key. Shortening a story to get rid of repetition (and you'd be amazed how much time we all spend repeating ourselves as we talk) or to clarify the storyline ("Oh, I should have mentioned that this was a really big guy" sometimes required the insertion of "this big guy" earlier in the story) was legitimate. Adding any words was not legitimate. Ever. Even if it was clear that the speaker was searching for the word "supercilious" to describe the relief official dealing with her mother, if that word never came up, it was never used in her story. And the shortening process sometimes left just a one-hundred-word story standing, after 4,000 words had been whittled down and thrown away.

I found that it was like carving a sculpture. Or, at a ratio of forty paragraphs read for every one selected, it was like making pure maple syrup, the ideal Canadian comparison.

Clearly, on a project of this apple-carton scale, none of the usual top-of-desk rules applied (and there were, in those days, no desktop rules to apply to non-existent computers, so everything was done by hand, in pen or in pencil, right on the cheap paper). I took over the front room of our house (Sally was understanding, and this was before the kids came along, which would have made it impossible). As I read each story, I would cut it, in pencil, as much as seemed necessary to leave us with a really great story, without a single word to spare. If a fine title sprang out of it, I'd add the title at the top. And alongside the title, I'd add notes on the chapters that the story might fit into.

For instance, a selected story might be about a boy (marked KIDS, accordingly), growing up on a Saskatchewan farm lost to the drought (FARMS), so it had two potential piles to go on. Kids' stories lay over by the window, farm stories down in the fourth row in the centre of the floor.

In due course, the shuffling and dealing on to the floor revealed that there were enough stories for a chapter on this, but not on that, which should be combined with this theme, and so on. When the chapter themes were established, the hard work of arranging the order of the stories *inside* each chapter began. I recognize now that it called for the same skills that come into play as I try to find the best order for a book of short stories by Alice Munro or Mavis Gallant. Each chapter had to start with a strong story, have stories with useful background information early on, then have a variety of voice, subject matter, pace, length, seriousness, or humour that in order forms a pleasing narrative arc, until the final story, which has to be strong, with a final line that will ring in your head — as when a hobo's tale of the lonely life on the road ends with the words "I was seventeen years old."

Each chapter, in other words, had to be arranged like a short story collection, which in a sense it was. The skills of editing fiction and editing non-fiction constantly overlap, as young editors are sometimes surprised to hear.

As for the overall shape of Barry's book, the order of the chapters posed a major editorial challenge. Obviously, stories from the early years of the Depression needed an early position, while later stories — about taking part in the Regina Riot or joining up to fight in the Spanish Civil War — deserved a place further on in the book. But, most important, we were dealing with our readers' minds, bringing them stories when we thought that they'd be ready for them. We knew, for instance, that the chapter on "Rough Justice" (where a greedy landlord in the Maritimes was tarred and gravelled one night for trying to raise a widow's rent, or where two cheating employers in Edmonton were badly beaten up and robbed) would shock people if it came too early in the book. After reading many chapters of decent people being badly treated without fighting back, however, the reader was primed for the "Rough Justice" chapter, cheering on the resisters.

Finally, I was able to pick the paper-clipped chapters off the floor, and deliver the messy manuscript to a printer. And here is a piece of history. In those days, children, people typed manuscripts, then they were edited with marks in pen or usually pencil, and then they went to people called "typesetters," *who retyped the whole manuscript*, from beginning to end. In this case, the ill-typed, heavily edited manuscript was so illegible that the typesetter/printer (Bob Hamilton, whom I worked with later) pleaded with me to set up shop in their building so that I could translate the constant tricky words right on the spot.

And there — if I had any doubt about the power of the stories in the book — I received inspiring confirmation of the book's appeal. The typesetters — hardened old pros — simply could not get enough of Barry's stories, and talked excitedly about them over coffee and lunch. It was clear that we were on to a winner. So clear that we actually set Barry to work on gathering stories about the Second World War — for a book later entitled *Six War Years* — long *before* we published *Ten Lost Years* in the fall of 1973.

I've gone into great detail here about the editorial role in piecing

Barry's books together, but let me be clear that I was the junior partner in all this. The historian Christopher Moore has stressed what stands out about Barry's achievement. "He really had a gift for engaging interviewees, and getting them to open up; not everyone who goes out with a tape recorder understands how vital that is. And he really did the work." That forty to one ratio stood him in good stead as he produced a string of bestsellers with other editors.

During the summer of 1973, while I was attending the AGM of the Canadian Author's Association, I told the assembled authors that they should get ready to work with new technology. In this case the new technology I was talking about was not a computer but Barry's tiny portable tape recorder. In my role of cocky young editor, I told them about the surefire success of the forthcoming book *Ten Lost Years*, which was going to open up the new field of "oral history."

Listening to my bold predictions was Hugh Kane, the head of Macmillan of Canada. When all of these predictions came true, he was the moving spirit behind the staid and very respectable Macmillan deciding to hire the cocky kid to be their editorial director at the age of thirty. So working with Barry and *Ten Lost Years* had a huge impact on my career.

A less permanent impact was to make me an academic authority in the field of oral history. My experience shaping *Ten Lost Years* (and *Six War Years* in 1974) established me as *the* Canadian publisher of oral history. As a result I was invited to give a serious paper on oral history at the Canadian Learned Societies' Conference in Montreal in 1975, and later it was published — gasp — in a scholarly journal in Australia devoted to oral history. I like to think that there may be historians on the banks of the Murrumbidgee who to this day are quoting me as the unchallenged Canadian expert on oral history.

In publishing terms, because I knew how much work was involved in creating a successful oral history book, I was able to steer clear of many people who thought that their new tape recorder was an Aladdin's lamp route to a book. Later I did publish successful books by Bill McNeil, based on his successful CBC Radio series "Voice of the Pioneer." I even published three books with the unstoppable Allan Anderson, *Remembering the Farm* and *Salt Water, Fresh Water* and *Roughnecks and Wildcatters*.

Allan was an old CBC hand and a heroic "lost weekend" drinker. When I wrote his obituary in *Quill & Quire*, his family forgave me for joking that if he knew the country like the back of his hand, "it was because the back of his hand had come in touch with so much of it." And when I say "unstoppable," I mean it. He once returned, chastened, from a national publicity tour. He confessed to me that on a live, thirty-minute Calgary TV show the host introduced him and got to ask the question, "Allan, why did you write *Remembering the Farm?*" Twenty-nine minutes later the host, despairing of arm waving, had to bellow an interruption, "I'm sorry our time is up . . . we've been talking to . . ." Allan had talked unstoppably *straight through the entire half-hour show.*

I developed the theory that Allan was a successful interviewer because people, desperate to stop his chattering flow, in self-defence would start to blurt out amazingly revealing stories.

Barry, by contrast, in his low-key, what-the-hell way, was a very easy guy to talk to — in a coffee shop, a bar, on a train, or in all the places he struck up a conversation/interview, often being invited home to continue it. He was born for the role, and I know that when he visited our Doubleday office in Toronto, people really liked him. One of our sales guys liked him so much, in fact, that later in Vancouver he confided in Barry that he was travelling from hotel to hotel in his western territory, accompanied by two very lovely, very sexy French-Canadian identical twins. Barry confirmed to me that he had met the glamorous young ladies in question, but admitted that — even as a highly skilled interviewer — he had not found a way to discover the details of the arrangement the three of them enjoyed.

*Ten Lost Years* was a phenomenal success. It flew off the shelves, to the extent that its success provoked articles wondering how on earth a book by an unknown author, about the Depression, for God's sake, could have such a success.

I have an answer. Many of the stories are so good you will never forget them. The book is still in print forty years after it appeared. The hardcover edition sold more than 200,000 copies and the paperback has sold much more than that. But here is why I use the word "phenomenal." In every other case, when a hardcover book is brought out in paperback, for half the price, all sales of the hardcover stop dead. In this case, long after the paperback edition of *Ten Lost Years* had come out, Doubleday was still reprinting the hardcover!

Why? I think I know. Word about the book was spreading slowly to people who bought very few books and never looked at book reviews. But they had known the Depression, and they had heard that this was a true and honest book about their lives, their times — and they wanted it. And to them — people of their generation — a book was a hardcover book.

I worked with Barry — in precisely the same way — to produce *Six War Years 1939–1945: Memories of Canadians at Home and Abroad* (1974), which was also designed by the brilliant Brant Cowie. I even continued to see it through for Doubleday after I had left to work at Macmillan.

In his Introduction to *Six War Years*, Barry took a typically modest stab at explaining why the book was important. "Wars are for generals to fight," he said, "and we keep things going in the few yards around us that we call our own. . . ." Later he wrote, "these stories, amazing though they may be, happened to the ordinary anonymous people you pass on the street every day. . . . This is not my book; it is your book, and I am passing it on."

The academic historians, of course, did not like what he was doing. To them, he was dealing in legend and superstition, stories that had no written records to prove their reliability. Pierre Berton, whom I published, ran into the same hostility and ignored it, taking comfort in his giant sales.

History itself came to Barry Broadfoot's aid when in 2010 there was a court case concerning Robert Semrau, a Canadian soldier accused of killing a badly wounded Taliban prisoner. A smart journalist recalled that there were stories about this sort of thing in *Six War Years*. They would never have made it into regimental histories or officially documented accounts, yet the anonymity of Barry's books produced two stories worth recalling in this context.

There is the story of Jan, a Jewish kid between age twelve and fourteen who spoke German and acted as an interpreter when a Canadian major was interrogating a sneering captive German lieutenant.

"There were five of us in the room of this house, the major, me, the guard, Jan and the prisoner. The major says to me, 'We're not going to get anything out of this shitheel.' And Jan, without a word, grabs up the major's Luger, which is lying beside him on the cot where the major is sitting, and bam, he blows this Jerry's head off. I mean, what there is left of a head, well it wouldn't fill a can of soup. Don't mean to be crude. There's blood all over the place. Everywhere.

"What are going to do? Shoot the kid? You don't court-martial him. No the major says, 'We'll forget this ever happened,' and the guard and I agree."

The second story concerns a group of Canadians holed up for the night in trenches not far from the Germans. Out in no man's land someone is screaming, on and on.

"It went on for two hours and it seemed like ten. You see, we thought he'd die. Not often did they last that long. But this one wouldn't die.

"Finally a guy says he is going out there. He's an Indian, and I think he was from around Cochrane, near Calgary, or maybe his name is Cochrane. An Indian — he gets killed about a month later. Anyway, the lieutenant doesn't say anything and this Indian slips out and Jeezus! It is one dark night and I ask the lieutenant if we should ask for a couple of flares just to help him, and he says no.

"In about fifteen minutes, all of a sudden the screaming stops. Just like that. Like shutting off a tap. A light switch. In about five minutes this Cochrane comes back and he says, 'Damn it to hell. What a shitty way to earn a living.'

"The sergeant after a while asks who it was out there, and Cochrane says he doesn't know. Well, was it one of our guys? Cochrane says he doesn't know. Was it a German? He says how the hell should he know.

"Then — and you might not think there are some very moving moments in a war in the mud and wet and shit — but Cochrane says, 'All I know was that there was a dying soldier out there and I just put my hand on his forehead and said a little prayer and then I put the knife right into his throat. I was just helping a poor soldier along the way.'"

After *Six War Years* (another huge success, though without the long-running stage play that keeps *Ten Lost Years* rolling along), Barry brought out seven other books. For me, the most impressive was

*Years of Sorrow, Years of Shame*, about what Canada did to its Japanese-Canadian citizens during the war. He told me that he didn't expect to make any money from it. He was writing it as a matter of conscience, writing out of his own shame at our behaviour.

Later, he and I worked together again on *Next Year Country*, about his beloved Prairies, and *Ordinary Russians*, about the country that had just been opened up by glasnost. We stayed in touch by phone or by Russian tractor factory notes. That was how I learned with pleasure of his marriage to Lori, an old sweetheart from his Winnipeg days; of his George Woodcock Lifetime Achievement Award for an Outstanding Literary Career in B.C., the award arranged by the heroically ubiquitous Alan Twigg in 1997; of the Order of Canada honour in 1996; and of his honorary doctorate that same year from the University of Manitoba. I suspect he didn't wear a turtleneck for these presentations, but I may be wrong. I'm confident, though, that if he spoke he would be modest, underplaying his role as a historian, and possibly even using the phrase "What the hell."

In 1998, when I began one of our occasional phone calls with the words, "Hi, Barry, it's Doug Gibson," I got a very strange response.

"Doug [*pause*] Gibson [*pause*]. I know that name."

"What do you mean, Barry?"

"Oh, I've had a stroke, and I don't remember every name."

It was true. The stroke had afflicted him with a failing memory and robbed him of his sight.

The next time I was out west, I went to Nanaimo and stayed with Barry and Lori in the house on Morningside where they now lived. His sight allowed him to stride forward, grinning confidently, and shake my hand with vigour — but finer work like reading was beyond him, although he tried.

We had a good visit, talking about old times, although he described himself as a "dead man walking." But now, for him, "what the hell" was a stoical way of facing up to what life had brought him. In leaving, I tried to tell him what an important role he had played in reclaiming Canadian history from the bloodless academics. They might scoff at the "unproven" rumour in *Ten Lost Years* of a brutal railroad cop found crucified against a boxcar. Wiser heads realize that the point of the story is that these club-swinging cops were so hated by the homeless men trying to ride the rails that to them the story was absolutely believable.

Christopher Moore, the Governor General's Award–winning historian I've quoted earlier, understood that. Late in Barry's life he made a pilgrimage to pay his respects to the old pioneer of oral history in Canada. On Barry's death in 2003 he told the *Toronto Star*, "*Ten Lost Years* and *Six War Years* are among the most powerful books anyone has written about Canadian history."

Not bad for an old newspaper guy. What the hell.

# MORLEY CALLAGHAN

Novelist, Short Story Writer, and Torontonian

In his 1965 book, *O Canada*, the august American critic Edmund Wilson described Morley Callaghan as "perhaps the most unjustly neglected novelist in the English-speaking world." Comparisons were made to Chekhov and Turgenev. In 1963 the *New York Times* had hailed Callaghan, saying, with unconscious sexism: "If there is a better short story writer in the world, we don't know where he is."

All the time Morley Callaghan, of course, was in Toronto, the city of his birth. Toronto was the base from which he made occasional forays but to which he always returned, setting his own life and most of his stories in the city streets he knew in his bones.

The Callaghans were an old Irish family, but they had fallen into poverty by the time Morley's father, Thomas, left Wales for London, and as a young teenager sailed to Canada as an indentured servant. It seems incredible now, but this form of genteel slavery was fairly common in Victorian times among penniless young immigrants, allowing them to work their way back to freedom. In Toronto, Thomas did that, gained an education and came close to going to university. It was not the perfect rags to riches immigrant success story but he rose to a white-collar job as a railway dispatcher, marrying a respectable woman named Mary Dewan, playing a role in the union movement, and continuing to study the ways of the world through the newspapers, which he described as "the poor man's university." He provided a happy home for his family.

Although the Callaghans were Roman Catholic, young Morley was sent to non-denominational public schools in Toronto, then went to the University of Toronto, where he was an active sportsman, learning to box well (as Ernest Hemingway would learn to his cost in Paris), and playing such serious baseball that icing his arm was regarded as important.

And he wrote. His entry in *Canadian Who's Who* noted proudly, "Has been writing seriously since 1923." The writing included fiction that was soon to make him a prodigy when he published his first book, *Strange Fugitive*, at the age of twenty-five. But it also included valuable part-time work for the *Toronto Star* newspaper, where he became friendly with another young reporter, an American with experience in Kansas City named Ernest Hemingway, who encouraged his writing ambitions.

Morley fulfilled his father's dreams by graduating from Osgoode Hall Law School in the heart of downtown Toronto, beside courts teeming with criminals of all sorts — and some of those criminals, such as prostitutes, thieves, and bootleggers, would become familiar to his readers over the years — but he chose never to practise law, becoming a professional writer instead.

In those days for a serious Canadian writer the literary world lay elsewhere. Soon, with the help of Hemingway, who was generous with his contacts, Morley was successfully mailing off stories to Paris (to *This Quarter* in 1926 and *transition* in 1927), and Ezra Pound bought two stories for an edition of *Exile*. New York was an even bigger draw, and Hemingway saw to it that on his visits Morley met the right people, including prominent writers like Sherwood Anderson and William Carlos Williams, and the legendary book editor at Scribners, Maxwell Perkins, who signed him up for the short story collection *A Native Argosy*, which came out in 1929, when Morley was only twenty-six.

Nineteen twenty-nine was a watershed year for the world, and for Morley Callaghan everything changed on a personal level as well. He married Loretto Dee (a notable beauty whose family had close, romantic connections with real live gangsters like "Legs" Lenihan, later gunned down in his flower shop in Detroit — we can only imagine the floral tributes at the funeral), and they followed their friend Hemingway to Paris.

Much later, in 1963, Morley wrote about his time there, in a memoir entitled *That Summer in Paris: Memories of Tangled Friendships with Hemingway, Fitzgerald and Some Others*. The others in that "very small, back-biting, gossiping neighbourhood" included Ezra Pound, Gertrude Stein, James Joyce, the painter Miro, and Zelda Fitzgerald, who was not sure if Ernest was turning her Scott into an alcoholic, or vice versa. It was the time of — pick your slogan — the Jazz Age or the Lost Generation, and it was an exciting time to be with that crowd in Paris, since 1929 was when *A Farewell to Arms* was published, joining *The Sun Also Rises* and Fitzgerald's *This Side of Paradise* and *The Great Gatsby* as the exciting new books of the decade.

When Morley's memoir came out many years later, however, Norman Mailer (reviewing it for the *New York Review of Books*) damned it with faint praise, calling it "a modest dull book that contains a superb short story about Hemingway, Fitzgerald and Callaghan." That "short story," of course, describes the boxing match when Hemingway, who fancied himself as a boxer, and even earned money in hard times in Paris as a hired sparring partner, invited Morley to join him in the ring. This was a mistake. Not only because Hemingway had just eaten Lobster Thermidor and consumed "bottles of white burgundy," but also because Morley was a good, well-trained boxer. Hemingway already knew this. In an earlier sparring match Morley had bloodied him, and in Morley's astonished words, "Suddenly he spat at me; he spat a mouthful of blood; he spat in my face." Hemingway laughed it off as a macho practice among bullfighters, but Morley was not amused.

In the fateful fight, where Fitzgerald agreed to be the timekeeper, Morley was even less amused when his pal Ernest, who at six feet towered over him and outweighed him by forty pounds or so, began to press the attack in this friendly bout. In Morley's words, "Ernest had become rougher, his punching a little wilder than usual."

So Morley knocked him down.

Hemingway, furious, climbed to his feet accusing Fitzgerald of deliberately letting the round run long because he wanted "to see me getting the shit kicked out of me." It changed their relationship forever, since his prowess in the ring really mattered to Hemingway. He once, famously, said, "My writing is nothing. My boxing is everything."

And Morley spent the rest of his life trying to be more than "the guy who knocked down Hemingway in Paris."

Safely returned to Toronto, Morley began to write at a great pace. He produced two novels (*It's Never Over*, published in 1930, and *A Broken Journey*, which appeared in 1932); Gary Boire has identified them as particular examples of "the obvious influence of American naturalist writers such as Anderson and Theodore Dreiser."

Then Morley really hit his stride, releasing three 1930s novels with biblically inspired titles. George Woodcock summarized his achievement in these Depression years as follows: "A sudden sureness of touch appeared in Callaghan's fourth novel, *Such Is My Beloved* (1934) and continued through *They Shall Inherit The Earth* (1935) and *More Joy In Heaven* (1937) which have an economy of form and a lucidity of expression and feeling that make these the best of all Callaghan's works and perhaps the best Canadian novels written in the 1930s."

And then the novels stopped.

To what extent this was caused by Morley's inspiration drying up, and to what extent it reflected a writer's realistic assessment of the fiction market set against the need to provide for a young family, now consisting of two sons, Michael and Barry, is impossible to say. But after 1937 Morley busied himself writing magazine articles (and his book for young people, *Luke Baldwin's Vow*, was based on a reworking of a *Saturday Evening Post* story), plays, a film script, a semi-fictional history (*The Varsity Story*), and doing a lot of broadcasting work for CBC Radio, which put bread on the table. The exception was *The Loved and the Lost*, a novel that appeared in 1951, set in Montreal and dealing with a white woman who dated a black man in the jazz scene in that city. It was, for its day, a daring novel, and won the Governor General's Award; it continues to be read in courses today.

In his marvellous book about Canadian Publishing, *The Perilous Trade* (2003), Roy MacSkimming tells the story of the launch of that book "set in the underworld, which Callaghan had come to know by mixing with boxers and gangsters in a bar and grill on Dorchester" (now René Lévesque Boulevard, where I was later to die a thousand deaths with Pierre Trudeau). John Gray of Macmillan, along with his colleague Frank Upjohn, "decided to launch *The Loved and the Lost* at Montreal's tony Ritz-Carlton hotel, inviting guests such as Frank Scott from McGill and the city's mayor, Camillien Houde." Now Mayor Houde had done time in prison during the war, and in Roy MacSkimming's elegant phrase was "famed for his underworld contacts." As the party moved on to the dodgy Dorchester Street establishment and the booze flowed, everyone was having such a fine time that the mayor decided that the great writer should sign his "golden book" of distinguished visitors at city hall. "Gray and

Upjohn piled into Houde's limousine with Callaghan and his wife, Loretto, some newspaper cronies, and the oversized mayor, and were chauffered to City Hall at two in the morning. Having forgotten his keys, Houde ordered his driver to break in through a window, and the signing was enacted in the mayor's chambers, sanctified by the ceremonial passing of a silver flask." It was an interesting Montreal version of the ancient tradition whereby honorees received the keys to a city, what you might call a real breakthrough.

But apart from this unlikely burst of excitement, the flurry of attention caused by a fine collection of stories in 1959, and above all by Edmund Wilson's 1965 announcement of his neglected greatness, Morley Callaghan spent almost a quarter of a century working away quietly. He was universally regarded as a survivor from his great days in the thirties, a man with not much writing future, a burnt-out volcano.

Here I was lucky enough to enter the scene. When I was hired in March 1974 to become the editorial director of Macmillan of Canada, I was inheriting a fine list of distinguished authors built up by the legendary publisher John Gray. The authors included not only the magisterial historian, Donald Creighton (a lean, sepulchral figure who inspired shock and awe when he stalked the corridors, concocting lines as famous as the opening to his epic John A. MacDonald biography: "In those days they came usually by boat"). There were other fine Canadian historians, including two of the best, with the worst possible professional surnames, Careless and Wrong.

The fiction list was equally distinguished, consisting of names like Hugh MacLennan, W.O. Mitchell, Robertson Davies, and Morley Callaghan — "If," they explained to me, "he ever gets around to writing another book. He hasn't done anything since 1963."

I must admit that I found that there were mixed feelings about Morley at Macmillan when I arrived. He was respected as a grand old man, now over seventy, with a distinguished past (*Hemingway! Fitzgerald! Joyce!*) His involvement with major writing events like the Kingston Conference of 1955, where a future for Canadian writers and publishers was discussed, stood his reputation in good stead. So did his published recognition that in the book world Canada (besieged by cheap overruns from British and American publishers with huge economies of scale in their favour) was "a country that is no publisher's paradise." But true to his parents' union sympathies he had played an active role with the Writer's Union, a stance not guaranteed to make him popular with the local Capitalist Oppressor, his Canadian publisher.

I heard tales, too, of how jealously Morley (and it was easy to get on first-name terms with him) had protected his turf as Canada's Great Novelist. Apparently when Macmillan held the launch party (almost literally in this case) for Robertson Davies' astonishing novel *Fifth Business*, all of literary Toronto was aboard the floating water-front restaurant near the site of the fictional Boy Staunton's death in the harbour. At the height of the party Morley appeared, and, flanked by what one witness described as "his two big sons," he made a dramatic progress around the room before making an equally dramatic exit. A point had been made.

John Gray was among the Macmillan people who did not appreciate Morley's approach. In MacSkimming's words, "Gray sometimes confided to colleagues that, much as he admired Callaghan, he felt more comfortable with other Macmillan authors who were less prickly and combative, and, frankly, more British . . ."

The "British" comment is interesting, because Gray himself came from a very traditional Upper Canadian family that had sent him to a private school, which may have been where he learned to keep his handkerchief up his sleeve, like a British officer. He. had even got the job in publishing (for which he proved to be ideally suited) in the first place because of "the way he played bridge." None of this, I suspect, endeared him and his style to the indentured servant's son, who was so "prickly and combative." In fact, if the typical Australian represents someone with no time for airs and graces but with an instinctive support for the underdog, even against the forces of law and order, I must say that Morley was the most "Australian" Canadian I have ever known. It's clear that he would have been on the side of outlaw Ned Kelly or of Jack Duggan, "The Wild Colonial Boy" of the song, both of whom defied the British-based authorities.

Later, John Gray brought me and Morley together in an unexpected way. After his retirement, John Gray remained on Macmillan's board, and after board meetings he would often visit my office for a chat about books and authors. He was a great storyteller, a quality that none other than W.O. Mitchell once told me, flatteringly, that all good publishers possessed. I remember with special delight Gray's tale of Prime Minister Mackenzie King once visiting the Macmillan Bond Street office and insisting that the group should move two doors up the street to visit the former home of his ancestor, William Lyon Mackenzie. The bachelor prime minister was the only member of the party unaware that the historic Mackenzie house had fallen on hard times and was now a house of ill repute. When the portly PM stood reverently outside the ancestral abode, head bowed, one of the ladies inside took his stance for shy, bourgeois hesitation. Throwing up the window, she loudly proceeded to invite him inside with very explicit promises. According to Gray, the sidewalk party left in a hurry.

Later I had the pleasure of working with John Gray on the first (and, sadly, only) volume of his memoirs, 1978's *Fun Tomorrow*. (One reviewer noted that he was a man so modest that while describing his service in the Second World War, he never actually got around to mentioning the Military Cross he had won.) As he wrote the book Gray was dying of cancer. In the end, thank to heroic efforts from the printer, Hunter Rose (headed by Frank Upjohn's son, Guy) I was able to rush to his hospital bedside the first, specially bound copy of his memoirs on a Saturday. He died on the following Monday.

The funeral was what brought me and Morley into uncomfortable contact. It was a predictably large event at a major Toronto church, and I was sitting in a pew alongside the half-dozen main representatives of Macmillan. Shortly before the service began, Morley appeared and edged his way along the pew ahead of us to sit directly in front of me.

Before I had a chance to tap him on the shoulder and say hello he launched into a loud monologue with his neighbour in the very audible tones of a somewhat deaf old man. (And he had a crooning, lilting way of talking, lingering on the letter l.)

"Well," he told his neighbour. "This is a sad day." Then without warning he asked, "Well now, what do you make of this young fellow Gibson who has taken over the editorial side at Macmillan? I've worked with him, and I find . . ."

My seatmates were all in an agony of delight. Agony because this was wonderful stuff, and I was twisting around in the pew, practically shrouding my ears and chanting "*Can't hear you, can't hear you.*" Agony, too, because they were publicly mourning the loss of their beloved president, and could not be seen to smile, let alone guffaw. The entire pew was rocking with suppressed laughter.

But not from me.

Morley's dissection of my character went on for quite a long, loud time, but I can report that while love can make a man blind, sheer embarrassment ("*I can't believe this is happening!*") can render him deaf. I never did get around to tapping Morley on the shoulder, and I got out very fast at the end of the service.

As it happened, Morley and I got along very well, working together on five books in the seventies and eighties (his seventies and eighties, also), and I'm proud that I was involved in the old volcano rumbling into fiery life and producing major fiction again after almost twenty-five years. One critic, Eric McMillan, has even singled out these later books for special praise, noting approvingly that "as he grew older, Callaghan's writing grew progressively livelier and looser."

Early on I decided that it would be fun to get to know Morley better, so I took him to a boxing match out in the suburbs. Morley had seen the Cassius Clay–Mohammad Ali fight in Toronto with the unstoppable George Chuvalo (whom Jimmy Breslin, the New York sports writer, described as "fighting with his face"). So I took Morley by cab (as a mere editor, I could not afford a car) to George Chuvalo's positively last appearance against a fighter named Pretty Boy Felson.

Now I know a little bit about boxing, having fought for the Scottish Universities boxing team against the evil English team. (We won. I lost. Indeed I lost so badly that after the surgeon had finished rearranging my nose, he broke the news apologetically that there should be no more boxing. I was not inclined to argue. In recent years an inspection of my nose by an otherwise typical Toronto doctor — you know, white coat, certificates on the wall, medical instruments for examining ears and noses — led him to look up my nostrils and exclaim "*My God, what a disaster!*")

But Morley knew far more. As we watched the bouts on the under-card he predicted the likely results, every time. And when the brave, bull-like George Chuvalo finally cornered the dancing "Pretty Boy" we both knew that the result was inevitable. I remember, too, that in the absence of cabs at the suburban arena we took a bus back to the subway. Far from being offended by rubbing shoulders with the fight crowd, Morley loved it, and seemed to thrive on it, a frail old man in a sea of excited young fans.

Very late in his life that frail old man was involved in a fight with an intruder he caught in his house one night. Morley's house at 14 Dale Avenue (still in the Callaghan family) sits almost symbolically on the front lines of the prosperous Rosedale district. Just to the south, across one of the deep ravines that cut through Toronto, lies the main city, now joined by a footbridge named the Morley Callaghan Bridge. The towering high-rises represent a different (and much less prosperous) world, and it was presumably from that direction that the intruder came.

He deserves no sympathy, for he attacked Morley physically, leaving visible wounds. Yet Morley, old, bald, and frail, refused to go down, and the attacker must have felt helpless in the face of Morley's blazing defiance as the old man stayed on his feet, trying to fight back, swinging at the thief.

The newspapers, rightly, made much of this attack on an old man in his seventies but Morley, when I called in alarm, shrugged it off. He was fine, there was no need for a fuss. You wonder how the thief described the incident to his pals; I suspect there is little honour among thieves for inconclusive fights with little old men.

Morley's career — simply surviving and raising a family as a writer based in Toronto — is a testament to what a fighter he was in every way. One of those ways was insisting on being seen as a North American writer. One critic, Gary Boire, has ascribed to him an ambiguous position as someone who was determined to get away from the "colonial" influence of London, yet — like the country as a whole — found himself swinging to a position where American influence became the new colonialism. Callaghan, he says, "can be read as the quintessential anti-colonial colonial." It's an interesting theory. "The Wild Colonial Boy," indeed.

Yet what was most striking for me is how Morley came out with all guns blazing against Toronto — and, by extension, Canada — with our first book together, *A Fine and Private Place* in 1975. You remember how Edmund Wilson placed Morley among the international greats and — at the very least, by implication — denounced Canadians for overlooking this great talent in their midst?

That, in a nutshell, is what *A Fine and Private Place* is about. I found myself in the middle of a public brawl where Morley took on the Canadian literary establishment.

The novel's central character, Eugene Shore, is an elderly writer, well respected abroad but almost unknown in his own country and ignored in his own city. Although that city is never named, it is clearly Toronto. There are references to Jarvis Street, the Park Plaza Hotel, Britnell's bookstore and even a publisher on Bond Street (the Macmillan office I attended was at 70 Bond Street).

More important, the districts through which the characters walk, even the cafés they visit (like the Riverboat on Yorkville), are so explicitly described that the reader could almost follow their movements on the ground, all the way to the climactic event at the meeting of Sherbourne and Elm Streets, just north of Bloor.

Many real-life people are described unkindly (including a Northrop Frye character), unless they take a positive view of the work of "Shore" and his New York critic/admirer "Starkey Kunitz." It is astonishingly personal, and Morley allows himself to discuss his own work, and his own style, by having one of his characters, a graduate student named Al Delaney, decide to write a book about Shore.

At one point as Al and Shore sit over a late night dinner, Shore says, "'Do you know something, Al?' And now he had a deprecating little laugh. "Tonight, listening and talking to you I had a feeling I never expected to have in this town. I suppose I've been starving for years for some conversation about my own work.'"

(I am reminded of a conversation Morley and I once had, returning in my car from a successful reading Morley had given at Burlington's famous bookstore, A Different Drummer. The late-night setting led me to raise the name of another author, asking Morley what he thought of him. Back came the reply: "Oh, he likes my work well enough.")

The entire book, with the sour Andrew Marvell quote as its title, is a remarkable piece of revenge on an unappreciative city. Its bitterness caused a sensation when it came out. Callaghan admirer George Woodcock did not like it, calling it "the story of an unappreciated novelist that clearly has personal implications and is used to present a flattering self-analysis and a contemptuous dismissal of the characters who are blind to the worth of the novelist and clearly represent Callaghan's critics."

Over the years, many have raised questions about Morley's unadorned writing style, and some, such as John Metcalf, have parodied it. But it is hard to improve on the spare, direct storytelling in the book's key paragraph, where the plot twist has been carefully set up by conversations with a rogue cop who does not like Shore. "Seven days later, sometime after midnight, Eugene Shore was struck by a hit-and-run driver. He died on the way to the hospital. There was the smell of liquor on him."

*A Fine and Private Place* was hugely controversial in Canada, and sold perhaps 10,000 copies in hardcover. We heard later that in Russia the translation sold over half a million copies.

Those Russian readers — no doubt also admirers of Chekhov and Turgenev — were lucky in that they got a rare experience: the chance to read a strikingly accurate description of Toronto. This was one of Morley's paradoxical strengths. He could write clear, evocative, objective descriptions of the city with which he had a love-hate relationship. He liked to walk the streets, early and late, visiting the courts, noting how the sun fell on the melting snow in the alleys, catching the yeasty evening smell from the waterfront breweries, dropping in at nightclubs or cocktail bars, and generally catching the spirit of the districts his characters inhabit.

This is a rare talent, and of all the books I have edited that deal with the city that has been my home, Morley's work stands out. So, too, I should mention, does that of Richard Wright. Before he went on to fame and fortune as the author of *Clara Callan*, I worked with him on *Farthing's Fortunes*, a picaresque novel that gives a convincing picture of life in nineteenth century Toronto. Above all, in *Final Things* (shrewdly selected as worthy of mention for its Toronto atmosphere by Noah Richler in his thoughtful book, *This Is My Country, What's Yours?*) Wright gives a depressingly accurate picture of the shabby apartments around Allan Gardens, a few significant social rungs above the desolate walk-up Queen Street apartments caught by Alistair MacLeod in *No Great Mischief.*

Morley's own house on Dale Avenue is worth a special description. It is a tall, handsome, orange brick building, set behind a lawn raised above street level, and I think it is important to understand it, if you want to understand Morley. Certainly Barry Callaghan chooses to begin his 1998 memoir of his life with his father, *Barrelhouse Kings,* with a description of the house. And although Barry is a controversial character (don't let that man near a microphone!) if you want to get a sense of Morley at home, and of Morley's conversation, read Barry's book. He has caught his father perfectly.

I say this with feeling, because all the time I was at Macmillan I lived quite near Morley's house. I often used to walk past and see — just as Barry has described it — Morley sitting there, cocooned in light in the front window of his study, gazing blindly out into the night, thinking. And writing.

I used to like dropping in to visit Morley and his wife, Loretto, who had clearly once been a very great beauty, and was no longer able to be very active. In their big drawing room, surrounded by interesting art, Morley enjoyed receiving visitors and directing conversation in a sort of literary salon. Clenching his pipe in his worn, old man's teeth, he really *listened*. I have a strong image of his blue eyes focused intently on the speaker as this long-necked little old man, with his wispy-haired head to the side (a little like a cartoon ostrich, I thought), absorbed what was being said about politics, or — often — about writers and how their standing was rising or falling. I once took Jack Hodgins, then a very young fiction writer from Vancouver Island, along to meet Morley, and the encounter between the generations was everything we had hoped.

Barry's book talks about how, in the 1950s, Morley and he liked to watch from the front windows of the house as their Rosedale neighbours returned from their work downtown. They would count homburg hats, denoting establishment jobs that Barry and Morley liked to deride. It's my speculation that Morley — the son of the former indentured servant — liked his position as a householder in what was perhaps Toronto's most respectable "old money" district, but also (and above all) relished his role as an outsider and an observer.

The second book of his that I edited, *Close to the Sun Again* (1977), dealt with a former naval captain who after the war became a captain of industry, like the homburg-wearing men in the houses around Morley on Dale Avenue. Like so many of his books, it deals with the clash between worldly success and wider, vague, spiritual longings. Critics have noted the lasting influence on Morley of the theologian Jacques Maritain, and on his choice of extreme examples to portray

these contrasting values, such as priests or prostitutes. Indeed, prostitutes feature in two of our other books together, *No Man's Meat
and the Enchanted Pimp* (1978) and *Our Lady of the Snows* (1985),
where Kipling would have been surprised to find the title's use of his
admiring description of Canada. As for outsiders, in *A Time for Judas*
(1983) he deals sympathetically with Christianity's ultimate outsider,
in an ingenious reworking of the Bible's story of the crucifixion.

During all of the time we worked together, Morley was his own
literary agent. This meant that he and I negotiated the terms of
his publishing contract directly. He loved that. "Well, here we are
like rug traders at the old bargaining table," he would say, rubbing
his hands with glee. It was easy to make a deal with someone who
enjoyed the process so much. And after I left Macmillan, and Morley
moved on to make a deal for his last novel, *A Wild Old Man on the
Road* (1988), I remember feeling a sort of detached sympathy for the
people at Stoddart, who almost certainly — as rumour had it — paid
the old rug trader far too much for his last book. And I note with
pleasure that the final title includes one of his favourite adjectives,
"wild," which provoked many editorial discussions between us.

I must say that despite his "prickly" reputation I found him very
easy to work with on an editor-author basis. His usual accreditation
to me in my signed copies of his books neatly reflects the professional roles that we both played: "To Doug Gibson, the editor."

In my talks to young people in the publishing world I am usually
asked about the outrageous confidence that I, still a young man,
showed in cheerfully suggesting changes to the work of senior
accomplished writers like Morley Callaghan, the toast of the literary
world long before I was born. But I summarize the answer as "just
doing my job."

I often go on to give two examples of the minefield where an
editor tiptoes. When I started work as a junior editor at Doubleday
Canada, I happened to run into a young writer at a party who was
delighted to meet me because, as it happened, he had just sent in his
first novel to Doubleday.

"Look," he told me, " I know that the odds are against my book
being accepted — but if you do turn it down, when you send it back,
would you please send along some comments — you know, tell me

what's good about it, what's not working and needs to be improved, and so on?"

I hedged, saying that we didn't usually go into such detail when we sent a manuscript back, but I would see what I could do. Well, the manuscript was okay, but we couldn't see anyone actually spending money to buy it, so I sent a regretful letter returning the manuscript.

Back came a letter — in these days before email — saying, thank you, but you must have forgotten our conversation where I asked you please to give some details about what's good and what's bad about the manuscript. Please give me a report like that, he asked, stressing that it would be very helpful to him, and so on.

So I dug up my Reader's Report and gave it a much kinder gloss: "The dialogue is thoroughly convincing . . . a fine sense of place . . ." but suggesting that the pacing needed to be tightened at this point, while this character needs to be more clearly established at the outset. And so on.

Kindly, encouraging stuff.

Back by return of post came a letter that began, "Dear Mr. Gibson, Who the hell do you think you are?"

I learned a great lesson there. First, obviously, not to get into helpfully reviewing manuscripts that you are rejecting. Second — and this wider lesson is the truly important one — that in the realm of publishing, especially publishing fiction, you are dealing with hopes and dreams.

And then, to hammer home the lesson, I go to the other end of the spectrum, and tell of an unforgettable encounter with Morley Callaghan.

On this occasion Morley phoned me at the office in a fever of excitement. He'd just finished a novella, and he was pleased with it, and could I come by his house in Rosedale and read it? Well, I argued strongly against such a visit, using words like "unprofessional." But this was Morley Callaghan, now a widower, and around the age of eighty, and not only a legendary figure but my friend, and very insistent. So I gave in, and went that evening to the big house that I knew well.

Morley greeted me at the door, restraining Nicky, a giant poodle with a tiny brain, I'm afraid, and brought me inside and guided me to a chair in the big drawing room. He got me set up there, very solicitously, gave me the manuscript (typed on his old machine, as

I recall), then retired with Nicky across the hall to where — as the door opened briefly to reveal — a TV set was blaring out a Stanley Cup final game.

I started to read. After five minutes the TV roared again, and Nicky was bounding around the room with Morley in irritated pursuit, here to ask me if the light was good enough. Yes, fine thanks, Morley.

Then another five minutes passed, and we had more TV, more Nicky, more pursuit around the room, and kind enquiries as to whether I wanted a glass of water. No, thank you, Morley, I'm fine.

When it happened again five minutes later, it all became clear to me. Morley needed — really *needed* — me to tell him that this new manuscript was good. Not, I want to stress, because my opinion was worth its weight in gold. No, he needed to hear it because, as a widower, he had spent so long on this work, his face pressed right up against it, that he really didn't know if it was any good. So he needed an objective, professional opinion, saying, "This is fine, Morley, relax."

And it was, and I said so.

That book, *Our Lady of the Snows*, featured a Toronto prostitute as the central character. Morley's interview with Peter Gzowski, the host of CBC Radio's *Morningside*, drew memorably from that topic. My friend Peter (whom I write about in a later chapter) was a superb, honest interviewer, and an author's appearance on his program had a dramatic impact on any book's sales. But his staff knew that like a good boy from Galt (and I am married to a girl from Galt, now Cambridge), he was somewhat prudish on the air — for example, made very uneasy by four-letter words. There was no danger of that with Morley, the experienced old CBC Radio hand, but he was a respected senior man of letters with a decisive on-air manner that made him very hard to interrupt. So my friend Hal Wake (who now runs the Vancouver Writer's Festival and tells fine stories of those days) recalls being part of Peter's team in the control booth listening with delight as Morley, asked about the book's theme, began decisively: "Now Peter . . . you . . . know . . . prostitutes. You . . . know . . . prostitutes. And you know that . . ." And by now it was too late for Peter to make any protest or diversionary move, and the control booth folks were almost rolling around on the floor. And Morley, I suspect, was not unaware of the impact he was having.

A final story about Morley Callaghan, which also tells us a lot about Alice Munro. She was once on the Toronto subway when she saw Morley, by then a widower, tottering aboard her car, looking old and frail and ill. She went over to him and reintroduced herself, and sure enough, Morley confessed that he was sick and was going to his doctor's. Alice was alarmed enough by Morley's condition that she got off a stop early and took his arm to help him; and being Alice Munro, she admits that she did so with some awareness of her own kindness in the matter. And just as she was about to help the poor shuffling old man across the road, he pulled back his head, looked her in the eye, and said, "You know what's the matter with your work, don't you?" — and proceeded to tell her.

He was a fine, feisty fellow. When he died in 1990, the funeral at St. Michael's Cathedral was even better attended than the fictional funeral for Eugene Shore. He had lived to a great age, and the minor slights (like the autographing session in a Toronto department store that was so ill-attended that I had to rope in a passing friend, the editor/literary agent John Pearce, to pose as an eager book-buyer) were long gone. He was now part of Canadian literary history, with several of his books ensconced in the New Canadian Library and taught in universities across the country. He had received his share of honours and honorary degrees, and was a Companion of the Order of Canada.

It was a solemn service, with all of the great, formal dignity St. Michael's Cathedral could provide. And then, as the coffin was borne out past the silent congregation towards the great entrance doors, everyone jumped. A Dixieland jazz band stationed out of sight above the entrance had burst into full cornet and trombone and clarinet action, blaring out, "Just a Closer Walk with Thee." Then the tempo changed up to "St. James' Infirmary," (a tune with the significant, defiant lyrics *"Put a fifty-dollar gold piece on my watch-chain / To show the boys I died standing pat"*). Suddenly everyone was smiling and chatting, delighted by the uplifting surprise. We were all stepping lively as we moved behind the coffin through the old cathedral doors, and out into Morley's Toronto sunshine.

# W.O. MITCHELL

Character, and Creator of Characters

W.O. For millions of Canadians the initials alone were enough to identify him. They knew W.O. Mitchell as the author of a famous book called *Who Has Seen the Wind* and a series of stories, immortalized on CBC Radio and beyond, about Jake and the Kid. And if they had ever seen him in person or on television, they knew that he was a wild-haired old guy with a salty tongue and a scratchy Prairie voice. A real character. And they liked him.

It went beyond liking for those who had read his books — thirteen in all — and seen his plays and laughed till they hurt at his public performances. Peter Gzowski summed it up best at the tribute to W.O. staged by the Calgary PanCanadian Wordfest in October 1997; he said that other Canadian writers may sell more books, may be richer, may even be better known around the world — but that "there is no writer in the country who is more or better loved than W.O. Mitchell."

I suspect that the news of his death at home in Calgary on February 11, 1998, produced widespread grief from coast to coast, with people far beyond the literary world feeling that they had lost a friend. He was a Canadian icon, a link with the old Canada of farms and small towns that, defying urban reality, many of us still tend to think of as home.

On the Prairies, his status was special, and I found that walking a block with him on any Main Street in the three central provinces was a slow but lively business: within twenty seconds it seemed he could find a common link — a relative, a former neighbour, a doctor — with anyone who hailed the familiar figure.

Other Prairie authors have talked and written about how his work opened up possibilities for them, and all of them come fully equipped with their share of affectionate "W.O. stories," since nobody ever forgot meeting him. The Alberta writer who said that she didn't know you could put gophers in a book until she read W.O. Mitchell humorously noted his inspiration.

Gophers, I should add, were to play a prominent part in the rich vein of Mitchell lore. When he wrote a role for a gopher squeak in the CBC Radio version of *Jake and the Kid*, he ended up producing the most convincing squeak himself, and being paid for it. The old Depression Prairie boy who had ridden the rails during those ten lost years needed no prompting. Thereafter gophers started popping up in his scripts with profitable regularity — until an edict came down from on high, and the gophers squeaked no more.

His special hold on Prairie people is easy to understand. He was one of them — from Weyburn, then Winnipeg, then High River, and then Calgary — and for them the brief sojourns elsewhere didn't really count. When he wrote about the land and its people, he showed that their everyday life and its setting could be the stuff of literature, and they appreciated what he was doing, in every sense. Discussing his last collection, *An Evening with W.O. Mitchell*, the newspapers in Saskatoon and Regina produced precisely the same phrase in their different reviews. In something more than a coincidence that phrase was "he belongs to us."

Coincidence — and history — dictated that I should be smitten by the man. Everyone who has read *Who Has Seen the Wind* will remember that at a time of sorrow in young Brian's household the old Scottish granny takes down the family Bible and reads, "This is Maggie Biggart's book. It was given to her on her wedding day in Dunlop, Scotland — May — 1832." Like many of the details in his books, this reference is to a Mitchell family link. As it happens, Dunlop, Scotland, is a small town of fewer than a thousand people, even when all the dairy farmers are in town.

I know this because the Gibsons have lived in Dunlop for generations, and I was raised there, and my mother, the Jenny mentioned in the dedication, still lives there. So when as a young editor in 1974 I found myself working on a new edition of *Who Has Seen the Wind* illustrated by William Kurelek, I realized that running into this fellow Mitchell was significant. Over more than twenty years we were to work together on ten books.

There were strong indicators from the outset that working with W.O. would be an interesting proposition. The signing of the contract was marked by a celebratory lunch at the Westbury Hotel hosted by my boss, the convivial, white-haired Hugh Kane. He and

I and William Kurelek — a quiet, gentle man — watched enthralled as Bill (for so I was learning to call him) launched into a cutlery-rattling imitation sermon by his creation, hypocritical preacher the Reverend Heally Richards, beginning with the shouted words "Brothers and Sisters!" Our fellow diners — stolid Harold Ballard look-alikes — were not amused. There were complaints. When the flustered maître d' reached Hugh Kane, Kurelek and I gaped while money discreetly changed hands, and Bill was persuaded to resume a normal conversational tone.

Not, of course, forever. The Westbury Hotel incident was almost repeated before my eyes in a Victoria dining room when Bill's delight at embarrassing a TV interviewer with the full-volume punch line "So when did *you* last have an erection?" resulted in a few old ladies nearby almost fainting into their soup, and the head waiter hovering. After that dinner, I recall, Bill persuaded me to take along some personal remaindered copies of his books to the reading, and to stand there and sell them to the crowd, to his great benefit. He was a charmer.

I have never known anyone around whom stories clustered in such numbers. He was, shall we say, incident-prone. If I were walking on the street with W.O. and two pigeons collided in the sky and fell on our heads, I would have regarded it as a normal hazard of being in his company. Pierre Berton told of visiting the Mitchell household in Toronto during W.O.'s stint as fiction editor at *Maclean's* magazine. As Berton told it, when he arrived for dinner an indignant mother-in-law was leaving, suitcase in hand, the house was on fire, and the children were outraging the neighbours in imaginative ways. (In Toronto there was even a petition to persuade the terrible Mitchell kids to leave the neighbourhood.)

The three Mitchell children went on to lead respectable lives but, as you would expect, produced their own share of stories. Once W.O. contacted his teenaged daughter Willa, then living a deter-minedly independent life in Vancouver, and they had a talk in his Hotel Vancouver room. Taking a crowded elevator down to the lobby with her, he pressed a fatherly twenty dollars in her hand. True to her Mitchell genes, she loudly denounced this sum to their fellow passengers, noting that most guys usually gave her far more. For once, W.O. was reportedly speechless.

From the Alberta foothills my friend Andy Russell (author of

*Memoirs of a Mountain Man* — and you can imagine how much fun I had editing and publishing *that* book) recalled hunting trips with groups that included our man. According to Andy — a master of embellished campfire yarns — one goose-hunting expedition set W.O. digging his pit off to the right. After the geese had come in, the silent gun on the right was noted. A search party found W.O. red-faced and buried up to the shoulders in caved-in-dirt. On another occasion Andy and some pals looked down on a field containing W.O. and a very inquisitive bull. Trying to cross a barbed-wire fence in a hurry, W.O got the crotch of his pants hung up on the top wire. As the bull cruised closer his manly predicament brought joy to the watchers — almost as much joy as his later imaginative account of how his pants got torn.

On another occasion, when he was in the car with his wife, Merna, near their summer place at Mabel Lake in B.C., he impatiently assured her that a wasp in the car was no cause for concern. Until, that is, the daring wasp crawled up W.O.'s shorts and stung him in the groin. As Barbara Mitchell tells it (in *Mitchell*, the second volume of the biography she and her husband, Ormond, wrote, after the first volume, *W.O.*), "Fortunately, they were right in front of the Enderby drugstore. W.O. bolted out of the car, into the drugstore, and up to the dispensing counter. In as quiet a voice as he could muster, he asked for ammonia. Flabbergasted, the druggist and shoppers looked on as W.O. held open the top of his shorts and doused himself with half the bottle. Relieved, he casually asked the druggist, 'How much is that?'"

He knew that he was "incident-prone," but prided himself on his powers of recovery. In my role as publishing educator I used to run the first week of the Banff Publishing Workshop, founded by the brilliant Yuri Rubinsky. Each year, teaching about thirty keen young would-be publishers at this mountain retreat, I made a point of bringing in an author to talk about the publishing process from the author's point of view. These young people were spoiled, meeting people like mountain man Andy Russell, historian of the West James Gray, and Robertson Davies. One year it was W.O. who, unsurprisingly, ranged widely with his comments on an author's life. In fact one central anecdote was his tale of an outboard failure in mid-lake when he was at the summer place near Enderby. Trying to fix the outboard, he spilled gasoline all over his shorts (his only garment). A quick glance around assured him that no boats were nearby on the silent lake, so he slipped out of the now-stinging shorts and crouched to work on the engine. Standing up later, arching to ease his back, he found himself ten feet from a sailboat quietly drifting by, full of pop-eyed female sailors. Rarely at a loss for words, outside of Vancouver hotel elevators, W.O. claimed that he instantly inquired, "What class is that boat?"

Presumably his ill luck with things such as matches and gasoline (oh, the stories I could tell!) persuaded him to stop smoking in favour of taking snuff. His snuff-taking became legendary. Indeed, such a strong smell of snuff accompanied every Mitchell manuscript that I could identify it almost before the package hit my desk. (And I was touched when his family sent me a snuff box after his death. Just opening that box, now in our dining room, brings him back.)

At Banff he tried to do some snuff missionary work with my girls, Meg and Katie. He sprinkled snuff on the dent where the base of the thumb meets the back of the wrist. Then, high drama. "Watch closely, now! *Sniffff!* Now, where did that go?"

Four-year old Katie, in deep-voiced disgust, replied, "Up your nose."

Later, back in Toronto, Katie joined us for a Mitchell book-signing session at Britnell's, the dearly departed bookstore at Yonge and Bloor. Katie was reaching the haul-back-on-Dad's-hand stage, accompanied by the four-year-old whine, "Daaaad, let's go!," when W.O. intervened.

"Katie, I need your help," he said plumping her up on the table beside the pile of books to be signed. "See this page? Every time I say '*Katie!*' you open the next book there, then put it down right in front of me. Okay? '*Katie!*'" It worked like a charm, and as a production line team they charmed the lineup as they finished the entire pile of books.

Once, for the cover of a collection of his plays entitled *Dramatic W.O. Mitchell* (1982), I took him to the photographer's studio to encourage him to be dramatic. It was, I discovered, like asking the Atlantic Ocean to be wet. He was a man of gigantic enthusiasms. On one visit to the Macmillan office, he was asked to look at an ailing potted plant. This led to an enthralling, arm-waving, audience-generating account of the titanic battle he had waged against the evil forces of the mealy bugs at his greenhouse at home in Calgary in defence of his beloved orchids. In the same spirit, his alder-smoked salmon was, apparently, beyond compare, like his youthful prowess on the diving board. In fact, he led a life of superlatives: a fairly good Chinese meal would be the product of the Best Goddamn Chinese Restaurant in Canada. And his enthusiasms for people were equally strong: If some of his swans were actually geese, there are many worse faults in a man's view of the world.

Ironically, for a writer who gained great fame in the bookshops, he seemed to set great store by success in the movie theatres. This continued to elude him, despite constant excitement about this proposed deal, and that potential director, and that interested star. He was so disappointed by Allan King's version of *Who Has Seen the Wind* (not bad, in my view of it) that he took to calling it "*Who Has Seen the Waltons*" until he was legally constrained from doing so. When he himself was the subject of a movie, Robert Duncan's NFB documentary *W.O. Mitchell: Novelist in Hiding*, he was incensed by the thesis that he spent too much time "being" a writer, giving the public performances that he loved, and not enough time actually writing. His anger (and he really did, on occasion, hoot with rage) was so fierce that he turned out more books in the next ten years than in the previous thirty.

Robert Duncan was on to something, although he didn't give full weight to the fact that, as a writer, W.O. had suffered the terrible misfortune of creating a classic with his first book. One result was that for many years, whenever he sat down to write, *Who Has Seen the Wind* crouched like a huge crow on his shoulder, silently defying him to write another book as good. Perhaps it was only in 1981, after he brought out *How I Spent My Summer Holidays* (a dark story's deliberately sunny title, which I favoured, although it drew some criticism) that he felt free to write with no crow on the shoulder. That 1981 book was controversial. But in their biography, Barbara and Ormond Mitchell note that "George Woodcock, who had always been dismissive of Mitchell's work, grudgingly admitted that *How I Spent My Summer Holidays* 'compels one's attention with a vision that seems to have stepped straight out of the Puritan nightmare.'"

Working with him on that pivotal book reminded me that for all of his eccentricities, when it came to his writing, he was deadly serious. His biographers remind me that at a late stage in the editing process, I managed to persuade him that we needed an extra scene, to make the relationship between the two main male and female characters clearer to the reader. Right there in the Macmillan offices, W.O. commandeered a typewriter and an empty office to produce the extra scene. Conversely, when I tried to persuade him to place some harsh, shocking material farther back in the book than the opening pages, we discussed it at length, but he was adamant that though it might be commercially risky (frightening off some readers), it was artistically necessary.

But there is no doubt that W.O. was the opposite of the typical author, who likes the quiet, private life of a writer, but has to be pushed to do any promotion. W.O. so loved the promotion tour that he gave the impression of doing the troublesome writing stuff just as a preliminary for THE REAL THING, the promotion tour, the interviews, and the readings.

His public performances, of course, are legendary. All of the doubts that he associated with the lonely act of writing ("like playing a dart game with the lights out," he once famously observed), were removed by the instant response of the audience. As a one-time actor, he loved "the immediate thrust of a live audience as it responds to story magic," and it showed. His performances were immaculately professional: voice husking or thundering, fist raised, white hair flying, mouth creased in a foxy grin, or eyes wide in innocent astonishment at a double entendre raising a laugh. His performances, now fortunately captured on audio cassette, were unforgettable, and he himself was perhaps the most outrageous character he ever created.

He was such a stellar presence — and such a mischief-maker — that anyone introducing him before a speech had an impossible task. I learned this, to my cost. If I gave him a well-deserved reverent introduction ("a man whose work has altered the course of Canada's writing, one of Canada's cultural treasures"), he would get to the lectern, lean on it, look around, then say, with impeccable timing, "Aw, horseshit!" So if the next time around I gave him a funny, irreverent introduction, using his own "folksy old Foothills fart" description, he would come up, look over his glasses, and gravely give us ten minutes on "the role of literature in society," while I squirmed, and people wondered why that rude lightweight had been asked to introduce this fine, scholarly old gentleman.

Another irony: This larger-than-life performer, not short of ego, valued selfless work. A couple of years before his death, when his health was failing, I asked him what, looking back on his long career, had brought him the most satisfaction. He thought hard and then said, "The teaching, I think." Grateful former writing students who had learned from "Mitchell's messy method" at Banff, Calgary, Toronto, Windsor, and elsewhere, will know why. Perhaps the fact that both of his sons, Orm and Hugh (the juvenile fire starters who alarmed the neighbours), grew up to become teachers, is not an accident. It's interesting to note, too, that he was a fine judge of talent. He was proud to be the first professor to use in his class the stories of a young author named Alice Munro. Throughout his life he remained a fervent admirer, putting "Sweet Alice" in a special category. Very late in his life Alice sat by his Calgary bed, holding his hand and talking gently to him till Avie Bennett, observing this, was overcome, and removed himself from the room.

My own relationship with him was almost uncannily close. Let me give two examples. When we decided to publish the short story collection *According to Jake and the Kid* (1989), we agreed on the sixteen stories to be included. We knew that the tough part would be arranging them in the best order, so when he next came to Toronto we set aside a whole afternoon in his room in the old Four Seasons Hotel on Jarvis Street to shuffle and deal the stories in order on to the bed. We were done in *under twenty minutes*, both of us in total agreement: "Yes, now this one!" "Okay, then this would be next!" "Right, so we'd need this more serious one next!"

And so on. Bang, bang, bang.

This was so extraordinary that much later his biographers asked me to account for it. I could only give a feeble answer about trying to give a short story collection an overall shape, starting off with a strong story that establishes the character and the setting, then trying for a trajectory that mixes serious with humorous, blends long stories with short, and you know, um, er, ends on a strong story . . . I trailed away. Barb and Orm looked disappointed, hoping for an overarching principle. The truth is that W.O. and I knew what it was — even if I, for one, couldn't explain it.

And I certainly can't explain the matter of the title change to the novel that we had always called *Trophies*. Since it concerned a university professor, with framed degrees on his wall, who goes after a grizzly bear hide on a hunt that goes so badly wrong that he is seriously mauled, the title always seemed perfectly fine, and we had both accepted it as final. Until one morning, at home, I started to think that the place where he encountered the grizzly, Daisy Creek, was too good a name not to use in the title. How about, let's see, *After Daisy Creek*?

I rushed in to the office and tried the new title idea around. Everyone liked it, especially the all-important sales people. Great. Time to call Bill.

"Bill, I was thinking that *Trophies* is a good title, but it occurs to me that maybe we can do better . . ."

He cut me off, excitedly. "Yeah, and I've got a great title, a real doozy of a title. It's just perfect!" (Oh, great, I thought. Now I not only have to talk him into the title that everyone here likes, I've got to talk him out of this new one. Ah, well.)

"So, Bill, what's your new title?"

"*Since Daisy Creek!*"

I felt an eerie ringing in my ears.

"Bill, that's pretty good. Um. When did you think this one up?"

"Oh, just this morning."

Talk about an author and editor being on the same wavelength.

We were not on the same wavelength when Bill was rushing to deliver a new novel in time for fall publication. The final chapter had to be in my hands by the end of May. Through the winter he would deliver chapters, and I would rush to call him back to tell him the new stuff was really good, well done, keep going!

At the end of May he called to say he had done it, the book was finished, and the final chapter was in the mail. At great, congratulatory length I told him what a pro he was, and how delighted I was.

Until I read the final chapter.

It was terrible. Sloppy, slapdash, with a vital scene recounted "offstage." How do you tell the legendary W.O. Mitchell that his work is no good? Carefully. With great difficulty. I lost sleep over having to make the phone call, which eventually went like this.

"Bill, you know I've been very pleased with all of your chapters as they came in?"

"Yeah."

"And you know I'm no use to you if I don't level with you?"

"Yeah."

"Well . . . I have to tell you that this final chapter is no good."

Pause.

"I know."

"What do you mean *you know*?"

"Oh, hell, I was just rushing something off to you by the end of the month because I promised I would. But it's no good. I've started rewriting it already."

"Why, you son of a . . ."

I expressed myself vigorously, and he laughed, and I put it down to working with a wonderful, terrible, larger-than-life character.

Later, when we published *Roses Are Difficult Here* in 1990, I was responsible for a spot of censorship that he teased me for at readings across the country (and he loved, in his biographers' words, "to wind me up"). He would interrupt his tale of the arrival of Santa Claus in Shelby to confide to delighted audiences that in his original version, the runaway horses in Rory Napoleon's team of "reindeer" were originally roared at by Rory as . . . well, let's just say the term Bill used resembled "sock-kickers." I was the villain identified as "Dougie" Gibson, his normally sensible editor and pal. Shamefully, I had said, "There goes the library market" and had insisted on changing the instructions to the runaway horses to read "Whoa, you bay bastards!" In his readings — and even sometimes in his signings, for God's sake, as his fan and heir Stuart MacLean tells me — Bill insisted on restoring the original and in poking fun at me.

We were more than just a good, professional author-editor team. We were friends. That became clear when I left Macmillan in 1986 to set up Douglas Gibson Books at M&S. W.O. was a very loyal man who had stuck with Macmillan since 1947, but he decided that his primary loyalty lay with me. "I'm comin' with you," he said. And to my delight, he did.

He was, of course, only half a person. The other half was the redoubtable Merna Mitchell, known to most of us by the full appellation "Fercrissakesmerna." As his loving, caring, and remarkably tolerant wife for more than half a century, she deserves a book of her own. She was more than a glasses finder and a snuffbox retriever, she was the organizing principle in his life, to the extent that any arrangement made with him was worthless unless entered into the agenda by Merna.

Their relationship — sustained by what I called "the power of mutual recrimination" — was a constant delight to their many friends. No phone call to their house was ever complete until the phone had been wrested away so that the previous speaker could be joyfully contradicted by his or her spouse. Orm and Barb quote me in *Mitchell*, saying: "I remember there was one wonderful incident that went on for two, three minutes while I sat there looking at the ceiling while the phone was being passed from one to the other and they were having this spirited debate, grabbing the phone from one another, as to whether they were wasting my time by passing the phone. It was always two for the price of one. I always came away laughing and delighted."

When that stopped happening, I knew that he was losing the long battle against prostate cancer. Confirmation came the day he was too tired to recount a juicy anecdote and simply said, "You tell Doug the story, Merna."

The last time I saw him was on a cold October day in Calgary. Opposite his house, in the park where we had once walked and talked about plot twists, the last cottonwood leaves were falling. Inside the house a hospital bed was set up in the family room, where he received twenty-four-hour-a-day care. Merna, Orm, and Barbara had warned me that the morphine produced good days and bad days, but this was a good day, so he would recognize me.

To cover my predicted dismay at his appearance, I had prepared an opening joke: I praised Merna's gallant reading of one of his stories at the previous night's tribute, suggesting that all these years we had had the wrong member of the Mitchell family performing his work in public. He snorted at that, and we were briefly back to the affectionate insults that marked our relationship. He complained at one point, however, that the drugs were taking away his memory. There was not much to say in response.

But like a great comedian he had prepared his punch line. When I announced that it was time for me to go, the others tactfully disappeared. I stood by his bed saying my goodbyes, trying to tell him how much he had meant to me, and not doing a good job of it. Merna returned to say, "Bill, he really has to go now, the taxi's here." A few more words from me, then he turned, looked me in the eye, put out a hand to shake, and said, "Well . . . goodbye, Jimmy."

This was awful.

But the alarmed noises from Merna and the others were cut off by the mischievous grin spreading across his now-boyish face. And I blundered out of the room, marvelling at the grace that had turned a hard farewell into a brave joke.

Goodbye, Bill.

CHAPTER 8                                                      1913–1995

# ROBERTSON DAVIES

Man of Letters, Oracle, and Ugly Duckling

*"I feed my fires with quotations."* — Murther & Walking Spirits

*World of Wonders* was the first book by Robertson Davies that ushered me, a young editor, into his world. Its title provides a neat summary for that world in 1975, where to me everything was a little brighter, a little more surprising, and much more interesting than the everyday world offstage. It was a larger-than-life place, fully floodlit, and Davies was at its centre, ideally cast for the role of Man of Letters.

For a start, he looked like Jehovah. Not since Alexander Graham Bell — or, a mischievous thought, Karl Marx — has there been a head where flowing white locks and well-shaped beard combined so artfully to produce a leonine look, perhaps the look of the bust of Mendelssohn that adorned the piano of the house where he grew up, learning how a true artist should appear. It is impossible to think of Robertson Davies without that trademark beard.

Then there was the voice. Elderly ladies who as girls in Kingston took part in theatricals in 1932 that were directed by young Rob Davies still talked more than seventy years later about his marvellous voice, and how impressively he could use it. Over the years thousands have heard that voice resound around theatres and lecture halls all over the world. He not only performed readings from his work, he gave so many speeches that I was able to publish a fine selection from them entitled *One Half of Robertson Davies* (1977). He provided the title, based on the old Chinese proverb that "The tongue is one half of a man: but the other half is the heart." (I believe that quotation is genuine; he was not above inventing scholarly origins for his titles, such as *Fifth Business*, for the pleasure of misdirecting academic researchers.)

Within the limits I later discovered at the Art Gallery of Ontario, he enjoyed exercising that voice. In the 1980s I once saw him use it to great effect from a stage lectern, to dispel the friendly, avuncular effect he had chosen to create at the outset. He had just begun to give a literary talk when a news photographer bustled to the front of the house and started to scuttle around his feet, popping up like a gopher to flash shots from below that were certain to be revealing nostril shots, and were blindingly distracting. Davies stopped his reading and took off his glasses. His normally beguiling voice snapped out, *"Would you please not do that!"* and he beamed down a terrible smile. The photographer, a member of a profession not renowned for its shyness, leaped away as if scalded, as indeed he had been.

From a surprisingly early age, even during his teenage years at Queen's, that voice had chosen to adopt an English accent. Introducing her selection of interviews with those who knew Davies, *Robertson Davies: A Portrait in Mosaic,* Val Ross recalls meeting him in the McClelland & Stewart office in 1991: "He spoke with an English inflection to his vowels — remarkable for someone born in Thamesville, Ontario, who had spent seven of his eight decades on this side of the Atlantic."

Remarkable, indeed. But then this was the boy who at Upper Canada College briefly sported a monocle, and at both Queen's and Balliol College, Oxford, dressed in a floppy-hatted way that seemed designed to attract attention. He carried everything off with style, every stride, every gracious turn to meet an acquaintance, every introduction, every bow, and every raised eyebrow. More than one literary critic has suggested that perhaps this fine novelist's greatest character creation was himself, the iconic figure who strolled in an old-fashioned tweed overcoat through Toronto's Queen's Park or the nearby campus, brandishing a cane. After his death his daughter, Jennifer Surridge, suggested that "one of the reasons he developed his personality, one of the reasons he developed a character [her word] at Upper Canada College, was he didn't like people to learn things about his personal life."

*"Charisma embraces; style excludes."* — Question Time

Certainly it seemed to me that later in his life, as the beard grew snow-white, he used the Jehovah image as a protective shield. It failed miserably (blew up in his face, you might say) on the opening night of the Stratford Festival — he was a perpetual member of the board, and took his supportive duties seriously — when a bold woman emerged from the crowd outside the theatre to give his beard a tug, turning to report happily, "Yeah, it's real!"

I was partly to blame for a later incident in Winnipeg. He had been reluctant to undertake the full national tour to promote his latest novel. Was it really necessary? he wondered. I found myself forced to point out that his friend and rival, W.O. Mitchell (who *loved* touring) had been setting the country — and his new book sales — on fire, while his own sales languished in comparison. So he gamely agreed to go on a pre-Christmas cross-country promotional tour, and, as luck would have it, at the end of a tiring day of interviews he ran into a waitress (evidently not a student of the best Canadian writing) who received him raucously: "Hey, are you Santa Claus?"

"No, madam," he responded. "But I have sharp claws!"

Novelist Timothy Findley was a friend who watched the public performance over the years. At the grand celebration of Robertson Davies' life that we held in Convocation Hall in Toronto the week of his death, he perceptively suggested that perhaps only the Davies family knew how much it cost him in emotional energy to keep up the role of Robertson Davies.

Very early in our working relationship, which deepened over the years into a friendship as we worked on eight books together — my copy of *The Cunning Man* is inscribed in his fine italic hand "For Douglas Gibson ('my partner frequent') Sairy Gamp a.k.a. Rob Davies." — I caught a glimpse of this, a peek behind the costume. We were together in a side room at the Art Gallery of Ontario, about to face a crowd of perhaps 400 people assembled to hear him read from his new novel, *World of Wonders* (or possibly *The Rebel Angels*). I was to introduce him, and was pacing nervously around the room where he and I waited, as the hum of the assembling audience rose in our ears. My twitchy pacing took me close to the stolid figure of the author, and I was astonished to hear that composed, Jehovah-like figure uttering low, shuddering breaths.

I stopped pacing, and looked at him in disbelief.

*"Butterflies?"*

"Oh, yes," he said, mournfully.

"Still? After all these years, and all the hundreds of speeches?"

"Yes," he added, gravely. "Always."

This was a revelation, and a very encouraging one. Even Robertson Davies got really nervous before a speech! Further questions revealed that he thought it essential to be keyed up before a performance. And for him, the ultimate professional, every reading or lecture or speech was just that, a performance. He had too much respect for the craft of the performer — lecturer, actor, singer, musician, or magician — to wander on unrehearsed and unprepared and unexcited. *But those shuddering breaths!* Who would have thought it, or even believed me, when he swept confidently onto the stage, like a galleon under full sail.

*"How fully does one ever know anybody?"* — Murther & Walking Spirits
The quotations that punctuate this essay, like the one above, come from James Channing Shaw's selection, *The Quotable Robertson Davies*, which I published with pride in 2005. That wide-ranging book, with comments from "Academia" alphabetically all the way to "Youth," seems to me to provide two very important lessons about him. First, that he wrote a great deal, on many subjects; a book full of selected quotations from a slim, narrowly defined body of work would make little sense. Much more important, it shows that from his early years as a writer Davies sprinkled his plays, essays, and novels with witty epigrams and shrewd comments on the strange ways that human beings behave. A writer who is striving to produce epigrams (such as the apposite line "A great writer must give us either great feeling from the heart or great wisdom from the head") is very different, I suggest, from a writer who just gets on, unambitiously, with telling the story or making the case. Davies liked to aim at the role of oracle, and the selection of quotations show how often he hit the mark, giving the readers of his novels memorable flashes of wisdom to ponder.

*"Whom the gods hate they keep forever young."* — Fifth Business
From his earliest years, many of his friends were aware that he was exceptional. Some even tended to store his letters, confident that a great future — of some sort — awaited him. They were not to know that he had several lives to live before he found his greatest role.
*Robertson Davies: Man of Myth* is the title of Judith Skelton Grant's masterly 1994 biography. Her opening paragraph gives the perfect summary of his career — or, more properly, his careers:

While he was growing up, his father, Rupert, a newspaper owner and editor, moved the family from the village of Thamesville to the town of Renfrew and later the city of Kingston, all in Ontario. Davies was educated at Upper Canada College in Toronto, Queen's University in Kingston, and Balliol College in Oxford. A brief career as an actor was followed by more than twenty years as a journalist (he was both a columnist and editor of the *Peterborough Examiner*), and for another twenty years he was master of Canada's first graduate college and a professor of drama at the University of Toronto.

All this, she notes, fails to include his lives as a playwright, and above all as a novelist, the life that brought him world fame.

### *"Canada . . . the Home of Modified Rapture"* — The Lyre of Orpheus

Davies knew only too well that world fame was dangerous for a Canadian. He was all too familiar with the Canadian "tall poppy" syndrome, where those standing above the crowd are likely to be cut down; he had been a tall poppy most of his life, from the days when the Polish kids in Renfrew, a town he hated, used to beat up the smart kid who lived in the big house. One of his favourite stories was of attending a Vancouver cocktail party when the momentous news was shouted into the room that Lester Pearson had won the Nobel Peace Prize. The wondering silence that followed was broken by an older woman who rattled the ice in her glass fiercely as she declaimed, "Well! *Who does he think he is?*"

Alice Munro understands these things well. In 1978, when I published *Who Do You Think You Are?*, a title that resonated with Canadians, the American and the British publishers (alarmed by the fact that Malcolm Bradbury had recently used the same title) preferred to publish the book with the meaningless title *The Beggar Maid*. Rob was amused by this, and sympathetic to Alice, whose work he admired. Later he was kind to his fellow author from Ontario at a PEN event in New York in 1986. Alice recalled him inviting her for a drink. "And," she says in Val Ross's book, "it was like being with a member of my family. It was very comfortable. I felt so relaxed! And he was making me relaxed, of course, by letting me have the sense of our being alike, from small-town southwest Ontario."

Then, the Alice Munro touch.

"Yet we are not really alike. We come from different classes. I was the kind of girl who would have come to do his mother's ironing . . ."

*"You can't really form an opinion about somebody until you have seen the place where they live."* — The Cunning Man

In July 2008 Jane and I went on a literary tour of Southwestern Ontario (designated "Sowesto" by Greg Curnoe, an artist based in its centre, the city of London). We first visited Alice Munro country, following the old pioneer Huron Line from Stratford to Goderich, and paying special attention to the stretch of flat farming country watered by the many-branched Maitland between her birthplace in Wingham and her current home in Clinton. We roamed around her father's old haunts at Blyth, where we saw a play based on a Munro short story, and we had dinner with Alice and her husband, Gerry, in Bayfield, on Lake Huron.

The next day our pilgrimage took us to Thamesville, where a plaque indicates the former home of the Davies family, the place young Robertson was born and spent his first, impressionable years. Not far from the modest house was "The Pit," the gravel pit on the edge of town that was to feature in the early scenes of *Fifth Business*. Indeed Judith Skelton Grant's chapter on Robertson Davies' time in Thamesville contains a map of the little town that Davies produced for her from memory that is, in her words, "astonishingly accurate. There are simplifications, and a few minor errors, but one could easily use it to walk around Thamesville today." To do so — even in a season far removed from snowballs — is to enter the world of young Dunstan Ramsay.

Less than an hour away from Thamesville, closer to Lake Erie, lies the third point of the triangle that marks an astonishing concentration of small-town writing talent born in the first half of the twentieth century. The town of Dutton is the birthplace and family home of economist, diplomat, and towering writer John Kenneth Galbraith. The farm where he was raised doing chores lies just outside Dutton. These chores made even a prolific professor's life seem easy by comparison. He wrote that when Harvard colleagues worried that he was perhaps working too hard, publishing too much, "back of the query lies their natural concern for union rules. Only with difficulty have I suppressed my reply: 'The trouble with you, my friend, is that you've never worked on a farm.'"

The farm in question is identified by an official roadside tourist site notice (apparently written by Galbraith himself, to good effect). It is further identified by an improbable Inuit monument, surely the only Inukshuk to be found on a Sowesto farm, and no doubt a useful landmark pointing the way for any off-course Inuit dog-team heading west on the 401. Davies, who set his play *Question Time* in the Arctic, has a shaman make a comment that applies perfectly here: "Not being serious is a civilized luxury."

Dutton and the nearby farming area is the setting for Galbraith's classic memoir, *The Scotch*, a frank and funny account of growing up in an old-fashioned rural community, where "the formula 'It was good enough for my auld man so it's good enough for me' combined a decent respect for one's ancestors with economy of thought." I was an abiding admirer of this book, Galbraith's personal favourite, and I persuaded him to update it for a new edition that I brought out at Macmillan. Later, I was able to bring the book to McClelland & Stewart, where we published it with a cover showing a tartan-clad couple very like Grant Wood's classic couple with a pitchfork outside a barn. A framed 2002 letter from Galbraith hangs on my wall as a result.

Dear Mr. Gibson,

I now have the latest edition of *The Scotch* with the wonderfully imaginative cover which should give the book a wide response in central Iowa or thereabouts. I can only assume that Grant Woods would be greatly pleased though not perhaps as much as I am.

After a number of equally complimentary paragraphs this author of important books like *The Great Crash* and *The Affluent Society* concludes:

I think this is the first time I ever wrote a publisher to tell of the elegance and intelligence of his creation. I do so here with both sincerity and enthusiasm. Do inform all concerned of my pleasure,

Yours faithfully,
John Kenneth Galbraith

Clearly, Galbraith could be generous. But he could also be merciless in his satire. The good townspeople of Dutton have now

— just — forgiven Galbraith for his portrayal of their community in *The Scotch* (although Margaret MacMillan, who as a historian notes these things, tells me that a Dutton branch of her family has still not forgiven Galbraith's slighting reference to their farming practices). But the local library, a fine modern building, is named the John Kenneth Galbraith Library, and each fall a JKG literary prize is awarded in town. In 2008 I presented the prize, having been roped in by fierce local whirlwind Jenny Phillips to head the jury for my old friend's prize.

That official visit allowed us to visit the Galbraith family farm, now in private hands and off the tourist trail. Accompanied by the three Galbraith sons and a granddaughter, we were shown around the old barn, where a childhood carving revealed that as a boy he was just plain "Ken Galbraith," while a visit inside the farmhouse showed that the family who bought it from the Galbraiths have not made many changes to what was clearly the home of "A Man of Standing."

Any reader of *The Scotch* will soon see why Galbraith was such an admirer — indeed, such an influential admirer — of the works of Robertson Davies. His apparently relaxed writing is as honed and as carefully polished as that of his Thamesville-born contemporary, who warmly returned his admiration. Davies, I recall from conversations with him, especially enjoyed the story in the book that tells of the adolescent Ken smitten by the charms of a neighbouring farm girl. She comes to visit his (blessedly absent) sister, and Ken and she walk together through the orchard and sit on a rail fence, while "the hot summer afternoon lay quiet all around."

At this point their attention is drawn to the nearby herd of cows:

As we perched there the bull served his purpose by serving a heifer which was in season.

Noticing that my companion was watching with evident interest, and with some sense of my own courage, I said: "I think it would be fun to do that."

She replied: "Well, it's your cow."

*"Never neglect the charms of narrative for the human heart."* — The Cunning Man

Galbraith continued to have an eye for a good story. Once I was chatting to him by phone, regretting that a recent Gibson family trip to Boston had not allowed us to meet at his office. I lamented the fact that at the start of the long drive back to Toronto I had announced to the car that I would exceed the fifty-five-mile an hour limit, and take my chances. All went well until the New York Thruway, when a dispute over an apple in the back seat distracted me, and I was pulled over. When the trooper asked if I was aware that I was exceeding the speed limit, I began to hum and haw, as you would expect.

Whereupon four-year-old Katie burst out loudly from the back seat, "But *you knew*, Daddy! *You knew* you were going too fast. You told us you were going to speed because . . ."

She was hushed into silence, but Trooper Swanker (for it was he) was not amused, and New York State became much richer. After a spell in Ottawa clerking at the Supreme Court, Katie is now a lawyer, still with a strict regard for truth.

Galbraith loved that story, commenting, "Oh, the inconvenient honesty of our children!" He shared a similar story from the days when he, driving frequently between Boston and JFK's Washington, had amassed so many speeding tickets, to the disgust of his wife, Kitty, that she had to take over the role of driver. On one journey, he told me, she was driving uncharacteristically fast, and in the front seat he was warning, "Kitty, slow down, you're going to get a ticket." She ignored his advice, with predictable wifely comments.

So he was delighted when there came the wail of a police siren and she was pulled over. The traffic cop walked heavily to her window, flipping open his charge book. When he asked her if she was aware that she was speeding, Galbraith could not hold back. "She certainly was, officer. I've been telling her for half an hour, 'Kitty, slow down. You're going to get a ticket.' *And now this*!"

And he sat back, vindicated.

The officer looked at him, then looked at Kitty. Closing his book with a sigh he said to her, "Ma'am, with a husband like that, you don't need trouble from me." Then he walked away.

To his eternal credit Galbraith told that story against himself, and it entered Galbraith family lore. And, of course, for a tight-fisted Scotch-Canadian economist, it had the perfect ending.

*"Whose esteem is sweeter than that of an expert in one's own line?"* —
Fifth Business

It was because of his admiration for Robertson Davies that my
path crossed Galbraith's again just after Davies died. It's important to
understand that from the earliest Deptford novels (*Fifth Business*, *The
Manticore*, and *World of Wonders*), Galbraith had been so impressed
by the work of his Sowesto near-neighbour that he had made it a
point of pride to do missionary work on his behalf, spreading the
word about this marvellous novelist across the United States. Soon,
to my great pleasure, it became predictable that each new Davies
novel would be greeted by an enthusiastic lead review in an influential place like the *New York Times* or the *Washington Post Book Review*
section. And since it was by Galbraith, it would be well written, and
enticing, with that air of easy spontaneity that he once said he managed to acquire about the fifth draft. His missionary work — and of
course he was not alone in his enthusiasm, so he was pushing at an
open door — was very effective, and helped to create the huge audience that Davies enjoyed in the U.S.A.

In 1982 Davies wrote about receiving an advance copy of a
Galbraith review for the *New York Times*, one that called him, as
quoted by the blushing author, "not merely one of the best writers
of this time but of the century. A Puritan upbringing forbids me to
believe this. But I am glad to have it said, and by a man with a loud
voice."

At considerable personal cost, at the age of eighty-six, Galbraith
travelled from Cambridge to Toronto to participate in the Davies
Celebration at Convocation Hall. By then he was frail and old, and
afflicted by deafness, but as he paid tribute to the other writer from his
area, he still stood tall among the assembled authors. They included
Margaret Atwood, Timothy Findley, John Irving, Rohinton Mistry,
Jane Urquhart — along with the Massey College Master, John Fraser,
and me; together we two had planned the event. It was a glorious
evening, with the great historic hall well attended, and many thousands of others watching it live on CBC's Newsworld channel. All of
the speakers were invited to speak briefly about Davies, then to read
a favourite passage from his work. To lessen the chance of overlap,
I chose an unlikely passage in *The Cunning Man* where the aesthete
priest Charles Iredale is punished by being sent to the country to

board with Amos McGruder and his sister "Miss Annie." The delicate urban sophisticate finds himself eating mush off an old oilcloth in a smelly kitchen where "too often there was hair in the butter."

Worse, Miss Annie wrote and performed hymns of praise, accompanying herself on a wheezing old organ.

> Her star piece, with which she concluded every Sunday-night concert, was set to the tune of the once-popular waltz song "Let Me Call You Sweetheart." In Miss Annie's recension it began —
> *Let me call you Jesus,*
> *I'm in love with you —*

I sang this verse, very badly, in front of an amused audience. Learning that I had sung in public, on television, caused my daughters, safely off at university, more dismay than if they'd heard that I had taken my clothes off for the cameras. But the evening was a huge success, and as the platform party and the Davies family left the Hall, with our communal singing of "Adeste Fideles" still echoing from the walls, we were swept up in a great, roaring wave of affection. The celebration had done its work well.

*"Learn to enjoy the pleasures of talk for talk's sake, without thinking you have to reshape your life every time a new idea comes along."* — The Cunning Man

In private, Davies was a great storyteller, a collector of many pointed anecdotes. I was privileged to hear these stories in several venues: across the table in the semi-somnolent dining room at Toronto's very traditional York Club (where he mischievously set an adulterous row in *The Cunning Man*); in the midtown apartment that he and Brenda, his devoted wife of fifty-five years, maintained for midweek visits from "Windhover," their country home nestled among the Caledon Hills; and above all in the Victorian study that he created at Massey College, where the visitor sank gratefully into a comfortable chair surrounded by old theatrical prints and fresh, sometimes uproarious conversation until his secretary, Miss Whalon, intervened.

Miss Whalon, known to her friends as Moira Whalon, was half of a remarkable working relationship that speaks well of both parties. A native of Peterborough, she was working for the local Lock

Company when word reached her that the editor of the *Peterborough Examiner* needed a secretary. She was hired by young Mr. Davies and remained his secretary as he moved on to be appointed as the founding Master of the University of Toronto's Massey College in 1963, and in time to become a world-famous author.

Her dedication to duty became an affectionate joke between them. An American publisher once remarked that a just-arrived Davies manuscript was the most cleanly typed manuscript he had ever seen in a long career. This was a mistake. Miss Whalon's passion for continuing excellence was aroused. In those days when type-written errors could be erased only with great difficulty, she spent countless hours re-typing and re-re-typing thousands of pages, until the manuscript was indeed the cleanest in the world.

Miss Whalon kept a protective watch on the time of the man she affectionately called "R.D." How to address Davies was a problem that afflicted almost everyone. "Professor Davies," although safe and somehow appropriate, was very formal; "Master," while he held that position at Massey College, seemed vaguely Oriental and undemo-cratic, even obsequious; "Doctor Davies" was appropriate, because his string of honorary degrees began in 1957, and late in his life was extended, to his great pleasure, by honorary degrees from Oxford and the University of Wales, yet the title was clearly formal; "Robertson" seemed a form of very formal informality; "Rob" seemed positively impertinent.

It took me many years to work up to "Rob." This was a man who had been publishing books literally before I was born and somehow, despite his endless courtesy and kindness, it seemed presumptuous. So we worked away together on his books, he addressing me as "Doug" by phone and in person, and signing letters as "Rob," while my let-ters went to "Professor Davies" and my phone calls began. "Hello . . . there." I observed the same shyness in many others, including Peter Gzowski ("What the hell do I call him?") over the years.

Of course, his public persona was based on the fact that he looked God-like, if God had condescended to wear what Val Ross at that 1991 meeting in our offices called "full Edwardian rig of blazer and flannels." The fact that he also could speak in fully formed orac-ular paragraphs left people awestruck. I remember on one occasion, in 1986, inviting him to address the Banff Publishing Workshop.

Thirty-six bright, articulate young people who wanted a career in publishing formed the audience, their numbers swelled by Banff Centre administrators who wanted to hear Robertson Davies speak about author-publisher relations. Davies spoke wittily and well for half an hour. From the chair, I got the ball rolling by asking the first two questions, then threw the meeting open for questions. Suddenly, every one of these clamorous students, disrespectful rebels given to peppering all of our speakers with dozens of hard questions, fell silent, heads bent in shy study of their fingernails. When I complained later to them that this had turned me into an on-stage interviewer, which was damned hard work, the explanation was, "Yes, well [shuffle] but this was . . . *Robertson Davies!*"

It astonished them to learn that behind the God-like mask was a kind man, no stranger to shyness, as the Art Gallery of Ontario story showed. If his shyness was at odds with his God-like appearance, so was his kindness. I recall a time of sorrow in my own life, when our conversation in his study went helpfully on for many minutes, and Miss Whalon was gently waved away when she tried to intercede on behalf of the next appointment. He was, as his readers know, a wise man, and his advice was sympathetic and good.

He once admiringly ascribed to Stephen Leacock a "sense of a large world in which the minds and passions of men are unchanging but ever-renewing," and he was armed with the same cool, classical approach, always fascinated by the things that human beings get up to. Sometimes, as you would expect of a man who wrote thoughtfully about Jung, his speculations were deeply psychological; he was intrigued, for instance, by the fact that his admired friend Hugh MacLennan had twice married women older than himself. He saw this as significant.

But above all, he loved funny stories. I cherish the letter to me where he recounts with joy the tale of how English author Michael Holroyd broke the news to his mistress of long standing (if that is indeed the right phrase) that he was getting married, then was amazed when she took it badly. "But I thought you would be delighted to be on the periphery of my happiness!" said he, in hurt surprise.

Few authors came back with more stories from the compulsory relay race to which we subject our authors that is called "the promotional tour." Pride of place goes to a U.S. publicity director's mistake that saw Davies sent to promote *The Rebel Angels* on a radio station in Washington, D.C., that specialized in black Christian speakers and soul music. Davies, introduced, he claimed, as "a cat who's written a book called *The Rebel Angels*," chose to have fun with the deeply religious audience, breaking the bad news that Matthew, Mark, Luke, and John could not be reliably classed as Christ's contemporaries. The phone lines lit up with devotees protesting that *"They walked with Him!" "They talked with Him!"* while the hip interviewer punched the air with glee. A close runner-up was the tale of the Ontario municipal official at a Stephen Leacock Award ceremony who, letting his oratory flow, described Davies as a "man of many faucets."

*"It has long been a contention of mine that if you truly value a book you should read it when you are at the age the author was when he wrote it."*
— One Half of Robertson Davies

Davies came late to fame. It was in response to Val Ross's question that he suggested that the animal he most resembled (when we might have expected a lion, or a phoenix, or even a manticore) was the Ugly Duckling. "You see," he went on, "no one thought much of him when he was a duck. But when they found out he was a swan, opinion changed. I may not be the world's foremost swan, but I am not a duck."

I suspect that behind this surprising statement lies an even more surprising fact. The fact that in mid-life, despite a series of successful careers behind him — as a book reviewer at *Saturday Night* magazine, where he was called "the best in North America" by New York's Alfred A. Knopf; as a columnist and editor at *The Peterborough Examiner*, where he was a long-running, very prolific success; as a respected professor teaching drama at the University of Toronto; as the founding Master of Massey College; and as a successful family man who had married well and happily, and raised three healthy daughters — he saw himself as a failure. He may have written and published a number of books and plays, but he had been disappointed in his great ambition — to become an internationally renowned man of the theatre.

The transformation into a swan — which may have surprised even the Ugly Duckling — came when he published *Fifth Business* in 1970, when he was fifty-seven years old. It was such a leap forward from his previous Salterton novels, which were lighter fare, that he was often asked what had changed. "People died," he would reply, darkly. Val Ross has shrewdly pointed out that the whole book is the retort of a retired schoolmaster who feels that his life has been undervalued.

While he did not wake up to find himself famous, like Byron, he found that something had changed. Now he was regarded as a serious novelist, and that was the route he chose to follow. He wrote some further plays, for adults and for children, and he even wrote a grand old opera entitled *The Golden Ass*. But it was clear that now this was a side interest. The swan was fully launched on a career as a novelist that would make the world sit up and take note as the elegant white shape glided by.

*"You might as well ask a spider where it gets its thread as ask a writer where he gets his ideas."* — One Half of Robertson Davies

We can see that his life provided R.D. with much of the material that he spun into novelist's gold. We see the influence of Thamesville and Upper Canada College on *Fifth Business*. Renfrew, for all of its horrors, gave good material to *What's Bred in the Bone*. Kingston, of course, pervades the Salterton novels. I remember that the excellent John McGreevy made at least two fine films about R.D. In one he has Davies borne in a horse-drawn carriage around the elegant streets of Kingston, telling tales of the town. Once he recalls the Queen's professor of English who gave an idealistic course for inmates at one of Kingston's flourishing prisons. The apparently innocent course title was "Literature as a Means of Escape." "And that," says Davies, facing the camera, *"is true!"*

His time at Oxford and at the Old Vic gave him not only a lasting accent, but also an awareness of the wider world. Above all, it gave him a wife.

*"There is more to marriage than four bare legs in a blanket."* — A Jig for the Gypsy

Entire books have been written about less interesting figures than Brenda Davies. The Australian granddaughter of a Scot from Shetland who amassed a fortune, she rose swiftly to become the stage manager at the Old Vic. There she met the young Canadian from Oxford, and slowly a romance developed. When they married and came to Canada she found his family less than warm. (R.D.'s mother was such an old-fashioned character that he once told me that he remembered as a boy having to *kneel* before her to deliver an apology.) But Brenda soldiered on, raising their three daughters, running the household, and doing all of the practical work, like driving — in effect organizing his home life.

It can't all have been easy, because we know that R.D. lost a year at Oxford to depression, which Judith Skelton Grant discovered to her surprise, after he had tried to conceal it from her. Brenda tended to speak of his ups and downs as examples of Welsh temperament, inherited from his father, but Davies himself wrote about the Black Dog of depression. But through all of the *sturm und drang*, the moves attendant on the career changes (and only a former stage manager could have adapted so swiftly from life in Peterborough to the juggling role of Master's Wife at an all-male residential college in the heart of Toronto), she was a reassuring presence, a constant source of support to him, and a good friend to many.

Among them was Shyam Selvadurai. He has written about the unlikely pairing that we, his cunning publishers, put together, whereby he, a young, slim Sri Lankan–born first novelist, would (like a lesser rock group) "open for" the sturdy establishment figure of Robertson Davies at a number of promotional reading events in Ontario. I was among the minibus passengers the night that we "hit" Hamilton, and I was pleased to see that the contrast between the readers intrigued the audience, helping to launch Shyam's career. Unlike him, I was not surprised to see the warmth that arose between him and Rob and Brenda Davies.

*"One must visit a wise man from time to time to discover what one already knows."* — The Cunning Man

Davies knew his city and his province in his bones, and I once suggested that he and his alter ego, Samuel Marchbanks, were perhaps the Last of the Upper Canadians. One of his most perceptive and provocative statements was that the great Canadian dramatists were Ibsen and Chekhov. Once, speaking of change from the Ontario of old, he described a Chekhovean scene in Cobourg, an old town on what used to be called "the Front," where pioneer settlers arrived by boat. In the years after the Second World War, as tides of new immigrants were sweeping in to utterly change the old rural province of his youth, the local establishment in the town had turned up for a production of Chekhov's *The Cherry Orchard*. In accordance with tradition they were dressed, he liked to recall, in dinner jackets "green with age." At the end of the play, these people stood around in the lobby confessing that they really did not see what this fellow Chekhov was getting at . . . while the metaphorical sound of trees being felled echoed symbolically outside, across the Ontario countryside.

As he aged, some of the advice he gave to others was notably practical. Don Harron, the broadcaster, writer, and comedian, was inspired by R.D.'s ability to continue with his creative work; so as a hard-working writer eleven years younger than the Master he earnestly asked him what to expect with advancing age. "Frequent urination," sighed Davies.

His last completed novel, 1994's *The Cunning Man*, was, he told me, an attempt to reveal the way that the city of Toronto had changed over his lifetime. He watched that development, and the changes in his province and his country, with a keen, caring eye (he once joked that Canada was not so much a country to love as "a country to worry about"), continuing to work hard into his eighties. In that, as in all of his work, delivered in polished form, he was a total professional.

*"It is men's work, rather than their recreations, which create trouble."* — Samuel Marchbanks' Almanack

But what was it like to edit Robertson Davies? Here, after he moved to follow me to McClelland & Stewart, is a very frank letter he wrote to me about the process, giving the author's point of view:

> Herewith the typescript of *Murther & Walking Spirits* which now embodies many of your suggestions and alterations. Not all, for I thought some of them needless, and some inadvisable, because I sense that your notion of the novel is different from mine; you have edited always for a rigorous clarity, and I feel that a certain fuzziness is essential to the nature of the book, which is, after all, about a man whose perceptions are not those of ourselves . . . Kicking and screaming as I wrote, I have shoehorned another generation into the Gage-Vermeulen family,

to meet your objection that everybody lived too long; I did not feel when
I was writing that a statistical realism was needed, but you do, and now
you've got it, though it creates a lump in the narrative that I do not like
. . . Because I have incorporated all the changes directly on the pages,
the typescript is not as tidy as I — or Moira Whalon, who takes great
pride in such things — could wish. But I think it is clear, and if you or
anybody concerned finds my writing difficult, I can explain by phone.
Here and there, my comments on your criticism are a little saucy — a
protest against a too-literal reading. Do not take it personally.

I have altered a couple of chapter headings.

I welcome enquiries, protests, loud screams, or whatever.

The saucy comments in the margins included a reference to my
role as a "Scotch dominie," but of course the process simply shows
both of us doing our jobs as professionals. I would raise frank questions about the manuscript, and he would accept or reject them.
That was our unvarying practice, and it worked.

What is perhaps equally interesting is what went on at the start of
the editorial process. I was aware (and his letters confirm this astonishing fact) that after spending years writing his latest novel, Davies
was always gripped by self-doubt. Was this new book a falling-off,
even a failure? Had he been wasting his time?

Knowing this, I made a point of setting to work as soon as I
picked up the manuscript, and reading it straight through, deep into
the small hours if necessary. This meant that the next morning he
received a couriered letter giving my reassuring response to the new
book, possibly indicating a few areas that struck me as needing more
work. But the main implied message was "Relax, this is very good."
And, incredibly, he needed that sort of fast reassurance.

*"Those who find a Master should yield to the Master until they have out-
grown him."* — What's Bred in the Bone
It has often been said that Charles Dickens was the great inspiration for the Davies novels. The comparisons are obvious. The
swirling cast of characters, often with Dickensian names and
speaking with distinctive accents. The witty, formal descriptive language, suitable for declaiming aloud. And the elaborate plots, in
which coincidence often played a role. No criticism angered Davies

more than the suggestion by some reviewers that his coincidences were unlikely. "Those boobs!" he exclaimed. "Can't they see what's going on around them?"

I once found myself in a Dickensian scene with him in the middle of Toronto. In my formal dark blazer and my full beard I picked him up from Massey College (similarly attired, I noticed) to take him downtown to speak at a book industry event at the Convention Centre. Approaching our destination, I started to pull into a parking lot — *and the attendant at the lot next door went mad, shouting and gesticulating fiercely at us.* Rob and I were amazed by his behaviour, but ignored him, and parked the car and started to get out. And he *came after us*, yelling.

I had visions of a Pickwickian street scene with me in the role of Sam Weller, defending my elderly companion when it came to fisticuffs. I slammed the car door and set off towards our assailant. He backed down instantly, waving his hands appeasingly. What he said was this: "I'b sorry. I t'ought you were Greek priests."

Too late, we realized that we had missed the chance of getting the Greek priest special parking rate, instead of the orthodox one.

*"We all need to take aboard so much rubbish to keep ourselves human."* — Murther & Walking Spirits

It seemed to me that, for all his great artistry as a novelist, in a sense Davies remained a newspaperman. From 1942 until 1963 he lived in Peterborough, a town of 30,000, and as the editor of the only newspaper in town he got to know almost everything that went on. Judith Skelton Grant gives details of battles over birth control editorials with the local Catholic bishop, and a scandal over a local judge's attempt to influence the police commission. And that, of course, was only the material that made it into print. For a future novelist, the constant stream of events, tragic and comic, must have been inspiring. All human life was there.

Even more important, it taught him to write, and write, and to do research. Every reader of his novels knows that they are full of arcane knowledge — from the care of Gypsy violins, to magician's tricks, to the medical knowledge to be gained from excrement — and that knowledge was hard won. In the days before computer searches, it represented an enormous amount of reading or consultation with experts. He worked extremely hard on the facts, true to his journalist origins.

His old Peterborough colleague, Ralph Hancox (whom I got to know well when we were part of the group setting up the Simon Fraser University Masters in Publishing Program) tells of his playing hard, too. As a prank the two newsmen invented a scandalous story about one of the town's revered founding fathers. They even carefully aged the fake supporting document, then brought the matter to the local historical society, which promptly suppressed it.

*"If you want to attract real, serious attention to your work, you can't beat being dead." —* A Mixture of Frailties

Since his death in 1995, I have been involved in publishing four posthumous books by Robertson Davies. *The Merry Heart*, where I provided the introductions; two volumes of letters selected by Judith Skelton Grant (*For Your Eye Alone, Letters 1976–1995* and *Discoveries, Early Letters 1938–1975*); and *Happy Alchemy: Writings on the Theatre and Other Lively Arts.* There have been many academic articles about him, and an academic conference where a young speaker talked learnedly about the role of a character named Doug Gibson, and was surprised when this figure from the distant Davies past rose at question time to announce, "I am Doug Gibson."

At that conference Judith Skelton Grant told a story, repeated in Val Ross's book, of how at the end of an easy, relaxed dinner party at her house, she discovered that Davies's paper napkin had been ripped to nervous shreds.

There will be more books about Robertson Davies, and even other books by him, since his daughter, Jennifer Surridge, is preparing selections from his voluminous diaries. A treat in store.

When Robertson Davies died, the newspapers of the world were full of tributes. I even contributed one for the *Globe and Mail*. But the best, of all those that came to my attention, was another *Globe* piece, this one written by Robert Fulford.

It began:

The death of Robertson Davies on Saturday night was like the abrupt disappearance of a mountain range from the Canadian landscape.

Perhaps there's something ungrateful about grieving over the loss of a great figure who lived among us for eighty-two years, but when the news came over the telephone it was hard not to feel a sharp sense of loss. Though his reputation went around the world, it was in Canada that he occupied an enormous space, now left sadly empty.

After singling out his last novel, *The Cunning Man*, as "like a magnificent farewell tour, a revisiting of the many places and themes he had taught us to love," Fulford sums up his achievement: "As always, he mixed wild imaginings with the hard facts of our past. Our leading fantasist was also a realist whose baroque tales rested firmly on Canadian reality."

After speaking of Davies as "a show that ran longer than any other in the history of Canadian letters" he concludes by quoting the final paragraph from *The Cunning Man*.

The narrator answers the phone to find that it's a wrong number, with a voice asking if this is the Odeon theatre.

No, this is the Great Theatre of Life. Admission is free but the taxation is mortal. You come when you can, and leave when you must. The show is continuous. Good-night.

# CHAPTER 9

# JACK HODGINS

Islander, Teacher, and Inventor of Worlds

"Donnelly Family Exterminated!" was the 1880 headline. News of this most un-Canadian crime quickly spread from Lucan, Ontario, along with the details of how a group of vigilantes in that farming community had attacked a local family by night and wiped them out. Although some relatives survived the "extermination," there were five deaths, three men and two women. Horrible deaths they were, too, thanks to "Pitchfork Tom" Ryder, and two other members of the mob who used their spades on a victim's head. Although there was a witness, a boy hiding under the bed, no one was ever convicted.

Who were these people, and where did they come from? Family legend has it that "Big Jim" Hodgins was the unofficial founder of the London-area community, arriving in 1832. As a local agent for the Canada Company he was so successful at recruiting Irish immigrants from feud-scarred Tipperary (his brother Adam had to be smuggled out in a coffin, for his own safety) that, to quote Ray Fazakas in *The Donnelly Album*, "within a generation there were at least forty-six different Hodgins households in the township." Adam's grandson, "Running Joe," eventually moved west to Vancouver Island, to produce, in due course, a grandson named Jack Hodgins.

So we have a Hodgins ancestor, "Big Jim," bringing over scores of Irish immigrants to invent a new world in Upper Canada, just as in Jack Hodgins' breakthrough novel, *The Invention of the World* (1977), we have Donal Keneally, a nineteenth-century giant, persuading an entire Irish village to come to Vancouver Island to set up a community. Interesting.

The Donnelly story came to my door in the shape of Thomas P. Kelley, the author of two sensational mass-market books about the Black Donnellys. He was a larger-than-life character, with the air of a carnie barker, who was in his sixties when he arrived at my Doubleday office to pitch me a new Donnelly book. He came with his wife, a shy, silent, silver-haired lady who wore genteel white gloves for the occasion. She watched proudly, her purse on her lap, as he leapt about, grunting, telling the exciting Donnelly tale, with imaginary spades swung, to sickening effect. Then, carried away by his narration, he jumped onto my desk to continue his arm-waving oration.

My desk was in its usual cluttered state, piled high with letters and layered manuscripts from many authors (who must have been surprised by the boot marks on their pages when they were returned). Sadly, once he had scrambled atop my desk, Mr. Kelley's nerve failed him. An older gentleman, not in good training, he found that he needed my steadying hand to climb down, while his wife looked on affectionately.

I did not publish his book, though over the years I did bring out several books about the Donnelly killings, by the preacher Orlo Miller and the lawyer Ray Fazakas. And the case of the author who leapt excitedly onto the editor's desk did enter publishing lore, as evidence of the lengths that authors will go (or perhaps the heights they will scale) in order to get published.

Jack Hodgins did not have to climb such heights to get published, but I remember that it took us at Macmillan a shamefully long time to decide to sign up this genius from Vancouver Island. This was different from taking on the latest book from Robertson Davies or Morley Callaghan. This was my attempt to bring a brand new, promising young author to our list, and I knew that it was an investment in his career that would almost certainly lose us money at the start. As Margaret Laurence put it later (reviewing that first book, *Spit Delaney's Island*) most publishers "feel about as welcoming towards a volume of stories as they would to sudden attack of paper-eating termites in their warehouse."

I didn't feel that way, and our slow caution in signing Jack was not caused by my facing obdurate superiors. George Gilmour, the president, was a nice Maclean-Hunter man who took a hands-off attitude towards editorial decisions, while Don Sutherland ran the trade division. A former Chinese scholar, Don went on to head McGill-Queen's University Press. When he participated in meetings with his Quebec publishing industry peers, the discussion was, of course, in French. At the end of a tiring day, the "foreign language" synapse in Don's brain sometimes produced a flow of idiomatic Mandarin, which surprised and delighted the French colleagues with whom he was debating.

Hugh Kane, too, was anything but an obstacle, although over many years at M&S as Jack McClelland's right-hand man, Hugh had often tried to rein in his enthusiastic boss. Lured away by John Gray to succeed him as the head of Macmillan, Hugh (a white haired, red-faced little dynamo with thick glasses), had found himself side-lined by Maclean-Hunter's takeover in 1972. When I arrived in 1974 I was horrified to find that he was not even invited to editorial meetings, which I chaired. I fixed that, to everyone's benefit. And instead of sulking, Hugh was busy changing the world of Canadian children's books forever.

At the time there were no Canadian bookstores for children, and only May Cutler's Tundra in Montreal published specifically for children. In fact, things were so bad in Canada that in 1972 I had made the infamous joke: "If all publishers are born gamblers, the men and women who publish children's books are the sort of people who jump out of a tenth-storey window in the hope that an open truckload of mattresses will be going by."

When I arrived at Macmillan the corridors in the stately old building at 70 Bond Street were alive with gossip of how Hugh was championing a crazy project, a couple of children's books by a poet named Dennis Lee, illustrated by Hugh's old friend Frank Newfeld, that would need to sell *ten times* the usual number of copies sold by Canadian children's books before they broke even. The whole thing was going to be a disaster.

Dennis Lee, for his part, remembers that Hugh's faithful support included discovering the ideal title for the main book. After a trial run, with Dennis reading some of the poems from his still-unnamed book to a group of Toronto kids, Hugh told him excitedly, "I think we've got our title, Dennis. Did you see how at the end the kids were dancing around chanting to each other, 'Alligator Pie, Alligator Pie'?"

The rest is history. The success of the book was encouraged by Hugh's determination to keep rolling the dice, indeed to keep Dennis rolling across Canada, giving endless readings and performances. Once, in Fredericton, Dennis sauntered into the local bookstore and introduced himself to the lady bookseller, who remembered Hugh Kane the salesman very affectionately. Dennis, not an overbearing man, politely offered to autograph the copies of *Alligator Pie* and *Nicholas Knock* that she had on display. The owner thought hard and then, with the precise phrasing of a diplomat, said, "If it were Pierre Berton or Farley Mowat, I'd say yes, but *in this case* I don't think so."

Which brings us back to Jack Hodgins. Jack was, and remains, a tall, lean, gangly figure, so loose-limbed that his hands and feet seem to be perpetually surprised to find themselves stuck so far away from him. He is such a nice, unassuming guy that humiliations like the one that befell Dennis in the bookstore happened to him all the time. As you will soon see, they were gleefully collected and cherished by this man with a love of a good story, or to put it another way, a passion for narrative.

In the end, after a delay caused by excessive caution, we signed up Jack, and I began one of my most rewarding author-editor relationships. Over the years I have been proud to publish twelve books by Jack, from short story collections to novels to a travel book set in Australia (*Over Forty in Broken Hill*), all the way to his classic book on the art of writing fiction, *A Passion For Narrative*.

"Jack Hodgins, he got curly hair" was the first recorded comment by my daughter Meg (aged two) on one of my authors, after Jack had visited the house for dinner. (I remember fondly that at a return engagement at Jack's house outside Nanaimo, his kids, Shannon, Gavin, and Tyler, kindly took me outside to see their pullets in the yard overhung by arbutus trees.) Jack's hair was curly then in 1976 and it's curly now, although it's less springy, and a purist would notice that it has gone grey. But Jack is still impossibly boyish, lean, and active. And he's still shy, in a stooping sort of way that allows him to rear back with a sudden smile or a laugh, as the conversation — or the instructive talk about the craft of fiction — demands it. Those who have seen him in action in a classroom know that he is that very rare blend of a shy person who is also a natural teacher.

As a writer, he arrived with a bang in 1976 with *Spit Delaney's Island*. The book produced many reviews like the *Montreal Gazette*'s: "Jack Hodgins has done for the people of Vancouver Island what John Steinbeck did for the inhabitants of California's Salinas Valley and William Faulkner for the American South."

The stories in the collection were set on the Vancouver Island that he knew well, having been raised in the logging/small farming community of Merville in the Comox Valley. Like the community itself, the stories were filled with memorable characters, but Jack Hodgins was careful to explain, as he told Jack David (a promising academic soon to become a notable publisher) in an interview, "I'm one of them. I'm not an outsider looking at them and laughing at them and saying, oh ho ho, look at those funny people who live on this funny island. They're not funny to me at all, except where they share the same feelings that I have. When I laugh at them, I'm laughing at us, all of us."

Margaret Laurence called the book "remarkable" in her *Globe* review, and wrote of Jack's ability "to convey human beings in all their uniqueness and nuttiness, and an ability to convey a sense of place — that Island which is both a vivid geographical place and an island of the spirit." It was clear from the chorus of praise — and the resultant book sales — that an important new writer had arrived.

I had deliberately tied Jack to Vancouver Island by putting a fine Emily Carr painting on the cover of *Spit*, and it delighted me to see how quickly Jack did indeed become *the* fiction writer portraying the Island to outsiders. I was not aware that in the process I was sharpening a double-edged sword; over time a writer who brilliantly describes a region can run the risk of being downgraded to the easy description "a regional writer."

Jack and I have worked happily together as author and editor over the years. Family legend goes that once Dianne, his wife, as his first reader, objected that a passage of magic realism went much too far, that no reader would believe it. Jack sniffily rejected her advice — until the day the same passage came back from my desk with the words *"No! No! No!"* written on it. More often, in my role of editor, all I needed to do was highlight a passage as being not quite right, and Jack would supply a brilliant revision that solved everything.

I am proud of the friendship that has allowed me to make many visits to Jack and Dianne's home in Victoria. One other marvellous side benefit for me was that I got to know the Island well. I learned that as you travel from Victoria north over the Malahat to the logging museum at Duncan (where I saw a "crummy" that had rolled straight out of Jack's writing about loggers), then up the highway to Nanaimo (where he taught high school) and beyond up to Campbell River, en route to Port Alice (a.k.a. "Port Annie, Pulp Capital of the

Western World," where his fictional hero Joseph Bourne resided) or, if you choose, west past the "goats on the roof" and the forest giants at Cathedral Grove to Port Alberni, then further west through the mountains where the roadside snow lies deep in winter to Ucluelet or Tofino, land of the surfers — why, you have travelled through the equivalent of a dozen little European countries, each with their own geography, climate, and culture. And that's not counting the Duchy of Saltspring Island, where Jack and I once gathered and ate the best blackberries in the world, in the lineup to the ferry.

I know, of course, that islanders anywhere — in Skye, in Toronto, in British Columbia — are different, proudly different. My former wife Sally's fine 1984 book, *More Than an Island* ("a model of civic history" according to Jane Jacobs) was a history of Toronto Island that made that point very clear. But I was amused to have the difference confirmed whenever I went to Vancouver Island.

I preferred to come by ferry, either through Active Pass to Sidney or straight to Nanaimo, nearer to Jack's home territory, the ferry gliding in past the Gabriola Island "galleries" shown to me by my friends Rufus and Bee Churcher.

Even aboard the ferries, the characters started popping up. Once I stepped outside to the outer deck and found a small family softly singing hymns into the wind — dozens of hymns. Ancient Mariners would accost me with dramatic stories of fishing fortunes made and lost at the whim of the Weather Gods, and so on, until I suspected that Jack had hired this cast of Vancouver Island "characters" for my benefit.

The UBC scholar and critic W.H. New went beyond *Spit Delaney's Island* to look at the cumulative impact of Jack's first two novels, *The Invention of the World* (1977) and *The Resurrection of Joseph Bourne* (1979): "By the late 1970s then, with three books appearing in rapid succession, Hodgins seemed to burst upon the literary scene in full bloom. This was an experienced writer, writing something 'different,' not an imitative apprentice. Journalists trumpeted the arrival of a major talent. Interviewers asked where he'd been. Readers sat back and enjoyed."

Bill New reminds us that where Jack had been was on Vancouver Island, apart from the spell he left to get a five-year teaching degree at UBC, where he took a creative writing class with Earle Birney.

Then he taught high school in Nanaimo, and wrote and wrote and wrote, the years of rejection allowing him to become what the world calls "an overnight success."

*The Oxford Companion to Canadian Literature* is intended to be a sober record of undisputed facts, yet it singles out *The Invention of the World* and *The Resurrection of Joseph Bourne* as "two immensely good-humoured and formally innovative novels." "Immensely good-humoured" is absolutely right. The perceptive Toronto critic W.J. Keith caught exactly the same spirit by praising Jack's work for its "sprightliness." Some critics have in fact complained that his books are devoid of truly evil characters. The human villains tend to be unlikeable and cranky and grumpy, but never truly malevolent and evil. True evil is to be found not in people — who for Jack are always capable of redemption — but, in *Broken Ground* (Jack's superb 1998 historical novel), for instance, by impersonal forces like the meat-grinding machine of the First World War, or the casually malevolent forest fire that destroys a new community in the woods — ironically a soldier's settlement granted to survivors of the war.

To me, *The Invention of the World* is Jack's greatest book. It begins brilliantly, with the reader directed to watch the man who waves us aboard the ferry to the Island. "Follow him home," we are told, and we soon learn that he is trying to reconstruct the whole island and its history. One of the book's sections, in fact, consists of his Barry Broadfoot–style recorded interviews with old residents as he tries to take intellectual possession of the place. "And he will act as if he himself had set all this down in the ocean, amidst foamy rocks and other smaller islands where sea lions sunbathe and cormorants nest and stunted trees are bent horizontal from the steady force of the Pacific wind."

The rest of the book is woven out of an astonishing variety of brightly coloured strands: a love story, a study of a nineteenth-century Irish village, a comedy of manners (the culture clash between wild loggers just out of the bush and prim, weight-watching townsfolk), a retelling of a pagan myth, a portrait of tough pioneer days in the rain-forest, a mystery story, and a wry look at our constant search for Eden.

The final scene, one of the greatest in Canadian literature, takes us to the crowded wedding reception that really takes off when

Danny Holland (axe throwing champion and former lover of Maggie the bride)

> pulled the starter on the chain saw he'd hidden under his bench, swung it up over his head, roaring and belching blue smoke, and let out a wild yell of delight. Then he turned and, before anyone realized what he was up to, cut a door-size hole in the wall right through to the ladies' washroom. The battle that followed, it was generally agreed, was all the fault of a man named Herbie Purkis from Beaver Cove: when the hole had been cut in the wall, he was upset, it seemed, that for one startled moment the whole assembled crowd was given a flashing peek at the creamy white buttock of his surprised and fumbling wife.

The brawl that follows sets the loggers, armed with roaring chainsaws, against the people of the town, who fight back with other weapons. Besides hurling insults "like hand grenades . . . They raised their prices, they cancelled appointments, they cut off supplies."

After the brawl has destroyed the hall, it's time for wedding speeches and Danny Holland himself crawls up to the stage. His speech is typical:

> And since he, who had more manhood in his little toe then all the rest of these bastards put together, and since he had been the one, don't forget, who had been the first to, been the first to . . . He eyed up the bride who, sitting in a pile of debris, eyed him back with a vengeance, and found that he had forgotten what he'd come up here to say. It didn't matter, he said, because they all knew this one thing for sure: you can't beat a goddamn wedding for fun.

Reviewers inside Canada noted that at last Canada had a Bunyanesque answer to the magic realism of the Latin American writers like Gabriel García Márquez. Abroad, people sat up and took notice. Gordon Lish, the esteemed fiction editor of *Esquire* magazine, went so far as to say, "Jack Hodgins' *The Invention of the World* joins Robertson Davies' *Fifth Business* as the decade's most distinguished achievements in Canadian fiction."

It was like *Fifth Business* in another way. For all the praise, and a number of prizes, it did not win the Governor General's Award.

As with Davies, a later jury seemed to make up for the omission by awarding the prize to the *next* book: to Davies for *The Manticore* and to Jack for *The Resurrection of Joseph Bourne*.

By a happy coincidence the G.G. Awards were given out in Vancouver that year, so I had the pleasure of sitting beside Stanley and Reta Hodgins, Jack's quietly thrilled parents, and the rest of the beaming Hodgins family, led by Dianne, a very good beamer. The winning book starts with a giant wave out of Alaska that leaves strings of kelp hanging all over town and a fishing boat stranded up a tree, but the Granville Island vulnerable waterside setting for the award didn't seem to worry anyone. And the French-language recipients, far from Winnipeg, were all gracious.

Over the next thirty years (up till 2010's *The Master of Happy Endings*, which I, in my semi-retired state, did not publish) Jack has brought out other fine novels and short stories that combined comedy and tragedy. He won his share of prizes and recognition, becoming both a Member of the Order of Canada and a Fellow of the Royal Society of Canada. Yet even as he continued to bring out "sprightly" books that were distinctive in tone and subject matter, his book sales never really took off in the way I believe that they merited. All too often his new books received reviews like this one, for his 2003 novel, *Distance*: "Without equivocation, *Distance* is the best novel of the year, an intimate tale of fathers and sons with epic scope and mythic resonances. . . . A masterwork from one of Canada's too-little-appreciated literary giants."

That review by the writer/bookseller Robert Wiersema ran, significantly, in the *Vancouver Sun*. And you, dear reader, may be wondering why the book never came to your attention — and why you have missed so many of Jack's books. You should know that the question baffles me, his editor and publisher, too.

One explanation may lie in the fact that the best book of criticism of his work — *On Coasts of Eternity*, edited by J.R. (Tim) Struthers, which I recommend to everyone wishing to know more about Jack and his work — was well-published by a Vancouver Island press, Oolichan Books, with a fine Vancouver Island painting by the famous Island painter E.J. Hughes. I wonder if all this is significant. Somewhere along the line, I believe, the Canadian literary establishment decided that Jack was "a regional writer," rather than a writer from a solid regional base who used it to draw fictional messages that could apply anywhere. So it may well have been significant that it was the *Vancouver Sun* that ran a review calling him a "too-little-appreciated literary giant."

I have two theories for why this damaging change (which others may claim never occurred) took place. One is the fact that in 1994 the Giller Prize appeared on the scene. There is no doubt that Jack Rabinovitch's brilliant annual tribute to his wife Doris Giller has been a wonderful thing for Canadian writing. But it has changed the landscape for our fiction writers. If you are among the five writers nominated for the Giller, you're in luck, and booksellers and reviewers and interviewers will be all over you, as ordinary Canadians hotly debate the merits of your book and its rivals. The process is magnified ten-fold for the lucky winner — and I have published half a dozen of them over the years, and know the impact well.

But if you are the author of a book of fiction that is *not* short-listed, you might as well not have published it. Potential interviewers melt away, attention dies, nobody cares. Your book is written off. This happened several times to Jack. His 1998 novel, *Broken Ground*, for example, won the Drummer-General Award, given each year by A Different Drummer Bookstore to the excellent book most unjustly neglected by the juries of the big literary prizes.

To make matters worse, Jack was now "a regional writer," *from the wrong damned region.* Thanks, largely, to the work of Alistair MacLeod (ironically, one of Jack's greatest admirers) writers from Atlantic Canada became the new flavour of the decade. To make matters even worse, the Canadian fiction world seemed to become steadily more Toronto-centric. As the man who once jokingly told a magazine writer that Jack's literary roots are so strong that "If he ever moves off the Island I'll kill him," I watched morosely as — to take just one example — David Adams Richards moved to Toronto and saw his career take off. *Post hoc ergo propter hoc?* Who knows? I have nothing against Dave — I like him and wish him well — but all my editorial life I have fought against the idea that you need to move to Toronto to hit the literary big time, and maybe I was wrong.

That certainly was the burden of my talk to the 2008 conference organized in Vancouver by Alan Twigg to celebrate B.C. writing. I rained on the parade by apologizing to Jack (who was uneasily present) for my bad career advice, lamenting the fact that the mountains separating B.C. from the rest of Canada seemed to have increased in height in recent years, at least in the mind of the central Canadian publishers. Amidst the general scandalized reaction, it was forgotten that B.C.'s Daniel Francis, discussing the non-fiction scene, later made exactly the same observation, lamenting that Doug Gibson had "stolen my thunder."

One of the reasons that I have loved publishing Jack is because he soon became a lightning rod for Appalling Author Promotion Tales. This section will be devoted to examples of the sort of humiliations endured by authors promoting their book — at readings, autographings, or other public events.

When Jack won a prize for *Spit Delaney's Island* he was flown to Halifax to be the guest of honour at the Canadian Authors Association AGM. When Jack shyly turned up at the evening cocktail party reception he was greeted with cries of "Ah, there you are!" and "Thank goodness you're here," and propelled behind the bar. He was instantly too busy filling drinks requests and mixing inexpert cocktails to explain that he was not the barman. The charade went on for the entire party, not helped by Jack's liberal hand with the martinis, and the next day the conventioneers were openly surprised that the award had been won by the inefficient barman.

On another occasion Jack was invited to read at a high school. The frightening PA announcement just before lunch went something like this. "The bell will ring in a few minutes. You will go to the gymnasium to meet . . . (very, very long pause) . . . *a writer*."

What Jack learned when he showed up was that the reading would be given in the gym to the ten resentful kids who weren't fast enough to get away. They sat scowling on the bleachers and Jack stood on the gym floor, trying to read loudly, while the basketball team noisily practiced alongside. *Bam, bam, bam, squeak, swish, bam, bam, bam, bam*.

In *A Passion for Narrative* he tells of doing a Canada Council reading tour in the Yukon, which at one point involved a flight in a bush plane over herds of migrating caribou. A pickup truck took him north from the airport, the driver warning him that the population of the mining town would be, you know, down the mine, but the librarian would no doubt have arranged an audience. The library, however, was locked up, and they had to chase around the village for a key. In the end, his audience consisted of one person, "the Anglican priest, dressed in full regalia, as though for a wedding or funeral . . . The minister sat in the middle of the front row, trying very hard to look big. Just as I opened my book to start reading to him, a wide smile spread across his lips. 'Now you know what it's like to be me every Sunday morning in this place.'"

While we're on the subject of religion, in Canada the only type of authors who can be guaranteed good treatment by everyone on the book promotion trail are hockey players. Montreal veteran sports writer Red Fisher summed up an important part of my life as a Canadian publisher with his book title *Hockey, Heroes, and Me* (1994).

When we published Jean Béliveau's memoirs, for instance, the response was so overwhelming, with crowds turning up at every event across the country, that in Winnipeg he ran out of steam and Avie Bennett flew out to encourage him to keep going. He appreciated our help to the extent that when I came across him, years later, at the Montreal Salon du Livre signing autographs for a worshipful lineup of hundreds, and he spotted me lingering nearby, *Jean Béliveau stood up and walked across to greet me as "Mr. Gibson," shaking me warmly by the hand.* Meanwhile, the awestruck crowd racked their brains to remember which NHL team I owned.

Gordie Howe was even more personal. Once, at a cocktail party he playfully announced his presence by moving up beside me, on my blindside, gently checking me with his hip. Now Gordie is renowned for mysteriously getting bigger the more clothes he takes off, and I can report that when he gives you even a friendly check, you stay checked. It was like having a building move against me.

We worked with Gordie and his wife Colleen on the book *After the Applause* (1989), by Charles Wilkins. Colleen was such an active force promoting Gordie's interests that she never stopped talking. As in never. It was a real problem, but Ken Dryden (and you'll find my encounters with him in my Paul Martin chapter) shrewdly noted that by behaving in such a demanding fashion, "Colleen lets Gordie be Gordie" — the amiable, slow-talking, beloved hockey icon from Saskatchewan.

Bobby Orr is in a class by himself. He once helped us with a picture book about the NHL by providing a foreword. I drove from downtown Toronto to a Mississauga mall for a book signing that was due to start at 7:30. But as I drove in at 6:30, something was terribly wrong in the mall, with parking unavailable and the roads jammed. Even getting into the bookstore was bewilderingly hard — and then I realized that the hundreds of people standing in a line snaking through the store and out of the door into the parking lot were there to meet Bobby.

My role was to stick with him and make sure that the line of autograph seekers moved along efficiently, with nobody taking up time to babble endlessly at their hero. I saw how expert Bobby was in his "Bobby Orr" public role. Worshipful dads would come along with their ten-year-old sons — "His name's Robert, but we call him Bobby" — and instantly Bobby would be chatting easily with the kid, establishing that, yes, the young admirer was a defenceman on his team, with Bobby hoping that he was offence-minded, and there would be happy laughter all round. Every single member of that lineup went away with their signed copy, thrilled by their genuine full-eye-contact friendly meeting with Bobby Orr. And even in his smart modern suit and fashionable haircut, you could still see the joyful crew-cut kid, photographed flying through the air after scoring a vital goal.

Bobby even stayed half an hour extra to make sure that no one was disappointed. Then the bookstore staff took us behind the scenes where they had piled up hundreds of extra copies of the book that they hoped Bobby would sign. So I stepped in to run interference for Bobby and get him out of there, "letting Bobby be Bobby," if you like. Bobby was grateful, and we had a friendly chat the next day, but I never did get him to write his own memoir. Canada's bookstores and their parking lots might not be able to handle it.

One of the hazards of publishing hockey heroes is the fact that invariably — apart from my good friend Dryden — they have been helped by a ghostwriter. So one of my delicate tasks before they set out on the tour to promote "their" book was to make sure that they had read it. This was important. The publishing world knew the cautionary tale of the Great Player — a real golden boy — who had "written" a hockey-coaching book. At the sales conference great stress had been laid on how closely the Great Player had been involved in writing the book, sharing his experience and wisdom. Finally — tada! — the Great Player was brought into the room, as a sort of climax before the lunch break. The applause was deafening, both for the glamorous man, and for the book that was going to make them all rich.

After the applause, in response to a request for questions, one brave sales rep asked him about the advice he had given in the book about the slapshot.

"How the hell should I know," the Great Player laughed, "I haven't read the fuckin' thing."

Sales estimates and promotion plans for the book shrank audibly. The lunch was not a success.

Margaret Atwood did not have a good slapshot — except metaphorically, as debating opponents know — but from her first book signing (soon to be described) she has amassed a number of interesting promotional experiences. I was involved in one of them, when I was behind the scenes with Margaret before she was to give a reading at the National Library in Ottawa. She had just completed an American publicity tour, and we laughed together at how amazingly enthusiastic American audiences were, with people happily employing superlatives about her reading being the best they had ever attended in fifty years. Canadians, we noted, were much, much, more reserved.

Then Margaret went out and gave a fine reading — in that carefully level, understated voice that repays very close attention — and afterward I joined the autograph-seeking line of book buyers. When I reached the front I said, "Hey, Margaret — that was . . . *not bad*."

She was crushed.

"Oh, Doug," she said, "I was hoping for *not bad at all!*"

The Canadian crowd around us got the joke, and liked it very much.

Margaret is one of the authors represented in a splendid British book about authors' humiliations, appropriately entitled *Mortification: Writers Stories of Their Public Shame*, edited by Robin Robertson. Her contribution concerns her first autographing session, in Edmonton, where she was set up in the Hudson's Bay store at a little table beside the men's socks and underwear department. Surprisingly, book buyers did not flock there to see her and to buy *The Edible Woman*.

In that book of shame William Boyd, the Scottish novelist, tells of a day from hell spent promoting a thoughtful new novel in Cleveland in the 1990s. One live on-air radio host announced his book title, welcomed him to the show, then said, "Now William, tell us about your Princess Diana."

It got worse. The host was such a commercials-driven personality that after a few minutes he posed the unexpected question: "Do your carpets ever get dirty, William?" and he was off on a subtle segue to a carpet-cleaning commercial. There were other such segues.

In all of the sad stories in *Mortification*, the saddest is perhaps the tale of the poet visiting a small, unexciting English town to give a reading. In the question and answer session he was challenged by a young member of the audience to explain what one of his carefully polished poems "really means." He worked hard to explain it, pleasantly and helpfully reconstructing the poem, in very simple terms, to be met with the response: "Well, why didn't you just write that, then?"

Returning home to his shabby, lonely, damp hotel room he noticed a used bookstore. Wallowing in his own misery he went to check if a rejected copy of his book was on the shelves. It was. Who, he wondered, would give up and throw away such a precious book? You can imagine his feelings when he carefully opened it at the title page and found, signed in his own hand, the words "To Mum and Dad . . ."

One story filtered though from the West Coast after a tour by the brilliant British lawyer, dramatist, novelist, and Rumpole creator, John Mortimer. A not conventionally handsome man, he was standing up at the front of the room addressing a crowd of adoring matrons when someone whispered to his publicist that he should be told that his fly was wide open. "Oh, he *knows*," she replied, glumly.

If costumes are involved, the possible humiliations expand. Don Harron (a.k.a. the rural Ontario sage Charlie Farquharson) once wrote a spoof on the Canadian establishment in the guise of "Valerie Rosedale," who was, as the name implies, a stiff, formally dressed WASP lady of a certain age. The costume — in which he toured the TV studios of the land — was hilarious. But as Don waited to start a day of Halifax promotion, standing in the lobby of the Lord Nelson Hotel, the house detective — trained to spot troublesome transvestites — sternly told him to move on.

I once picked up Don in his Valerie costume, taking him for an appearance at the Canadian Bookseller's Toronto convention downtown, from his Annex home. As I escorted him down the sidewalk to the car a neighbour lumbered towards us, in the last gasping, wheezing stages of a very vigorous jog. He staggered to a stop, courteously, to allow Valerie to mince across the sidewalk in front of him. Don — a trained actor — produced his most basso-profundo voice to say man-to-man, "Hey there, Giorgio, how the hell are ya!"

We got into the car with the gasping neighbour, hands on knees, squeaking plaintively "Don? *Don?*"

Farley Mowat — as my chapter on Harold Horwood recounts — once disgraced himself at a Writers' Development Trust private dinner. John Irving, the amiable American novelist married to the former Canadian publisher Janet Turnbull Irving (a woman with her own stories about how poor, unjustly treated Colin Thatcher phoning from prison can turn from an amiable "Hi Darlin'" phone friend into a hissing, threatening bully in half a second), once gamely went as the "guest of honour" to one of these fundraising dinners in a private Toronto home. He is a very nice man, so with a sense of his own responsibility he worked at being the life and soul of the party, telling stories and making friendly contact with everyone around the table.

There was only one problem. The woman seated beside him was clearly unhappy. She sat there with her arms folded, scowling at everything he said. Finally, with the conversation drawn elsewhere, he took the chance to speak to her privately. "Look," he said, "I've obviously said something to offend you. I don't know what it was, and it certainly wasn't deliberate, but I'm sorry about it."

"No, no," she said, "It's nothing you've said. It's just that — well, I've read all of your books, and I thought — I guess I thought you'd be more . . . more . . . *interesting.*"

John told me this in a Montreal parking lot and I laughed so hard that I hurt my leg falling against a car. The way of an author — even a popular, celebrated author, engaged in doing good charitable work — is never easy.

L.R. Wright was still dazed when she called me after her very first interview. "Bunny" Wright was a sensible adult person, who went on to fame with her crime-fiction series, but she was reduced to incoherence by her very first interviewer's very first question.

This was on a live morning TV show in Calgary and the host (think hair and teeth) introduced her as follows: "Our next guest is L.R. Wright, a Calgary writer whose first book, *Neighbours*, has just won this year's 'Search for a New Alberta Novelist' competition. Welcome Ms. Wright. And after looking through your book I have one question for you. *Why are there no pictures?*"

The correct answer, of course, is "Because it's a novel," with the added words, "you moron" entirely optional.

What happened, Bunny reported, was that she was so thrown by the question that she gaped into the bright lights — and bright teeth — and said, "*Pictures?* I never really . . . *pictures* . . . Nobody at the publisher's . . . *pictures* . . . I don't know why . . . it just never . . . *pictures* . . . ?" And so on. Throughout the rest of the interview she was in a daze, confronting the question why she had never thought of pictures in her book.

Just west of Calgary, at the Banff Centre, Roddy Doyle (an alert, wiry elf of a man) delighted us all by explaining that he had taken local warnings about unusual hazards very seriously. Like me he was staying in the Banff Centre for the Arts, and we had all been warned that it was rutting season for the elk that roamed the campus. This was new to him, Roddy explained, in his North-Dublin accent. He was prepared for most of the hazards facing a touring author, but these had never before included "the danger of being focked by an elk."

The Russian poet Yevgeny Yevtushenko was in a class by himself. Born in Siberia in 1928 he gained worldwide fame by writing anti-Stalinist poetry that was nicely calibrated to make him a popular literary hero while staying out of jail. When he came to Toronto in 1984 he had recently published a novel, *Wild Berries*, which M&S had distributed, so I looked after him on his visit.

He came loaded for bear. His novel had just received a bad review from the *Globe*'s literary critic William French, and Yevtushenko apparently came off the plane saying "Vhere is Vhilliam French?" That evening I introduced the two at a cocktail party and Yevgeny, sat down with Vhilliam. It was a terrible thing to watch. Yevgeny, tall, glamorous (wearing, I recall, a sharp metallic silver suit), and very passionate, leaned close to Bill French. "Vhilliam," he said, apparently affectionately, "I am a mann (hand on chest). You are a mann (hand on Bill's chest). So vhy, Vhilliam, you must drop leetle bits of deert (and the long expressive fingers crumbled grave dirt in the air) on my book."

Bill's background in London, Ontario — and even in the squabbling world of Canadian books — made him no match for this Siberian brigand, and he made the mistake of claiming that he had quite liked the book, really. Memory quails at the response. The finale was when Bill's adult son joined the party and Yevgeny formed such a friendly attachment to him that he kissed him long and lingeringly full on the mouth, before his father's eyes. Yevtushenko is an accomplished heterosexual, and this was not an accidental case of culture clash.

The next night Yevtushenko gave a reading at Harbourfront. I was backstage partly to look after him (ha!) and partly to give out the door prize at the intermission. When the lucky winner whooped her success, I peered into the audience and made a very unwise joke: "Hey, it worked! See you back at the office tomorrow!" I did not realize that most of the audience were recent Russian immigrants, who were familiar with that sort of casual corruption. They took it seriously.

They were there to see their great hero, Yevtushenko, but first they had to outwait the English author, Fay Weldon, reading a witty little home-counties domestic novel. Sadly, she read too long. The crowd grew restive. Backstage, around me, Yevtushenko was going wild. His entourage — a cellist, and an American reader that he had insisted on flying in, thus insulting his official Canadian reader, my poet friend Al Purdy — was also restive. Al, a big, shambling guy, was nursing his hurt pride with the help of beer. Poor Greg Gatenby of Harbourfront was trying to handle Yevtushenko, who was stalking around backstage, sparks flying off his gesturing hands as he insisted that "that vhooman" must be taken off.

Ultimately, as Fay Weldon read on, Greg did his high-school-vice-principal walk onstage and announced that it was time for Fay to leave. "What, right now?" she protested, and he ushered her towards the side of the stage.

Now things moved fast. Poor Fay was so distressed that she blundered offstage into a sharp, shin-high box of equipment and fell to the ground, moaning. I rushed to her aid, but she is a sturdily built lady, and she was weeping, and it was not easy. To make matters worse the Yevtushenko entourage — the mad Russian, rival readers, cellist, cello, and all — was thundering past us, even over us, as they stormed the stage.

The stage manager and I dragged Fay to a seat, and she was glad to accept his offer of an aspirin. She soon recovered as from the wings we watched Yevtushenko perform. From our side view we could see that he worked the microphone like Sinatra, now whispering close, next drawing back to make the hall ring with his declarations. "My God!" exclaimed the awestruck Ms. Weldon.

The duel of the English readers was frightening to see. The sulking Al ("You wouldn't believe what's going on," he'd confided to me) was reading in a monotone. When he finished the English version Yevtushenko would leap at the microphone, practically waving a sign that said, "That was *terrible* — now listen to how it *should* be read, in the original Russian."

It was an astonishing performance. The crowd loved it so much that when finally the entourage bowed its way offstage I found myself taking Yevtushenko by the shoulders and turning him around for an encore with the (entirely unofficial) words: "Back you go, Yevgeny."

What I remember best is that his Cossack shirt was so soaked with sweat, he might as well have been in a warm shower for several minutes.

When Jack Hodgins wasn't enduring amazing promotional ordeals (like the time in Sydney when the Aussie who had befriended him in the audience insisted on accompanying his new mate, beer in hand, up onstage for his reading, to sit at his feet) or writing wonderful books, he was teaching writing. His UBC training led to many years teaching in high school, then spells teaching creative writing at various places, as well as his full-time post at the University of Victoria from 1985 to 2002.

He was a remarkable teacher, as I saw whenever he wheeled me in as a visitor who could talk to the class about the real world of publishing. It was a lunch at the Faculty Club at the University of British Columbia before one such session where (as Jack explains in the afterword to *A Passion for Narrative*) his editor "saw me take a pile of handouts from my briefcase in preparation for the class." I read them, and said, "Jack, this is terrific. Do you do this all the time? We should publish a book!"

"Not a chance," he said, "I'm not going to be another one of the writers who write books on how to write books."

For twelve long years I worked on Jack, and eventually, in 1993, the first edition of *A Passion for Narrative: A Guide for Writing Fiction* came out. Together with the revised edition (2003) it has sold over 25,000 copies in Canada, and is the Canadian classic in the field. Jack writes, "To my horror, one student who had moved several times from one university to another across the country told me that he'd been assigned the book three times by three different instructors."

Jack goes on.

> My publisher, flush with excitement over the advance sales figures, had his own plans for the book. Shamelessly, he contacted every publisher in the country, commiserated with them on the anguish of trying to find something helpful to say in the hundreds of rejection letters they have to write every week, and offered them free copies of *A Passion for Narrative* if they would recommend it to all the writers they rejected. Astoundingly, most publishers took him up on it.

I'm especially proud of the word "shamelessly." Almost as proud as I am of the dedication to the revised edition where, after a graceful bow to his teachers Earle Birney and Jack Cameron, Jack writes, "and to Douglas Gibson, editor from the beginning, and friend, whose initial suggestion and continuing interest made this book possible."

"And friend" is very good.

# CHAPTER 10

# JAMES HOUSTON

Artist, Author, Hunter, and Igloo Dweller

When James Houston received an honorary degree from York University in 2001, as his publisher I was asked to summarize his career for the lunchtime crowd of special guests. "James Houston," I began, "is the most interesting group of people you will ever meet."

The list of characters includes: *accomplished artist*, instructed as a boy growing up in Toronto by teachers including Arthur Lismer; *soldier*, as a long-serving member of the Toronto Scottish Regiment and the illustrator of the Canadian Army's Second World War marksmanship training manual, *Shoot to Live*; in fact he was such a marksman that an old friend at his funeral told of once asking him just how good he was, Jim shyly responding that he could hit a playing card at a hundred paces, and when the friend was under-impressed, Jim moved his hand from palm out to hand-edge out, adding, "Sideways"; and a serious *art student* in post-war Paris (until, he said, his mother became suspicious), who returned to set up a *commercial artist's* studio in Grand-Mère, Quebec, its deliveries handled by a kid on a bike named Jean Chrétien.

It was in the role of artist on a sketching trip that Jim Houston was visiting Moose Factory, at the southernmost extension of Hudson Bay, when his life changed. It was 1948. A bush pilot friend offered him a free seat on a medical emergency trip by float plane north into the heart of the eastern Arctic. When they arrived at Inukjuak, or Port Harrison as it was called at the time, Houston found himself surrounded by smiling Inuit — short, strong, utterly confident people who wore sealskins and spoke no English. His book, *Confessions of an Igloo Dweller* (1995), records that "their eagerness to shake hands, their wide smiles and friendly way of laughing, their gruff sing-song voices, excited me. I had never dreamed of seeing people like these unknown countrymen of mine." By the time the medical plane was about to leave, to rush a child — gnawed by dogs — to hospital, Jim Houston had decided to stay. He had found his most interesting role of all. Or perhaps it had found him.

That day, as the plane flew away, he was aware that "I didn't know anyone's name, of course, and only the two words of Inuktitut that everyone knows, 'igloo' and 'kayak.' These people spoke no other language." But it all worked out. He was led by the arm to a corner of one of the summer tents, and a pile of fish and other red meat lying on the gravel was pointed out to him. When eventually the tea he drank had to be drained from his system, he records, "that brought some young sightseers out to check, I guess, that everything was normal." His memorable first chapter ends with the words: "People lay down close on either side of me and we all went to sleep."

Jim Houston's decision to stay among his new friends changed the course of his life. It also changed the North, Canada, and the world of art. Discovering that his neighbours were almost casually producing wonderful soapstone carvings, the sort of thing he associated with museums, he took a sackfull of them south and found a Montreal gallery that was eager to sell them. After his first meeting with the Canadian Handicrafts Guild (now known as the Canadian Guild of Crafts), which had long been baffled by the problems posed by the North, one veteran exclaimed, "We've found our man!" With the support of the Guild he returned to the Arctic, using a barter system with the Hudson's Bay Company that allowed the Inuit sculptors to be paid for the work they handed in. Jim would allot tokens worth two blankets for this sculpture of a seal, or a rifle and a set of shells for this mother and child piece, and in the barter economy they could be cashed in at the local Bay trading post.

He took the carvings south, and they were so well received that he pushed to expand the system. In 1949 the first Montreal sale was organized, with great success. In Montreal he met (and soon married) Alma Bardon, a journalist from Nova Scotia. Their son, John Houston, summarizes what happened next: "Then word came through from the Canadian government that there was funding to go further north, to Cape Dorset. Instead of the trip to sunny Mexico they had planned, the couple spent their honeymoon bouncing around on a dogsled, sleeping in igloos, on their way west along Baffin Island's southern coast to a place called Cape Dorset."

Jim established himself in Cape Dorset in 1951 with the mission of encouraging the Inuit throughout the north to exercise their artistic skills. He was, as his successor, Terry Ryan, said, "like Johnny

Appleseed," sowing the idea of creating Inuit art, and often doing it by dog team on prodigious travels across the trackless land, his Inuit companions miraculously using occasional silent Inuksuit as their only guides.

For more than a dozen years, he spent his time spreading the idea of art and in turn being educated by these kindly, patient people who became his friends, and who named him "Saomik, the left-handed one," when they were not nicknaming him, affectionately, for his prominent chin or bushy beard. He stumbled amusingly through their language, slept in their igloos, ate raw fish and seal meat, wore skin clothing, travelled by dog team, hunted walrus, and learned how to build a snow house. And they especially liked to have him in their boats when it was time for hunting seal or walrus, making use of his shooting skills, in those days when a food cache filled from the land and sea was very important.

As a result of his extraordinary efforts, year after energetic year, in his other role as *promoter/impresario* he brought Inuit art to the attention of the outside world. "No James Houston, no Inuit art," said one American museum director. Right idea, right place, right time, and, above all, right man.

In time, Jim and the gallant Alma (who went on to make her own huge contribution to the Inuit art world) raised two sons, John and Sam, in the North (the boys once bursting into tears when they learned that their playmates' taunts were true — they were indeed white). But he took time off in 1958 from his government job administering southwest Baffin Island (where technically he was responsible for every human being and sled dog in a territory of 168,000 square kilometers, or 65,000 square miles) to go to Japan to study printmaking at the feet of the old master Unichi Hiratsuka — a visit that was controversial with one relative who had been a Japanese POW.

A hunting trip with his friend, the legendary artist Osuitok Ipeelee, was what originally led to the creation of Inuit prints. Osuitok observed that creating exactly the same picture of a sailor on each Player's cigarette package must be boring work. Taking the walrus tusk Osuitok was carving, Jim demonstrated the principle of printing with the incised tusk, some seal lamp soot, and toilet paper. *Confessions of an Igloo Dweller* recalls Osuitok's reaction: "'We could do that,' he said, with the instant decision of a hunter. And so we did."

Returning to Cape Dorset from Japan, Houston introduced stone-block printmaking techniques to the repertoire of artists who are now world famous; the prints of Kenojuak Ashevak, Osuitok Ipeelee, Pitseolak Ashoona and many others now hang in homes and galleries in scores of countries. The cumulative economic impact of his work in the North runs into millions of dollars each year. Its importance for individuals was stated very clearly in a letter of condolence to his family from an Inuit artist: "He put bread on our table."

Not that he always avoided culture clashes. Once, as his book records, he instructed the Inuit printmakers in the use of paper money, explaining that, for example, ten-dollar bills were worth twice as much as these blue five-dollar ones. Then to emphasize that paper money was useful, like their artistic work, he stressed that "bigger money can be made from printmaking than from trapping foxes."

With that phrase ringing in his ears, he went home, proud of his new role as economics instructor — until the next day, when on the printmaking drying line he found "big money" in the form of "a huge, chest-wide stencilled print of a green dollar bill." Big money, indeed.

Elsewhere he tells of his failure to introduce competitive games like basketball and soccer to a society based on co-operation, so that basketball defenders would *help* the attacking team to get the ball finally through the hoop. It was indeed another world (arguably, a saner one) clearly described, and sensitively understood, by a man who bridged both worlds. In the words of *The Encyclopedia of Literature in Canada*, "Houston's passionate involvement with Arctic life, legend and art enabled him to record an ancient culture at a critical turning point in its history." Add *anthropologist* to his list of careers.

Having helped to set up the Cape Dorset co-op and seen it running smoothly (as it continues to this day, under his good Northern friend Jimmy Manning, who grew up playing with the reluctantly white Houston boys), in 1962 Houston decided to leave. It was time for another career. His parting gift, as he sadly left the people he loved, speaks for itself. A crowd had gathered as he prepared to step into the plane that was taking him south. A spokesman stepped forward.

"Left-handed, we have something for you, tunivapovit, a small gift from many here."

He held out a small, brown paper bag. It was old and crumpled with what looked like seal-fat stains that made irregular shiny blotches. . . . Light as a feather, it seemed to contain nothing, just a crumpled bag. . . .

I opened the bag and reached in. Inside was a clutch of small, tightly folded letters many people had pencilled in Inuktitut. I drew out a handful of one- and two-dollar bills, each one wadded up tight. There were a lot of them in that little paper bag — thirty-three Canadian dollars.

"What are these for?" I asked.

"A gift for you," Kiaksuk said. "Everyone gives them to you. You're going away, everyone says, to try and make more money."

As you can imagine, Jim Houston was in distress as he climbed into the plane and "left that unforgettable place that had so long been my home."

In April he was in Baffin Island, eating raw seal meat and worrying about his dog team (and worrying even more about the breakup of his marriage, which had led Alma to take her sons to Britain, in John's words, "to get some space.") In May he was living in mid-Manhattan, wearing a dinner jacket pressed by a butler and worrying about his new role as a designer at Steuben Glass.

Now, of course, in the world of glass design, James Houston the *master designer* is a legend. He wrote excitingly in his memoir, *Zigzag*, about the challenges of creating over 100 sculptures in glass — which some have suggested were inspired by the ice he knew so well — for the collector's market. A show at Ashley's in Toronto in the 1990s prompted a McClelland & Stewart salesman to marvel at the fact that Steuben had brought out all of their best work to this display in Jim Houston's honour. He was astounded when I told him that all of the pieces there had been created by Jim. It seemed like a full life's work.

The move to Manhattan also created James Houston, *author and illustrator of children's books*. From 1965 to 1998 he wrote seventeen children's books, including *Tiktaliktak*, *River Runners*, *Ice Swords*, *Drifting Snow*, *The White Archer*, and *Frozen Fire*, winning national and international awards, and becoming the only three-time winner of the Book of the Year Medal given by the Canadian Library Association. When he delivered the prestigious Helen E. Stubbs Memorial lecture in Toronto in 1999, it was clear to me that the worshipful assembled audience regarded him as a supreme children's book author and illustrator, who perhaps did one or two other things on the side.

Among the "other things" was *writing bestselling adult novels. The White Dawn* (1971), a tale of nineteenth-century Yankee whalers stranded in the Arctic for a winter, amid deteriorating relations with their Inuit hosts, was a huge international bestseller, selling millions of copies around the world and becoming a major Hollywood film. Jim helped to write the screenplay and was the associate producer, with great tales to tell of the clash in the North between filmmakers on a Hollywood timetable, with the million-dollar meter running, and a lead Inuit actor drawn away from "playing" by excellent hunting weather. There's an unforgettable scene in *Zigzag* when Jim flies off in pursuit of the truant actor and gently explains that what he's doing — "um . . . the playing" — is really important to all these white people from the South. As a favour to his pal Jim, the hunter came back to "play" some more (Shakespeare would have approved). His role was to lead the final assault on the film's star, Timothy Bottoms, which outraged some of the Inuit observers on the set, older women who shouted, "Bad, bad to kill that boy!" and "Bad, bad to kill Timothee!" The movie is still available on TV some nights, and shouting at the screen is always an option.

Other historical novels followed, including *Ghost Fox* (1977 — set in eighteenth-century New England and Quebec, near North Hatley), *Spirit Wrestler* (1980 — set in the Arctic in the 1950s), *Eagle Song* (1983 — set in Nootka Sound on Vancouver Island, before white settlement), and *Running West* (a fur-trade novel set in the eighteenth-century Canadian West that won the Canadian Authors Association medal for fiction in 1990). All are linked by the provocative theme of an aboriginal society in uneasy contact with white settlers, and, unusually, encourage white readers to see themselves in the role of strange intruders. Presumably there are worshipful adult readers out there who think of James Houston as exclusively a *writer of thoughtful, well-researched historical novels.*

I saw him in action when he researched his final novel, *The Ice*

*Master* (1997), which is also about whaling. Together we clambered all over the *Charles W. Morgan*, the very last New England whaler, now moored at Mystic Seaport Museum in Connecticut. We peered into every bunk and every try pot, like small boy stowaways eager to find an apple barrel to hide in, like Jim Hawkins in *Treasure Island*. He liked to call me Dougal, and when he named the drunken Scottish mate in the novel Dougal Gibson, he liked it even more, and when I was present for a slanderous reading (as I was at Richard Bachman's Burlington bookstore, A Different Drummer), his delight knew no bounds. (His interest in Arctic whaling history was longstanding. In his early years up north he was thrilled to meet a very old, very wrinkled, Inuit lady. Did she remember, he asked gently, ever meeting the old whalers, the "Yankee men" or the "Dundee men"?

"Remember *meeting* them? I danced with them and slept with them!" she replied, approximately.)

I came onto the scene late. When I became M&S's publisher in 1988, I had to stop taking on top authors for my Douglas Gibson Books imprint, since that would have been unfair to my colleagues. But Jim Houston, a major M&S figure (perhaps encouraged by his contemporary and old friend Jack McClelland) insisted on working with me as his editor, and I could not resist. We worked happily together on his last two novels, and on his three books of memoirs. And on the memoirs I was genuinely useful, helping this quite private man tell his own life story.

As you can imagine, I enjoyed spending time with this fascinating man as often as I could arrange it. With my two daughters, Meg and Katie, both at Harvard, I was often "in the neighbourhood" of the Connecticut home of Jim and his second wife Alice. Whenever we got together (and once it was in Toronto on a strangely busy Tuesday night, when it was hard to get a table for dinner, and the roses at our table seemed excessive, until we realized that it was February 14th) he would tell me amazing stories about the people he had met and the things he had seen and done in the North, and I would urge him to put it all down on paper, since it would make a book that I was desperate to publish. But, despite the fact that he was one of the most creative and energetically productive people I ever knew, with a sketch or a painting or a new novel or an art documentary or a glass sculpture or a children's book always on the go, nothing ever happened.

Finally, it became clear what the problem was. Sure, he had all these great stories from his days in the Arctic, but he didn't know if he threw out all the letters from his Ottawa bosses in 1956 or 1957, or if the bear attack was 1959 or 1960, and so on. Most of the dates, and the order of events, he felt, were too vague for him to put in a book. And some of the stories would provide a ten-page chapter, others only half a page.

"Jim, it doesn't matter a damn," I told him. "Just get the stories down on paper. Give them dates when you know them, otherwise you can ignore the order of the chapters, and leave that to me. And forget about having chapters that are the same length; they'll be just as long or as short as the story you're telling. But for God's sake get to work on this — your memories of those days and those artists are priceless."

That was what he needed to hear, and he set to work on collecting stories, and telling them in the usual understated Houston way. When *Confessions* finally came out in 1995, the reviews confirmed the wisdom of this style of book, with the *New York Times* saying, "You just want to see another piece. Hear another story."

Working with him on that book of Northern memoirs, followed by *Zigzag: A Life on the Move* (1998), and *Hideaway: Life on the Queen Charlotte Islands* (1999), as well as on his last two novels, meant that I was too late to see Jim in his role as a volunteer *art teacher* in Harlem in difficult times in New York, or in his role as a New England *sheep farmer*. That particular zag came after his divorce and his encounter in Manhattan with a "super girl" called Alice Watson, who was working in the book division of American Heritage Publishing Company. They got married (in the Yale Dwight Chapel that I knew so well, from the outside) and moved to Rhode Island to be close to her native Connecticut, as was only right for a Yale professor's daughter. It was a very happy marriage.

In due course, Jim and Alice stopped counting sheep and retired to the peninsular Stonington, Connecticut, to an old white clapboard house that boasts evidence of damage from the cannon of evil British ships. It was at one time occupied by Whistler's mother, who apparently continues to pay nocturnal visits to the guest bedroom, but not on any of the five occasions when I was there.

Strolling about the historic old fishing town, Jim seemed a typical retired citizen, craggily handsome, jovially greeting other New York corporate retirees. But on occasion the irrepressible old Arctic hand would leap out. Once, looking south from Stonington Point with my binoculars, I was excitedly hailing the arrival of a flock of Brant geese, the duck-size migrants that are always a beautiful sight to a keen birder. Jim saw them differently. "Very good eating," he remarked, sticking out his square jaw and gazing far into the distant past. Then he chuckled, and rounded his eyes at me in the distinctive smile that charmed companions in Manhattan nightclubs, Scottish castles, Parisian ateliers, and Baffin Island igloos. And when he sat, leaned forward, spread his hands, and started to tell a story, he was one of the world's best. The ultimate *storyteller*.

I once saw him in action before a crowd of bored and restless school kids in Calgary. He and I had spent the previous evening at dinner in the Palliser Hotel's Rimrock Room with the legendary "mountain man" Andy Russell, with Andy and Jim trading grizzly and polar bear stories. I could have sold tickets, and a tape recording could have made my fortune.

The following morning, as part of the Calgary Book Festival, Jim was due to speak to roughly 300 fourteen-year-olds crammed into a former movie theatre. With an hour or two to spare, I went along, and found Anne Green, the usually composed Head of the Festival, pacing the lobby in despair. All three speakers were now ready, and the kids were thrumming with impatience. But the chair was held up (as it turned out, behind that local Albertan hazard, a cattle drive). So I volunteered to chair the meeting, and to introduce the authors. Problem solved, let's go.

I was ill-prepared for my first two introductions, but I was ready for Jim, who was to speak last. "You already know this man's work, " I told the surprised kids. "How many of you have been to the Glenbow Museum, along the street here?"

Every hand went up, except for the cool rebels'.

"And you know when you go in, the main staircase winds around a huge hanging plexiglass sculpture, seventy feet tall?"

Heads nodded.

I pointed to Jim. "He did that. He's the sculptor who made that giant piece, called *Aurora Borealis*. And he's also a man who has spent a large part of his life in the far North, living in snowhouses, igloos, driving dog teams, and eating raw seal meat." (Cries of "Ewww!" and general consternation, especially among the girls.)

And so on.

When Jim rose to speak, he went to the front of the stage, spread his tweed-jacketed arms wide, and said, "I'm a really old guy! And I've had a *hell* of an interesting life!"

They clapped, they cheered, they loved him, and they couldn't get enough of his stories. You can guess where all the questions were directed at Question Time. (Apart, that is, from a thoughtful girl who came up to me privately in the aisle, to ask "How do I get to do what you do?" Just possibly, my enthusiasm for the publisher's life might have peeked through. I hope she made it.)

In 1999, the Canadian Museum of Civilization staged a special show, *Iqqaipaa*, on the early, Houston years of Inuit art. Maria von Finckenstein was the exhibition curator, and Jim was involved as a special advisor to the show, to which he lent twenty pieces from his personal collection. After the official ceremonies, about a dozen of us, including Governor General Adrienne Clarkson (my predecessor as publisher at M&S) and the chief sponsor, my pal Duncan McEwan, followed Jim around as he chatted about individual pieces — how he watched this one being completed, or got to know the sculptor, and what was special about the rock in this piece, and so on — priceless information that now is gone. Fortunately, Jim wrote some notes about Inuit art, and his own astonishing career has been documented here and there, as in the late Charles Taylor's fine book *Six Journeys* (1977) and in many magazine pieces, although each one usually concentrated on only one of the many Houston lives. Jim's extraordinary career did not go unrecognized; the best-known photograph of our craggy northern legend was taken by the legendary Irving Penn.

There is yet another life to describe. In 1968, he was asked by the government to tour British Columbia to write a report on redeveloping Northwest Coast Indian art. He travelled widely and was especially impressed by the Queen Charlotte Islands. In *Hideaway* he describes standing on the bridge over the Tlell River watching its waters "as smooth and brown as buckwheat honey" and falling in love with an old green cottage right beside the bridge. Next year, he and Alice bought the cottage, appropriately named "Bridge Cottage." They spent the last part of each summer fishing for salmon (Jim was such a keen fisherman that he cast flies after them across the world, and Alice was no slouch) and enjoying the company of their friends. Notable among these was Teddy Bellis, a Haida friend and neighbour, who liked to interrupt Houston's cocktail parties for off-island visitors by asking loudly if they were "enjoying eating dog." He would let them consider their canapés thoughtfully for a while before specifying that they were eating dog salmon, very tasty.

Jim and Alice loved their West Coast hideaway. When I visited, I recall that the tidal pull on the Tlell was so strong that I had to swim full out to stay in place opposite the cottage and avoid being swept down into Hecate Strait, while Jim stood there making "Mao, the Great Helmsman" swimming jokes.

Jokes and stories were a large part of conversational life around Jim, but I'm not entirely sure that he was joking when he instructed me not to marry Jane until he had "had a chance to check her out." In the event, all went well, and he approved. In fact, on our first Stonington visit, he even told Jane an astonishing story, just for her, with me off helping Alice in the kitchen, about a polar bear attack on his sled dogs. On the trail, he explained when Jane asked, there was no need to tie the dogs up. They had lost their ability to hunt, and stayed with the sled, their source of food. The only thing they would attack was a marauding polar bear, which was such a killing machine that they were programmed to attack it en masse, instantly, in self defence.

On this occasion he and his hunting companion (it may have been Osuituk) had halted for the night and set the dogs free, when a bear appeared over a nearby rise. The dogs went for it, and the bear used its scythe-like claws to gut the first dog, flinging it aside, yelping, trailing yards of red guts. Seeing the other charging dogs, backed by two fur-clad humans scrambling for their guns, the bear turned and disappeared.

Jim grabbed his gun to attend to the dying dog.

"What are you doing?" said the other hunter. "You don't need the gun. Nanuk, the bear's gone."

When Jim explained that he was going to put the hopelessly

gutted dog out of its misery, his friend stopped him, saying in effect, "That's not your decision. "

Jim went over, and with the side of his boot tried to scrape the entrails back into the stomach cavity. The other dogs gathered around, and started to lick the wound clean, helped by the antiseptic northern air. *The dog lived, to pull again!*

I was impressed by Jane's account, but mildly irritated to hear it. I thought that I had coaxed all of his best stories out of him for inclusion in *Confessions of an Igloo Dweller*.

On our last visit Jim's health was going downhill. The treatment against shingles over so many years, he said, had shot his liver. When we arrived to stay overnight, Alice announced that Jim had been in bed all day, but would be at the dinner table in his dressing gown. That gave me an idea. When he came carefully down for dinner, he found me dressed in *my* dressing gown, openly amazed that he was so up to date with hip Toronto dinner fashions for men. Within seconds the outfit did indeed feel natural, and he was soon telling more stories.

Of course, I shouldn't have resented that new story he told Jane. He was a man whose stories, like his many lives, were too rich and varied to be contained. The honours and the honourary degrees that were showered upon him are only one mark of his impact on the world. His books, drawings, and glass sculptures are everywhere. Above all, every Inuit print and every Inuit sculpture will always bear the invisible mark of James Houston.

Someone like Jim doesn't disappear from your life after his death. His continuing influence emerged right at his funeral in Connecticut, held at the Mystic Seaport Museum, hard by the whaling ship that he and I had clambered over. The historic church, now used as a hall, was packed with dignitaries from most of his careers, along with Stonington neighbours who knew him just as a friendly figure whose stories always enlivened their dinner parties among the crystal and the old family china.

I was nervous about the lack of an officiating clergyman, and the crowded old church was tense and sombre. Then Oz Elliot, Jim's great friend who had run *Newsweek*, ascended the podium.

His first words were addressed to Jim's widow.

"Good morning, Alice."

From her seat in a central pew Alice replied, "Good morning, Oz," loud and clear. And the whole congregation visibly relaxed, ready for the speakers — including me and an Inuktitut speaker from much further north — to reveal many of the different aspects of Jim's life.

At the reception afterwards I was greeted by a fellow Canadian, a friendly chap named Richard Self, from Vancouver. *All the way from Vancouver?* Richard explained that he and his wife, Nancy, were close to the Houstons, having bought Bridge Cottage on the Queen Charlotte Islands. When I congratulated him, saying how much I had enjoyed visiting Jim and Alice there, he invited me to come back "any time."

Jane and I have a rule that invitations issued at weddings and funerals don't count. Yet a year later Richard followed up with a phone call out of the blue. Weren't we interested in coming to stay for a few days at the cottage on the Tlell? You bet! We rushed to make arrangements.

In September 2008 Jane and I arrived at Sandspit airport, found Richard and Nancy's car in the parking lot, and plunged into that glorious Houston *Hideaway* world for five days. Every day we watched the river ebb and flow just twenty paces outside the main cabin window, the view full of memories and guarded by bald eagles. It was the middle of the salmon run, and we spent many happy hours with our rods thrashing the water, following in Jim and Alice's wader-steps. Despite the helpful presence of their great friend (woodsman, artist, and expert angler) Noel Wotten, we had no luck. But we learned the most basic lesson of fly-fishing, that actually catching something is only part of the fun.

We roamed around on dry land, too, revisiting Rosespit Beach, where on a notably cold, clear day Jim and I had seen Alaska in the distance. I also remember that he commented admiringly on the "hardy" young Haida women who, in jeans and T-shirts, were standing waist-deep in the frigid surf, trying to net crabs. "Hardy" was one of the greatest compliments Jim could bestow.

Working on *Hideaway* had made me aware of the special nature of the Queen Charlottes, or Haida Gwaii, as it now is. With their basic food source provided by the plentiful salmon, the Haida had developed a reputation as great, fierce travellers, "the Vikings of the Pacific." Braving open seas in open war canoes, they had raided as far down the coast as California, and the slaves they brought back had allowed them to create a leisure society — a little like slave-based Athens — where there was time to develop great art. The art was both literary (in sagas brilliantly translated in recent years by Robert Bringhurst) and representational, as in their argillite carvings, or in the totem poles in the traditional distinctive designs popularized by Bill Reid (whose work hangs in our kitchen). And anyone who has ever strolled along the tangled driftwood-strewn beaches or the Emily Carr–inspiring deep woods will know where the inspiration for artistic shapes and the distinctive "ovoid curves" came from.

The fine museum in the Carr-totemed town of Skidegate (where Jim once took me to a community event), revealed much of this to us, with the introductory lecture for tourists given by another Scottish rolling stone, a former classmate of mine at St. Andrews.

Visiting Barbara and Noel Wotten we saw sandhill cranes dancing sedately down by the river, and visited the tree house (as in, "house carved out of the interior of a tree") that Jim's ten-year-old-boy spirit liked so much. . . . Jim Hawkins would have liked it, too. And Noel, who chainsawed a path to the tree for tourists, directed us to the site of the famous Golden Spruce, which we found lying, rotting and grey, in dark water. The tale of this sacred Haida tree — uniquely, a golden-coloured spruce — and the bizarre logging crusader/vandal who felled it, then disappeared in Hecate Strait before his trial date exposed him to public rage, is brilliantly told by John Vaillant in *The Golden Spruce*, a book that I wish I'd published. One That Got Away.

Whenever we encountered locals they remembered Jim fondly and asked about Alice, urging us to persuade her to come back for a visit. We're still working on it. But we almost didn't survive our own visit. It was a full moon in September, and the tides on the Tlell, just twenty paces outside our window, were up to twenty-three feet. We planned our epic kayak trip the mile or so down river to Hecate Strait with great care, going down at the end of the ebb tide. That was fine, easy paddling. Ten minutes from the ocean we felt the tide turn, and had to fight our kayaks through white water at the river mouth, before reaching ocean swells. We exulted in the view of mountains as we paddled north to the old beached wreck that Jim had told me about. Then Jane wisely suggested that with these giant tides, perhaps we should get back.

By the time we reached the river mouth, the white water was gone, submerged beneath many feet of salt water charging inland. Surfing in up the river was like riding on the back of a stampeding elephant. It was fun, of course, but when we reached Bridge Cottage, the landing beach had disappeared (along with Richard's fine Wellington boots, which I had left high and dry out of the water when we took off).

Landing, and getting out of the kayak without being swept sideways up the river a great distance was a problem that I solved by half-landing and then deliberately dumping myself and the kayak. That way I was able to drag the boat ashore and help Jane to land. Since I was already soaked it seemed the sensible thing (think ten-year-old boy) to strip off and try swimming in the current, just to see what it felt like. Jane, who has never been a ten-year-old boy, but has been a lifeguard, was not amused. There were no Great Helmsman swimming jokes from her.

Replacing the swept-away boots (we had half a miracle when one was swept back the next day, but half a miracle won't allow you to walk in — let alone on — water) took us on a memorable trip to Queen Charlotte City, and the fishing supply store named "The Best Little Lure House in the Charlottes." A trip to the local bookstore introduced us to the proprietor's parrot, which was able to produce uncanny imitations of visitors, and very alarming ones of deceased friends. It could even mimic phone calls, including a "Goodbye!" followed by a hang-up click and a realistic dial tone.

The Queen Charlottes/Haida Gwaii is that sort of place. Courtesy of Richard and Nancy, who have lovingly preserved aspects of the place like Jim's little writing cabin, while adding new marvels like commissioned totem poles, we were able to see why Jim and Alice spent so much of their life there.

Visiting Houston territory on the West Coast was one vivid reminder of Jim. Visits by Alice, John, and Sam to our Toronto home have been others. But a visit to Jim's Arctic was the best treat of all. I had never been North, except in my imagination, when I worked on Jim's books or on Don Starkell's *Paddle to the Arctic*. You can imagine my delight when, at John's suggestion, I was invited by Adventure Canada to join a cruise that was intended to follow the travels of James Houston.

We learned that John (an experienced filmmaker, and one of the best Inuktitut-English translators in the country) would be making a documentary about his father in the course of the voyage. My role — for which I would receive free passage — was to be a working member of the expedition crew and a lecturer on the Jim Houston I knew. It was a perfect circle: working on books about the Arctic with Jim now allowed me to see the Arctic and talk about my memories of Jim.

So in September 2008 Jane and I and roughly 100 other excited southerners flew north from Ottawa to Iqualuit. The clamming was so good that day that there was a bus driver problem.

"OK, Doug, you can get your bus on its way."

"All right, driver, we're all set. Let's go!"

"Uh, where to?" The driver was a last-minute replacement for a man gone clamming.

Even the commissioner of Nunavut, Jim's longtime friend (and actress in *The White Dawn*) Ann Meekitjuk Hanson mentioned the great clamming she was missing when she gave us a formal welcome to our tour of the town.

I should explain that Matthew Swan's excellent Adventure Canada cruises are for people for whom bingo-playing cruises hold no appeal. A cruise with them is above all a learning experience, full of fun, of course, but also lectures by anthropologists, biologists, art historians, and even people like me, giving useful background to what we are likely to see ashore.

And we rubbed shoulders with celebrities like the legendary Kenojuak Ashevak, the most famous Inuit artist of all, a beaming, tiny elder whom I got to know despite a language barrier. On our last morning aboard ship I suggested that we swap our Adventure Canada nametags. She laughed happily at the idea, and the swap was made — I suspect that she has not kept mine as carefully as I have kept hers, beside one of her magnificent prints; it's like having a calling card from Claude Monet.

Another northern celebrity aboard our ship meant a lot to me. A couple of days after Jim Houston's death in April 2005, Cape Dorset's Jimmy Manning joined me on Shelagh Rogers' CBC morning radio show, sharing our memories of Jim and passing on our condolences to John when he joined us by phone — a stumbling moment for me, in front of a million ears. So meeting Jimmy was a powerful experience for me, and we soon became friends, with Jane and I even visiting his Cape Dorset home, along with Alice.

We soon got into the cruise routine of sailing by night, and each day ferrying everyone ashore by Zodiac to visit Inuit communities along Hudson Strait. Wherever we visited we were instant celebrities — especially John and Sam (whose Inuktitut was a little rusty as he was embraced by former babysitters) and Alice, who had met many of our hosts before. Some of them sat quietly with her, crying over her loss; it became obvious that Jim's passing was their loss, too. The local people always met us warmly and entertained us, usually in the local school's gym. Naturally, local artists were not shy about showing their wares, and many sales were made.

When we landed at Ivujivik, on the Quebec side of Hudson Strait, right at the northeast corner of Hudson Bay, there was no welcoming committee.

Crisis!

"Doug, could you take over and get the guests to the Community Hall? I'm going back to the boat, to find out what's gone wrong with our contacts."

"Sure. No problem."

So in an Inuit community in Quebec (did they speak Inuktitut, or French, or English?) I led our trusting, camera-slung guests up a deserted main street. Not a curtain twitched.

Then off to the right I glimpsed a woman in a traditional long-tailed costume, heading away from us. She must be going to receive us in the mysterious hall.

"This way, everyone," I announced, and my hunch was right. When we reached a group of formally dressed women outside a large building, I went forward. Not only did I shake hands with them, I did the traditional eyebrow-raising thing (in the bundled-up North, you don't smile in greeting, you raise your eyebrows in a friendly fashion). And I got to say the words, grandly indicating the parka-clad group straggling behind me: "I'm Doug Gibson . . . *and these are my people!*"

Later, while looking after the loading of our returning Zodiacs, I had the chance to chat with the leading elder of the community, who had made a truncated speech of welcome.

"You mentioned Henry Hudson briefly in your speech back there," I said, "but I think you had more to say."

"Yes," he replied, glad to tell the tale. He was a large, solid man with a dark, squarish face, and his English was good.

"Henry Hudson came by here in 1610, with lots of beads to trade with our people, I guess for water and food. Now we still get some of our food in the traditional way, gathering eggs from seabirds' nests, high on the cliffs. And in our way of doing things, when you take an egg, you thank the bird by putting something in its place, like a little stone, okay? And it's kind of interesting, but to this day . . ."

My ears pricked up.

"To this day when our people put their hand in a nest, they sometimes find a Henry Hudson bead, put there a long time ago."

*"To this day?"* I said, stunned. *"You're finding beads brought here in 1610?"*

"Yes," he said, and at that point I was torn away, the last man to join the last boat back to the ship. Later I told this story to Margaret Macmillan, the famous historian, and she shared my astonishment that European trade goods from four centuries ago were still cropping up in the Arctic.

Back across Hudson Strait we went, in our beloved little red ship (I was to feel a real sense of loss when she sank in the southern Atlantic a couple of years later, with no loss of life) to Cape Dorset, the place that had been Jim Houston's home for so many years. It was an emotional return for Alice and Sam, and especially for John. Along with the little boy's mother, Heather, he had brought his five-year-old son Dorset on his first visit to the place he was named for. It was wonderful to see him being greeted with smiles and long hugs by the local elders who knew his grandfather well.

Thanks to the historic collaboration between Jim and the local Inuit, Cape Dorset is now a community based around the production of art. Strangely, in the same week I found myself visiting Cape Dorset, Niagara-on-the-Lake, and Stratford, three very different Canadian communities based economically on art and culture. As you stroll the hilly Cape Dorset streets, the sound of carving drills comes from many backyards and sheds. The constant artistic ferment caused one witty visitor from New York, Robert Graff, to compare it to Greenwich Village; not an obvious visual comparison.

The famous Cape Dorset Co-op was still there, in an expanded version of Jim's original building. And there we watched Kenojuak take off her coat and get right down to drawing what would be a new print, before our very eyes.

Later, when I saw John's film about his father, I was fascinated to see Jim talk about the fast, confident way Kenojuak's left hand moves as she draws. Jim asked her about that, and she told him that she just follows "a little blue line" ahead of her pen.

"A little blue line!" Jim snorts. "I wish I had a little blue line that would do that for me!"

To make his film, John took people like me out "on the land" and filmed us. I struggled to answer his questions about how the Arctic landscape met my expectations, and I talked, as we all did on the ship, about the extraordinary light in the north. More usefully, I spoke about what a "noticing" person his father was, as shown both in his art and his writing.

Later, on our last Cape Dorset day, our James Houston Memorial Cruise turned solemn when we assembled at the base of some striking red cliffs just outside the little town, to scatter half of his ashes, while the rest remained in Stonington. Scores of local people attended, some of the elders limping heavily across the rough ground in order to deliver their affectionate tribute to their friend Saumik, while some distance away young Dorset created his own Inukshuk from a little heap of rocks. After the family, and the elders like Kenojuak had taken their turn, among other friends I had a hand in scattering Jim's ashes in that quiet place.

Later, John brought his film crew to our house in Toronto (perhaps in the hope that I'd get it right this time). We sat in the front room, surrounded by James Houston memorabilia — books, a glass shorebird sculpture, some of the northern drawings he was always giving to lucky friends like me, and work by artists he had discovered. At the end of our filmed talk he used a shrewd filmmaking technique, asking me without warning what I felt like when I heard the news of Jim's death.

Other people in the film rose to that challenge with rare eloquence. I was wordless. What John chose to include in the film was my silent, bleak look, my face a gash of sorrow at the loss of a dear friend.

The prize-winning film, by the way, is widely available on DVD, and well worth watching. And its title is *James Houston: The Most Interesting Group of People You Will Ever Meet.*

# CHAPTER 11

# CHARLES RITCHIE

Diplomat, Diarist, and Charming Dissembler

Charles Ritchie should have been a spy.

By day, he worked as a diplomat: dispassionate, discreet, and diligent (apart, of course, from those afternoons when he slipped out to the movies). In his diplomatic role — in the words of the old Elizabethan joke, as "a man sent to lie abroad for the good of his country" — he was very effective at producing shrewd dispatches, as one of those legendary external affairs men whose sheer skill and dedicated professionalism allowed Canada to punch well above its weight in the international ring. By night — even when he was our ambassador to JFK and LBJ's Washington, or to Bonn, or to London — he emerged from his dark-suited carapace to become a wildly indiscreet diarist, a role that allowed him to be a gossip, a boulevardier, a ladies' man, and a gifted writer with a novelist's eye and ear, and an insatiable appetite for life.

After he retired in 1971, full of years and honours, he was persuaded to publish some of the daily diaries that he had kept all his life (far beyond the January 15 cut-off familiar to the rest of us). It appeared, certainly from the brilliantly written diaries, that in his life he did much of his best work in the bedroom. He was sixty-six when *The Siren Years*, an account of his life as a Canadian diplomat in London during the Second World War (including, as the title implied, the years of the Blitz), appeared in book form, to the astonished pleasure of reviewers and ordinary readers on both sides of the Atlantic. C.P. Snow (the distinguished British physicist, civil servant, and novelist, who knew something about diverse talents) hailed the 1974 book as "a brilliant discovery" and pronounced Ritchie "a natural-born diarist." Comparisons were made, perhaps inevitably, to Samuel Pepys.

In Canada, to the chagrin of ink-stained professional writers in garrets across the land, this retired civil servant's apparently effortless recycling of his late-night diaries won the Governor General's Award for Non-Fiction in 1974.

My path first crossed his in that year, before the book was

published. Within hours (it seemed) of joining Macmillan, in the unfortunate absence of all the company's leaders who knew Charles and had read his book, I was assigned the task of taking the distinguished visiting author to dinner. I was ignorant of the book's irreverent style, and of Ritchie's history of enjoying sparkling dinner companions (Nehru, for example, who ran in and out of the room, which also contained Lord and Lady Mountbatten, whom the Indian statesman knew very well indeed, or in Paris Greta Garbo, looking Garbo-like, and restricting her conversation to the husky words "Pass the salt"), so I played it all wrong. Like some earnest graduate student (oh, yes, I must remember to order wine for him) I plied "Mr. Ritchie," or "Sir," with questions about serious political issues such as the current unpleasantness in Northern Ireland. To which the beaky, horn-rimmed face gave politely measured responses. I shudder to think what his diary entry for that day must contain. But I fear that if his young dinner companion was described at all, such words as "earnest," "dull," and even "boring" must be at the core.

Charles Ritchie — and I'm glad to say that as I came to know him and his writing, and help him bring out his next book, *An Appetite for Life*, he soon became "Charles" — was *never* boring. In fact when in 1948, during his years in Paris, he once confessed to feeling ignored, a group of friends organized Ritchie Week, "a week of non-stop parties, dinners, even a ball in Ritchie's honour. . . . Old and new friends showered us with invitations. Whenever we appeared, a special anthem was played to signal our entrance. Verses were addressed to us — on the walls of the houses on our street someone had by night chalked up in giant letters the slogan 'Remember Ritchie.'" He tells us that a clutch of coloured balloons inscribed "Ritchie Week" were even let loose over Paris.

There is a great mystery at the heart of these memorable celebrations, one that challenged Allan Gotlieb, a disciple of Ritchie's who had a fine diplomatic career (and who took his advice to keep a diary). They were being put on for a man that the baffled Gotlieb, trying to plumb the depths of the mystery, calls "only a mid-level diplomat." Beyond that, Ritchie was a man without any obvious physical attractions, being in his own words, "beak-nosed and narrow-chested." Yet the Paris celebrations were organized for this skinny, mid-level Canadian by people who were, as Gotlieb put it, "at the centre of one of Europe's most sophisticated scenes." In fact, the moving spirit was Lady Diana Cooper, "the extraordinarily beautiful, aristocratic wife of the British Ambassador to Paris, Duff Cooper," and her chief accomplice was none other than the novelist-socialite Nancy Mitford.

"How does one explain this phenomenon?" Gotlieb asks. "The answer has to be found in Ritchie's extraordinary sense of style, his gaiety, his delight as a companion, his joie de vivre, and in the impression he gave of being a grand Whig aristocrat from the eighteenth century transplanted into the twentieth."

The Whig grandee comparison strikes me as very good. This, after all, was a man who in London chose to take his chances with the Nazi bombs raining from the sky, rather than protect himself underground because, he says, of "the insufferable conversation" in the bomb shelters. And, when he returned one morning to find his flat totally destroyed, he disarms the reader by lamenting the fact that he was left "with only one pair of shoes." Later, in a busy elevator in the UN building in New York, he asks for assistance in pressing the button to his floor on the Whiggish ground that he had "no mechanical aptitude."

Charm. That was what did it. In Nova Scotia, where he was born and raised, they say, "The third time's the charm." With Charles Ritchie it was every time. In international sport some people are said to "swim for Canada," or "row for Canada." Charles Ritchie could have "charmed for Canada," and in a sense that was what he did.

His diaries make it clear that he was not only witty, and the cause of wit in others, he was always seeking out new excitements, trying to be at the centre of incidents about to happen. *The Siren Years* is full of tales of lounging around P.G. Wodehouse's clubland, but also of hearing Churchill growling defiance in the Commons. Or T.S. Eliot dissecting a rival at a party. Or Charles himself, at one of the country-house weekends he charmed his way into, groping his way down midnight corridors, in pursuit of a bathroom, or my lady's chamber. We read of his frustrating progress with an American ballerina (a mention that decided a starry-eyed young Colin Robertson on taking up a romantic career in the foreign service). And, on a larger scale, we read of his determined attempts — ultimately successful —

to be one of the first civilians to arrive at the D-Day beaches, on the feeble pretext that he was bringing greetings from Canada. Yet he *was* there, in his civilian raincoat, getting only slightly in the way of the men wearing boots, and he was able to record his perceptions of Canadians at war, as opposed to the other Allied forces.

His extraordinary romance with Elizabeth Bowen, the famous Anglo-Irish novelist, is now common knowledge, and the subject of a revealing book of her correspondence, punctuated by his diary entries. The book, *Love's Civil War* edited by Victoria Glendinning (with an assist from Canada's Judith Robertson, daughter of the legendary Ottawa mandarin Norman), appeared in 2008, and laid bare a remarkable thirty-year love affair. Charles met Elizabeth in London in 1941. He was a charming, philandering bachelor, and she — a handsome, strong-faced woman ideal for the role of Coriolanus's mother — was unhappily married. By the time her husband died, Charles had married Sylvia, a second cousin, in 1948. Yet through all those years, until Elizabeth's death in 1973 (and Charles spent the last weeks of her life in England in order to be with her, visiting her in hospital and, as Glendinning puts it, "bringing champagne"), the two lovers wrote obsessively, sustaining a relationship that was only fulfilled in brief moments. They were never together for longer than a week at a time, meeting in hotels in Europe, London, New York, or at Elizabeth's home in Ireland. The letters, and Charles's self-revealing diaries reveal, in Jane Urquhart's words, "most powerfully, a world of love."

And Sylvia? In the heading of this chapter I described Charles as a "charming dissembler." No one outside a marriage can truly know what secrets lie inside it, but questions certainly arise here. At a Toronto party to launch *Love's Civil War*, a man who was in the Paris embassy when Charles phoned Sylvia to propose marriage in 1947 told me of a malicious joke that made the rounds there. In those days transatlantic phone calls were difficult, the line punctuated by crackles and whistles. So when Charles phoned Ottawa to propose marriage, the response that came from Sylvia, a woman not in the first blush of youth, was supposedly: "Yes (*whistle*), yes (*crackle*), I will! Er (*whistle, screech*), who's speaking, please?"

Opposed to that unkind story there are the numerous diary entries where he speaks of his affection for Sylvia, or "Syl." In December

1951, for instance, he wrote: "The most extraordinary phenomenon seems to be taking place in me. I seem to be falling in love with my own wife. It's not the first time this has happened, but never before, I think, with the force of this time. I find her beautiful. I want to go to bed with her all the time, and don't grudge her this hold over me."

And yet Charles, the natural spy (and Glendinning quotes Elizabeth Bowen saying that as Irish and Canadian outsiders in England they were both in some sense "spies") took better to a life of meeting "on street corners" than Elizabeth, who poured out her heart to him in an endless series of letters that make up the bulk of the 475-page book

In the summer of 1952, Charles deliberately left one of Elizabeth's letters out where it would be seen by Sylvia. . . .

And so it went, a fascinating three-person drama that makes for a fine book, which, I must confess, I did not publish. Three final points about this grand, only semi-secret love affair. First, Elizabeth Bowen dedicated her most famous novel, *The Heat of the Day* (1949), to Charles. Second, in his anguished final note about their love, after her death in 1971, Charles wrote, "If she ever thought that she loved me more than I did her, she is avenged." And finally, the affair took on the trappings of an international incident. Alan Sullivan, the recently appointed Canadian ambassador to Ireland, was accosted by a fiercely tweeded lady at the 1971 Dublin Horse Show. Having established his role she said abruptly, without mentioning any names, "Well. At least he was with her at the end!" and harrumphed away in her sensible brogues.

I never met Elizabeth Bowen, and Charles never raised her with me. In his role as godfather to Bob Rae, as "Uncle Charles" he once casually introduced Bob to the distinguished novelist. But to his godson he was happily married to Sylvia, and she played a full part in his life. Charles, I gather, was a fine, non-religious godfather; in fact, he told Bob of devilishly greasing his own hair before his confirmation, so that the priestly laying on of hands would be a memorable experience for the unlucky cleric. His godfather role consisted of useful occasional cheques in the mail, invitations to lunch, funny stories, and wise career advice. Since Michael Ignatieff was another godson, it was fortunate that the Rae-Ignatieff competition for the role of

Liberal leader followed Charles's death. When it came to career advice, even his charming diplomacy would have been hard-pressed by that situation.

I only met Sylvia in my role of visitor dropping in, and remember her as a charming hostess, her subjection in Paris to "Ritchie Week" presumably having prepared her for any conceivable social situation. My usual contact with Charles was by phone, and it began with my trying to persuade him that the success of *The Siren Years* demanded the publication of another volume of diaries. He was — or seemed to be — hesitant, but I persuaded him, with lines like "Just think of it, no work; you've already done the writing." And we worked happily together as the conscientious Pat Kennedy helped him to bring out *An Appetite for Life: The Education of a Young Diarist* in 1977. Its reception proved that Ritchie was what the reading public craved.

The first part of the book is set in the same Halifax that his contemporary Hugh MacLennan saw as Dickensian. Certainly the old garrison city saw London as closer than upstart Upper Canada, and it did seem to embrace the Pickwickian characters that walked its streets. Charles himself had to look no further than his own Cousin Gerald (the subject of a whole chapter in a later book). When Charles's mother, pulled by the London vortex, held her annual social gathering in the West End for her English friends, it was Cousin Gerald who startled the assembled ladies and gentlemen by calling very loudly across the room: "Did I tell you, Aunt Lillian, that I caught syphilis last Wednesday?"

Charles's mother responded magnificently. "That is not at all funny. Just sit down, dear." But the party broke up very shortly thereafter, the conversational flow never quite restored.

Young Charles dreaded Cousin Gerald's visits to their Halifax home, the Bower, which was kept with great difficulty by his impecunious widowed mother. I have twice made a furtive pilgrimage to the old mansion and been pleased to see it still standing. I wish all future occupants better luck than the Ritchies in the matter of household help. Their maid was known to serve porridge "with a pair of scissors in it."

On such fare it is no wonder that our hero grew up concerned about being "angular, beak-nosed, and narrow-chested," all adjectives that continued to apply. With his fussy little grey moustache and horn-rimmed glasses, to me he looked exactly like a mid-level bureaucrat, or a small-town bank manager sent in by head office to settle things down after too much excitement. Indeed, as the years went on, this wildly romantic writer with a novelist's eye, and ear, and imagination seemed to grow thinner, literally "more tightly wound." I remember seeing him near the end of his life, laughing aloud, head thrown back, with his old diplomatic colleague Douglas Le Pan in the lobby of the Château Laurier, and noticing that with his prominent nose he looked like a tightly wrapped umbrella.

In his dealings with women, it hardly seemed to matter. Conventionally handsome young athletes in his classes — at King's College in Halifax, or at Pembroke College in Oxford, or at Harvard, or at Paris's École Libre des Sciences Politiques — must have despaired at his success in attracting young women. It was not until his days at Oxford, where he occupied the room that had held young Samuel Johnson two centuries earlier, that he was relieved of the burden of virginity (a considerable burden, according to his diaries) by an older woman nom de plumed Margot Poltimer. She apparently made a point of conducting the same service, on (literally) an amateur basis, to deserving young Oxford men of her acquaintance.

According to *An Appetite for Life*, Charles had been left alone in a postcoital haze of delight (along the lines of "I've done it!") when there came a knock on the door. It was the porter introducing an American Midwestern couple of Dr. Johnson admirers who were in search of the good doctor's teapot. They excitedly roamed around the room speculating if the kettle, or the sofa onto which Charles and the willing Margot had so recently "subsided," might have belonged to the old scholar. To Charles's horror, the man approached the still-throbbing piece of furniture: "That sofa is a fine piece," he said. "Did it belong to the doctor?"

"Oh, Buddy," his wife cried, "that is *modern*."

Apart from that intrusion, Charles never looked back. Women continued to swarm around him. Even when he was in his seventies, a visit to his publisher's office would bring female staff tumbling out of their offices and turn gimlet-eyed proofreaders into giggling coquettes. Although he never actually kissed their hands, with a little bow, *he gave the impression of having done so.*

At Oxford he fell in with a *Brideshead Revisited* set. This involved him in high living and gambling that he could not afford. Worse, it involved him in friendship with upper-class twits who thought it amusing to fire a pistol from their college rooms into the street below, regardless of the danger to passing peasants. One young woman was hit in the leg. The magistrate took a lenient view.

There were specific *Brideshead* moments. Once Charles was invited by his friend Basil to spend a weekend at his stately home, which was "colonnaded like a Greek temple." There was to be a ball, so Charles had hired a white-tie-and-tails dinner outfit. Dressing for dinner he was defeated by the tie. He panicked, deciding that he would send a message to his host Basil and his brother Lionel to explain that he had been taken ill. Then he noticed a bell, and rang for the butler. That Jeeves-like figure shimmered into the bedroom and offered to help.

> He looked at my tie and said he could tie it for me, so he stood behind me tying the tie, both of us facing the mirror so that his arms were around my neck. He was chatting away about Mr. Lionel when to my amazement I saw in the glass that his hands had moved down from tying the tie and the next thing I knew they were under my hard shirt, stroking my body and feeling it. When I said, "Stop that at once," he took his hands away and looked quite discomfited, and he said, "I am sorry, sir. It was a misunderstanding. Mr. Lionel's friends always enjoyed it when I did that sort of thing for them" just as if he had handed me a delicious dish at dinner and I had refused it. Then he withdrew with dignity and a hurt expression.

Charles had come a long way from Halifax.

The success of each new book produced a successor, all under the wise editorial care of Pat Kennedy. *Diplomatic Passport: More Undiplomatic Diaries 1946–1962* came out in 1981, delighting readers with the tale of the newly arrived ambassador to Germany at a formal dinner in Bonn entertaining the two unilingual ladies seated beside him with the only German he knew, a recitation of "Little Red Riding Hood." This book was followed in turn by *Storm Signals* (1983) about his difficult years in Washington, when in his presence LBJ almost physically assaulted Lester Pearson, and finally by the book of reminiscences, *My Grandfather's House* in 1987.

With Pat doing the actual work, my own role as publisher was to persuade him that each success was not an agreeable fluke, and to persuade him to send us more to publish. This was a very agreeable task, since it involved me in being in constant touch by phone. There, the English-accented voice, complete with Oxfordisms like "I say!" was unmistakable. He was always full of news, not all of it reflecting well on the character under discussion. He received similar stories with a high cackle-cum-guffaw and the delighted words "How frightful!" Every conversation ended with an invitation "to foregather" the next time I was in what he called "The Nation's Capital."

We foregathered once at his summer home in Chester, Nova Scotia, at the elegant waterfront house with thick white pillars in front, which made the word "cottage" impossible. While Sylvia busied herself with treats like lemonade for the two little Gibson girls, Charles took us for a stroll around Chester. If a libel lawyer had been in attendance he or she would have been salivating at the prospect of any of these stories making it into print. Every dwelling we passed housed a skeleton — a daughter run off with a spectacularly unsuitable companion, a father evading jail with difficulty, a sailing or a golfing dispute that caused a feud with next-door neighbours — and every yard of the walk was marked by past snubs and scandals.

I remember especially pausing by a very large house, where the wealthy American owner, a society lady, apparently had told Charles, a Nova Scotian for four or five generations, that her son had just got engaged. "She's from Nova Scotia," she said, of the fiancée, "but you can take her anywhere." Charles was taken aback by this, and was still uncertain how he should have replied.

John Fraser, in his 1986 book, *Telling Tales*, recounts another time Charles was taken aback. The setting here was far from Chester, at a celebration of authors called the Night of 100 Stars at the Sheraton Hotel in Toronto. Charles, one of the honoured authors, was dressed in dinner jacket and "festooned with all the bric-a-brac (medals, orders, insignias) of his long years in high office." This cut no ice with the callow desk clerk when the elderly Charles, tiring of the evening, tried to get back into his room, where unfortunately he had left both his room key and his identifying wallet.

"Listen, Buster," said the desk clerk at one point in the altercation, and Fraser, an outraged passerby, stepped in to aid the distinguished diplomat in distress. It did not go well. Eventually Fraser snorted, "All right, my man, enough of this nonsense. Fetch the manager."

When the manager arrived, confronted by an agitated young man and a nervous older one, he misunderstood the situation.

"What seems to be the problem, gentlemen?" he said, but it was not asked in a friendly manner. "Do you two fellows want a room together for the night?"

In the end, hotel protocol was satisfied when Charles supplied a signature that roughly — but in the distress of the moment, only roughly — accorded with his registration card, and he was taken up to his room.

On another occasion, we did indeed foregather in Ottawa, and after lunch I made a pilgrimage with him down to the apartment at 216 Metcalfe Street, where so many of my letters and hot-off-the-press copies of new books had gone. We were greeted by Sylvia, but it was Charles who showed me around the comfortable old apartment, temptingly full of books. At the climax of the tour, he flung open his study door and said with full, deliberate irony, "And here is where the Great Work goes on!" I laughed and thought nothing more about it.

The scene moves now to Massey College at the University of Toronto on the evening of April 12, 2010. The head of the Quadrangle Book Club, an agreeable social organization that I have addressed in the past, is Ramsay Derry, a distinguished freelance editor, and he is talking about his work with Charles Ritchie. To my horror I learn that long before I and my colleagues at Macmillan saw the "diaries" to do the usual editorial smoothing before publishing them, he, and Charles had worked hard to "improve" them (my word). I had been aware, of course, that Charles, for libel reasons, if nothing else, had gone through the diaries removing incriminating (and possibly even boring) sections. I had been reassured by the sentence in the foreword to *The Siren Years*, where Charles wrote: "The diaries are as I wrote them at the time, save for occasional phrases which have been altered for the sake of clarity."

I had believed that to be true, had in fact marvelled to Charles at how well he wrote, even as a teenager. This new evidence from Ramsay cast doubt over much of what I had cheerfully accepted, without asking hard questions, and that Pat, as the editor, had faithfully put into book form.

The ultimate irony is that the person spurring on these "improvements" was, apparently, me. It seems that Charles's diaries speak of Macmillan (that would be me!) having such high hopes for his new books that he felt under pressure to give us/me really fine stuff, even if the new material was just that — new. "The Great Work," indeed.

I guess the moral is that if you are "running" a spy, he is likely to turn into a double agent.

But one final story shows the best qualities of my friend Charles. When Roy MacLaren was our minister for international trade, the former British prime minister Ted Heath turned up in Ottawa. Now this was a purely private visit, but Heath was, after all, a former PM, so it was decided to put on a lunch for him. About a dozen people were invited, including the long-serving ambassador who was the dean of the Ottawa diplomatic corps, and, to make up the numbers, the long-retired high commissioner to London in Heath's time, Charles Ritchie.

Now Heath, it should be explained, is not the warmest fish in the sea, and the editor of *Punch*, Alan Coren, gained undying fame by giving him the unlikely nickname of "Ted 'Mr. Bojangles' Heath." The lunch was proceeding when his stiff, unbending style emerged. The foreign ambassador, for whom English was not a first language, tried to ask Heath a question.

Heath did not understand. "What?"

The ambassador tried again.

This time Heath roared, "*What?*"

All eyes upon him, the blushing ambassador tried again.

This time Heath simply dismissed him, saying crossly to his neighbours, "Can't understand a word the man's saying."

Everyone felt very bad, but didn't know what to do. Charles knew what to do. He was retired, he didn't care, he was free to act.

As the party stood up and pulled their chairs back he raised his voice and called clearly down the table to the host, standing beside Mr. Heath. "Roy! I say. Roy! Didn't you think that Heath was *bloody rude*?"

General satisfaction. And if it is true that the definition of a gentleman is "one who is never rude unintentionally" Charles Ritchie proved that day to be a true gentleman.

# PIERRE TRUDEAU

Prime Minister, Author, and Haunting Icon

Shortly after the news of Pierre Trudeau's death was broadcast, I was sitting in the back of a cab in downtown Toronto. The cab driver and I shared our regrets about the news. The driver was a Greek who came to Canada as an adult in 1967, yet his heavily accented English allowed him to summarize elegantly how he felt: "I grew with him."

Late in his life, I was fortunate enough to get to know Pierre Trudeau, the author. At McClelland & Stewart we paid a great deal of money to publish his *Memoirs*, based on the 1993 CBC TV series that began each episode with him, clad in an elegant buckskin jacket, paddling a canoe on a misty lake. It was a brilliant image, and the series drew millions of viewers.

When the manuscript came in, however, bearing the company's hopes for a successful year, there were obvious problems with it. Such major problems, in fact, that after I had spent a sleepless night our chairman, Avie Bennett, and I decided that it had to be reworked: in rough terms, made chronological rather than thematic. We flew to Montreal, and Avie, who knew Trudeau, introduced me to him for the first time. Given a choice, I would have made our first meeting an easy, congratulatory one, but *c'est la vie*.

We sat in his prow-shaped office, jutting out high above the St. Lawrence River, with the snow starting to fall down past the deep windows. After the usual courtesies, Trudeau asked us what brought us to visit him. Avie turned the conversation over to me, and I started to explain why the book had to be rewritten.

Did Trudeau listen, shrug, and then say, "Sure, whatever makes sense to you"?

No. He leaned forward, the eyes narrowed in that look we all remember, and he started to make objections.

"But what about this?" "But what if we did this, what would happen to that?" On and on, a tough, unyielding barrage of questions. Had I considered this? How would I handle that? Obviously, I'd thought this through very carefully, so I was able to answer all his questions, while Avie watched like a fascinated tennis-match spectator.

If I'd ever said, "Of course, Mr. Trudeau, if you don't like it, we don't need to do this," I'd have been lost. Because he was grilling me *to be sure I knew what I was doing*. And in the end he leaned back, changed his tone, and said, "Fine, your plan makes sense. Let's do it your way." And thereafter, with *Memoirs* and the other three Trudeau books we published, we had a terrific working relationship, marked by his professionalism in getting proofs back to me or my colleagues exactly when he'd promised, every time.

There's a lesson here, I suggest, about Canadian politics. A prime minister runs up against people with all sorts of ideas, some of them excellent, some totally crazy. One way to spot the ones who do know what they're talking about is to grill them aggressively — and I can tell you, he was very, very good at it.

When the book was launched in Toronto (I'd been among the throngs at the televised launch at the National Library in Ottawa, and then had seen the dangerously surging crowds at the Ritz-Carlton in Montreal behaving with un-Canadian enthusiasm), we had to rope off sections to deal with the 1,200 people clustered in the huge hotel convention room on the waterfront. It was a very big deal, and I'd brought my fifteen-year-old daughter, Katie, and my cousin, Graeme Young, in town from Edmonton, and we'd taken a place on the TV camera island ten feet above the crowd.

When Trudeau began to speak, the huge crowd chanted, "Trudeau! Trudeau!" (even "Four more years!") and it was all very exciting. Then, after the usual "It's-very-nice-to-be-in-Toronto" stuff, he talked about his book and about working with Avie Bennett (onstage with him) and then others at M&S. And then Trudeau said, "But the man whom I especially want to thank, the one who pulled this together, is my good friend at McClelland & Stewart" — and I smiled modestly — and then he said, "my good friend *Fred* Gibson." And then he looked stricken and said, "Ah, Bob Gibson? Don Gibson?" Avie Bennett stepped forward and whispered into his ear. Trudeau said, "*Doug* Gibson. If he's here tonight, he'll never work with me again."

(This problem with names was not reserved exclusively for me. Barney Danson, who went on to long service in his cabinet, recalls a meeting in his riding where the PM came and delivered a barn-burner that ended with him urging the crowd to vote for, well, someone with the same number of syllables in his name as Mr. Danson.) I had my revenge at dinner that night — and this, of course, was shortly after Mr. Mulroney's term in office — when Trudeau and I crossed paths while changing tables. When he apologized for getting my name wrong, I was very gracious. "That's all right, Brian," I said, "I do it all the time."

Peter Gzowski witnessed this exchange; he liked it.

Happily, we did work together again, and McClelland & Stewart went on to publish *The Essential Trudeau* (with Ron Graham), as well as *The Canadian Way* (with Ivan Head), and *Against the Current*, on which Trudeau worked with his old comrade Gérard Pelletier.

I remember a lunch at the Beaver Club in Montreal (a cold day, which they appropriately called *un jour de fourrure* at the coat check), with those two old veterans at a time when provocations in Paris by Quebec's delegates (*plus ça change*) were once again causing trouble for Ottawa. Trudeau and Pelletier, once his ambassador to France, were mesmerizing as they described, with weary irritation, every possible move on the diplomatic chessboard.

In producing his memoirs, Trudeau relied heavily on the help of his former aide Tom Axworthy, then of his former biographer, George Radwanski. Yet as a former journalist and editor (at *Cité Libre*) and an experienced author (*Federalism and the French Canadians*, 1968, and many other publications) he cared about exact phrasing. My most amusing, strictly literary, memory is of an argument about poetry with him. Towards the end of the *Memoirs* he quotes the Rimbaud poem "Ma Bohème." The English translation, it seemed to me, could be slightly improved with a metrical twist of my own devising. By speaker phone, with Avie Bennett as referee, Trudeau sprayed spondees and declaimed dactyls as he demonstrated the rhythms of the original French, then the very different rhythms of the two English versions, expressing a strong preference for the original one. I was hopelessly outgunned, in two languages. We did it his way.

In later years, when I was in Montreal and had time to spare, I would call and, if it was convenient, drop in for a visit to his law office on René Lévesque Boulevard. Once, when he was in his mid-seventies, he took me to lunch. Instead of making for the nearest corner crossing, he set off straight across the wide boulevard named after his old rival. I was recovering from recent back surgery, so was appalled at what happened next. When the lights changed and three lanes of cars (Montreal cars!) hurtled towards us, he called out "Run!" with great cheerfulness, and sprinted to the other side through what seemed to be an unbroken stream of whizzing, honking metal.

As a non-Montrealer I remember thinking that, although the company was good, this was a really stupid way to die (immortalized on a Trivial Pursuit card as "the man killed along with . . ."). I also remember being surprised to live to tell the tale. And as we walked, to lunch, my pulse slowly subsiding, I noticed how, with nods, smiles, nudges, and turning heads, his fellow Montrealers reacted with pleasure to his presence among them. Rumours about his unpopularity in his home province were greatly exaggerated, in my experience.

In our conversations, his own pleasure was greatest when the talk turned to "the boys," and his face would light up as he spoke about his three sons, whose joint portrait graced the office wall behind him. I responded with tales of the great deeds of "the girls" although his Toronto encounter with Katie ("Fred" Gibson's daughter) had not been a memorable one, his small talk deserting him on that occasion. When his youngest boy, Michel, died in an avalanche in B.C., like all of his friends I was at a loss for helpful words. The funeral, which I did not attend, was a time of such national sorrow that one incident stands out; when the doors closed for the service, one enterprising reporter slipped inside — and was loudly "outed" by enraged colleagues. This was a time for sadness and mourning, not sly reporting.

Today, a signed photograph from Trudeau hangs on my wall. It speaks of "the best of memories." For me, that certainly is true. Perhaps my taxi driver friend put it best for all of us: "We grew with him."

Of course, a man like Trudeau doesn't simply disappear from your life on his death. He had been part of mine right from 1968, when I was around the Doubleday Canada office when we published Martin Sullivan's extraordinarily successful book about his rise to power, *Mandate 68*. I think, on reflection that it was our most successful book until we rushed out Harry Sinden's book, *Hockey Showdown*, about the 1972 Canada–Russia hockey series. (And if you think *you* cared about Canada's comeback, and Paul Henderson's winning goal, put yourself in the shoes of the gang at Doubleday — including a kid called Margaret Wente in the publicity department — who had invested a huge amount in a book about a hockey series that, it seemed for a while, Canadians were going to want to forget!)

So it was established early in my mind that books about Trudeau, like books about hockey, did very well. I was not involved in Walter Stewart's 1971 book, *Shrug: Trudeau in Power*, which, as you may have guessed, took a jaundiced view of the new Messiah. But I did edit other books by the unforgettable Walter, who listed his hobbies in *Canadian Who's Who* as "reading, walking, arguing." Frequently his arguments, as the managing editor of *Maclean's*, were with the editor, Peter C. Newman, who took a relaxed attitude towards what for Walter were points of principle, to be defended with high-pitched, eye-flashing eloquence. I had a grandstand seat for this long-running feud, as Walter and I worked together on a number of books, notably *But Not in Canada!* (1976) a sharp corrective to the smugness that was afflicting Canadians as they looked south of the border, unaware of the things that had also stained our history. Walter invited people who hated the book to direct some of their tomatoes at me, and some did.

I got into the Trudeau-publishing game in 1978, with a biography by George Radwanski. Later in his life, as privacy commissioner, George got into trouble for his spending habits (years later Ottawa-area restaurant owners were still bewailing "The Radwanski Effect" for the drop in business) but he was a talented writer, and the book, which included what would now be called hours of "face time" with Trudeau, was a success. It was clear then, however (and later, when his dining habits hit the news, and few of his colleagues came to his aid), that George was not universally popular in the press gallery where he worked, and where he was regarded the way high school jocks look at the very smart chess club president.

This emerged after George — who perhaps had not minimized the closeness of his relationship with Trudeau — asked a press conference question and was greeted in reply by the wrong name. I know how he felt, but the gallery took immense delight in this exchange, and I heard about it from many sources.

I also heard another story that speaks to what a clubby atmosphere — in the best sense — prevailed in those days. Now that Margaret Trudeau's bipolar disorder has been openly discussed, I can mention the occasion when the prime minister's wife made a late-evening appearance at the Press Club bar. Her behaviour was erratic, so those present simply crouched over their drinks and tried to ignore her group. Matters escalated when Trudeau arrived and tried to persuade his wife to come home, which she loudly resisted. All the journalists, most of them married men, crouched even lower in their seats. And after Margaret, in what we might call her Rolling Stone Phase, was finally persuaded to leave, nobody wrote about it. Think about that.

Somebody who stood apart from that clubby group, for a number of reasons, including her sheer, limitless talent, was Christina McCall Newman. A Victoria College graduate, she had gained a foothold at *Maclean's*, where she worked with the country's best writers, including the legendary editor, Ralph Allen, whose biography she wrote after his death. She married Peter C. Newman, and for many years they were the ultimate Ottawa Power Couple. During this time she turned out newspaper and magazine articles of such perception and style that they were instantly, from the first sentence, recognizable as her work. Soon everyone was waiting for her first big book, an in-depth study of the Liberal Party. I was the most impatient person in the queue. I had signed her up for this book, and had waited anxiously for it over several years. The wait was not without its exciting moments. At one point Christina, an impressive, elegant woman, with a very direct, level gaze, came to my office to tell me that she had decided that Macmillan was not the right publisher for her book after all, and that she wanted to get out of her contract and take the book elsewhere.

I can do a very direct, level gaze, too, and I gave her the benefit of it as I told her, politely but firmly, that we intended to honour the contract, and expected her to do the same. We were alone, our eyes locked for a very long time, before in the end she got up and left. She was not pleased.

Before the manuscript finally came in to us, there was a false alarm, including a phone call to me on the dock at North Hatley, postponing delivery for another year, which played hell with our budget for the fall, and spoiled my swim. But the final manuscript — beginning with a swing ("Lord knows the Liberals should have been ready for the election of 1979 when it was finally called on March 26 that year") — was everything I had hoped for. Its in-depth portraits of people like Keith Davey, Trudeau himself, James Coutts, Michael Pitfield, John Turner, and Marc Lalonde made them into characters out of a fine novel. I read it with delight, and told Christina that it should be called *Grits: An Intimate Portrait of the Liberal Party*. What we lost in Southern cookbook sales we'd make up in sales to Canadians who realized that this was a book for the ages. And so it proved. *Grits* set a new standard for political writing and we, dammit, published it very well.

The stage was set for Christina's next great work: a joint project with her new husband, Stephen Clarkson, a respected political science professor at the University of Toronto, and a successful author in his own right. Its overall title was to be *Trudeau and Our Times*, which perfectly catches Trudeau's importance to millions of Canadians. Despite the publication of many other Trudeau books, including Richard Gwyn's *The Northern Magus* (with its cover shot of Trudeau at the Grey Cup in a floppy hat calculated to offend) at M&S, we knew that there would be a huge audience for this new two-volume book.

Working with Stephen and Christina was predictably tricky. George ("Two legs bad") Orwell might have said, "One author, tricky. Two authors, very tricky. Husband and wife authors, tricky beyond belief." I noticed that Christina had picked up some power principles from her former husband, Peter C. Newman, whose whole career is marked by a fascination with power. A trivial example: every meeting I had with Peter, regardless of our plans to alternate locations, always ended up at his office. I was amused to see the same thing happen to my meetings with Christina and Stephen, and visiting their pleasant house in Rosedale was no problem for me, although they each seemed to spur the other on in their dealings with me. I suppose that it was a compliment of sorts that they chose to work with me as publisher on both volumes of *Trudeau and Our Times*. And they were well served by an editorial team that included the painstaking copy editor, Barbara Czarnecki. As for me, I find from the acknowledgements that I was "unfailingly inventive, enthusiastic, and patient." We all know what the "patient" means here. As for the "inventive," I'm pleased that both Barbara and Stephen graciously recall that I took the very first sentence about Trudeau, "He still haunts us after . . . etc." and changed it to "He haunts us still."

Those two volumes, massively documented, represent a great work of scholarship. They hide a great tragedy. For the last years of her life Christina was so unwell, afflicted by many problems, including an arthritic back, that she was in effect unable to write, and one of our finest pens was stilled long before her death in 2006.

Having played such an active part in what you might call "The Trudeau Industry," I continue to publish books about Pierre Trudeau. In 2005 my friend William Johnson alerted me to the fact that two friends of Trudeau, Max and Monique Nemni, had received his permission to study all of his papers and write his intellectual biography, about how his thinking developed. He was reading the manuscript in the original French, Bill told me, and it was so exciting and new that I should do the same, and consider publishing a translation, which he would be glad to provide.

I was initially reluctant. So much had been published already. But, with a sigh, I agreed to read the French manuscript. What followed was astonishing. I would emerge from my basement office to report to Jane that my French must be worse than I thought, since the documents quoted by the authors seemed to establish that my friend Pierre as a teenager and young man was anti-semitic, pro-fascist, and against de Gaulle and in favour of Marshal Petain, who had made alliances with the Nazis, who, after all, were not much worse than Winston Churchill's British forces. It was not my French that was at fault. Max and Monique, two federalists in Quebec who worked on *Cité Libre* and were friends of Trudeau, were appalled at what they had discovered in his private papers. For example, even as a man of twenty-three, Trudeau was ignoring the war in Europe and plotting a revolution to take Quebec out of Canada.

If the Nemnis (now Toronto residents, and good friends) were appalled by what they found, I was, too. But none of us doubted our duty to set the scholarly record straight, even if it put our friend in an unflattering light. *Young Trudeau: 1919–1944 — Son of Quebec, Father of Canada*, translated by William Johnson, came out as a Douglas Gibson Book in 2006. It shocked readers, and won the Shaughnessy-Cohen Award as the best book on Canadian Public Affairs. It has changed the world of Trudeau scholarship forever. It is unfortunate that the two-volume biography by John English, for all its merits, came out too soon after the Nemni book to be able to absorb its lessons in the text.

In late 2011 I will publish a second volume by Max and Monique dealing in detail with how our friend Pierre spent the years from 1944 till 1965 becoming the liberal and Liberal politician we all know. The title is *Trudeau Transformed*. It will prove that, indeed, "He haunts us still."

# MAVIS GALLANT

Short Story Writer, Canadian, and Parisienne

BOY EATS BUN AS BEAR LOOKS ON. The caption writing task confronting young Linnet Muir is newspaper work at its simplest, stripped to its essence. Easy. Then comes a dangerous thought: BOY EATS BUN AS HUNGRY BEAR LOOKS ON. As Linnet/Mavis puts it, this "has the beginnings of a plot." Soon her imagination is really rolling, with emotional questions arising about the boy being "a mean sort of kid" and the onlooking bear becoming "a starving creature."

No wonder Mavis Gallant (née Young) eventually left the newspaper world to become a fiction writer.

She will, of course, tell you that in the story where this occurs, "With a Capital 'T'," and in the other five allied stories, the first person narrator, Linnet Muir, is not her. She says so directly in the 1981 introduction to *Home Truths*: "The character I called Linnet Muir is not an exact reflection." To which I say that the first name Mavis (the Scottish word for a song thrush) and the short Scottish surname Young, translate amazingly well into Linnet (songbird) Muir (short Scottish surname). As they say, if it walks like a songbird, sings like a songbird . . . And all of the important autobiographical facts that we learn about Linnet, a young woman making her way alone in Montreal during the 1940s, seem to fit the real Mavis exactly. In fact, in the 2006 documentary *Paris Stories*, Mavis admitted to the interviewer, Lynn Booth, that "they were as close to autobiography as I have ever written."

Many of those biographical facts are known to her legions of admirers across the English-speaking world. Here is the sort of praise she has attracted. "There isn't a finer living writer in the English language" (*Books in Canada*). "She is a very good writer indeed" (*New York Times*). And "Mavis Gallant is a marvellously clear-headed observer and a rare phrase-maker" (*Times Literary Supplement*). American writer Fran Lebowitz summed up the adulation among other writers, noting, "The irrefutable master of the short story in English, Mavis Gallant has, among her colleagues, many admirers but no peer. She is the standout. She is the standard-bearer. She is the standard."

Born in Montreal, she was brought up by distant and ineffective parents, who sent her away to school as a tiny child. In an interview with the French scholar Christine Evain she recalled, "I was only four when I was sent to a convent school. In the bath we wore little rubbery clothes so we couldn't see ourselves. . . . And the nuns were not supposed to see us. And I had no one to help me with my clothes, and at four, you really need help." After her artist father died when she was only ten, there was even less attention. Mavis Young was shunted between seventeen different schools, some French, some English, some in Canada, some in the United States. Somehow, as the perpetual outsider, the observer of the new world around her, she managed to survive. Remarkably, at the age of fifteen, she was able to tell a schoolmate that she was going to write for the *New Yorker* and live in Paris — as the schoolmate reminded her many years later.

When she was eighteen she escaped New York and her mother's nerveless grasp. She made her penniless way to Montreal, presenting herself at the door of her old French-Canadian nanny ("Mavis! *Tu vis!* You're alive!"), who took her in. Then, Linnet-like, she set about finding an office job, initially at the National Film Board. In turn ("with so many men away at the war," as it was explained to her), this led to a job at a weekly newspaper, doing more than writing captions about buns and bears. She was an undeniably good journalist. For six years, even after the men came home, she worked for the weekly *Montreal Standard*. She may never have been "one of the boys" in the Montreal Men's Press Club, but she gained such respect for her writing skills that she was able to choose major assignments, like interviewing Jean-Paul Sartre. As she met and interviewed tides of refugees flowing into Montreal from all over Europe, some with numbers on their arms, she found herself increasingly fascinated by what had gone on "over there" on that mysterious continent that she had never seen.

Growing up in Montreal at the time, young Mordecai Richler noticed this young woman who had a newspaper column, with the photograph at the top showing her looking "jaunty." A woman columnist, not writing about recipes, or decorating tips, or society events? Mavis clearly had arrived. But there was still what we might call the "hungry bear factor" gnawing away at her. The non-fiction world of the newspaper was not enough. The world of fiction attracted her, and she had started to write short stories.

Many years later, in 1984, by then a world-famous writer that Canadians were belatedly claiming as one of their own, Mavis received an honorary degree from the University of Toronto. As her publisher, I was selected to give the speech introducing her to the packed audience filling the 1,500 seats in Convocation Hall. I'm sorry to say that I offended Mavis by telling the graduating class that this woman — dramatic arm gesture — represented their parents' "worst nightmare." I explained that having achieved a remarkably prominent position as a young woman at the top of the Montreal newspaper tree, "she threw it all away, to go off to Paris, to be a writer."

Starving in a garret was not actually obligatory, but it was likely. And Mavis, her marriage to a Montreal piano-player named Johnny Gallant long gone (without rancour, but with the great, lingering benefit of an elegant byline) was indeed on her own, with only one story sold to the *New Yorker* when she took the plunge. She gave herself two years to make it. To this day, when North Americans shake their head at this, and ask, "Why Paris?" she answers, sweetly (and Mavis is at her most dangerous when she says things sweetly), "Have you ever been to Paris?" And in *Paris Stories*, she adds, "I found for the first time in my life a society where you could say you were a writer and not be asked for three months rent in advance."

But it's true that she travelled around Europe, not restricting herself to dealing, like Henry James, with the safe theme of (North) Americans abroad. She travelled widely, marvelling at what she was finding about the impact of the War (no adjectives needed, just the War). "The Latehomecomer" is typical of the true stories that she stumbled across; how many English-speakers knew that German soldiers were still being held in near-slavery on French farms, years after the war was over? And it's distressingly true that as she wrote and sent off stories to her New York agent, without success, she went through hard times. Once, in Spain, she was reduced to selling her clothes for food. Then she discovered that several of the stories she had sent off into the void had indeed been bought by the *New Yorker*. The rogue agent had failed to inform her and had pocketed the money.

Soon a more prosperous pattern was established. With occasional trips here and there in Europe, later revealed in her work, Mavis established a base in Paris and wrote short stories for William Maxwell at the *New Yorker*. As the number swelled (eventually, with over 100 stories accepted and printed, Mavis stood at the top of the prestigious magazine's list, with only John Updike ahead of her total) her reputation grew. By the late 1970s she had published two novels — *Green Water, Green Sky* (1959) and *A Fairly Good Time* (a marvellous Gallant title) in 1970. Her short stories had been collected in *The Other Paris* (1956), *My Heart Is Broken* (1964), *The Pegnitz Junction* (1973) — her personal favourite, for artistic goals achieved — and *The End of the World and Other Stories* (1974).

In a fine article in the *Guardian* in 2009, Lisa Allardice wrote about Mavis's career: "A Canadian in Paris who has devoted her life to writing, she is one of the great chroniclers of exile, her fictional landscapes inhabited by misfits and lost souls, characters far from home, literally or emotionally." It is appropriate that one 1988 story collection had the excellent title *In Transit*. In fact Robert Fulford has shrewdly pointed out that the "grand theme" of Mavis's work "has been the movement of populations."

In summary, by the late 1970s, Mavis Gallant was a popular success everywhere in the English-speaking world. But not in Canada. In *Paris Stories*, Robert Fulford agrees that Mavis "was neglected in Canada." But he suggests that, on her part, "Mavis neglected Canada . . . She obviously didn't pay any attention to her publishing situation in Canada. She published with a Boston firm and a New York firm that had no distribution in Canada. So her books weren't even in the Canadian bookstores. So, you know, she wasn't even in the position to be neglected."

Enter John Gray. One day when I was at my desk at Macmillan, trying to expand the company's distinguished but small list of authors, a letter came in from Paris, addressed to the company in general. It was from Mavis Gallant, asking for news about the health of her old friend, John Gray. I wrote back, bringing her up to date on John's situation. Then I cleared my throat, as it were, to say that I had noticed her work and admired it greatly. I told her flatly that she, as a

Canadian, deserved a Canadian publisher, rather than relying on her New York–based publisher to distribute her work. As it happened, her last book had barely appeared in Canada — some mix-up in the American warehouse was blamed — so my timing was good. Mavis wrote back to say that she was delighted by the idea. In short order I had made an arrangement with her agent, Georges Borchardt (*not* the rogue agent), to publish her next collection of stories, *From the Fifteenth District* (1979).

We went all-out on that book, sending review copies everywhere, telling the Canadian literary world, in effect: "Look, there's this world-class author named Mavis Gallant, living in Paris and writing some of the best short stories the world has ever seen. She's one of us, a Canadian, and it's time we claimed her."

The reviewers read the book and responded with superlatives, recognizing a new planet in the Canadian sky. The book was a huge success.

Earlier, in the course of my campaign, I had told Jack McClelland of our plans, and he had scoffed at the idea that we could sell 4,000 copies of a book of short stories by Mavis Gallant. In his mind, Mavis was not the drawback. The received wisdom all over the English-language publishing world, as Jack knew well, was that short stories were hard to sell. With the superhuman help of Mavis and Alice Munro — and indeed of Margaret Atwood, whose superb short stories I later published, but never edited (a tip of the hat here to my renowned colleague, Ellen Seligman) — I planned to change that. To this day Canadian book buyers are revered by publishers abroad for their willingness to snap up books of short stories by these major figures, allowing short story collections to ride high on bestseller lists, as well as winning praise and prizes.

In the end, Jack bet me $100 that I would not be able to sell as many as 4,000 copies of *From the Fifteenth District*. Even in hardcover, we sold far, far more.

A word about Jack McClelland. In his history of Canadian publishing, *The Perilous Trade*, Roy MacSkimming's chapter title calls him simply "Prince of Publishers." He was very much a man of his wartime generation. As a dashing young naval officer he commanded a motor torpedo boat in England, conducting nightly raids against the deadly German E-boats in the channel. It was a pirate's life, and the losses were terrible. "I lived every day as if it was the last," he remembered.

Safely returned from the war to the family business, he took over the company in 1952, the year he turned thirty. His elderly father was still around. The famous designer, Frank Newfeld, claims that he once saw Jack — affectionately — remove his father from a board-room discussion that he had wandered into by wrapping his arms around the old man and carrying him bodily into another room, where he could potter around to his heart's content. In the hot M&S offices off the warehouse at Hollinger Road, where air-conditioning was for wimps, and leaving the vodka-bottle-strewn office before 8 p.m. was regarded as taking it easy, Jack was known for wearing his shirt piratically, very unbuttoned indeed.

The great, decisive moment in Jack's career was in 1963, when he dropped twenty-three of the twenty-eight agency lines that the company distributed. From now on there could be no turning back to the old days when selling books written and published elsewhere would support a small list of new Canadian titles. Now Jack was committed to the much riskier business of surviving by creating Canadian books from scratch. With the aid of his contemporaries Pierre Berton, Farley Mowat, and Peter C. Newman — and novel-ists like Gabrielle Roy, Margaret Laurence, young Mordecai Richler, and the even younger Leonard Cohen — he proceeded to do so, with energy and flair.

Almost everyone who was to play a role in Canadian publishing joined in the Children's Crusade that was life at the M&S office in the sixties and later. Names like Jim Douglas, Scott McIntyre, and Anna Porter later appeared on rival publishing company letterheads, but people like Allan MacDougall, Peter Taylor, John Neale, Peter Milroy, Patrick Crean, and Linda McKnight were also later to play a huge role in the book world. It was a hectic office. Once the fiction manuscript of a promising young writer named Margaret Atwood was "lost" for two years. She reminded Jack of this, in a remarkably friendly way, when her success in the world of poetry caused him to contact her to ask if she happened to have written a novel. If so, he said, innocently, M&S would be glad to see it.

Jack and his group of author pals worked hard and played hard.

There were tales of a "Swordsman's Club" in Toronto where very smart girls were likely to jump out of equally smart cakes, and M&S parties were legendary for the booze that flowed, with employees known to make their exit on all fours.

Famously, Jack worked hard to make Canadian books big news. To help promote the New Canadian Library, the paperback series started by Professor Malcolm Ross (which, you may recall, started out as an enormous gamble by Jack, but proved to be the battering ram that opened the sometimes resistant doors of the academic world to the study of Canadian literature), he created a snazzy blazer adorned with NCL covers (which is now preserved with care in the McMaster University Library Archives). He travelled the country in his "coat of many covers," distributing free NCL titles to surprised pedestrians on city streets. To promote a 1980 novel by Sylvia Fraser, *The Emperor's Virgin*, set in Ancient Rome, he staged a toga-clad chariot ride down Yonge Street, in a March snowstorm. He and the shivering author survived the trip, and the media loved it.

But apart from the brief ride down Yonge Street, it was all uphill work. The economics of publishing in a widespread, thinly populated country that shares a language with cheap books flooding in from abroad meant that even with the great books his major authors produced dominating the bestseller lists — despite my best efforts at Macmillan — M&S ran into financial trouble. Repeatedly. Even when the Ontario government, aware that an important national asset was in danger, arranged for a generous loan: more than once. It was like "the perils of Pauline" throughout the seventies and beyond, until at the end of 1985, Avie Bennett bought the company and gave it financial stability. As I have mentioned elsewhere, Avie brought me in to start my Douglas Gibson Books imprint three months later, on Jack's advice, and I owe both men a lot.

Jack was a strikingly handsome figure with a shock of hair like Kirk Douglas the movie star, hair that he wore fashionably long, even as it turned from blond to pewter. A fine speaker who liked the limelight and cared about national issues — with Claude Ryan he was co-chairman of the Committee for an Independent Canada, launched in 1970 — he remained a striking physical presence. Once, to stave off yet another financial crisis, he sold warehouse stock directly to the public, cutting out the booksellers; I remember that

Leonard Cohen, out of loyalty to his friend Jack, took the trouble to travel to Toronto to make a helpful personal appearance alongside Jack at the fire sale, which drew great crowds.

Just after he had outraged the entire bookselling community with this move, Jack showed up at the huge annual dinner of the Canadian Booksellers Association. I remember that while conversation at the tables in the crowded room faltered, Jack paused at the entrance, to light, very slowly, one of his ever-present cigarettes. Waves of silent outrage washed towards him, but the old torpedo boat commander had faced much worse, and clearly didn't give a damn. A favourite phrase.

Sometimes the physical presence was unwisely projected. His old colleague, Hugh Kane, told the story of a wedding reception for one of Jack's daughters that was held at the large McClelland family cottage on the shores of Lake Joseph in Muskoka, which Jack loved to cruise around with his family at the end of a summer day. On this occasion the polite reception chatter among the elegant guests was at its height when Jack burst from the cottage to run, naked, through the party and across the dock and hit the water in a racing dive. It was a scene not envisaged even in Charles Gordon's imaginative classic, *At the Cottage*.

Robertson Davies, who knew Jack, once described him to me as a "Peter Pan figure." He was not among the guests that day in Muskoka.

After Avie had bought the company, Jack did not enjoy his Lost Boy role as a senior advisor. I used to visit him in the front office courteously reserved for him, to chat and discuss publishing philosophy. But the arrangement with Avie did not work out — to my distress, since I admired both men, and even had illusions that I might help them get along. But Jack explained to me that it was hard to be a crew member on a ship that you had captained. Many years later, in 2004, when I was moved sideways at M&S after sixteen years as publisher and saw the company take a new direction, I knew what he meant.

From 1986 to 1988 I was on the sidelines at M&S, tending my separate Douglas Gibson Books imprint (and turning away from my door any M&S employee eager to share atrocity stories), while Adrienne Clarkson tried her hand at running the company. In the light of the comments from Jack that follow, it's important to stress how hard it is for any person, coming in as an outsider, to learn how to be a publisher in just a couple of years. That person would have to be very humble, putting all of his or her trust in more experienced colleagues, and very eager to learn. I was glad to see Adrienne make a great success of her time as Governor General, a position where every new appointee is expected to learn "on the job."

I had several superb assistants (most notably Valerie Jacobs and Gail Stewart) over the years. In every case I had to instill in exhausted new employees the truth that there is never enough time, or money, or people to do everything. There is no such thing as "a clean desk" at the end of a publishing day. There are always other manuscripts to be read, new plans to be hatched for promoting this or that new book, and new books thought up for this or that author.

Jack, who knew all about these pressures, did something wonderful for me when in September 1988 Avie persuaded me to leave the perfect cocoon that I had spun for myself at Douglas Gibson Books *(No meetings! Just work with authors you really like!)*, and take on the role of publisher of McClelland & Stewart.

The letter speaks for itself, and tells us a lot about Jack.

September 13, 1988

Dear Doug,

Just a note to congratulate you on your new appointment. I say, congratulate, but just possibly mean commiserate.

Because of the flood of stories and rumours — and I certainly did not invite them nor did I want to hear them — I am not surprised about Adrienne Clarkson's effective departure. It has been in the cards for some months. She is an extremely intelligent lady but it would have surprised me if she managed to survive in that new role for very long.

Welcome. You have the know-how and the experience and it should work extremely well. Obviously you are going to be busier than a one-armed paperhanger for a while but it will work out. Don't bother acknowledging this letter. You have enough to do. It is just to tell you that I am pleased personally to have the old firm with Doug Gibson as publisher.

Cheers!
Jack

It was a laying on of hands. And I never did get around to claiming the $100 for winning my bet about Mavis, who was born, in a striking coincidence, in the same year of 1922 as Jack McClelland.

After the huge success of *From the Fifteenth District*, I sent Mavis a surprising letter. It said, roughly, "Although you don't know it, you have written a very good new book, and I would like to publish it. It is called *Home Truths*, and it consists of your stories about Canadians at home and abroad. The table of contents I suggest is as follows . . ."

And after due consideration, Mavis wrote back. (Please note that we usually made contact by letter; phone calls to Paris were hugely expensive in the hard-scrabble world of Canadian publishing, where at Macmillan I tried to postpone my phone calls to Alberta or B.C. till after six p.m., when the rates dropped, since every cent counted.) She wrote to say that she agreed, but that she would like to drop stories B and C, but add stories Y and Z. So we proceeded with *Home Truths*.

Many years later, in 2007, she went into very frank detail about our relationship in an interview with French scholar Christine Evain:

*Mavis Gallant:* Douglas Gibson had been in Yale doing graduate work — he's a Scot — and as he was a foreigner, so to speak, he didn't know that I was "ungrateful, disgraceful, anti-Canadian" . . . Then [*after the publication of From the Fifteenth District*] he wrote to me and said: "I know you're going to say 'no' to this, but think it over. I'd like to publish a volume of your Canadian stories." This is what I wanted to avoid . . .
*Christine Evain:* The labelling.
*Mavis Gallant:* Yes! The ghetto! But then he'd said, think it over. And I remember I answered him and said, "I hope you have your shirt painted on your body, because otherwise you're going to lose it! But, go ahead!" *(Laughs)* And he had a title, *Home Truths*, which I thought was a clever title.
*Christine Evain:* From a marketing point of view, it was an excellent idea.
*Mavis Gallant:* He's very good at that! But, you know, I didn't know him then . . . I didn't even know he was a Scot.
*Christine Evain:* He has a very good feel for the Canadian market.
*Mavis Gallant:* He's brilliant at that. He's sometimes a bit eccentric, and so on, but, in the long run, he turns up trumps.

At my request — possibly an eccentric one — Mavis wrote a long, thoughtful introduction about being an expatriate Canadian. It contains dozens of gems such as this: "I have been rebuked by a consular official for remarking that Rome in winter is not as cold as Montreal; and it surely signifies more than lightheadedness about English that 'expatriate' is regularly spelled in Canadian newspapers 'expatriot.'" She even writes about the choice of language. Although we know she leads a French-speaking existence in Paris (with some of her friends surprised to learn that she is a famous writer, in English), here she says, "I cannot imagine any of my fiction in French, for it seems to me inextricably bound to English syntax, to the sound, resonance and ambiguities of English vocabulary. If I were to write in French, not only would I put things differently, but I would never set out to say the same things."

And so on. Marvellous stuff (*ambiguities*!) that shows how Mavis has always had a razor-sharp intelligence that she could easily apply to non-fiction, as in, for example, her accounts of the riotous events that she witnessed in Paris in 1968.

*Home Truths* was a spectacular success, winning the Governor General's Award for 1981 and sending me to Winnipeg on Mavis's behalf to joust with separatists, as I recount on this book's opening page. Much better, it brought Mavis Gallant home, in that over the next few years she received many Canadian honours, including becoming an Officer, then a Companion, of the Order of Canada.

It brought her home physically, too, since I was delighted to send her across the country to promote her work. We never quite got around to putting her in a toga aboard a chariot, but she might have surprised many by her response, for one of her many qualities is that Mavis is a good sport. At home in Paris she is a keen soccer fan. Knowing this (and following the same instinct that led me to take Morley Callaghan to a boxing match), I took Mavis to watch a soccer game. Two very different games, to be precise. One was a match for eight-year-olds in Rosedale Park where I, normally "Coach Doug," found myself racing around the field in the role of referee, to the great pleasure of Mavis on the sidelines. As if she had scripted it, an eighteen-month-old ran, unnoticed, onto the field, and to protect him I had to scoop him up and carry on refereeing with a child in my arms while the game raged around my feet for a surprisingly long time — with the child's parents no doubt distracted by discussions about house prices in Moore Park. Mavis laughed so hard we almost lost a famous writer, right there on the sidelines.

On the other occasion, at a slightly higher level, I took her to an international exhibition game at Varsity Stadium, and Mavis clearly knew what was going on, as she watched intently.

To add to the portrait of the *sportive* Mavis, I should add that she has dropped tantalizing hints about her love of horse racing (I can imagine her, among the jockeys, in the background of a Degas racing scene at Longchamp) and her skilful betting on the sport of kings. Peter Gzowski had the bright idea of inviting Mavis to watch the horses at Woodbine (naturally, she also spotted what was going on in his romantic life) during her time as Writer in Residence at Massey College in the University of Toronto in 1983–84. Her teaching time was not a total success, in that she did not (and does not) believe that writing can be taught. Her lessons, she claims, consisted of getting students to read good authors like Nabokov and E.M. Forster, and encouraging them to get on with writing.

Her spell in Toronto, however, allowed me to spend more time with her and to see how she terrified people. Even in the Gibson household she took on the role of one of Bertie Wooster's fierce aunts, teaching fourteen-year-old Katie Gibson the correct way to answer a telephone, for example, which Katie has never forgotten.

Another example: when the Toronto Harbourfront Reading Series held an event in her honour, it was full of worshipful attendees, onstage and in the audience. A high point was an onstage interview with her old friend Mordecai Richler, to whom she had once taken a gift of oranges when he was new in Paris, lying ill in his small room. (Charles Foran's fine biography of Mordecai adds the detail that the young writer was worried that spots on his elbows possibly indicated a venereal disease.) Now I had an interesting relationship with Mordecai, featuring a duelling correspondence with him over some long-forgotten point of pride. My assistant Valerie Jacobs would come into my office, beaming, bearing Mordecai's latest salvo in letter form; usually it began with head-shaking sorrow, "Gibson, Gibson." That night I sat with the Richler family at the event, expecting fireworks. But Mordecai had decided that whatever Mavis decided to answer — or refuse to answer — was fine with him. After her first response, delivered in friendly tones, "I've no interest in answering that," Mordecai was unruffled and, as I whispered to the family, it was clear that a very unconventional interview was under way. The interview continued along these lines, but her impatience with the questions of some audience members soon showed.

She has a formidable presence. She speaks in an accent that she says belongs to another era in Montreal, but to modern Canadian ears sounds English-influenced. She speaks with great, sibilant precision that can on occasion be mistaken for a hiss. As for her manner, with strangers she is such a reserved, dignified, and lady-like figure that she seems, metaphorically, to be wearing white gloves. Scores of journalists have come away from interviews with her, confessing that they felt intimidated.

Even her great admirer, Jhumpa Lahiri, suffered badly when she conducted an interview with Mavis, later reproduced in *Granta* magazine. Jhumpa, a well-known American novelist, almost worships Mavis. In an introduction to one of Mavis's books she describes her as a writer "who demands intelligence from her readers and rewards them with nothing short of genius." In the interview, however, the much younger American seemed to be playing the Disraeli-to-Queen-Victoria "authors like us" card a little too often, and Mavis was resisting. When Jhumpa, who obviously had a romantic view of the writing life in Paris, asked Mavis if she had ever worked in cafés, back came the sweet, sibilant reply, "As a waitress?"

Um, no, Jhumpa replied lamely, you know, for writing in. Game, set, and match.

I give these background details to set up my own humiliation at her hands in Montreal in 1998. The Quebec English-language writers' group, QSPEL, had honoured her by naming a prize after her. Because the Hugh MacLennan Prize for Fiction already existed, they decided that her name should adorn the non-fiction prize, since *Paris Notebooks* had established her credentials in non-fiction in 1986. Mavis, in Canada for other reasons, had arranged to attend the formal event to celebrate this prize at a downtown Montreal hotel. I was present as a member of the front-row official group. In the green room beforehand, with Mavis present, we went through the plan. Since there was no food or drink available, just a room with uncomfortable stacking chairs laid out in rows for an audience of

200, the plan was to move briskly, starting just after 6, and be out of there by 7:00. People had made dinner arrangements accordingly. Out by 7:00, we all agreed.

At 6:10 the QSPEL people started the meeting, very efficiently introducing me. I spoke briefly about Mavis's high standing in the literary world, and in turn introduced my great friend William Weintraub, the author of several urbane books, like *City Unique*. Bill was an old friend of Mavis from their journalism days together, and he spoke affectionately about them, before introducing Mavis.

It was 6:20 when Mavis handed me her purse and walked to the podium just ahead of where we sat. She thanked everyone for naming the prize after her, then said that because the prize was for non-fiction, she intended to read some of her own non-fiction, namely some diary entries. Having chosen the year (let's say 1995), she began: "January 1st. A grey day where the main event was . . ."

*One hour and twenty minutes later,* at 7:40, she said the words "July 1st, Canada Day . . ." *and kept going.* She was so absorbed in her reading that she was unaware of the constant procession of people slipping out of their seats and creeping away. Dinners were burning in ovens across Montreal, reserved tables were being forfeited in the city's busiest restaurants, but Mavis was on a roll.

For thirty minutes I had been on the edge of my seat, trying to catch her eye to give her a "cut" sign across my throat. But she was oblivious, lost in her reading. Now it was clear that she was going to read the diary for the whole year. Until — quick calculation — 9:00.

I conferred in whispers in the front row with Bill and Magda Weintraub. "Bill," said Magda, "You must do something!" Bill, a wise and witty man, just groaned. I, the son of a man who responded to an ancient minister's coughing fit by halting the church service and sending everyone home, realized that no one else was going to "do something." And I had taught my kids that in such a situation it's incumbent on you to be the doer.

Oh hell.

I rose and took the three longest steps of my life, to stand with my hand on the front of Mavis's podium. At the time, the phrase "own the podium" did not exist, but Mavis knew all about it.

"Excuse me Mavis," I said, " I think that people are very keen to have a chance to ask you questions."

She might have said, "Oh my goodness, is that the time? Of course, let's go straight to questions."

What she *did* say was "Questions? *Questions?* But I'm in the middle of my reading!"

I stood my ground. "Yes, but as I say, time is going on, and I know that people are very eager to ask you questions."

Mavis went over my head. Literally. She appealed to the crowd behind me, who were watching, thrilled. "Aren't you *enjoying* my reading?" And they, the cowards, gave her a supportive round of applause, and Mavis looked down at me in triumph.

I slunk back to my seat and gave Bill Weintraub the best line of my life. "Well," I said, evenly, "I think that went off pretty well, don't you?"

Now Mavis, enraged, was reading brilliantly. Every so often she would glare down at me and say something like "I *was* going read you the entry for September 20th, but" (angry turning of pages) "I'm told I must hurry up."

I sat there, arms folded, at peace with the world, while the audience suffered. Eventually Mavis finished at 8:10.

At this point my friend Linda Leith, who was soon to found Montreal's Blue Metropolis Reading festival, came to the stage and tactfully began, "Well, as we've heard, many people in the audience are keen to ask questions. Are there any questions for Mavis?"

One brave person asked a question, which Mavis batted away, along the lines of "I've no interest in answering such a question."

Linda asked if there were any other questions and a very, very stupid young man raised his hand. What, he wondered, did Ms. Gallant think of the criticism of her writing produced by So-and-so? Mavis flew at him, saying that she didn't believe in writers suing other writers, but what So-and-so said was so outrageous that she was sorry that she hadn't sued him, and — with angry finality — she refused to discuss him further.

"Well," said Linda, "if there are no more questions . . ." and she went on to comment on what a memorable evening this had been, and to thank Mavis.

As people rose to their feet and started to mingle, it was noticeable that nobody wanted to come near me. I was the burn victim, the scarred survivor of a flamethrower attack, and people bumped into one another or brushed against the wall to avoid coming anywhere near me. Apart, that is, from my old friend Pat Webster, who took me home (we agreed that probably the official front row party dinner could get along just fine without me) and fed me dinner. As I related the evening's events to my old friend Norman Webster, the legendary newspaperman, his eyebrows would rise in disbelief, and he would look at Pat, who would nod in confirmation. There are roughly 100 people in Montreal who will confirm the account you are reading.

It took some time for Mavis to forgive me. That evening she told Bill Weintraub, "I'll kill him!" But of course we got back on an even keel. She had followed me from Macmillan to my Douglas Gibson Books list at M&S, and we would continue to work together as old friends. Such old friends that in her Bertie Wooster fierce aunt role she inspected my new wife Jane at tea at the Ritz-Carlton in the course of a Montreal visit. Jane was on her best behaviour, and passed the test.

Since then, as ill health and the effects of osteoporosis have made travel harder for Mavis, there have been few visits to North America. There was, however, the triumphant evening in her honour in New York, where the authors who gathered to sing her praises from the stage included Michael Ondaatje and Russell Baker, both of whom have written introductions to recent collections by Mavis. Russell Baker has written about her choosing "to write in English, and in it fewer than a handful of living short story writers are her equal. William Trevor, and her countrywoman Alice Munro, perhaps, and — since the death of Eudora Welty — no American that I can think of."

Michael Ondaatje's admiring comments include the telling remark: "I know two writers who have told me that the one writer they do *not* read when they are completing a book is Mavis Gallant. Nothing could be more intimidating."

I must note that she has not always been well served by her New York publishers. After many years of researching a major book on the Dreyfus Affair, for example, she was told by her editor that big, lengthy books were no longer in fashion. According to Mavis, her despairing reaction was to burn the many hundreds of pages she had written, leaving no copies.

I can vouch for the fact that when we co-published *The Selected Stories of Mavis Gallant*, the New York publisher — unbelievably — gave precisely the same book the misleading title *The Complete Stories of Mavis Gallant* (1996). When we in Toronto caught a major error in the order of the stories, it was regarded by them as a major nuisance to fix, until I appealed to very high levels. And so it went, with panic-stricken calls from New York at the last minute, incredibly, asking Mavis to cut sixteen stories (including the vital Linnet Muir stories) from the end of the book. I did what I could, and the correctly titled *Selected Stories* continues to sell well in Canada.

Our 2008 visit to Paris included a visit to Mavis in hospital. Some weeks earlier I had failed to get an answer to repeated phone calls, and had called her New York agent, Georges Borchardt, to get someone in Paris to check up on her, please, since I had "a very clear image of her lying helpless on her apartment floor." He had someone check. The phone was broken, relax, Doug, no problem, she's not lying on the floor, relieved laughter all round.

Exactly one week later Georges called with a very different message. "Doug, do you remember that image you had of Mavis lying on the floor? Well, *it just happened*. She collapsed on Thursday, and the neighbours broke in with a locksmith on Sunday, and she's in hospital, but doing well." Georges wondered wryly about my using my talents elsewhere, like a circus, for example. Longchamp, anyone?

Jane and I visited her near the end of her fifty-day stay in the Broca Hospital in Paris. Despite the fact that she had lain unconscious for so long, without food or water, her brain, to the amazement of the doctors, was unaffected. When we reverently tiptoed into her hospital room, she wasn't there; her roommate, an Alzheimer's victim, was. Enquiries of the nurses about Madame Gallant revealed that she was an unpredictable gadabout, to be found who knew where. We were glad to find her in the cafeteria with a visitor.

She recovered completely, but her energy was affected. This led me into a new role with her 2009 book, *Going Ashore*. My editor's note tells the story of the book's origins.

This book was conceived in a Toronto-Paris phone conversation in 2007, when Mavis Gallant remarked to me that it was unfortunate that so many of her stories were out of print, or had never appeared in a book. This caught my attention. . . .

Intrigued, I encouraged her to compile a list of the "missing" stories, and promised to publish them. She was delighted, and asked me — in a typically direct way — if I could bring the book out before she died. We are such old friends that I felt able to answer with another question: "What are your plans in this regard, Mavis?" She laughed and started to make research enquiries.

Then serious ill-health intervened. . . . Later, in another transatlantic call, I gently suggested that, given the lack of progress on the new book, perhaps I should step in and take on the task of collecting the stories. "That," said Mavis, "would be noble of you."

Inspired by the adjective, I set to work.

With the help of friends like Christine Evain in Nantes and William Toye in Toronto, I was able to amass copies of the hidden stories. Despite serious ill health Alberto Manguel was able to write a brilliant introduction that speaks of "the profound, vital sense of revelation that comes from reading Gallant's stories." I put on the cover a photograph by Geoff Hancock that showed Mavis in her prime, smilingly posing in her cardigan in the sunny Tuileries Gardens. Mavis, although pleased, jokingly described herself as looking "like a gym teacher." The book by the gym teacher did extremely well, and was hailed by every reviewer.

Mavis, fighting ill-health, continues to work, slowly, at the series of diaries that I hope to publish, although when we chat by phone she evades my questions about her precise progress. I was pleased to learn from Lisa Allardice in the *Guardian* that in November 2009, Mavis was still able to get out to the famous Paris restaurant, Le Dome. There she is automatically given Picasso's old table.

As for Mavis and me, she will be cross that I have written this account of our relationship down through the years. But she will forgive me. As this excerpt from Christine Evain's interview proves, we know one another very well.

*Mavis Gallant:* Doug came to New York once when I was giving a talk, years ago. And he has a tendency to stand up at a gathering and talk about one. And he found out that I was at a dinner and he muscled his way in — he's very good at that: he just called and said, I heard that you're giving a dinner, and he came along. And I cornered him and said, "I've asked everyone not to give a talk about me, or single me out, or whatever." And he said, "You have *not* asked everyone, you just asked me!" And that was true. *(She laughs).*

In the fine documentary that I quoted earlier she speaks memorably about how she writes:

> The first flash of fiction arrives without words. It consists of a fixed image like a slide, or closer still, a freeze frame, showing characters in a simple situation. Every character comes into being with a name (which I may change), an age, a nationality, a profession, a particular voice and accent, a family background, a personal history, a destination, qualities, secrets, an attitude towards love, ambition, money, religion, and with a private centre of gravity.

The final words of her introduction to her *Selected Stories* also deserve to be remembered: "Stories are not chapters of novels. They should not be read one after another, as if they were meant to follow along. Read one. Shut the book. Read something else. Come back later. Stories can wait."

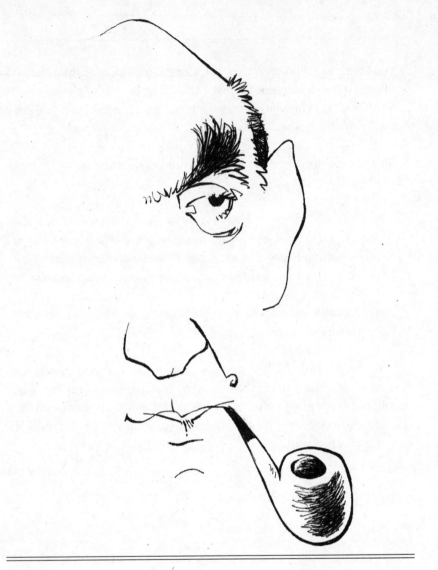

# CHAPTER 14

# PETER C. NEWMAN

## Refugee, Journalist, and Power-Seeking Missile

"That bastard Newman! You can't ever trust him!" It was 1968 and my boss, David Manuel, was furious. The letter in his hand contained bad news. Despite the existence of a signed contract, Peter Newman was cancelling his plans to provide Doubleday with his next book, which was certain to be a bestseller. He was cancelling the contract with regret, and returning, without interest, the money that had been advanced to him some years earlier.

But it wasn't just that. The letter to David — announcing, and feebly explaining, this decision — was a copy, and the envelope contained an original, signed letter from Peter to Jack McClelland, saying, in effect: "This should fool those guys at Doubleday."

David Manuel sent back the correspondence to Peter Newman with a curt note explaining that it seemed to have been intended for someone else. Then we sat back and waited to see how Peter Newman could get out of this situation of almost terminal embarrassment.

No problem. Back from his desk as Ottawa editor of the *Toronto Star* came a cheerfully unrepentant letter that joked about the unpredictability of the mails, glossed over the difficult facts, and went on to spread general good will and best wishes all around.

That day I learned why John Diefenbaker, who had suffered badly in Newman's 1963 book about him, entitled *Renegade in Power*, had called him "the bouncing Czech." Although Dief bore the fine people of Czechoslovakia no general ill will, it was not an affectionate nickname. So I learned very early in my career that there was more to Peter than met the eye. Clearly, this was a man who bore watching. As the years went by I found that watching him was a lot of fun.

Fast forward almost forty years. By now, after I had edited and published Peter's superb autobiography *Here Be Dragons* in 2004, we were friends. I had enjoyed my encounters with him down through the years, since I had seen him clearly from the start. I knew that he was a mischievous fellow, with his own agenda, and not a candidate for sainthood.

But after the predictable success of *Here Be Dragons* (stuffed full, as it was, of amazing stories involving Canada's major figures), I had tried, like a good publisher working to keep his major authors busy on another book, to get Peter going on a new project. He was always flattered, and always keen to get started on something in due course, but a little vague about when that might be, since he was so busy, as always, with newspaper and magazine work. I found it very hard to pin my friend Peter down.

So when Jane and I were invited to join Peter and his wife Alvy for a sail in their boat in Lake Ontario, I was delighted. I looked forward to getting to know Alvy better (since in a earlier conversation I had brushed away her objections that I would have no idea about the Peace River district she came from, and amazed her by establishing that she had been in high school in Fairview with my second cousin Fraser Robertson). And spending a whole summer Saturday in a yacht with Peter — an experienced sailor who has ventured right around Vancouver Island — at the helm, meant that I could find out what his plans were, for sure.

Except that the boat also contained Ray Heard and his wife. I don't know if Ray was actually assigned the task of talking all the time, of if Peter assumed that he would fall naturally into the role, but a tête à tête with Peter proved to be impossible. We had a fine sail, fine food and drink, nobody drowned, and nobody strangled Ray Heard. So I was still making no progress in getting Peter to start a new book, and still unsure about what his next project might be.

Until, that is, the morning of September 12, 2005, when Jane, an early riser, disturbed my morning drowse with the words, "I think you should see this."

*This* was the front page of the *Globe and Mail*, which revealed in a huge headline that Peter C. Newman had just brought out a clandestine book, *The Secret Mulroney Tapes: Unguarded Confessions of a Prime Minister*. These were tapes that Peter had made during the years of Brian Mulroney's time as prime minister. Peter had talked (perhaps the word is "flattered") his way into the role of Boswell to Mulroney's Dr. Johnson, and the two had chatted frankly over hundreds of Ottawa hours as the Prime Minister's life in office unfolded. The eventual publication, Mulroney obviously hoped, would be a team effort that provided him with a great legacy.

Then things went wrong, somehow, between them — it may have been the word "team" — and the project languished. But there were these many hours of tapes. . . .

As I lay there in what had been my restful bed I cast my mind back for any clues that this bomb was about to explode. No new Peter C. Newman book had been listed for that fall season by any Canadian publisher. Random House, it was true, had been offering booksellers an anonymous book for that month by a major author that would, they promised, be hugely controversial. Since Random House was a 25% owner of McClelland & Stewart (cynics might have added more), it was, in effect, a sister publisher and undeniably used the same design and production and sales and marketing teams, so it would have had to go to extraordinary lengths to keep the new book secret. (And that indeed was the case, with the book even being printed outside the country, in the United States, for greater secrecy.) So this news was a total surprise to me.

Then I remembered a lunch, some years earlier, when Peter had mentioned in passing that he had all of these tapes that he had made with Mulroney. I didn't get into the obvious problem that tapes of a conversation belong to both of the parties involved, because I simply told Peter that I was going to be publishing Brian Mulroney's memoirs, so was not interested in any other Mulroney projects, and we moved on to other topics. It occurred to me that morning that this vague thirty-second conversation, in Peter's world view, constituted fair warning.

That morning I was the only person in a world of screaming "Mulroney Betrayed by Newman" news stories to receive a phone call from both Peter C. Newman and Brian Mulroney.

Both calls were instructive.

Peter, who called shortly after 8 a.m., was not a whit apologetic. He was gleeful, like a kid who had just constructed a firework that had gone off with a very big bang. "Hey, Doug, you've seen the papers! I guess you know now why I wasn't rushing to take on a new book, ha ha ha."

For him this was wonderful fun. Such fun that I couldn't stay angry with him, and we parted affectionately, with Peter still chortling, and me shaking my head in disbelief.

The next phone call was from Brian Mulroney. He was well aware, of course, that I was a friend of Peter Newman's, since he had been keenly interested in the sales of *Here Be Dragons* and had regularly asked how his (ironically described) "old friend Peter Newman" was getting along. He knew, too, how likely it was that I would have known about a new big book like Newman's, so hard to keep secret.

Yet his call did not begin with any angry accusations. Instead he said, evenly, "I take it that you knew nothing about this new book by Peter Newman?"

"That's right, Brian. I've just read about it in today's *Globe*, like everyone else. It's a complete surprise to me."

"Okay. So he's betrayed both of us," Mulroney went on, and we proceeded to discuss the implications. Later that day Mulroney's office issued a press release that used words like "devastated" and "betrayed," noting that he considered the published material to be confidential.

I was, and remain, impressed by how Mulroney handled the call to me. A lesser man would have leapt to furious conclusions, and hard words might have been exchanged between us, before things were cleared up.

Thereafter, I stayed carefully on the sidelines as a legal battle was waged between them and their lawyers, with Random House (which did not publish Peter's next book) an unhappy participant. I understand that in the end Peter was able to keep only some of the proceeds from the book, while Toronto's Hospital for Sick Children is now much richer. Brian Mulroney has been quoted as boasting that he "ruined" Peter Newman. Who knows? But we do know that Peter, born in 1929, is still working noticeably hard as a journalist and an author.

On the other hand, Peter always was a hard-working, unstoppable force. His amazing life story is told in *Here Be Dragons*, over 700 lively pages. Some critics claim that the book may indeed be brilliant, but enjoys an extra sheen added by his imagination. Certainly, the sub-title: "Telling Tales of People, Passion, and Power" gives us a number of clues to Peter's astonishing career.

He was born in Moravia, now Czechoslovakia, the only son of a prosperous family that owned the town's sugar beet refinery, the largest in the country. Young Peter led a charmed — if somewhat lonely — life, until Hitler entered the picture. As a prominent secular Jewish family the Newmans were in danger, and as the Nazi net closed around them, they fled. Peter's grandparents were not so lucky, and died in a concentration camp.

Young Peter and his parents left everything behind. In order to travel light (something that was to become a family characteristic) Peter's father exchanged their cash for some supremely valuable postage stamps, worth hundreds of thousands of dollars in today's currency. To avoid attracting official attention they were given to Peter, part of his little stamp collection.

After the train left Prague forever, Peter's father noticed that his son was playing with a fine new cap gun. Asking casually where the stamp collection was, his father learned that Peter had traded it away for the cap gun to "another boy."

"And where is this other boy?"
"He was at the train station in Prague."
"I see."
My father was silent for a long while, as he no doubt pondered the vagaries of life. I don't think he ever forgave me, and I don't blame him.

Eventually, after fourteen months on the run in Europe they made it to Biarritz, on the Atlantic, just north of France's border with Spain. There, in one of the most exciting passages in the book, Peter records the night that he — a young boy of eleven, in short pants — and other refugees lying on the sandy beach were strafed from the air by a Nazi Junkers plane. His father, he reveals, had trouble getting the local French inhabitants to help the wounded, and the Newmans were glad to escape on the last boat to freedom, in this case London.

From London the family set sail for Canada, and in 1940 Peter arrived "a trembling eleven-year-old," in every sense a refugee. "Nothing," Peter wrote in his autobiography, "compares with being a refugee." I would argue that Peter has always remained one, living by his wits, making alliances for the moment, then moving on as a new source of power emerged. "Peter Newman doesn't have friends," so the joke goes, "he has sources." But he has the fixed, aware intelligence of the watchful outsider, the perennial refugee, and we are all better for it.

After a spell in Burlington, Ontario, his ambitious father saw him established at Upper Canada College, the breeding ground of the Canadian establishment, where Canada's shirts are stuffed.

Roy MacSkimming later described Peter's way of writing about the Canadian business establishment (the one that gave the title to one of his most successful books) as "half cheeky, half fawning." If you want to understand that interesting mixture of attitudes towards these leaders, you need look no further, I think, than the little Czech boy of thirteen who spoke little English, was shy and awkward, and not especially good at games, thrown into the macho WASP world of Upper Canada College. No wonder, in a burst of candour, he described himself as "a court jester" to the business world he wrote about, which was full of people he could never quite be like — and, at the deepest level, I suspect, did not want to be like.

Instead, after he went to the University of Toronto, he chose to become a journalist, and a student of Power.

Power. The word runs through his professional life as a writer. "Power is for princes" were the very first words in his first book, *Flame of Power*, which hit the bookstores in 1959. "Power," of course, makes its appearance in the subtitle of *Here Be Dragons* and — almost hilariously — in *Renegade in Power* (1963), *Home Country: People, Places, and Power Politics* (1973), *The Establishment Man: A Portrait of Power* (1982, when that still applied to Conrad Black), *Titans: How the New Canadian Establishment Seized Power* (1998). And for many years the name of Peter's business corporation, where his royalties flowed, included the magic word "Power." He was indeed to become, as my subtitle suggests, not a heat-seeking missile, but a power-seeking one. He would seek out sources of power, find them, and — eventually, when they disappointed him — attack them.

Equally important, the success of his first book hooked him on fame. Endearingly, as a new author he confesses: "I remember carrying my first copy in my briefcase for weeks, taking frequent peeks at it, in case it had somehow disappeared and the whole thing was a dream." Less endearingly, he recalled becoming "a praise addict." His lust for fame and acclaim was such that "from now on, I would sacrifice anything and anyone to the unquenchable fires raging inside me."

Fair warning, again.

And then he left the Toronto world of the *Financial Post* and *Maclean's* to become the latter's Ottawa correspondent. The world of Ottawa's press gallery, and the cozy way it covered politics and politicians, was about to change forever.

I came in touch with that old world in 1976, when I edited the autobiography of its Grand Old Man, Bruce Hutchison. He was indeed a remarkable man, the leading journalist of his day, who had somehow turned himself into a weighty international figure. When this lean woodsman from the West visited London or Washington he was received as the Voice of Canada, with access granted everywhere. His books — notably his study of Canada, *The Unknown Country* — were the age's most successful bestsellers. In Ottawa he was as powerful as the average cabinet minister.

Yet somehow he managed to maintain the image of a simple fellow who was never happier than when he was back home on Vancouver Island, working with an axe on the woodpile at Shawinigan Lake. That certainly was where the great photographer, Yousuf Karsh, chose to photograph him. To get the setting just right, Karsh started to order around Bruce's scruffy, roustabout companion, briskly getting him to hose down those leaves, or stand over there, right now. After the session when Bruce introduced the sawdust-stained helper as Chief Justice J.O. Wilson, Karsh "a gentleman of sensitive manners," could think of nothing to say and drowned his confusion by plunging, fully clothed, into the lake.

Bruce Hutchison was a fine and distinguished writer with millions of words, and millions of impressed readers behind him, when I entered the scene as his editor. And when people wonder aloud about my cocksure confidence in editing established authors like Robertson Davies or Hugh MacLennan, breezily suggesting this change, and cutting that sentence, they tend to ask: "Didn't anyone object to you making all these proposed changes to their polished writing?" And I answer that Bruce Hutchison was one.

I edited *The Far Side of the Street* the way I edited everything, and it was only when Hugh Kane came along and gently suggested that Bruce was a pretty old guy by now, and used to having his writing treated with great respect, that I realized that Bruce must be mad as hell at this young whippersnapper. Hugh handled it very well (as I was to try to do over the years as a publisher whenever authors and editors rubbed each other the wrong way). He suggested that I try to go easy on Bruce's writing — he had, after all, earned the right to be set in his old-fashioned ways, with a career that had started at the *Victoria Daily Times* in 1918. (1918!) Meanwhile, I suspect, he told Bruce that young Gibson was good, if sometimes a little overzealous, and would do a fine job looking after his book.

Certainly Bruce bore me no ill will. In fact, on a visit to Victoria I received The Ultimate Victorian Accolade: a roast-beef dinner with Bruce Hutchison at the Union Club, the ivy-covered building full of "billiard rooms" and other ancient traditions that sits right beside the Empress Hotel, very close to where I entered Canada as an unprepared immigrant. Bruce was the perfect genial host, the glasses glinting from his lean, tanned face as he drawled out stories of the famous characters he had known from Mackenzie King onwards — and, of course, his biography of King, *The Incredible Canadian*, had won the Governor General's Award in 1952.

*The Far Side of the Street* reveals an Ottawa Press Corps that was very different from what we now expect. One story from Bruce's book demonstrates the difference. The day that Lester Pearson entered Parliament as the leader of the Liberal Party was a momentous one. He specifically asked for his old pal Bruce to handle a coast-to-coast TV interview that night, although Bruce was not a TV interviewer. But as a working journalist he would today be expected to be objective.

Bruce's book tells how he cut short a visit to Washington and arrived in the House press gallery when Pearson was making his maiden speech. This was the historically ill-advised speech where Pearson ended by suggesting that, um, it would be nice if the majority Conservatives under Diefenbaker would resign and hand the government over to the Liberals.

In Bruce's words: "The bombshell dropped but exploded only in the jeers and laughter of the government benches. Even the press gallery laughed. Dexter [Grant Dexter, another newspaper colleague] and I were too crushed to laugh, the Prime Minister too delighted . . ."

The pair of "too crushed to laugh" objective newsmen rushed to Pearson's office and proceeded to plan the TV interview. Somehow, Pearson pulled himself together to produce a "cozy chat between two untroubled friends."

There, in Bruce's own words, you have an account of a very different press gallery than what we expect today. That was the chummy scene that Peter Newman entered in 1957. "Storming Ottawa's Barricades" was the title Peter gave in his memoir to this chapter in his life. The epigraph is equally descriptive: "'Journalists are like Germans,' a politician once complained. 'They're either at your feet or at your throat. At the feet to get information, at the throat when writing it up.' This," Peter wrote, "became my standard operating procedure."

In 1963 his *Renegade in Power: The Diefenbaker Years* "set the gold standard for political bestsellers" in Roy MacSkimming's words. This new genre for Canada, "an insider's book, anecdotal and thoroughly savvy," was a runaway success and sold 80,000 copies in hardcover. A new type of bestseller, "the Ottawa political book," had just been established, and Peter had installed himself as the leading political journalist of his time.

But he never belonged with his peers in Bruce Hutchison's old press gallery. "I had always been an outsider in the gallery, with little respect for the rules. . . . Every departing member of the press gallery is traditionally given a souvenir pewter mug with their name and years of service engraved on it. The fact that I was never 'mugged' was proof positive that my peers felt that I had not played by the rules of their game. They were right, and their slight made me proud."

By the time he left Ottawa in 1969 with his two books — the second, *The Distemper of Our Times*, came out in 1969 — setting new records in sales, he had established himself as a man in a class by himself. Even Bruce Hutchison was impressed. Reviewing *Distemper* he wrote of Newman, "He talks in a soft, disarming whisper, with a boyish smile. But once he finds the nearest typewriter his shrill voice, in print, sounds like an electronic bullhorn in a narrow cave. Oddly enough, he never realizes how much he is hurting politicians, who seldom complain, lest they invite a second blast. To him all this is just part of the game and in his strange innocence he wonders why anyone should be distressed."

And then, perceptively, Hutchison refers to Peter the refugee, and adds, "Actually, he is more distressed than his victims because he judges them unworthy of the nation he loves."

Peter's impact on Ottawa was not a solo achievement. He and the former Christina McCall, a young writer he met at *Maclean's*, were an extraordinary team. They became such a power couple (an appropriate Newman term) in Ottawa that on one occasion young Pierre Trudeau was to be found rolling amorously with a lady friend on their carpet, at one of their soirees.

Peter's own amorous life is worth more than a brief mention. He devotes a healthy part of his autobiography to it, noting that thanks to his repressed Upper Canada College days he got off to a very slow start. He claims that the sexual ignorance at the all-boys school was such that "we thought 'oral sex' was talking a good game."

He was to learn the talk so brilliantly that other men watched his success with scores of ladies in bewildered envy, wondering if it was the pipe, or the soulful brown eyes, or the big expressive hands, or the fact that bushy eyebrows are a little-known sexual magnet for certain women.

(I should explain at this point that I cannot comment on Peter's activities from the position of a sexual saint. Like most men, I have not led a monastic life, and between my first marriage to Sally and what I intend to be my last, to Jane, I have had the pleasure of knowing a number of fine ladies, notably a fair Southern Belle from Mississippi. I am grateful to them all. But compared to Peter I am a mere dabbler, a sexual dilettante.)

He had such a slow start, he claims that in his early days (when he was trying his hand, unsuccessfully, at being a wasp) he married his first wife, Pat, as a virginal bridegroom. On their wedding night he was appalled to find her protected — facially — by a mask of Noxzema.

The marriage did not last. Peter had met Christina at *Maclean's*, and when Pat became pregnant, as Peter tells it, they had an understanding that he would stay in the marriage only until the baby was born. What the world saw, however, was a man who chose to announce to his wife that he was leaving her when she was lying in hospital with their first newborn child.

In Peter's words: "I was not prepared for the social censure that followed." Some families never spoke to him again. But Peter's sense was that "I finally felt freed to see what my future would be with Christina, who held out the promise of being my ideal mate."

For many years they were a remarkably successful couple, socially in Ottawa, and in the pages of the magazines where they both wrote. Peter gracefully acknowledges her helpful role in polishing his prose, and recalls that they had a huge joint project in mind: he would handle the country's business establishment, while she dealt with the political one. But after they had moved to Toronto, where Peter became editor-in-chief of the *Toronto Star* in 1969, the joint book idea died. Over time the marriage fell apart. They split up, amiably, Peter says, and he went on to write *The Canadian Establishment* for Jack McClelland, and she went on to write *Grits* for me, as this book's Trudeau chapter describes.

Peter had been lured to the *Star* by its stance favouring Canadian nationalism, but found that like everyone else he was expected to be a courtier at the court of the all-seeing, all-powerful publisher, Beland Honderich. So it only lasted for two years. One of Peter's greatest achievements at the *Star*, however, was to attract the approval of the legendary Duncan Macpherson, the political cartoonist who was a great talent and a physical giant with a genius for making trouble.

One of *my* greatest achievements, as the editor of *Here Be Dragons* was — like any good editor — to enrich the book, in this case with a Duncan Macpherson story of my own. A very cruel person had once shown Duncan how to whip a tablecloth off a fully set table, and after a number of disasters at the Mark Hotel (he was in San Francisco with the luckless Allan Edmonds covering the Republican Convention there, and Edmonds grew used to wearily taking out his wallet to calm outraged restaurant staff) he succeeded in doing it. Flushed with this success — and almost certainly a drink or three — Duncan was pleased to see his friend the Russian ambassador sitting at a well-laden table, complete with wines and steaks, at Barberian's restaurant in Toronto. The ambassador restrained his two body-guards when they reached for their armpits at the approach of this large wild man, who told them to sit there while he showed them something amazing.

*Wheeeep! And crash, rumble, tinkle, splash, and curse.* With their steaks and wines in their laps the bodyguards were now clutching at their armpits in earnest, with the ambassador frantically restraining them, explaining that this was just his friend Duncan being Duncan.

I worked with him on a couple of book jackets — and his signed cartoon for the cover of *The Power & the Tories* hangs in our house — and even provided the running text for one of his annual cartoon collection books. I liked him very much, though other *Star* employees shrank away in horror when I announced that I was off to Duncan's office.

Stories clustered around him. One favourite of mine concerns the time he returned to the *Maclean's* art director's office with a dozen white storyboards the size of giant pizza boxes containing his work from a travel assignment. The art director, greatly daring, suggested an improvement here, a revision there. Duncan's face darkened. Sweeping up all of the giant whiteboards in his arms, he opened the window and threw all the cardboard pieces out. The appalled art director saw the illustrations for next month's issue floating like giant snowflakes down towards the traffic on University Avenue. Emergency rescue teams scurried downstairs, and there was no more talk of revisions.

When Peter left the *Star*, he reports, Duncan wrote a supportive letter that began, "The *Star* is losing the best talent they ever had when you leave." Peter was on his way to reform *Maclean's*, a period in his life that deserves a whole book, not just a part of a chapter.

But for now, let's follow the romantic trail. After Christina there were a number of ladies, notably Joy Carroll. She was an interesting partner for Peter since she was by profession a romantic novelist (and a Ph.D. thesis could usefully explore the link between her style and Peter's famous line that Joe Clark looked "like a deer disturbed eating broccoli.") Much more immediately important was the fact that she was married to a crew-cut writer named Jock Carroll. When she moved in with Peter, he took it badly. For weeks he made a point of returning her clothes and other intimate possessions to her c/o Peter C. Newman, at *Maclean's*. The many cartons, prominently and even libellously labelled to Joy and Peter (and the nouns and adjectives attached to their names were *very* uncomplimentary) crowded the corridors of *Maclean's*, where they were read, avidly, by Peter's staff. A lesser man might even have been embarrassed.

After the affair with Joy ended, Peter (now rising at 4 a.m. to write his latest book) would take likely ladies out to dinner and then, around dessert, say, "Look, I have to be in bed by 9:30, with you or without you." He reports that this line was surprisingly effective.

He doesn't, however, report that his early rising led to a bizarre form of competition with his neighbour, Abe Rotstein, who was also writing a book in the early hours. Their pride in being the first to light a lamp at their desk produced an unhealthy competition that led, it is claimed, to one competitor getting up, lighting the desk light in triumph, then sneaking back to bed.

Wife Number Three was Camilla Turner, another Maclean-Hunter editor and a notable fair-haired beauty, a number of years younger than Peter. They were married in 1975 with three best men standing up for Peter: Senator Keith Davey, Jack McClelland, and a young Montrealer named Brian Mulroney. And there is an example of what I call the power-seeking missile aspect of Peter's character. He had a nose for it. In 1975 very few national political reporters had paid much attention to the young Montreal lawyer. Peter sensed (I assume it is a sixth sense) the Power possibilities in him.

In the same way, scores of young journalists from John Fraser through Ken Whyte have been charmed to find that in their early years the mighty Peter C. Newman was taking the time to sit down with them and talk about their life, dispensing advice, and remaining available for further contact. This is an agreeable counter to the side of Peter that kept a black book listing people who had ever criticized him or his books in print. But it may simply be based on the demographic fact that young journalists grow up to be middle-aged journalists, some of them powerful middle-aged journalists. Peter was very good at spotting those who were headed for power. (As I write these words, the uncomfortable thought strikes me that my own constant contact with Peter over the years may owe something to Peter's power instincts in my own case; even more evidence, dammit, that assigning a simple role to Peter is never easy.)

Camilla and Peter lived a hectic life in Toronto (he records that a ten-second delay at the Maclean-Hunter elevator could throw off their schedule for the day, which explains why, when he and I were working together on a joint Macmillan-*Maclean's* publishing project, the alternate meetings at each others' office never quite worked; amused by the process, I would travel to his office, every time.)

Then Camilla followed him in retirement to the West Coast, where I visited them for dinner at their place in Cordova Bay, a visit notable for the acres of subterranean files Peter had amassed there to impress visiting publishers, and for my spotting an interesting painting that looked like a Klimt, and was.

They seemed very happy there, and Peter was able to indulge his passion for sailing. I once visited him aboard his navy blue yacht in Vancouver's Coal Harbour and he showed me how he had set up a writing room there, complete with mahogany trim. I was jealous, and sorry to have to get back to Toronto.

But the marriage to Camilla didn't last, and other ladies came into play, exhaustively listed in his memoirs in a way that leaves the reader admiring his memory. One of these named lovers was Barbara MacDougall, the distinguished Conservative Cabinet minister. Her brother-in-law, Michael Enright, was a former (very disillusioned) colleague of Peter's for many years at *Maclean's*. When someone suggested to the raging Michael that "Peter Newman is his own worst enemy," he replied, grandly: *"Not while I'm alive!"*

To complete his romantic circle, in 1993 Peter met "the woman of [his] dreams." Alvy Joan Bjorklund from Peace River country (where I've canoed down the mighty Peace) was less obviously smitten — "as we said goodbye, she devastated me with a firm handshake and an equally firm 'Goodnight, sir.'"

But they got beyond that — she was lovely, friendly, and straightforward — and they married. He was sixty-six and she was forty-two. She has since spent many years pursuing a doctorate in Europe, so in their married life they have moved more than ten times. She was not deterred, before marrying Peter, by overhearing one disapproving matron say of him, "He's had three wives and God knows what else." Readers of his memoirs, which seem almost boastful as they list names, will have a good idea of "what else."

As for his career as an author, a shrewd stock market investor would be well advised to study Peter Newman. When it comes to seeing new career opportunities in the book world the man is a genius, seemingly gifted with second sight, or the power of prophecy. He was gifted at spotting prosperous wagons where he might hitch a ride and at cutting ties with wagons (perhaps named Ignatieff) that were going off the road.

Having established himself as the best political writer in the

country, he put the helm hard over and sailed into the almost
uncharted waters of Canadian business at the highest level with *The
Canadian Establishment* in 1975. It was a huge success, eventually
selling 250,000 copies and spawning several other business books
from him in the same style. Along the way M&S handled an injunc-
tion from Paul Desmarais of Power Corporation (there's that word
again) by undertaking to sticker a requested correction over the
offending passage *in the warehouse*; M&S staff stuck 75,000 corrections in one weekend, and a legend was born.

The last of these spinoffs was Peter's admiring look at Conrad
Black, *The Establishment Man*. Yet when Conrad came to grief, falling
afoul of the U.S. legal system and spending years in a Florida jail, it
was Peter (travelling light, as always) who wrote some of the most
savage accounts of his fall, both in magazines and in *Here Be Dragons*.
Although, to be fair, it is possible that Conrad and his wife Barbara
Amiel were more exercised about the book's paragraph that tells the
world about Barbara, between marriages in London, accepting a
dinner date invitation from Algy Cluff, the chairman of the *Spectator*,
with the warning: "There's one thing I have to tell you. I won't be
wearing any knickers."

This seems an appropriate point to pay tribute to Peter C.
Newman the writer. His research is astonishing, he knows what will
interest people (you have to admit it), and he wrote it up entertain-
ingly, tossing conventional prose expectations on a virgin-sacrificing
fire (as you see). He is a great believer in the "Hey, Mabel!" school
of book writing, where you try to include lots of stories so good that
readers will read them out excitedly to their spouses or companions.
It's a good model for any writer to emulate.

Having milked the business world dry with half a dozen bestsellers (which almost on their own had kept M&S afloat), Peter
decided to enter the world of Canadian history writing previously
owned by Pierre Berton.

A brief word about Berton who, in Peter's words, "had enough
energy to light a city." Unlike Peter he was a fine, lively speaker, and
his promotional tours were not the difficult process that Peter the
refugee gamely but awkwardly undertook, leaving Canadian Club
audiences glad to see him, even in a fur hat, but underwhelmed by

his speech. By contrast Pierre was a big, booming force of nature, who had been used to practically dictating how his own books were to be published at M&S. I inherited him, and recall a meeting in the boardroom where Pierre, a large presence, sat with his agent/manager Elsa Franklin, to discuss his new book, *Niagara*.

Had I read it? Yes. And I had only one suggestion from that first reading. "It would be good, Pierre, somewhere on that first page, to remind readers just how big the Falls are, and how much water goes over every second."

Pierre sat straight in his chair and trumpeted in that well-known voice: "I will not alter the artistic integrity of my work for mere commercial purposes."

This was terrible. Pierre Berton was offended to the depths of his artistic soul. What should I do?

I burst out laughing and said, "Come on, Pierre, you do it all the time!"

And he, to his eternal credit, burst out laughing, too. Later he signed his copy of *Niagara* to me, with a flourish: "To Doug, who saw it through."

Jack McClelland would have been delighted to see through Peter's new historical project, a history of the Hudson's Bay Company. (After a spell at Thunder Bay's Sleeping Giant Literary Festival held inside the magnificently re-created Fort William, I'm sorry that the Northwest Company lost the fur trade battle, but the HBC history was still a wonderful project.) But M&S was not exactly flush with cash, and Peter's agent (and mine), the incomparable Michael Levine, saw an astonishing prospect here. In effect he took Peter away from his old pal Jack and, in Roy MacSkimming's words, "negotiated a half-million-dollar package deal with Peter Mayer, international CEO of Penguin who was building a hardcover program in Canada. The advance was the largest for any Canadian author to that point. Newman's departure started a trend that would see many of the country's top authors, and many emerging authors as well, migrate from Canadian-owned publishers to the multinationals." That has been the main trend in Canadian publishing in the last twenty years, and the power-seeking missile, always ahead of the trend, was the author who started it.

I have skipped lightly over Peter's years as the editor at *Maclean's* from 1971 to 1982. Peter once described it as an important mission to save a vital Canadian institution (his chapter on these years is modestly entitled "Captain Canada to the Rescue"). On another occasion he wrote caustically, "My job description was to save *Maclean's*, not to be the indulgent daddy of the dysfunctional family that edited it."

"Newman stories" (and he boasts about being "the most cussed and discussed" journalist of his era) abound from those days when the magazine was wrenched from being a monthly general interest magazine into a weekly news magazine. And opinion is sharply divided. Scores of the most talented writers in the country were attracted to the Great Experiment. Some failed and some thrived. Among those who thrived was Ann Dowsett Johnston, who remembers that Peter's habit of posting weekly public memos pointing out pieces from the last edition that he liked was "inspiring and effective." To others it was like grade school, and a formal production system for teacher's pets.

Rona Maynard is one deeply critical voice. In her memoir *My Mother's Daughter* (which I published, having published her mother, Fredelle Bruser Maynard, before her) she writes about her days at *Maclean's*: "What I hadn't bargained on was the toxic emotional climate — equal parts awe, suspicion and resentment — that Newman inspired in the entire office. He slunk in and out on his way to interviews with titans, a tall, hunched figure whose thick black eyebrows gave him an air of impenetrable world-weariness." Later she calls him "a famously reluctant personnel manager" whom she was glad to leave in her past. Later, of course, Rona was able to apply the lessons she had learned when she became the popular and successful editor of *Chatelaine*.

Still, the stories go on about the *Maclean's* hothouse in those days, and the exotic plant at the centre. There are hundreds of such stories, worth an entire book.

I was delighted when our long acquaintanceship led to a full author-editor relationship. Ironically it came about in sad circumstances, where I had played the role of the villain. As president of McClelland & Stewart I had felt obliged to cut our ties with the boutique non-fiction publishing house of (John) Macfarlane, (Jan) Walter, and (Gary) Ross. When, given the tough Canadian book market, nobody proved to be interested in buying the house, for all its merits, I closed it down. Naturally, we honoured all of their existing contracts, making sure that fine books like Roy MacSkimming's *The Perilous Trade* (no comments please) were properly published.

Among the Macfarlane Walter & Ross, authors that we inherited in this way was Peter C. Newman, and he and I gravitated together, with me becoming his editor. I enjoyed working with him — although his deadlines continued to expand and he went on writing "like it was 1975!" — a time when publishing, ironically, did not require modern long lead times.

And there was one memorable moment when I met him for dinner in the main dining room at the Royal York Hotel. Now this, historians will recall, was close to the epicentre of the Great Toronto Fire of 1904. This time, Peter came in wearing his distinctive Greek fisherman's hat (hey, maybe *that's* what women like) and I was relieved when he finally took it off, and put it on the table near the festive candle that lit the table.

Some minutes later there was a terrible smell and Peter grabbed the cap, now singed and almost smoldering. What with one thing and another, it was a fairly oily item, very combustible, and the thought flashed across my mind that like Chicago and Mrs. O'Leary's cow, downtown Toronto had almost been swallowed up in flames thanks to a fire started by Peter's damned Greek fisherman's cap. Flame of Power, indeed.

# CHAPTER 15

# BRIAN MULRONEY

Boy from Baie Comeau, Prime Minister, and Author

My first contact with a Conservative prime minister came the day I sat on Olive Diefenbaker's hat. This was in a Royal York Hotel suite, of the type I got to know much later when I was the president of the Toronto St. Andrew's Society, and we held the traditional St. Andrew's Ball for 700 tartan-clad people at the hotel. The grateful hotel people granted a free hospitality suite to the lucky president, so that between bouts of whooping and whirling to the pipes of the 48th Highlanders in the ballroom below, the prez and his/her pals and official guests could relax over fortifying drinks.

There were no fortifying drinks in evidence the day that David Manuel and I were ushered into the presence of Mr. Diefenbaker and his wife. They were visiting Toronto on that 1968 day for political reasons, since the recently deposed Tory leader was still a very active member of Parliament, and a crowd-pleasing draw. But that day he had other things in mind. He was enjoying being courted for his memoirs by every Toronto-based book publisher.

At Doubleday Canada my boss David Manuel had learned of this particular visit, and had arranged a pilgrimage to his suite on very short notice. I, a beardless boy, was pressed into service ("You've got a tie? Good.") to form a sort of mini-entourage, to make our desire to publish the Grand Old Man even more obvious, and (like a hired mourner) even more solemnly impressive. That was my role.

Unfortunately I was so over-awed that when the former prime minister answered the door, shook our hands, ushered us into the suite, and, in that familiar high yet rumbling voice, invited us to have a seat, I sat down on Olive's hat. It was a little straw number, as I recall, heavily lacquered, and very fragile, resting there unnoticed on the low couch.

As I sat, *at the very first crackle*, a sort of miracle occurred, a hat-avoiding piece of levitation, a Canadian equivalent of the Indian rope trick. Somehow, as I started to squash the hat, my thigh muscles sprang into action, and I shot upwards again, leaving the precious hat badly crushed, but not totally destroyed.

What happened was physically impossible, and my thighs were sore for days, but it happened. (I now believe every story I read of wispy 100-pound mothers lifting two-ton trucks off their children in an emergency. This, too, was an emergency.) And Olive was very nice about it, as she rescued the hat and dusted it off, insisting that there was no real damage done.

We did not, however, succeed in persuading Mr. Diefenbaker that Doubleday Canada was the company to which he should entrust his memoirs.

That honour went to Macmillan of Canada, so when I moved there in 1974 our paths crossed again. Not that I had any direct contact with the man who was always "Mr. Diefenbaker" to us (even behind his back, although he also liked "Chief"), as we published his three sets of memoirs. Two stories from those days. First, on one of the occasions when he "lost" the proofs of the urgently needed book — as happened with all three volumes — Hugh Kane flew to Ottawa and visited him in his office, which was dominated by a huge, historic, glass-topped desk. When in Hugh's presence the proofs were "found" again, everyone was delighted, and the Chief basked in the general congratulations. The atmosphere was so relaxed and congenial, in fact, that Hugh felt able to perch happily on the edge of the great desk.

There was a loud crack, and like the Lady of Shallot's mirror, the glass top "cracked from side to side."

Fortunately, by this stage in his career the former prime minister was somewhat deaf, and there were papers on the desk concealing the extent of the damage. So, although he was a man of some courage who had fought with the artillery during the war, Hugh chose to look theatrically at his watch ("My goodness, is that the time?") and apologize for having to dash away to catch a plane back to Toronto.

Later, when Mr. Diefenbaker was promoting his just-published book, a Macmillan colleague named Shirley Knight Morris was in charge of escorting him by limousine from TV station to radio show to newspaper interview. It was so hectic that in the limo taking him to an afternoon signing session at Simpsons department store, the kind-hearted Shirley looked in alarm at her aged fellow passenger, grey-faced, hunched, and slumped in such utter exhaustion that she seriously thought of redirecting the limo to the nearest Emergency Department.

But as the car stopped outside the Yonge Street store, a crowd formed on the sidewalk, and a remarkable transformation occurred. In the back seat Mr. Diefenbaker reacted to the sight and sound of the crowd like an old warhorse scenting battle and hearing the exciting sound of bugles again. Before Shirley's astonished eyes he seemed to inflate, his puffed-up cheeks regaining their colour, his nostrils flaring, and his spine stiffening. In ten seconds he lost about twenty years, as he bounded out of the car to shake hands and meet "his people" — and to sell hundreds of books to fans who were delighted by his vitality.

I found the same vitality, at all times, when I worked with Brian Mulroney. Unlike Mr. Diefenbaker (who relied on the hidden pen of an unfrocked academic — a man I found supremely unlikeable — named John Munro) Brian Mulroney wrote his *Memoirs* himself. Every word. In longhand.

That had not always been the plan, after Avie Bennett used his excellent contacts with people like Mulroney's old pal from St. Francis Xavier, Sam Wakim, to entice Mulroney to sign up with M&S to publish his memoirs. At the outset, there had been some thought of having a writer work with him, and I had secretly approached one or two likely candidates. But in the end Brian — as he soon became — decided to do it himself, with the aid of a hard-working researcher based in Kingston named Arthur Milnes.

I know that Arthur — a sturdy, down-to-earth fellow who has always been fascinated by political history — now spends a fair portion of his life explaining that, no, he did not write Brian Mulroney's *Memoirs*. In fact, his role was clear. He was the researcher who went on ahead of the author, producing research notebooks that reminded Brian what he had been doing, week by week in, for example, 1986. Armed with these reminders — and often with the results of specific follow-up research requests — Mulroney sat down and wrote his memoirs.

This hands-on approach is so unusual in the world of political memoirs that as the book's editor and publisher I decided to emphasize the fact that Brian Mulroney really had written it himself. That's why the hardcover edition has endpapers, right beside the book jacket, that show, clearly and legibly, pages from his hand-written manuscript.

The front cover of the book is predictable — a full-face, full-colour, smiling photograph of Brian Mulroney in his prime ministerial prime. It's instantly recognizable, it's a good photograph of a beaming, good-looking man, with even the slightly undersized mouth (about which the cartoonist Aislin was so fundamentally rude) showing a fine set of white teeth. And the author liked it. That's the way that ninety-nine percent of publishers around the world would have "packaged" the book.

Yet, on reflection, I think it was a mistake. A mistake, because it showed the side of Brian Mulroney that many people love to hate. The super-confident — even cocky — guy who's got it made, the guy who loves the limelight, loves the prime minister's role that leaves him waving to the crowds like a star on a red carpet somewhere.

Only a national psychologist could explain this fully, but I believe that one of the reasons why so many Canadians came to dislike Brian Mulroney, viscerally, in his role as prime minister is that he *enjoyed* it too much. This star "presidential" role — and you can think of Brian Mulroney beaming alongside Ronald Reagan onstage in Quebec City, their Irish eyes-a-smiling — played very badly in a country that liked the idea of Marion Pearson mending the curtains at 24 Sussex Drive. We want our prime ministers (unless they're named Trudeau) to reflect the great cares of office, and to do so with humility.

By contrast, Mulroney was the guy who beamed his way through events, loved leaping out of limos in his Gucci shoes (and you remember how controversial his Gucci shoes were?) and was delighted and proud to be where he was, a Hollywood prime minister. I fear that the cover we chose played to that unpopular image and prompted the emotional response: "Oh yeah, Mulroney — I never liked that guy."

On reflection (and I did suggest this at the time, knowing that it was a long shot) I think that on his *Memoirs* we should have run a cover showing Brian Mulroney as a little boy — shy, squinting at the Brownie camera — back in Baie Comeau.

I first met Brian — and he was always Brian, just as Diefenbaker was always Mr. Diefenbaker — in Montreal. I was in the city and had arranged to meet him in his office at Ogilvy Renault, in a glass and steel skyscraper on McGill-College Avenue in the heart of downtown. And what, you may wonder, is a celebrity lawyer's office like, once you penetrate the reception area, then the corridors with lines of filing cabinets and doors leading to conventional lawyers' offices, with English and French both floating in the air, and are ushered in by Francine, his assistant? Why, a comfortably furnished room with a couch and the sort of informal yet expensive furniture that you'd find in the living room of a well-to-do family's modern cottage. There are even framed, signed photographs from old friends like Teddy Kennedy, and what with the comfy couch and the armchair, it's more like a relaxed living room or den than an office — even if Francine is only a few steps away.

That was where we first met, and where I had my first fun with him. At the time, Brian's hated nemesis, Jean Chrétien, was going through very hard times in Ottawa, his leadership threatened by the Martin forces baying at his heels. Putting on a concerned expression, I suggested to Brian that it was terrible what was being done to poor Mr. Chrétien, implying that as a former PM and party leader, he must be sympathetic to Mr. Chrétien's plight.

He gaped at me. Then, seeing the grin break out on my face, he started to relax, laughing and saying in, almost, these words: "That son of a gun, it couldn't happen to a better guy" — and we were off to a good start. And we were to remain on good terms, with only one major fight ahead of us.

He is such a controversial figure that dozens of people have asked me: "What was it like, working on his book with Brian Mulroney?"

There is often an unspoken hostility behind the question, so my reply often surprises people. *"I enjoyed working with him, and I like him."*

Let me explain first how we worked on the book. He would write it, chapter by chapter, in chronological order, and Francine would send the neatly-typed chapters to me, usually in hard copy. If it came electronically, I would print out the pages (there was no electronic "track changes" wizardry on either side of this author-editor relationship) and then I would edit them, making changes, shifting paragraphs, and so on, as seemed appropriate. Then I would hand these edited (and thus very messy) pages over to my trusty editorial assistant, Aruna Dahanayake, at M&S, and he would produce *a clean copy*. I felt that, psychologically, this was very important. That was what went back to Brian, along with an explanation of the changes I'd made, if they were not obvious. He would see that version, and both there and later, when they checked the proofs, he and the tireless fact-checker Arthur would have a chance to amend the text to their satisfaction. As always, the author — the man with his name on the cover — had the privilege of having the final word.

And this process went *really* smoothly. I have a lot of time for an author who will carefully handwrite his book at great length, working hard at every stage to get things right, yet take the advice of the expert, which in this case was me, on the line-by-line writing.

Two stories about the process. First, the book contains no fewer than forty pages of photographs of his life, from old family photos from Baie Comeau, through campaign shots (and Robert Bourassa, no novice at the game, once said admiringly, *"Brian, c'est un maudit bon campaigner,"* a damn good campaigner), through posed shots involving other leaders like Thatcher and Reagan and Kohl and Clinton and Mandela, all the way to the last shot of him and Mila leaving Rideau Hall, hand in hand, on their way to private life. To select, and lay out in order, and label with proper captions, such a wide range of photographs requires a lot of space, and the Gibson dining room table was pressed into service. After some weeks, this was causing domestic pressure — hell, we had abandoned our summer holiday plans, in order to get the book through — so I asked Brian to get me the last missing photos as soon as possible, on the grounds that "Jane wants her table back."

"Tell her I'll buy her a new table," he joked, and when he met her for the first time at the Toronto launch of the book he was able to tell her instantly, "The new table's on its way!" Politicians are good at that sort of instant connection; he was great at it.

Secondly, his passion for accuracy (and for trying, dammit, to mention all of his friends in the acknowledgements) meant that he was making changes to the book right up until the last minute. I told him that Thursday was absolutely the last drop-dead day for making changes, since the final version was going off to the printer on Friday.

On Friday Arthur Milnes was on the phone, asking me to make one more change. "Absolutely not!" I said. "It's too late. Brian knows that."

"Yes," said Arthur, clearly not relishing his role as middleman. "I told the Boss that, and said that you'd refuse to make the change. And he said" (and here, dear reader, you can hear the deepening Mulroney voice), "'Tell Doug that I know that he's the finest editor in the country, and I *know* that he would never let a book go to press that contained a mistake that he had a chance to fix.'"

It was shameless. And it worked.

I swore, then *ran* through to the typesetting department, where we were able to insert the change before the text went off to the printer by courier, ten minutes later.

As you can see, I found that he was a genius at what you might call, in my case, man-management (and note the role he got Arthur to play here, too). In his political life, the success he had in keeping together the fractious Tory caucus, made up of perennial outsiders with high malcontent potential, even while the party was sliding in the polls, was astonishing — and unbelievable to all those who had never been exposed to the Mulroney charm. He was tireless in reaching out by phone to potential allies, day or night. I gather that even opposition MPs found that when tragedy — a son's car accident, a spouse's cancer, a parent's heart attack — struck their family, one of the very first phone calls offering sympathy, or help, even the name of a doctor, came from Brian Mulroney. Of course it was good politics; but maybe it was something more, some unspoken recognition that we're all in this thing together.

The journalist L. Ian MacDonald was a close friend who worked over the years with Brian. In the *National Post* he summed up this quality: "With Brian Mulroney it is *always* personal." He went on to tell the story of a friend who had just split up with his wife and was staying with his infant daughter in a hotel. The PMO switchboard tracked him down to allow Brian to try to console him.

The conversation went on for about half an hour, the friend later recounted. "You have more important things to do than this," the friend finally told him, "You have a country to run."

"Nothing is more important than this," Mulroney replied.

This attitude also meant that if you became his enemy, it was going to be a long, bitter business. "His time will come" was one of the phrases colleagues remember him using, nursing his wrath to keep it warm. And both his book and his private conversations were full of references to the enmity of the media. At one point he writes (cleverly using a member of the media to make his point): "It is hard to operate, year after year, in what columnist George Bain described as an atmosphere of unremitting antipathy, cynicism and disrespect. In my experience, things became so bad that I felt the press was not just filtering our message (an appropriate function) but actually blocking it." His private references to the CBC and the Toronto media were much less printable.

But if you were his friend, then everything was possible — and, famously, his administration suffered from old friends who took advantage of his instinct to help out an old buddy, the way you would in Baie Comeau.

In 2009, the CBC radio political program *The House* was interested to hear that I was starting to write this book, and wanted to interview me about it. It was a kindly interview and when the admirable Kathleen Petty broached the subject of Brian Mulroney's 1,100-page *Memoirs*, she threw me a softball lob by asking me how much larger this book would have been if I had not been there to edit it.

My reply surprised her. I explained that if anyone found the book too long, I was the one to blame. For as the early chapters about his life in Baie Comeau emerged and proved to be quite lengthy, he and I had a meeting in that Montreal law office/cottage living room.

He asked me: "Look, I've written a lot about growing up in Baie Comeau. Should we cut all that out, or cut it way back? Are people really going to be interested in that stuff?"

"Yes, they are," I answered decisively. "In fact, it's so interesting I wouldn't cut it back at all. It explains who you are and — in the fullest sense — where you come from. So keep it. And keep going at the pace you've established. And if that means that we end up with a long book, that's fine — we end up with a long book about a long career."

So, blame me for the fact that the book is so long. Conversely, blame me for the fact that after 1,100 pages the book ends when

Brian Mulroney leaves office, in 1993. The book had to end some-where, and that seemed to me a sensible end point, although I had a further reason for ending the book there, as I will reveal.

In this chapter's subtitle I call Brian the "Boy from Baie Comeau." I believe that the phrase helps to sum him up, and to tell us a lot about his complex personality. If Abraham Lincoln was "the Log-Cabin president," Brian Mulroney was the blue collar kid who made it all the way to the top. Before the book came out, few people knew that he grew up in a house so poor that for a spell he and his brother had to sleep in the basement beside the oil burner, to make space for a paying boarder. Think of that!

And think of the fact that his father, who worked at two jobs, would sit, exhausted, at the end of a long summer day, worrying about the family finances — which young Brian was boosting with his summer job. His father would say hopefully, "We're almost over the hump," and on the way, he implied, to the Promised Land of Financial Security. Financial security, at last.

When his father died after a long illness at home ("In the evening I would take him in my arms like a child — he was losing weight very quickly — and carry him downstairs") Brian stepped in, as a very young Montreal lawyer just starting out, to look after his mother and to see his younger siblings through their education. He had prom-ised his father that he would, although money was really tight.

In his biography, *Mulroney: The Politics of Ambition*, John Sawatsky has suggested that we should see Brian Mulroney as essentially a French-Canadian with an Irish name. It's an interesting thesis, and there's certainly no doubt that his bilingual background left him totally at ease with Quebecois friends, joyfully at home with them.

My own suggestion is that, even more important, Baie Comeau left him with a deeply engrained concern about money, and a sense of being an outsider, on the periphery. His memoirs record what a major expedition it was to drive the "fourteen-hour odyssey" to Quebec City, an ordeal for his father and the family car. The North Shore roads are better now, but even halfway, as you cross the Saguenay by ferry, you are very conscious of the hours of rough country that lie between you and the city lights.

So perhaps he was always the kid from the poor little mill town far away, who, like the hero in some novel by Balzac, was determined to make the city sit up and notice him. A story from his early days in Montreal, when he was starting to spread his wings, seems to back up that idea. In the 1970s Bob Lewis (later to become the respected editor of *Maclean's*) was a young, Ottawa-based journalist. He had lunch with an up-and-coming Montreal lawyer-businessman named Brian Mulroney, and in the course of the conversation asked Brian where he was living now.

"You know the mountain in Westmount?" he replied. "Right at the fucking top!"

Bob saw the reply as significant, and remembered it. Balzac certainly would have approved of it.

In those days Brian was a drinker, and not always a good one. Which leads me to another quality that I liked immensely as I worked with Brian. He had the guts to be honest. How many other Canadian politicians' memoirs would contain a whole section — three and a half pages long — that begins with the words "It is time to talk about my drinking"?

After an account of his drinking history, he tells of falling ill on a visit to Romania, and being flown home. "As I slowly recovered, I had some welcome free time to reflect on my life. That was when I realized that I would have to come to grips with the fact that I had developed what could only be described as a serious drinking problem."

So, he explains, on June 24, 1980, "I quit drinking." Cold turkey. He has never had another drop. He knows that he can't handle it; and he goes on to hope that "this account will help others to combat this tough disease." One of the most moving moments in the book is when a prominent journalist, caught up in the same personal struggle, sends him a note in 1990 from that anonymous community, saying ". . . you continue to be an inspiration to all who fight the battle day by day. God bless you — we're all rooting for you."

It's important to recognize just how far the kid from Baie Comeau went. Somehow the money was found to send him to university, then he became a lawyer, and then a very successful businessman (running the Iron Ore Company of Canada), who was fascinated by the world of politics. Against all the odds, this young guy from Quebec — a Conservative from Quebec! — who had never held elected office outside his St. Francis Xavier University model parliament days, rose to become the leader of the eternally fractious Tory party.

Let me tell you a story that shows just how bitterly divided the Tories were, a story that involves the Royal York Hotel, John Diefenbaker, and Flora Macdonald. In 2009 Flora, by then a distinguished former cabinet minister under Mulroney, was the guest of honour at the St. Andrew's Ball, and I spent time with her in the hospitality suite haunted by Olive Diefenbaker's hat, and then got to whirl her around the floor in "The Gay Gordons." She is an inspiring example to us all with her work — in her eighties! — in Afghanistan, sleeping in her sleeping bag on rough floors, among rough people. Not as rough on her, however, as her old enemy within the Tory party, John Diefenbaker. Once, when she was running for the party in the constituency of Kingston and the Islands, he publicly "endorsed" her by stating that she was "one of the finest women ever to walk the streets of Kingston." Ho. Ho. And remember, she was running *for his party*. Cynics say that in those days Conservatives tended to be all in favour of circling the wagons because it brought their targets much closer.

That was the sort of party that Brian Mulroney inherited in 1983, having contributed his portion of bitterness by ousting Joe Clark. Yet, with the help of the ever-gracious Joe, who buried a number of hatchets in his own hair, he managed to turn it into a winning electoral machine; he ran the most successful election campaign in Canadian history, winning 211 seats and taking office in September 1984.

Now that Mulroney's historical reputation has taken a hit, it's important to remember that millions of Canadians voted for this man, and voted for him again in 1988, in "the Free Trade election." By the time he stepped down in 1993, he had been one of Canada's longest-serving prime ministers. His time in office had seen major events at home — Free Trade, the introduction of the GST, the failed Meech Lake and Charlottetown agreements (and the book has a very full appendix, giving a blow-by-blow account of the Meech Lake negotiations, still a source of disappointment to him). And "disappointment" does not begin describe his disgust at the betrayal of his old friend Lucien Bouchard, who abandoned him to create the Bloc Quebecois. It is no accident that the book's photos include a shot of Bouchard's wedding reception . . . held at the home of his old friend Brian, at 24 Sussex Drive.

Outside Canada, he had to steer us through major world events such as Tiananmen Square, and the fall of the Berlin Wall, and he played a role in bringing down the Apartheid regime in South Africa, to the fury of Margaret Thatcher. He even successfully pressured his old friend Ronald Reagan to do something about acid rain.

But for many observers his greatest achievement was his leadership of the Tory caucus, which supported him through thick and thin. After the GST was brought in and the economy also hit trouble, the record-low ratings of public approval of both leader and party made for very thin times indeed, later demonstrated by the Conservative MPS being cut to two — *two* — in the next election. But the caucus stuck with him to the end. He seems to have been a genius at keeping them onside, taking caucus meetings very seriously, involving the caucus in election planning, keeping them busy and out of mischief (although he never uses these words). Then there were the invitations for a chat at Sussex Drive, and the phone calls when they hit personal difficulties. I know that in his phone calls with me he was always amazed by Jean Chrétien's difficulty in keeping the support of his caucus, and it brought him much pleasure.

I found that in our conversations he was always glad to chat about mutual friends like the unforgettable John C. Crosbie, but what was really interesting was to hear him dissect current politics and politicians. His instincts were uncanny ("Here's what Ignatieff should do . . .") and his information superb, so that he was usually a step ahead of the newspapers. When, in the midst of his judicial difficulties, Stephen Harper cut him off — in effect forbidding his MPS to contact Mulroney in any way — it seemed clear that Harper was the loser, since Mulroney's advice, especially on Quebec, was invaluable. It is striking how Harper's reputation for sensitivity to Quebec has since taken a nosedive.

Physically, Mulroney's features are well known, thanks to grateful cartoonists across the land, and the big Irish chin is just as prominent as the photos show, as is the shillelagh-dented forehead. By the time I got to know him well he had survived his near-death experience in the spring of 2005. It is not widely known, but he was so ill from pancreatitis, following lung surgery, that the hospital in Montreal at one point summoned the family to say goodbye to him. But he fought back, from an illness so serious that I remember an M&S board meeting where Dr. John Evans (an expert medical man, as well as his many other skills) frowningly explained to us that this man, in whom our hopes were invested, had a very, very serious disease, from which his recovery would be slow.

When he came back, I noticed that he moved slowly, with a sort of dignified decision. That may not have been just as a result of his illness; even when he was younger, he was not known for a loose, athletic gait, and his arms were usually held a little stiffly at his side.

The *Globe and Mail*'s Michael Valpy cherishes a story about those arms. Valpy was an old Africa hand when he covered Mulroney's trip to Zimbabwe in 1987. There, his host Robert Mugabe revealed a hilarious culture clash. In Africa it is common for two men to walk holding hands as a gesture of friendship. The Canadian Press corps was delighted to see how uneasy Mulroney, as a regular Canadian guy, was with this hand-holding by Mugabe — and this was long before the dictator became such a pariah that no sensible statesman would want to hold his hand. Valpy and the others watched with glee as Brian started to take evasive action, putting his hands behind his back, like the Duke of Edinburgh. When Mugabe was not deterred, reaching behind his back to fish out his nearest hand, Brian would twist his joined hands even further away, until he was barely able to walk a straight line. It was a fine, comical Quasimodo moment, not mentioned in the *Memoirs*, for some reason.

I never really got to know Mila, apart from a warm welcome to the house in Montreal (at the top of the, you remember, mountain) when I was invited for a working breakfast with Brian, served by the nice gentleman who later drove me downtown. I remember another equally warm welcome when the household was full of clothes, spread out on the stairs, ready to be packed for Florida, where they spend a lot of time in the winter. But after the book's launch party at the Royal Ontario Museum, there was a small private dinner, given by Peter Munk in a room high in the museum, where all of the family and a few close friends were invited. I enjoyed meeting the tight-knit family, but took the chance to draw Mila aside, to thank her for her decision, when she read the book's proofs, not to ask her husband to cut out the revealing pages about his drinking, as other wives might have done.

Mila just smiled, wisely. In the book her husband pays tribute to her wisdom, and his good fortune in having her in his life. When L. Ian MacDonald asked him what he regarded as his most significant achievement in life, his unhesitating reply was "Having a good marriage." This is a theme to be explored later, when I deal with Karlheinz Schreiber.

As the book's publication date approached, the excitement associated with any new book's appearance began to grow. But this was special, since I knew how much Brian had invested in this one opportunity to get his version of events on the record and to establish his place in history. As Brian confessed to L. Ian Macdonald, "I now understand why you writers get the jitters before a book comes out." As usual, the first copies, hot off the press, were sent by courier from the printer to our production department, then rushed to me, then fired off to the author. The "new book" thrill, every time, even for jaded old publishing types is extraordinary. It's a little like seeing a newborn baby, and this particular book was the weight of a fine, healthy baby.

Soon Brian came from Montreal to the warehouse near the Toronto airport, where we set up a sort of bucket brigade to help him to sign as many copies as possible, copies that were to go to influential people in the book world or special friends. I have photos of that day, and I remember how hard Brian worked at the signing — hour after hour — and no one should ever forget to use the words "hard work" when they consider Brian's career. He was great with the employees we'd assembled to get the books under his pen, and they clearly enjoyed meeting him.

But I noticed that even at his relaxed, friendly best, as he joked with the guys bringing in heavy cartons from the warehouse, he never stopped being Brian Mulroney, the former prime minister. He seemed to me to carry with him an air of gravitas, and he always thought before he spoke, in the well-known baritone. He never quite dropped his guard. In private, of course, he could shed that cloak, and could laugh and joke and tell fine, funny stories. He was, as this book's title suggests, a storyteller.

I should stress that I am not posing as a close friend of Brian and his family. I was not a member of his inner circle, and could never expect to be that. But, as with any book I take on, I was fighting alongside the author to make the book a huge success. So on the day of the launch party at the Royal Ontario Museum I was glad to be able to make a genuinely enthusiastic speech, recommending the book to anyone who cares about our politics, and later to be a supportive presence backstage when Heather Reisman interviewed her friend Brian before a packed crowd at her Bloor Street Indigo store.

Then came publication day, on September 10, and the reviews came in. Some reviewers clearly started from a hostile position, others were offended by the work involved in reading such a long book. But by and large, the reaction was one of pleasant surprise. Most reviewers noted that the book was — and remains, dear reader — a fine book that not only takes us inside a rags to riches life, but through many tumultuous years. In short, the book was hailed as a major book about a major life.

After publication day, I knew that my job was done. *Memoirs* was in every bookstore, the sales were so good that it was shooting up the bestseller lists, and the reviews were good. Now I was able to pass the torch to my M&S colleague, Josh Glover, who had set up Brian's forthcoming coast-to-coast publicity tour and who (with a background in the music industry that made him familiar with the foibles of rock stars) was ready to accompany Brian every step of the way.

With my mission accomplished, it was time for me to get away, to take Jane on the holiday that had been sacrificed to getting the book out. So we went off to James Houston's former cottage in Haida Gwaii for a glorious week, described elsewhere in this book.

I returned from this wonderful time away from newspapers and TV to find that Brian was mad as hell at me. It seemed that I had, in his reported words, "deserted" and "gone fishing" when the political campaign started. He took my desertion so seriously, felt so betrayed, that my worried M&S colleagues feared that he might never speak to me again.

He was giving a reading to a huge crowd at the Royal Botanical Gardens building in Burlington, and I showed up while he was having a private meal backstage. He did not seem pleased to see me.

"I hear you're mad at me," I began. "We should talk about it."

He waved everyone else out of the room, and we got down to it. It turned out that we were in a culture clash, not a real quarrel.

His political training was so strong that in his mind the climax of the book's publication was "the leader's tour" — and, as he put it, he expected "all hands on deck." Hence his outrage when he learned that goddamn Gibson had "gone fishing," while the author tour was on.

I came back at him — and we never raised our voices — explaining my role as editor and publisher, where my main duty was to produce a good book and get it in the stores. That accomplished, and with good reviews flowing in and the book zooming up the bestseller list, my job was done. With an M&S man accompanying him every step of the way on the well-planned author tour, there was no point in my sitting around the office, waiting to hear that everything was going fine. At this stage, my help wasn't needed any more.

We saw eye to eye in the end. And that was our only quarrel in the entire complex business of bringing out the book, and in what happened afterwards.

The book was indeed headed for great, surefire success, with the reviews and the word-of-mouth reaction just what we had wanted, and the sense that Brian's role in history had been undervalued now taking hold, and then — as I put it to the next M&S sales conference — "We Wuz Schreibered." Just a few weeks after the book came out, both the *Globe and Mail* and CBC News broke sensational stories about Karlheinz Schreiber paying large sums of money to Brian Mulroney. Since Mulroney's successful suit against the Canadian government had left the impression that he barely knew Schreiber, and had left no impression at all that he had accepted large sums of money from him — resulting in the famous $2,100,000 payment from the government to the aggrieved Mulroney — it was a huge story.

Day after day, it dominated the news. Day after day the number of people who looked at Mulroney's smiling book cover and started to rethink their dislike of the man dwindled. The book sales slowed, then stopped. Our surefire bestseller died, smothered under the pile of sweaty veils that the dancing Schreiber continued to drop. He continued his enticing "Dance of the Seven Hundred Veils " ("Oh, the secrets I could tell you!") before any forum that would listen, thus postponing his extradition to Germany on criminal charges. It was obvious then — and even more obvious in retrospect, since the bombshell revelations never came, and Schreiber is in a German jail — that he played the Canadian justice system like a violin.

I watched all this appalled twice over. First, I was horrified by what it was doing to the sales of what I knew was a very good book, one that for the first time took you into the prime minister's office and sat you behind the desk as problems came flying across it. Fascinating stuff — but all Schreibered.

Second, of course, I was concerned about what it must be doing to Brian. I knew how deeply he cared about his reputation, and how hard he had worked to rehabilitate it, to make Canadians remember his achievements, and not the murky stuff associated with Schreiber. And now this.

I stayed in touch with him by phone. And I can tell you that the man could give classes on how to handle phone conversations. I might call expressing sympathy for something that was going terribly wrong, and before too long he would have sucked me into his — entirely plausible — view of the world, where I hadn't noticed this pattern at the *Globe*, or this contradiction in CBC reporting, and so on. He was resolute and impregnable — although his opponents would have used very different adjectives about his self-belief.

On TV I watched his day in the hot seat testifying before the parliamentary committee led by Paul Szabo, who did not seem up to the job. On the phone Mulroney had produced brief, entertaining character sketches about some committee members, but it was a long, hard day for him, under attack for much of his time in the spotlight. At the end, I remember the cameras catching him and Mila stepping into their limo. I felt sorry for them as they faced the long ride back to Montreal after such an exhausting day.

Some days later, I asked him, very sympathetically, how he had spent the rest of that awful day. He reported happily that they had held a huge party for dozens of people at home that night. I was, and remain, amazed by this. But maybe it goes to show that politicians (even if they are not as old as Diefenbaker) draw energy and strength from crowds. I suspect, too, that all of his friends that night slapped him on the back and assured him that he was great, and none of the committee laid a glove on him. And I'm sure that at some level he believed it.

There is a story that the old Tory guru, Dalton Camp (whom I tried, too late, to get to write a book for me), once gave his friend

Brian a kindly scolding. He noted that Brian had quit alcohol, cold turkey, then quit smoking four years later (with more withdrawal aches). So why, Camp asked in exasperation, couldn't he quit his "hyperbole habit" the same way? By this Camp meant the habit of exaggeration that sometimes gripped him when he rose to his feet in the House, or faced a tempting microphone. Jeffrey Simpson once wrote shrewdly about this, noting the change that seemed to come over him on occasion at question period. Rising to defend a Cabinet member against a routine Opposition attack — let's say, his post-master general — Brian's oratory would soar until the postmaster general was likely to become not just a valued Cabinet colleague, but the finest postmaster general since Confederation, and so on. It was as if he was carried away by his own oratory.

I never experienced that oratory, but in his phone calls I did expe-rience his amazing ability to get you to see the world his way. The mechanics of the call are beautifully handled, too, down to the final "Well, my friend, it's been great talking to you, but I mustn't keep you any longer . . ." and so on. When I called him unexpectedly at home, at a very difficult, post-Oliphant time, his Rolodex mind pro-duced the jaunty final line, "Say hi to Jane!"

I never asked him directly about the Schreiber affair. My decision that the book should end with him driving away from Harrington Lake and out of office in 1993 — a time when, I suggest, the boy from Baie Comeau was so conscious that he was going to be unem-ployed that he was vulnerable to the Schreibers of this world who are trained, like truffle hounds, to smell out people who might be open, even temporarily, to accepting unwise money — was not just based on the book's length. I knew that the whole Schreiber affair was best left for another book, because it would be hard for Brian to put it in a good light, and his treatment of it would dominate the news cov-erage of the entire book.

I stuck to my decision not to ask him about Schreiber because a "What really happened?" question implied disbelief. So I watched the game play out through the long days of the Oliphant Inquiry, and beyond, with a sinking heart.

When Justice Oliphant summed up the affair in May 2010, the report was not kind to Brian. I wanted to phone him, but could not think of anything encouraging to say. In the end I phoned and began, simply, "I was just wondering how you were doing."

And that proved to be enough. As always, he carried the conversation, telling me that everything was fine, the family was all well. He even took comfort from a column by his old sparring partner Jeffrey Simpson, which said some very damning things, but also suggested that history remembered Sir John A. for much more than just the Pacific Railway scandal. He was in good spirits (he may even have used that phrase) and noted that Mila had said, "We've come through worse than this before."

When people look at the whole Schreiber affair, the automatic question is *Why did he do it?* Mulroney has acknowledged that taking money from Schreiber — although not, he has always insisted, in a context linked in any way with Canada's legitimate Airbus purchase — was a terrible mistake.

But what about the secret meetings, the special New York bank account, and so on? It doesn't make sense.

In a similar baffling situation Sherlock Holmes came up with a way to find an explanation: *"Cherchez la femme."*

Which brings us to Mila.

What follows is pure speculation, but it is based on three well-known facts. One, that Mila loathed Karlheinz Schreiber. Two, that she wanted Brian to have nothing to do with him. And three, that she was, and remains, a strong influence on her husband. Given those facts, an interesting theory emerges, explaining why Brian (concerned about maintaining a good lifestyle for his family, and worried about having no obvious source of income when he left office) met Schreiber in secret meetings, took money from him in cash, stashed it in a secret bank account in New York, and revealed it to auditors and tax authorities only when the story was coming out. All of this, I suggest, takes on a fascinating plausibility when seen through the lens of Mila. Brian Mulroney would not have been the first husband to try to keep secret from his wife his dealings with a business associate she disliked.

Pure speculation, of course, which I owe to an anonymous person close to the situation. I have never raised it with my friend Brian, for whom I wish a long and healthy retirement that conquers the curse of diabetes, and many more readers for his excellent book.

# CHAPTER 16

# ROBERT HUNTER

Greenpeace Founder, Writer, and Very Merry Man

I have visited thirty-four countries in my journeys around the world, have swum underwater with dolphins, stood on ice in the path of an onrushing icebreaker, parachute-jumped, dodged great white sharks and motorcycle gangs of whale factory workers in Australia, faced angry mobs in Newfoundland, founded a religion, run with the bulls in Pamplona, survived numerous storms and other near-disasters at sea while commanding a converted minesweeper in the North Pacific, stuck my head in a killer whale's mouth and have nearly drowned, or been stomped, run down or crushed many, many times. . . . What a fabulous existence!

That sounds like Bob, all right, with only the infectious little heh-heh-heh chuckle missing at the end. But that's only a tiny part of this guy's life. Let's try to do better, raising awareness of a man who would have been an icon in many other countries, but who was much too Canadian to take himself seriously, even when *Time* magazine in 2000 named him as one of the century's Top Ten Eco-Heroes. Others on the world list — like Rachel Carson and Jacques Cousteau — are probably better known all over Canada than he ever was.

His life began normally enough in Winnipeg, although he and the education system did not always play well together. After a spell of this and that, this man who would gain fame for jousting gallantly with the law fell afoul of it. He was jailed in Flin Flon for — brace yourself — selling encyclopedias without a license. Soon he was working as a nineteen-year-old journalist at the *Winnipeg Tribune*. According to Martin O'Malley, a colleague there who watched him with admiring amazement, "he regarded journalism as a respectable way to run off with the circus." He devoured books, serious books, by serious thinkers. "Hunter read the way most of us breathed," said O'Malley. And he wrote, too. In 1968 he brought out his first novel, *Erebus*, with M&S in Canada and Grove Press in the U.S., and a promising career as a novelist beckoned.

But by this time Bob had moved to Vancouver, where — besides introducing blue jeans to the *Vancouver Sun* newsroom — he was astounding solid citizens as the first counterculture newspaper columnist in the country. Three times a week *Sun* readers were exposed to his column, headed by his outrageously long-haired photo. But in addition to peace and love and other hippie staples, he was able to introduce really subversive new ideas, including the belief that the air and the water and the land around us are important and deserve to be protected. "Bob Hunter Writes as If Your Life Depended on It" ran one full-page *Sun* ad.

Given that approach, Bob took a dim view of the U.S. government's 1971 plan to explode a nuclear bomb at Amchitka Island in Alaska, which is — as the tsunami rolls — only a short distance from the British Columbia coast. In the wake of the 1964 Alaska earthquake, many B.C. citizens were alarmed by the planned explosion, and some even formed a "Don't Make a Wave Committee." As things developed, the group, including citizens like Jim and Marie Bohlen, Irving and Dorothy Stowe, and Ben and Dorothy Metcalfe, decided that it would be a good idea to head off the nuclear explosion by sailing a ship into the test zone.

With money raised by a concert featuring James Taylor, Joni Mitchell, and Phil Ochs (hey, this was big stuff), the fishing boat *Phyllis Cormack* was leased, and set sail from Vancouver in September. That ship would later get a more familiar name: the *Greenpeace*.

And among the twelve men on board was the *Vancouver Sun*'s Bob Hunter, writing up a storm.

The U.S. authorities made sure that the boat never got near the test, but the publicity generated by the grand gesture created such a storm of protest that the nuclear testing program at Amchitka was abandoned.

Now Bob had the bit between his teeth. He could see how wit and daring — and publicity — could allow protestors to confront and beat the authorities, and in due course Greenpeace was formed, with Bob as the founding member and first president. Nobody in the organization was taking notes about who thought of this idea first, or invented that policy, and since success has many fathers, there are differing accounts of the early years at Greenpeace. I like the simple tribute paid by Paul Watson on Bob's death in 2005: "Without Bob there would have been no Greenpeace."

That would be the Paul Watson, skipper of the *Sea Shepherd* who in the famous photograph is standing on an ice floe with Bob Hunter, shoulder to shoulder, hand in gloved hand, their backs turned to the sealing ship charging straight at them, confident, like the lone Chinese protester facing down the tank, that they can *will it to stop*. They did.

Nowadays, of course, Greenpeace is a huge international organization. Its German arm, for example, is housed in a $35 million building. As Bobbi Hunter, Bob's widow (who, he boasted, was descended from Vikings) recalls, this is a little different from the $50 rent that they paid in the early days in Vancouver, long before there were even salaries. But any time Greenpeace does something brave or clever or media-attracting (and deciding to put their nimble zodiacs between the whales and the harpoons of the whaling ships is all three), I hope that they remember that the policy was established by a laughing guy from Canada with a great sense of mischief.

I first got to know Bob in 1986, long after he moved on from the Greenpeace presidency in 1977. I'm surprised that it took us so long to meet, because as a publisher I was a sucker for tales of intrepid travellers, and you don't get much braver than sailing *towards* a nuclear explosion. But I have had fun publishing people like Fiona McCall and Paul Howard, who built a boat *in their Toronto backyard*, and then sailed it around the world, with four-year-old Peter and big sister Penny completing the crew, as described in *All in the Same Boat* (1988) and in *Still in the Same Boat* (1990). More recently there's the saga of Silver Donald Cameron, who with Marjorie sailed their little boat all the way down the Atlantic coast from Cape Breton to Florida, then on to the Bahamas; the title, *Sailing Away From Winter*, catches the spirit very nicely.

Above all, if you want intrepid, there's Winnipeg's own Don Starkell, whose 1987 book *Paddle to the Amazon* takes the reader — in an open canoe — all the way from Winnipeg, down the Mississippi system to the Gulf of Mexico, up the Orinoco to the headwaters of the Amazon, and all the way to Belem, on the Atlantic. I later had the fun of recreating the start of the 12,000-mile trip, paddling in the bow of *Orellana* as we headed south on the Red River. I was relieved when Don turned us around; I wanted no part of the seas in the Gulf that swamped them with such regularity that one of his teenage sons — the sensible one — quit and headed home, leaving the other to complete the trip with his dad.

That book was a great success, leaving Don desperate to come up with a new voyage. To my horror — and I tried to talk him out of it — he came up with *Paddle to the Arctic*, where he would take a kayak from Churchill (at the base of Hudson Bay) all the way through the Northwest Passage, dragging the kayak when the sea froze.

"But, Don," I argued, yelling down the phone, "this will be worse than encountering alligators, and Sandinistas in war zones. There'll be no possibility of help, no friendly villagers to feed you, and the only creatures that'll be glad to see you will be hungry polar bears!"

But he went. And he almost made it. Just thirty miles from Tuktoyaktuk, his destination, the freeze-up he had been racing settled around him. For thirty-three hours he was trapped offshore in the kayak, the frozen sea too solid for him to make any progress, and too soft to bear his weight when he tried to roll out and stagger ashore. Eventually he did, and a rescue helicopter from Tuk found him and rushed him to hospital, technically dead. He recalls that the nurse kept taking and retaking his vital signs, unable to believe that he was still talking. Later he called me from the hospital to tell me that we had a hell of a story. I told him to get well.

He lost a number of finger and toe joints to frostbite. But years later I was roaming around the Red River, trying to get the rising sun framed in the west window of St. Boniface Cathedral, when I saw a movement in the willows at the river's edge. A kayak, in Winnipeg, at 7:30 in the morning? It had to be Don. A shouted conversation ("Doug Gibson of McClelland & Stewart?" he called, incredulously) took me down to the Corot-like willow-shaded scene, where we bumped elbows. Then he, late for an appointment on the Assiniboine, was able to demonstrate that even with his short fingers he was able to paddle his own kayak, and glided away. A remarkable man.

The first book Bob Hunter and I published together was a total disgrace. That is, if you believe his political opponents, who dragged it out in the middle of an election campaign that involved him running in an Ontario provincial by-election in 2001 as a Liberal, because of his belief that the party was serious about its green policies. Certainly, from the title onward, *On the Sky: Zen and the Art of International Freeloading* was not, let's say, a typical VOTE FOR ME campaign document. Instead the 1988 book was a hilarious, gonzo journalist's not-totally-reliable-account of Bob's adventures posing as a travel writer. There his buddy Gaz (a *real* travel writer) teaches him the sacred text Thou Shalt Not Pay, and Bob sets out to have selfish, shameless fun, staggering around in foreign parts at other people's expense.

In the Bahamas, stoned out of his mind, he finds himself representing the white race in a grudge game of pool against a black giant backed by the locals (with Gaz bringing him to his senses just in time to lose). In Germany, fuelled by excellent free beer, he defies the guide with "teeny-weeny *sieg heils*." In atheistic Cuba, whenever the guide (note the theme here) uses the wearying phrase "Our Glorious Leader," he crosses himself ostentatiously. Then there's a duel with boats on a narrow, sky-high French aqueduct, and the crazy business of running with the bulls through the streets of Pamplona; you knew we'd get to that. And the religion? Well, he really liked the fun job of marrying people.

The book was a modest — wrong word — a moderate success and regarded with awe by middle-aged men stuck in the nine to five routine, who dared to dream. And Bob and I spent much of our editorial time together laughing.

Physically, he was tall, a six-footer, and slim and erect, with a dark beard that ebbed and flowed, and a perennial neat ponytail. His posture concealed a bad back (that damned parachute jump!) that got him into trouble in airport corridors, as he strolled along, carrying a newspaper, while tiny Bobbi struggled beside him with a mountain of bags as big as herself. He recalled: "In Calgary once, a guy in a Stetson said to me: 'Someone oughta kick yore ass, ya goddamn pimp.'" Bob bore it manfully.

I remember especially one evening when I visited the New Westminster farm where he and Bobbi were raising Will and young Emily, and he claimed that though we were less than an hour east of downtown Vancouver, you could fly in a straight line to the North Pole and never pass over another dwelling. Much more important, he showed me the sweat lodge that some local Natives had sought permission to build on his property. He was, he said, becoming more and more interested in Native issues, having been made an honorary Kwakiutl for his work as a media adviser with them.

His interest in the injustices done to Native Canadians, past and present, survived the family's move to Toronto in 1988. One thing led to another in our discussions, and soon, with the editorial assistance of Pat Kennedy, we were able to publish *Occupied Canada* by Robert Hunter and Robert Calihoo. This true story of how the government cheated his family out of their Alberta reserve comes from Bob's friend Calihoo, who learned the history as he studied it in jail. Thanks to Bob's inspired writing, the book is a thought-provoking retelling of Canadian history from the Native point of view. And it won the Governor General's Award for Non-Fiction in 1991.

I like to think that I was a natural publisher for *Occupied Canada*. I once made a complete break from an author — as late as the 1970s — who insisted on using the word "redskin" to describe the Natives clashing with the NWMP. Stupid stuff. (Although I note that when white guy Bob took his first, exhilarating session in "his" sweat lodge, the steam's impact on his pale skin produced many politically incorrect redskin jokes from his Native pals.) Much more important, I became involved very early in my career with what was then called "the Indian problem." In 1970 I edited and published *How a People Die* by Alan Fry. I described it as "a documentary novel about the tragedy of the North American Indian," and it was searingly honest about the social breakdown on some reserves. At one point a frustrated white official asks, "How do you talk to a man who doesn't share your notions about work or money or wife or kids or sanitation or what the hell he's going to live on tomorrow or next year and reach him where he's really alive inside and he can reach you back?"

At another point a character describes the Indians he works with as "the hardest god-damned people on earth to help."

Obviously, this was dynamite. What made it even more explosive was the fact that Alan Fry had worked, in the field, with the Department of Indian Affairs since 1954, and had been a district superintendent dealing with the people in a number of reserves since 1958. When the book came out he was working on Quadra Island, just off Campbell River. His meetings with the local band leaders gained their acceptance of the book, which they agreed was tough but honest. Yet when the book became a Canadian bestseller, in his own wry words (in the second edition of this classic book, published thirty years later), "A considerable fuss followed." Pressure came on him from angry Native leaders from elsewhere, and his job was saved by the leaders of the local band telling outsiders to back off, making it clear "that my future in the service was their business only." In the end, he resigned in frustration with the department bureaucracy four years later.

It's too bad that the protesters didn't read the excellent reviews that *How a People Die* received. N. Scott Momaday, the highly respected American-Indian author, wrote in the *New York Times*, "This small book is one of the most sensitive and incisive statements on the subject of human alienation that I have seen."

The *Saturday Review* was equally enthusiastic: "Fry tells of what he sees, and what he sees is bound to shock the comfortable novitiate in the business of cultural survival . . . it evinces a concerned passion for just solutions to the manifold problems of a neglected minority. Read it soon."

Sadly, thirty years later the book's tough account of the problem continued to be relevant, not ancient history about the bad old days. So relevant, in fact, that my friend Howard White reissued it through his company, Harbour Publishing.

And Alan Fry, the grandson of Roger Fry of Bloomsbury fame? He went on to write *Come a Long Journey*, a novel about a white guy and his old Indian friend canoeing together down the Yukon River that the *Winnipeg Free Press* described as "an epic of human relationships." And later, in *The Revenge of Annie Charlie*, he dealt playfully with white-aboriginal relations in the B.C. interior.

But his resignation left him in a financial fix. He solved it with his axe. Growing up near Williams Lake (as described, before my day, in his first book, *The Ranch on the Cariboo*) he had learned how to fell trees and turn them into cabins. So that's what he did on his property at Quadra, where his only asset was his house, and the big second growth Douglas fir that grew around it. He felled enough trees to produce a two-storey log cabin, a thing of beauty that I visited. Now, after the expenditure of a few dollars for chainsaw gas and nails, he had not one, but two houses to sell.

With the proceeds he set off for the Yukon — and, remember, I'm following all this with fascination, in my downtown Toronto office — and set up a tepee on the shores of Lake Laberge. There he lived *year round*, enduring winters so harsh that manufacturers of outdoor camping gear would send him free samples of things like sleeping bags for testing in extreme conditions ("stark blessed naked at forty below," he recalls), and writing for me a how-to book, *Survival in the Wilderness*.

Then this widower met a woman, and for some reason she preferred to live in a house in Whitehorse, not in the tepee. I'm still in touch with Alan by phone. Some years ago he gave me a pair of moosehide mitts, *made with his own hands*. They are much too grand to wear, but I look at them hanging in my den, and dream.

Over the years, sensitized by my early experience with Alan, I was proud to publish many books about our aboriginal situation, such as those by Native authors like Basil Johnson, and Louise Halfe, and the many authors in the anthology *All My Relations*. I think, too, of books like *Strangers Devour the Land* by Boyce Richardson, Michael Harris's *Justice Denied* (about the Donald Marshall case), and Gordon Sinclair's *Cowboys and Indians*, about the shooting of the native leader J.J. Harper on the Winnipeg street location that Gordon showed me one night. And of course there have recently been the three books I worked on with James Bartleman, the first aboriginal Lieutenant-Governor of Ontario. Of these, *Raisin Wine: A Boyhood in a Different Muskoka* (2007) is to my mind the most powerful.

Other contacts with the Native world were more personal. Once in Saskatoon I was walking west, getting to know the city on foot. I slowly realized that Saskatoon is unusual, in that the tough part of the city is in the west end. The number of cheque cashing outlets and pawnbrokers was increasing, so I decided it would be smart to cross the street and head back into town. As I did so, a pair of western-style swing doors at a tough-looking bar crashed open, and a big guy came out at a run, headed straight towards me. He was huge, an Indian, maybe six-foot-three and 220 pounds, and he stopped his charge and fell into step beside me.

"Heading into town?"

"Yes," I said.

"Okay if I walk along with you?"

"Sure."

There was a long pause. Stride, stride, stride.

Then he said, "See these boots?"

He indicated his Swedish-style wooden-soled boots. I nodded, not sure that I liked where this was going.

*"Are these women's boots?"*

Now I pride myself on being honest, but if he had been wearing stiletto heels, with red pom-poms, I'm pretty sure I would have found some overriding macho qualities to them. As it was, I was able to assure him that, no, they were not women's boots. I didn't try the word "unisex."

"Ah, that's good," he said, "'cause I just kicked the shit out of a guy in that bar for saying they were — and, you know, I wouldn't like to think I did that, and he was, you know, right."

I assured him that he had acted justly, with the full backing of the fashion authorities (not my exact words), and we walked happily together into Saskatoon. It turned out he was from the Yukon (no, he didn't know Alan Fry) where he had just been part of a big strike (I forget if it was in gold, or in diamonds) and was using his share to drive across Canada for the first time. He was giving a big party at his motel that evening, and it would be great if I was free to come. I apologized, saying that I had plans for dinner with Guy Vanderhaeghe (who has written scenes of white-native conflict on the Prairies, notably the Cypress Hills massacre in *The Last Crossing*, better than anyone). I've published Guy's work right from the start with *Man Descending* (1982), which I came to Saskatoon to launch, and he is a good friend as well as a great novelist. When I told him and Margaret over dinner about my encounter, he loved the story, but felt I had made the wrong choice for the evening.

I certainly made the wrong choice when I agreed to be on a Writers' Union AGM panel discussing "Racism in Canadian Publishing." The previous publisher on the panel had withdrawn, for some reason, and I was there as late replacement and Target-in-Chief. With some sense of irony I dressed in my nice blue blazer, and looked very white and suitably insensitive.

It went as you would expect. I happened to be sitting beside an aboriginal representative named Lenore Keeshig-Tobias. If her name is not familiar to you as a writer, I can suggest in her defence that she was kept pretty busy by panels like this. In fact, we were held up while she went back to her room to get the speech that she had written. When she arrived, she sat next to me, where I occupied the end seat.

This vantage point meant that I was the only person in the room who was aware that as Lenore expertly whipped up anguish and white guilt in the audience and then became so emotional herself that she was unable to continue, *she broke down at precisely the point where her typed speech ran out.*

I had an uncomfortable time up there, as Target-in-Chief, but I survived. Until the following Monday, when the *Globe and Mail* report on the entire AGM was headed "Racism in Canadian Publishing Denounced," along with a photo beside the headline of me, looking very white. Just as bad, the article had me categorically denying that there was any racism in Canadian publishing. When I called the journalist, a friend, he was apologetic; it made a better story. Later, a miracle occurred. A writer named Libby Scheier wrote a piece on the AGM for *Saturday Night* magazine. When she contacted me in the course of her research, I said, "Oh, no, I've been burned once!" "I know," she said, "and my article is going to set the record straight!" And, by God, it did.

More recently, I've had happy personal contacts with the Native world. As a member of the Historica national council (a group set up to promote interest in Canadian history) I strolled into my first meeting where about 100 of us were spread out among ten-person tables. I chose a nearby table, walked over, and introduced myself. It was only hours later that I learned that, by good fortune, I had sat at the Aboriginal Table, and by that time we were getting along really well. So well, in fact, that a strong tradition was born. So strong that when a few years later I and Georges Sioui, the great historian of his people, the Huron-Wendats, met in the corridor for an excited catch-up conversation that led to us slipping in late to another table, we were reprimanded for not sitting at "the table." ("What's the matter with you guys?" said Rarihokwats, the amazing non-lawyer who knows more about Supreme Court land claim rulings than any lawyer with a string of degrees, smiling.)

That attitude of friendly irreverence is to be found on every page of Bob Hunter's book, *Red Blood: One (Mostly) White Guy's Encounters with the Native World*, published by me in 1999. It's a fine account of Bob's surprising lifetime encounters with such people as the Huron who appears out of the trees when eighteen-year-old Bob is just realizing that his romantic plan to stay out all night in the January woods in zero degrees, without a tent, is going to kill him. Later, after his spell working as an adviser to the Kwakiutl band, he confesses to realizing, "It was a grinding line of work, being an Indian chief. It required, I quickly realized, the patience of a saint." Then there is the journey with a group of B.C. chiefs to intercept the Columbus fleet of 1992. How these well-intentioned pirates overcame the internal onboard battles between the Saintly Vegans in the galley and the Native Trappers, meat-eaters to a man, is hilarious. Almost as funny, in fact, as the boarding of the Spanish ship to extract an official apology to aboriginals from Spain for all the post-Columbian unpleasantness.

But my favourite Bob Hunter tale is his account of winning the Governor General's Award with Robert Calihoo. At the official dinner, at the top of Toronto's Bank of Montreal Tower, both Bob and his pal Calihoo, a proud graduate of Stoney Mountain Penitentiary, are slightly ripped.

> Sixty storeys up we emerged from the elevator into an enormous dining area, with a string quartet playing, looking out over the lights of the biggest concentration of wealth and power in Canada. Surrounded by the nation's economic, political, and literary elite, we were guided to a round table where we joined our publisher, the urbane, erudite and merry Doug Gibson, as well as, among others, one of the vice-presidents of the bank itself (presumably a human monster beneath the veneer of charm and breeding), and his delightful and attractive running-dog trophy bride.

It all falls apart. Calihoo and the banker do not see eye to eye on the role of banks, the merits of the Free Trade deal, and pretty much everything else.

"Despite the urgency of maintaining decorum, voices began to rise at our table. . . . My wife finally couldn't take it any longer and yelled at Royer: 'Will you just shut up!' That created quite a stir at surrounding tables."

A brawl seems to be imminent.

There was a ten-second pause at the end of which the banker's wife — a nice, north-Toronto respectable lady, who hadn't expected this as part of the 'for richer for poorer' deal, finally cracked, letting out a small scream. We all sat there, interested. Gibson, unable to resist a joke, said, 'Well, I guess you had to be there.' Which was met with chuckles or glares."

It was indeed a night to remember.

The magical thing about *Red Blood* was that in the course of writing it, Bob discovered that he had a Native great, great grandmother, making him one thirty-second Native, and making him very happy. Meanwhile, in addition to the string of books he was producing (by the end of his life he had written or co-written thirteen) he had two great gigs at CityTV in Toronto. Every morning, before breakfast, a cameraman would show up at the Hunter house, and Bob, *in his bathrobe*, would chuckle his way through the morning papers, giving the story behind this headline, and the reason why this paper is playing up this story, and ignoring that one. Great, cynical, informative stuff. Oh, yes, he was also contributing a column to *Eye Weekly*, writing the odd documentary, and making a couple of movies, too (in the dim past he wrote ten scripts for *The Beachcombers*, with Bruno Gerussi slapping his forehead). That is besides slipping off occasionally to risk his life with Paul Watson on the high seas. I remember him laughing when he told me about a Japanese whaler throwing a knife at him. I protested that knives were sharp, pointy things, but Bob enjoyed the high-seas action too much to care.

For some reason, Hollywood never quite took the plunge with a movie about him, though they came close. Over the years names like Kevin Costner were floated ("Hey! *Dances with Whales!* I like that!") and Bob was taken to Hollywood and chauffeured around at great expense more than once. He told me of a Major Breakfast Meeting, held at The Right Hotel, with A Very Big Player. At the end, the Very Big Player leaned across the table and gripped Bob. Looking him in the eye, he said that he was going to make this movie, "Not just because it'll be a great movie, but because, Bob, *I really, really like ya!*"

Bob felt obliged to do a little modest Canadian gripping in return, and came home elated. (He never heard from the guy again.)

By day, in those later years he was the CityTV environmental reporter, attending press conferences, investigating sewer spills, and so on. He was so good at it that the ruling Liberal Party tried to get him elected as an MPP, but the Gods of Irony would not allow it.

In 2002 he brought out perhaps his most serious book (if you can ever use that word about Bob Hunter without qualification): *2030: Confronting Thermageddon in Our Lifetime*, which suggested that we only have till that pivotal year to clean up our global act, before the damage becomes irreversible. He wrote, in what was almost his last testament, in the book's prologue: "Those of us living now in the industrialized countries should be thankful that the barrier of time appears to be firmly locked, because if they could ever break through, the people of the future — starting with Dexter's [his grandson] people — will surely come back to strangle us, the ancestors from hell, in our sleep, for having squandered the Earth's legacy in a handful of generations."

The book is part of an impressive legacy. I'm proud that in his presentation copy for me Bob wrote:

Doug, I phoned you twice to say, "I can't do this." But I was afraid of your . . . silence.
  Cheers,
  Bob Hunter

Prostate cancer took Bob in 2005, after he had tried everything to preserve the life he loved. A park just east of Toronto is named after him, and he lives on in his wife and kids, in his books, in Greenpeace, and in many memories.

A final, personal note. Gail Stewart was my faithful assistant for eleven years, before cancer took her. She had such a protective attitude towards my excesses that, just as she was about to leave, she reacted with horror to the news that another wise, restraining assistant on our staff was also about to leave: "Oh, Doug!" she cried, "Who's going to *stop* you?" Gail knew instinctively that Bob Hunter was precisely the wrong man when it came to influencing me, that we egged each other on. Every time we left the office together, her face told me that she worried that after our lunch we would both end up in jail.

I remember Bob and I were laughing ourselves silly over something (possibly the fact that I had created a sly new publishing joke, by indicating in the caption to the cover photo of *Red Blood* that the hideous "Wild Man of the Woods" mask face was on the left, and the Hunter face on the right) at a restaurant, when the waitress asked, "Are you guys brothers?"

A wonderful compliment, all things considered.

# CHAPTER 17

# ALISTAIR MacLEOD

Teacher, Fiction Writer, Stone Carver, and Dancer

Alistair MacLeod's people left the Scottish island of Eigg in 1790 to come to Nova Scotia. Proud memories are long in the Western Isles. When he won the international IMPAC prize for *No Great Mischief* in 2000 a local paper ran the headline . . . "Eigg Man Wins Prize."

Yet that appropriation is almost appropriate. In the words of the authority on Scottish emigration, James Hunter, to read Alistair MacLeod's fiction "is to be constantly aware of the extent to which his literary world is one that draws no sharp distinction between the Scottish and North American components of the Highland experience. The one — for Alistair MacLeod at least, is simply an extension of the other — the act of emigration denoting no sharp break with what had gone before."

Alistair was not born in Nova Scotia's Cape Breton, although his summer home was built there by his great-grandfather, born in 1838. Alistair's own father was a miner, and his trade took him out west, to Alberta and to Saskatchewan, where Alistair was born. But the family home was and remains in Cape Breton, on the west coast, at Dunvegan near Inverness. In the context of James Hunter's account in *A Dance Called America* of callous captains of emigrant ships simply setting shivering families ashore, it's interesting to note that the old French name for the Inverness coast was "Taille de Corps," which might be translated as "The Wade-Ashore Coast."

Alistair went to school in Cape Breton, and finding that, in his words, he was "good at school" he kept going, first to teacher's college, then to a year's teaching in a little country school, then to attend St. Francis Xavier University. He supported his education there and at the University of New Brunswick and while getting his doctorate at Notre Dame, with the hard, dangerous jobs — fishing, logging, and mining — that he portrays with such knowledge and sympathy in his books (along with the dogs and horses that he describes so well).

In his authoritative survey, *Scotland's Books*, the noted St. Andrews University scholar Robert Crawford calls *No Great Mischief* a "great

Scots-Canadian novel" (a very interesting term) "by a writer nurtured by the Gaelic-speaking community of Cape Breton." That puts it very well, since knowledge of the old language varied even among brothers, and Alistair himself knows far less than his Cape Breton wife, born Anita MacLellan, who is fluent in the ancient tongue.

After their marriage in 1971 they had six children, whom they raised in Ontario during the school year. Following a brief teaching spell in Indiana, Alistair has spent a lifetime as a much-loved teacher of English and Creative Writing at the University of Windsor, right across the river from Detroit. In summer they all return like pilgrims to their spiritual home in Cape Breton, looking west to Margaree Island.

In the midst of this busy life, he started to write short stories. He wrote very slowly, at the rate of one or two stories a year. And they were wonderful, and people — including Hugh MacLennan, I recall — noticed, and recommended them to their friends.

His very first story, "The Boat" (1968), is told by a teenage son whose mother wants him to go on fishing with his father (a singer of Gaelic songs), while the old man wants to free him for a wider choice in life, and will go to any length to provide it. The last line of that very first story is to be found in anthologies across Canada and far beyond: "There was not much left of my father, physically, as he lay there with the brass chains on his wrists and the seaweed in his hair."

In that first collection, *The Lost Salt Gift of Blood* (1974) all but two of the seven stories are set in Cape Breton. One of them, "The Road to Rankin's Point," tells us very precisely about the Scottish history of the area. The grandmother on her fiddle plays old Gaelic airs from Lochaber, and we learn of an inscription on the rafters in the barn . . . "We are the children of our own despair, of Skye and Rum and Barra and Tiree." Near the end, when the grandmother dies, the storyteller says, "for the first time in the centuries since the Scottish emigrations there is no human life at the end of this dark road."

That first book of short stories made Alistair MacLeod's reputation, and soon he was earning money in the summer at the coalface of writing instruction, teaching at the Banff Centre for the Arts. That was where I met him, around 1980, when he was a much-admired teacher working alongside my old friend W.O. Mitchell. The Banff sessions were the source of many anecdotes, not least Alistair's side-splitting account of his epic winter trip by taxi with W.O. from Calgary to Banff. ("Oh gentlemen," wailed the lost driver, a man not raised among midnight blizzards and white-outs, "I do not believe there is a Banff!") W.O. and Alistair were very different personalities, yet remained the best of friends, in Banff and in W.O.'s guest years at the University of Windsor, where Alistair politely listened to every word read aloud (in exultant tones, I can testify, from many phone calls with W.O.) as his colleague's new novel emerged on paper.

Alistair wrote more privately, creating a short story at the rate of roughly one a year, which meant that it was not until 1986 that his next seven stories appeared in the collection *As Birds Bring Forth the Sun*. All of these stories are set in Cape Breton and deal with Highland heritage. As for the title story, Edinburgh University's Colin Nicholson has pointed out that the story of the great grey dog — *cu mor glas* — that foreshadows death, was collected by ethnologist Calum Maclean from "a shepherd in the mainland district of Morar, south of Skye." He continues: "Off the western coast of south Morar stands the island of Eigg, which Alistair MacLeod's ancestors left for Cape Breton in the 1790s, and by beginning the title story of his second volume with the simplicity of 'Once there was a family with a Highland name who lived beside the sea,' MacLeod makes regional identification at once territorially specific and mythically resonant."

Certainly, the "mythically resonant" story collections made such an impression on the editors Carmen Callil and Colm Tóibín that they stretched the rules to include them in their Modern Library book, *The 200 Best Novels in English Since 1950*. The Irish novelist Tóibín even said: "Reading these two books, knowing that I could tell other readers about them, was the high point of the Modern Library project for me."

Given his reputation around the world as a short story writer, you can imagine the excitement that greeted the news that Alistair MacLeod was working on a novel. Slowly, of course, earning the affectionate name that I have given him, "The Stone Carver," as he inscribes every perfect word with loving care. I was able to play a role in encouraging him, because when I became the publisher at

McClelland & Stewart ('The Canadian Publishers,' as we boasted), I was lucky enough to "inherit" my friend Alistair as an author. And my guerrilla campaign to get him to finish and deliver his manuscript led to the great Canadian literary equivalent of the urban myth of alligators in the sewers.

For ten years Alistair MacLeod and I have been living in the midst of just such a myth. As it spins more wildly out of control, we compare notes, bemused by the directions the myth takes, aware that we seem to be in the grip of something bigger than both of us. The once-simple story of how I encouraged Alistair to finish the novel that became *No Great Mischief* has taken the following turns. In Nova Scotia, local legend has me flying to Halifax then driving to Cape Breton (soon, presumably, it will be in a storm, with the closed Canso causeway, under water, proving no obstacle to the wild-eyed publisher), and then rushing on foot to Alistair's writing cabin to wrest the manuscript from his grasp. Even in Ontario, the range of stories can make a reader dizzy. Sometimes the manuscript is exchanged for a bottle of whisky in Union Station. Sometimes the exciting new versions involve my driving to Windsor, dashing into the office of Professor MacLeod and grabbing a manuscript written by hand on exam paper notebooks. Best of all is the story first aired in the *National Post* — a story that was very popular in the halls of McClelland & Stewart — where the delivery of the manuscript's final chapter at the M&S office causes me to burst into tears of relief.

Alistair has perfected the art of being non-committal about such stories, perhaps a legacy of his years as a Creative Writing teacher reluctant to stamp out any fictional spark. Presumably by the time this account sees the light of day the legend will have expanded in other directions, possibly involving parachutes and guns.

The true story is as follows. Alistair published both of his short story collections with McClelland & Stewart. I became M&S's publisher in 1988, but of course already knew Alistair's work well. Indeed, I had got to know him in person at the Banff Centre, and one summer in the mid-1980s, when the Gibson family was touring the Maritimes, we visited the MacLeods near Inverness. Between juvenile soccer games on the grass in front of the house, Alistair showed us around his corner of Cape Breton and I remember walking that grassy track to his spartan clifftop writing cabin, which faces west to Prince Edward Island. It struck me at the time that, with the sound of the wind and the waves and the constantly changing view, I would get very little writing done there.

From 1988 on, I was keenly interested in how much writing he was doing in that cabin, or elsewhere. Over the years, as it became clear that the work he had started in 1986 was a novel, and as Alistair's readings from the novel at events across the country produced a groundswell of excitement, my contact would consist of a cheery phone call every six months or so, asking how the writing was going. This would produce charmingly vague responses from the Windsor (or, in summer, the Cape Breton) end of the line. So vague, in fact, that I would rely on information from a friend in the M&S warehouse, a member of Alistair's extended family, for reports on his progress. There were many other friends and admirers, "MacLeod-watchers" (like the "Kremlin-watchers" in the old days who could read significance into the arrangement of Soviet officials on a reviewing stand), who would pass on scraps of information about what he had read at this event, or mentioned about his manuscript in that interview or meeting.

All the while, of course, Alistair was holding down a demanding job teaching English and Creative Writing at Windsor (to the great benefit of his appreciative students), instructing a summer course at Banff, and raising their six children with Anita, not to mention undertaking the annual family moves between Windsor and Cape Breton. So I did not feel able to harass the man beyond the point of regular encouraging phone calls, letting him know that there was continuing interest at M&S, and in the wider world, in his next book.

This changed around the beginning of 1999. All of my "how's it coming along" questions — which Alistair has accurately likened to the "are we there yet?" questions from the kids in the back seat on a long car trip — had extracted no hard information about what proportion of the manuscript was now written. The book, despite my repeated offers, was still not under contract, presumably because Alistair was reluctant to commit to a specific delivery date. But messages from the "MacLeod-watchers" and my own sense of his situation led me to step up the pressure. My main motive was commercial. I could see that very few of the major figures in Canadian literature would have a new book in the fall of 1999 — Alice Munro had appeared the previous year; Margaret Atwood, Michael Ondaatje, Rohinton Mistry, and Jane Urquhart, among others, were not due for another year at least — so a book by a respected but not yet widely known author like Alistair MacLeod would have a chance to rise to the top, would have, to change the metaphor, room to breathe. Publishers keep an eye on these things.

So my phone calls became more frequent, and more urgent, especially after Alistair rashly allowed that it was possible that he might finish the book in time for fall. This was a key moment of misunderstanding: when Alistair said "fall," he meant that he would finish the book in the fall; what I chose to hear was that he would finish in time for us to publish his book in the fall, after the usual months of publishing preparations. I have referred to him as a stone carver, chipping out each perfect word with loving care. Certainly my confidence in the excellence of his writing was such that — without having read a word of the manuscript — I felt able to put the book in the Fall 1999 catalogue (going to the printer at the end of May) and to write him a letter in April outlining very precisely the generous terms we would offer for the new book, for which we would hold "a place of honour" in our fall list.

In the midst of this campaign of harassment, I learned that Alistair would be reading in Toronto. Unluckily, I had a clashing previous engagement in Ottawa (at the opening of a James Houston–inspired show on Inuit Art at the Museum of Civilization) that same evening. But the next day I flew back early from Ottawa and called Anita to find out where to see her husband while he was in Toronto. She told me where he was staying and mentioned that he was catching the 4:30 train back to Windsor. Failing to catch him before he checked out, I decided, with our Chairman Avie Bennett's amused encouragement, to try a direct approach.

So it came about that the unfortunate Dr. MacLeod, peacefully reading a book in Union Station at 4:00, found a bearded man in a coat dropping down to sit beside him on the bench with the words: "Isn't this amazing! Here I am patrolling Union Station in search of a bestselling novel for this fall, and I happen to run into you!"

We laughed, but I was able to emphasize the urgency of the matter, in person, and to tell him how certain I was that the literary world was eagerly awaiting this book (something that Alistair, a truly modest man, found hard to believe, even though I assured him that I was right on this). Above all, I was able to urge him on to a final sprint as he approached the finish line of this long distance race. Alistair was politely non-committal. When the Windsor train was called and a queue began to form, there was a fine moment when I offered to carry his briefcase, with a look of frank, open-hearted generosity, and Alistair laughed and clutched the bag protectively to his chest. Laughing, but still clutching.

To keep the pressure on, I put the book in the M&S catalogue, writing a description of the novel that stands up remarkably well, given that I had not yet read a word of it, or learned more than a sentence of two about it from the tight lips of the author. (When the manuscript later came in, containing the two lines of poetry that immediately preceded the two lines I had chosen to quote in the catalogue, I knew that the gods were with us.)

At this point the title changed. It had originally been *No Great Mischief If They Fall*, but Alistair phoned to report that he had just learned of a Scottish book with the same title. Not necessarily a problem, I said, since titles are not restricted by copyright. "Ah well," said Alistair, "unfortunately, the name of the other book's author is MacLeod." In one second the book became *No Great Mischief*, as nature surely intended.

As we neared the end of May the pressure on both of us increased. The catalogue was about to be printed at the end of the month, and it is not good for a book to be announced and then postponed. My phone calls about needing to see the manuscript by mid-May were not bearing fruit. Finally, on a Wednesday I called Windsor to tell Alistair that, because we were nearing catalogue deadline and because our sales conference was the following Tuesday and I could not face forty or fifty people and describe the merits of a book I had not read, I was flying down to Windsor on Friday to pick up the manuscript.

He was appalled. No, no, it wasn't ready, I shouldn't do that, don't come, and so on. But I told him that I was coming, hung up, and didn't answer my phone for two days. (At the airport on Friday morning, while my office was calling Alistair to let him know I was indeed on my way, I ran into Heather Robertson, the well-known author, who asked where I was going and was fascinated to hear about my mission. One year later Heather was to be part of the jury that unanimously gave the Trillium Prize to *No Great Mischief*.)

Arriving in Windsor, I startled the cab driver by asking to be taken to the nearest liquor store. He swung around nervously, checking for indications that I would pass out — or worse, throw up — on his back seat. Then, armed with a bottle of Talisker, a fine malt from the appropriate part of the Highlands, I went on to the MacLeod house.

At the door, I received a courteous but reserved reception from Alistair, and I was glad to have the Talisker to present. We sat in the front room with Anita and chatted for a bit about our families, and it was very pleasant. But there was an elephant in the room that we were all ignoring. After all, I had barged into their lives with the express intention of wresting the manuscript out of his hands. To make matters worse, no manuscript was in view. Much worse, above the piano I could see the MacLeod clan coat of arms with its terrible, blood-chilling motto: "Hold fast."

I did not comment on this.

Eventually, I produced a contract for the book and laid the large envelope on the coffee table, noting that they should treat it with care because it also contained a cheque, and then wondered aloud what *he* had for me. And Alistair rose in silence and left the room — *and came back carrying a manuscript!* Needless to say, it never left my possession from that moment until I was back in Toronto, jubilant from having read a wonderful piece of literature.

But not, it proved, a complete one. That same day, after Alistair had taken me to lunch in downtown Windsor (and significantly he was greeted in the parking lot *and* outside the restaurant *and* by another diner in the restaurant) and told me about the book's plot for the first time, he drove me to his office at the university. I noticed many handwritten scraps of paper. In response to my question, Alistair admitted that he wrote in longhand, and the absence of secretarial help in summer vacation time meant that his final chapters were being held up while he asked others to type it for him as a favour. I reeled at the thought of this bottleneck and promptly arranged for him to send his remaining handwritten chapters to us by courier and we would arrange to get them typed and on a disc.

And so, for the next six weeks or so, a package of ten or twelve or fifteen pages written by hand on yellow paper would arrive every few days at the M&S office, and I would take it for typesetting to two young interns, Medbh Bidwell and Adrienne Guthrie, graduates of the Simon Fraser University Master of Publishing Program. They were initially a little hesitant about this menial typing assignment, although I assured them that they were playing a role in Canadian literary history: they soon came to agree, as their wonder at the material they were typing grew, along with their impatience to find out what happened next.

In the course of these frantic weeks, I had occasion to call Alistair in Cape Breton. The phone was answered by a MacLeod son to whom I introduced myself as the man who was ruining his father's summer, ha ha. "Oh yes," he said, heavily, and passed the phone to Alistair.

My reaction to the final chapter was misunderstood by the *National Post* but will be easily grasped by anyone who has read the book and its last line: "All of us are better when we're loved." I was moved to tears.

My role in editing the book was almost non-existent. The early material, typed in a variety of faces over the years, was so polished that it needed almost no attention from me. Alistair's style is distinctive — sparse punctuation, a frequent preference for "which" instead of "that," much use of "perhaps," and dialogue punctuated very simply by "he said" so that a variant like "expostulated" would bring the whole chapter crashing down — and it is so deliberate and the rhythms so clear that pages of the manuscript would fly by untouched by editorial hand.

On occasion my own Scottish background proved to be very useful. For example, I knew a lot about Montrose's rebellion, having played the role of Montrose in a St. Andrews procession — cavalier's hat, breastplate, sword, thigh-boots and all (not to mention the runaway horse, and the ruined centuries-old lawn) — so I was useful in clarifying the odd historical detail. By way of general helpfulness I was able, for example, to remind Alistair of T.S. Eliot's lines about Rannoch Moor when he was describing that area, and I was sound in the general area of Scottish history and, by extension, Wolfe's battles at Beauport and upstream on the Plains of Abraham. (And if you shake your head at the ubiquity of Scots in Canada, consider that the aforementioned Abraham was "Abraham Martin, dit l'Écossais.")

Another Scottish aside: Rannoch Moor is where Alan Breck Stewart and David Balfour spent a hot day being hunted by English redcoats in *Kidnapped*. Robert Louis Stevenson, who knew something about Jekyll and Hyde personalities, has been credited with making these two characters represent the two sides of what might be called the Scottish schizophrenic personality: David, the sober, plodding, industrious common-sense Presbyterian Lowlander (good material for lawyers, bankers, teachers, engineers, and doctors), and Alan Breck, the wild, creative, romantic Highlander, an ideal man to set up a fur trade route, to conquer a kingdom, to cry over a sad song, or to fight against the odds in wars around the world. Working with Alistair — a Highlander to the bone — it was hard not to find myself being tugged into the ethnic role of my Lowland ancestors. In terms of the historic events of the book, these ancient Gibsons were presumably all in favour of Bruce (another Ayrshire man) and Bannockburn, where they were on the same side as the MacDonalds; but they were opposed to Montrose, dead set against "Bonnie Dundee" ("Bloody Claverhouse") at Killiecrankie, and notably unenthusiastic about Bonnie Prince Charlie. Now, centuries later and world away, here I was, David Balfour–like, urging the commercial advantages of finishing a novel like a sober man of business, on Alistair, a Celtic visionary and a great artist. It was, and is, a sobering thought.

Understandably, I was useless as an editor when it came to Gaelic. A toast, a greeting, a few swear words, enough topographical features to be able to tell a ben from a loch, that was the extent of my knowledge, although I grew up in an Ayrshire village with a Gaelic name. So I called on the assistance of a Toronto husband and wife team originally from Scotland, and they raised a number of proofreading questions that Anita (the expert in the household) was able to settle. By the end I was familiar enough with the language that, to my great satisfaction, I caught a typo in the Gaelic dedication.

The expert copy editor, Heather Sangster, maintained the same light-handed editorial approach, recognizing that the deliberately oral way of storytelling adopted by the author right from the start ("as most people hearing this will know" — page three) called for deliberate repetition of certain phrases, such as "the modernistic house in Calgary." As always, such a skilled copy editor caught inconsistencies that had somehow escaped the eyes of both author and editor over many readings.

In terms of the text, my chief role was to work with the designer to produce a book page that did justice to the writing. The type-face is clean, traditional, and easy to read, with plenty of "leading" (rhymes with "heading") space between lines. There are 43 chapters in the 283 pages of *No Great Mischief* so to start each new chapter on a fresh page would be disruptive to the reader's eye and would make the book seem padded. Hence our decision to allow a six-line spacing between chapters, and to mark each chapter opening simply with a numeral set against a Celtic design.

The book was not divided into formal chapters when it came to my office. I consulted Alistair by phone and undertook to divide it into chapters as seemed best to me, with occasional one-line breaks in the middle of a chapter when something less than a full chapter break seemed appropriate. I am happy to report that when we first saw the proofs of the book, formally divided into chapters, Alistair and I agreed that I had got it right the first time, with the exception of one paragraph, which was moved back into the preceding chapter.

After that it was merely a matter of giving the book an appro-priate look, which Kong Njo, in his role as art director, did with his usual skill, tactfully ignoring my suggestion that the MacDonald tartan might show up somewhere on the cover. Incidentally, at a Cape Breton launch for the book, the hall was decorated in MacLeod and MacDonald tartans, not to mention variants of the McClelland and the Stewart tartans. Had this particular Gibson been able to be present, his Buchanan tartan might also have put in an appearance.

In the course of presenting the book to our sales conference, that famous conference in June 1999, I did something unprecedented. I used music to convey the sense of the book. To be precise, from my Puirt a Baroque Halifax recording, I played "Niel Gow's Lament" in the background while I talked about how the music of the Scottish Highlands and of Cape Breton pervades this marvellous book. And the sad, slow music of the fiddle was worth a thousand words.

The publishing success of *No Great Mischief* is history, and it is history that was written around the world, as publishers in a dozen other countries, from Turkey to Japan, revealed the wonders of the book to their readers. For many readers, I suspect, one of the most moving scenes, in a book that almost overflows with them, is the incident where the narrator's sister from Calgary visits Moidart, the part of Scotland her family left two centuries ago, and meets a woman walking on the beach.

"You are from here," said the woman.
"No," said my sister, "I'm from Canada."
"That may be," said the woman. "But you are really from here. You have just been away for a while."

My friend R.H. Thomson tells me that when Toronto's Tarragon Theatre staged David Young's adaptation of *No Great Mischief*, in rehearsal that scene was so powerful that it stopped the show dead. It had to be cut.

The book's wisdom and good-heartedness have taken it far beyond those to whom that passage speaks most directly. Commentators in Canada have spotted this. In an essay entitled "From Clan to Nation," David Williamson has written of the book's warm inclusiveness as it deals with other migrant groups in Canada, "all imagined as fellow citizens. In that respect, at least, the book is a virtual instrument of citizenship."

Similarly, a senator with a French-speaking background, Laurier LaPierre, might have been expected by shallow readers to disapprove of the book's treatment of the French-Canadian miners in the camp. *Au contraire.* He went so far in his approval as to read aloud for Hansard the passage dealing with the impromptu concert involving both the Cape Breton miners and the rival clan of French-Canadians in the camp.

A special pleasure for me was seeing the success of *No Great Mischief* as early as October and consequently urging Alistair to let us publish his collected short stories in the spring. On that subject, let me note that there have been very few criticisms of any aspect of the novel, but some critics have complained that the dialogue in Alistair's work does not always sound realistic to their ears. My reply is that they have never talked much with Alistair MacLeod.

As far as I can reconstruct it, the phone conversation about the next book went as follows:

"Alistair," I said. "Would you have any other stories besides the fourteen that are in the two story collections?"

"Yes," he said, "I would."

"And how many do you have?"

"I have two," he said.

"And what are their names?"

"One is called 'Island,'" he said, "and the other is called 'Clearances.'"

"And are they short or long?"

"Oh, they are both quite long."

"Well," I said, "in the spring I think we will bring out a book of your collected stories and we will call it either 'Island' or 'Clearances,' and we will do very well with it."

"Do you think so?"

"Oh yes," I said. "And I have been right before."

And we both laughed.

I had indeed been right about the success I foresaw for *No Great Mischief*, and I was right, too, about the success of the collected short stories. I called that book *Island*, since the other possible title, *Clearances*, might have appealed to people with Scottish Highland heritage, but would have had unfortunate commercial connotations in the bookstores. As it was, *Island: The Collected Stories of Alistair Macleod* was such a hit that it instantly joined Alistair's novel *on the same bestseller lists* that spring.

Since then Alistair and I have met on many occasions to celebrate his success; the awards and honorary degrees really are too many to list here. But I remember our visit to Dublin, for example, in 2000, when his novel won the worldwide IMPAC annual award. The ceremony was held at Dublin Castle, and I enjoyed seeing the great entrance flanked by the Irish and Canadian flags. I strode in alongside Alistair, Anita, and their six grown-up children, including Kenneth, a musician who brought along his fiddle, just in case. The black-tie formal event began with a reception held in a spacious Georgian room, full of giant portraits of periwigged proconsuls, and the well-handled music of a string quartet. After the grand dinner and the speeches (including impressive talks by Irish politicians, all of whom seem able to quote literature by the yard, and poetry, some might say, by the metre), the string quartet was replaced by a group of young folk musicians in jeans. Kenneth went over to join them, and soon the red-haired Canadian in a tuxedo was giving a lively demonstration of what inspired the simile "like a fiddler's elbow."

Even better, under his influence, a Cape Breton square dance set was formed. With Canadian novelist Jane Urquhart gamely joining in to make up the numbers, the MacLeod family reeled and jigged to the music, while the encircling Dublin literati clapped and yelled delighted encouragement. Even the London-based organizer, a sophisticated PR man who had seen it all, was impressed. "In future years," he shouted to me above the Celtic whoops, "people will say, yes, this was a fine evening — but you should have been here *the year the Canadians came!*"

Closer to home, I have attended official celebrations in Windsor, where Alistair is warmly greeted on the street, as befits a dedicated teacher who has given so much to the city over the years and a writer who has made them proud. His time as a Windsor parent features years spent watching sports, including the track and cross-country events that later informed his son Alexander's Giller-nominated collection of short stories, *Light Lifting*. Another notable case was young Daniel's high school basketball team, which was heavily African-Canadian in its make-up, and very successful. Alistair recalls returning in the car from one triumph with red-haired Daniel, who has the milk-white skin that often goes with very red hair. To Alistair's amusement, Daniel was exulting that "those white guys" on the other team "can't jump like we can."

I can report that any Windsor literary evening event is likely to turn into a *ceilidh* at the MacLeod house, with daughter Marion at the piano and voices raised in song, including mine. And a 2010 summer visit to their Cape Breton home led to Jane and me being invited to a square dance that night in the fire hall at Scotsville. We did our best, and had great fun, inspired by the example of Anita and Alistair whirling their way sedately through the dances with quiet pleasure, among friends of all ages.

I was with Alistair in Kitchener-Waterloo at the climax of their first "one book, one community" event, now a popular annual feature, where everyone is encouraged to read, and discuss, one chosen title — in this case, *No Great Mischief*. Alistair was shown a blizzard of paper comments by citizens who had read his book. He asked if he could keep one. It said: "This is the first book I ever read. I liked it so much I think I will read another one."

I have attended with pleasure many of Alistair's unforgettable readings. Once I even stood in for him (he was in Calgary) at a reading in the old Chapters store on Bloor Street in Toronto. The plan was that the five finalists for a first-novel award would appear in turn from their hidden place backstage, read, and return backstage. No problem. Except that as I stood backstage the incredibly stupid MC (and I'm about to prove that) introduced *No Great Mischief* in a few words, then said: "Anyone who has ever heard Alistair MacLeod read from his work knows how much he brings to the reading. When we hear his voice, it opens . . ." And on and on, while my shoes filled with my heart's blood, and the audience craned forward in their seats, eager for this great treat: *Alistair MacLeod himself!* Finally, she said, briskly, "Unfortunately he can't be with us tonight, so here to read in his place is Douglas McIntyre!" I walked on to see the audience slumping back in stricken disappointment. I was just getting into my "rise above it" stride, moving into the reading, when the MC dashed on again, grabbed the mike, and said "Um . . . *Gibson!*" (Ah well, in recent years Alistair and I have both been selected as "Canada's Scot of the Year," so it's good for us to have experiences that keep us humble.)

At a York University event I once intervened to help him. I attended the reading with Avie Bennett, York's chancellor, and he and I were introduced from our prominent seats, front and centre, in the packed auditorium. After Alistair's fine reading, he asked for questions, noting that like any student before an exam he had tried to anticipate the questions he would be asked, so he had prepared a number of fine answers. Questions?

Shy silence.

Then more silence.

Finally I stuck up my hand.

"You?" Alistair was surprised, but ready for my now-welcome question.

"What is your first answer?" I asked.

General hilarity at this zen-like question, not interrupted by the sound of one hand clapping. But it broke the logjam, and the questions flowed.

In Vancouver, in 2009, Alistair generously travelled to speak at the Writers' Festival's special tribute to Alice Munro. At a lunch beforehand, speaking for Alice (who was unable to attend) I thanked all of the participants and explained that my editorial role with Alice was simply to tell her to stop writing, and to extract the manuscript from her. This prompted an explosion from Alistair, who told the table, "Ah, he's very good at that!"

With the passage of time my beneficent visit to Windsor to encourage him to deliver the manuscript has been upgraded to, in his words, "a home invasion." That is, when he is not taking the opposite tack, teasingly describing how for many patient years he would vainly try to get me to take a look at the manuscript of *No Great Mischief*. People like that version. I worry that some may believe it.

Since Alistair is so busy giving speeches and accepting prizes around the world, he is not doing much writing, dammit — or, to be precise, he is not admitting to me, when I ask, that he is doing much writing. Some years ago, in 2004, knowing how eager the world is for more Alistair MacLeod, I set out to turn his Christmas story "To Every Thing There Is a Season" into a fine little illustrated book, with the same title. I found an excellent traditional Cape Breton illustrator (Peter Rankin, a relative of Alistair's) and asked him to provide drawings of the lanterns and the sheep and the horses and the sleighs mentioned in the story. All was going well, and Peter had provided drawings that tied in perfectly with the text, so that — according to my careful plan — every double-page spread of text would have at least one little piece of illustration appearing beside its mention in the text. Hard to arrange, but possible. Yet when, late in the afternoon, the designer began to lay it all out, *it didn't work*. It was so bad that we decided to quit at the end of the day and try again tomorrow.

At 4 a.m. — as my wife will attest — I sat bolt upright in bed, saying, "The cows! The cows!" Somehow the illustration of cows in the early pages had gone missing, throwing all the later pages off. An editor's life is one that stretches the full twenty-four hours — till the cows come home, you might say.

In September 2009 Alistair and I both went on the Adventure Canada cruise from Ungava Bay down Harold Horwood's Labrador coast, and Alistair gave a lecture about his work, while I gave a talk about just how Alistair and I worked together in shaping his novel. Introducing me, Alistair went so far as to say that "no one has done more for Canadian Literature than this man, Douglas Gibson." I was almost wordless in response to this overly generous assessment.

A month later I was at a conference in Scotland, where I spoke about Alistair's work, and about my pleasure at seeing his work prominently displayed in bookshop windows in Scotland. It turned out that Alistair is so well known — and loved — in Scotland, even in tiny places like Ullapool, that when in my speech I asked the rhetorical question, "Has success changed Alistair MacLeod?" it met with a ripple of laughter.

His genuine modesty was on display when I took French scholar Christine Evain to interview him at a Windsor restaurant. My role was to introduce them, and then sit, smiling, while she asked him penetrating questions about his work, and Alistair fought his modest inclinations to shrug off questions about his art (a very un-MacLeodish word) and tried to answer them. My smile became a beam when Alistair reminded us — and I had forgotten — that he added the last paragraph of "Clearances" at my suggestion. This meant, of course, that the final line in the book is one that can be applied to all of the stories of Alistair MacLeod: "They will be with you till the end."

His success around the world has not, of course, changed Alistair one little bit. He is perhaps the most grounded man I know. So he is still the sturdy, heavy-striding, flat-capped, ruddy-faced figure that Scottish and Irish journalists have variously compared to "your local publican," and to "a farmer come to town to sell his cows." As soon as he appears on a platform to read (which he does far too often, in the eyes of an editor desperate to get him writing again), everyone in the room realizes that this not-completely-comfortable man is, above all, authentic, with no false airs. Humour and laughter, yes, to be sure, and solemnity when appropriate, but nothing false.

And when, after much throat-clearing, this shy man begins to read in what Elizabeth Waterston shrewdly calls an "incantantory" way, you realize —along with neighbours who have never heard the words "oral tradition" — that you are in the presence of a great artist.

It is true that "All of us are better when we're loved." What is also true — and people seem to sense this — is that all of us are better for being in Alistair MacLeod's presence. Even a phone conversation with him will leave me feeling that the world is a better place, after he has talked about his family, and I have told him about the latest deeds of my tiny grandchildren, Lindsay and Alistair.

# CHAPTER 18

1938–

# PAUL MARTIN

Successful Businessman, Very Successful Finance Minister,
and Prime Minister

My experience working with Pierre Trudeau and Brian Mulroney recommended me to Paul Martin, and I was pleased when he approached me in 2006 to edit and publish his memoirs. I liked the idea that a pattern was developing where working with Doug Gibson on your memoirs was a necessary rite of passage for former prime ministers. In that light, I was sorry that Jean Chrétien had broken the pattern and become The One That Got Away, his memoirs ghost-written by the skilful Ron Graham and published elsewhere.

On the other hand, I had done the next best thing by publishing Chrétien's protegé, Eddie Goldenberg. Eddie had worked with Jean Chrétien for over thirty years, was his principal secretary for all of his time as leader of the Opposition, then had held the role of senior policy adviser or chief of staff for the prime minister throughout his time in office. In short, Eddie, while an ideas man, was also the man who made Jean Chrétien's trains run on time, making sure that things got done, and that troubles — and troublemakers — went away.

His book, *The Way It Works: Inside Ottawa* (2006), was a masterly account of the power system in the nation's capital, and suggested how Eddie, the brightest and the liveliest of companions, could conceal an iron fist inside his neat velvet gloves. More than one reviewer admiringly compared his book with the works of Machiavelli. Eddie, although in private a prince of a guy, had absorbed the prerogatives of power so completely that after making many last-minute changes to the book — to my open exasperation — he greeted the couriered arrival of the very first, hot-off-the-press copy of his book (always a thrilling moment for any author) with the response, "Doug, I've got the book. It looks great!" Two beat pause. "I guess this means it's too late for any more changes."

At the launch party for Eddie's book, held in Ottawa's Rideau Club, with the Peace Tower looming outside its windows, the retired but far from retiring Jean Chrétien was in loud, jovial attendance. I took a couple of awestruck McClelland & Stewart colleagues over to introduce them. He was well primed for the encounter. As a simple guy, he explained, he was ignorant about the ways of Canadian publishers. So he went on to wonder aloud how anyone could publish a bad book like Jeffrey Simpson's *The Friendly Dictatorship* (a book that I had commissioned, about the dangers of a Canadian parliamentary system that was increasingly allowing power to centre in the prime minister's office, specifically *his* PMO). Surely I had nothing to do with a terrible book like dat, he smilingly assumed. It was not actually a "Shawinigan handshake," with his choking hands around my neck, but it was the Rideau Club cocktail party equivalent.

I cleared my throat and affirmed that I myself was the publisher. Somehow, in the general hilarity that ensued, I never got around to defending Jeffrey Simpson's accurate thesis (dramatically confirmed by a later occupant of the all-powerful office). Or to mentioning the interesting fact that the book's striking cover — a full-colour photograph of a Latin-American dictator in full white, medal-bedecked uniform, with Jean Chrétien's smiling, "friendly" face super-imposed — was actually a photo of me. The broken finger on my left hand — an old sports injury — is evident in the book cover dictator's cheery wave to bookstore browsers across the nation. (The background to this lies in the fact that my M&S colleagues — appalled by my mischievous idea for a very eye-catching book cover — had objected that getting a male model for such a photo would be prohibitively expensive. No problem, I assured them, and my quick visit to Malabar's, the costume people, was soon followed by an equally quick visit to my pal Peter Paterson's photographic studio. A publisher's life is full of variety.)

Naturally, the fact that through Douglas Gibson Books I had published this lively, opinionated book by Jean Chrétien's right-hand man made my relations with my new author, Paul Martin, potentially difficult. A publication-day cartoon by the wicked *Globe and Mail* editorial cartoonist, my friend Brian Gable, didn't make my life any easier. Entitled "Book Launch," it showed a giant copy of *The Way It Works* strapped to a rocket-launching vehicle, arriving at the door of a home labelled "Hon. Paul Martin," while a delivery man hammered on the door, shouting "Special Delivery from Jean Chrétien."

Everyone even vaguely aware of Canadian politics during the last twenty years knows how hostility between the Martin team and the Chrétien forces split the Liberal Party into two opposing camps. Yet Paul Martin never assumed that by publishing Eddie Goldenberg's book (which, coming from a Chrétien partisan, is not exactly kind to Mr. Martin), I had in any way taken sides in the feud.

Throughout my publishing career, in fact, I always took great care not to take sides. Publishers, I believe, should be like the Red Cross — carefully neutral, available to all sides, and able to bring a degree of civility to every dispute by allowing all sides to make their case to the wider public. To understate matters, it seems to me that, in a democracy marked by free speech, this is a fairly important role.

That belief lay behind my contacting Barbara Amiel, way back in 1979, when I saw her (ironically, on television) complaining that the Canadian media was so biased against her right-wing views that she would never be able to publish a book about them. In 1977 I had worked with Barbara and her then-husband, George Jonas (a witty, languid chap, always drawling epigrams while waving a cigarette holder as if rehearsing for a new Oscar Wilde play), on their award-winning true-crime book, *By Persons Unknown*, a strange story involving one Peter Demeter. So I had no hesitation in calling her up the next morning to throw down a challenge.

"What you say about Canadian publishers is not true, Barbara. If you want to write a book about how you've arrived at your political views, I'll publish it."

And so we did. Working with Ms. Amiel was always an interesting experience, since you never knew which Barbara was going to show up in the office to deliver the next chapter. It might be the smiling, charming, even winsome Barbara. Or the narrow-eyed, brisk, efficient, professional Barbara. Or the troubled Barbara, so troubled that a routine enquiry about her health could lead to a back-of-the-hand-to-the-forehead response, whispered in tragic tones, "Oh, I've just been throwing up blood into my wastebasket at *Maclean's*."

On that occasion, appalled, I tried to rush her to St. Michael's Hospital, just down Bond Street from the Macmillan office, but, no, she insisted on bravely continuing our meeting. My wastebasket remained in pristine condition.

The only time we got into a fight was over the book's title. She wanted to call the book *Confessions of a Fascist Bitch*, or simply *Fascist Bitch!* Showing unusual restraint (maybe unwisely), I insisted on toning this down, and the compromise was a book entitled *Confessions*, with flap copy that began: "Before cooler heads prevailed, this book was going to be entitled *Fascist Bitch!*" Most reviewers, I must note, gleefully took their cue from this line.

Down through the years, from my neutral position I have happily published authors from all over the political spectrum. Signing up David Lewis for his memoirs, *The Good Fight*, over lunch one day, I mentioned that we would pay royalty rates of X and Y. The old NDP leader asked if these terms were absolutely standard, and would he get the same from any other publisher?

"Yes, yes!" we assured him.

This led him to muse aloud about how the much-touted free-enterprise system in practice seemed to produce much less actual competition than advertised. We had no good response. But we did get a good book, and I did enjoy publishing books by his daughter-in-law, the ebullient Michele Landsberg, the wife of another NDP leader.

On the dark-blue side of the political spectrum, I enjoyed publishing Preston Manning, the leader of the Reform Party that turned Canadian politics upside down when he brought his grassroots party out of nowhere to become the official Opposition in Parliament. Preston proved to be a thoughtful man, and *Think Big* proved to be a thoughtful book. His essential decency was shown by his decision to throw a little party (hey, starting parties was what he did) at the University of Toronto residence where he and Sandra were staying for a term. This informal affair was for all of my M&S colleagues (from the editor, Jonathan Webb, onward) who had played a role in the production and the publication of the book. This was a gesture unique in my experience. People really liked it, and really liked the Mannings.

Before my time as publisher (when Adrienne Clarkson was in charge), to show that "political correctness" had no role in their publishing decisions, M&S had released the memoirs of the man who had planned to break up Canada, René Lévesque. I recall that when he toured the office at the time his book was launched, I was hard at work in my Douglas Gibson Books area, accompanied by twelve-year-old Meg, who was spending a PD day at her dad's office, reading and drawing. René interrupted his tour to sit down with her, discussing her drawings with a genuine interest that you can't fake with kids, and resisting urgent calls to resume his office tour. Meg enjoyed their talk, and remembered him so warmly that she was distressed when she learned of his death. He was a French-Canadian *mensch*.

To round out the roster of political parties that we published — and I've already mentioned Red Tories like John C. Crosbie, me son — I'd add Elizabeth May, who was not yet the leader of the Green Party when we published her *Paradise Won* in 1990, but her green colouration was already dyed-in-the-wool. As, to be fair, was ours, when we published *The Canadian Green Consumer Guide*, back in 1989, selling 150,000 consciousness-raising copies. I still feel guilty when I use paper towels in the kitchen.

Paul Martin, I'm sure, was unaware of all this background when he approached me through his lawyer, Bill Ross (the son, in this very small world, of the Hudson Bay trader in Inukjuak who had confirmed to James Houston that, yes, the local Inuit were still producing sculptures that were so traditional they looked as if they belonged in a museum). But I'm sure that Paul was aware of my experience working with Pierre Trudeau, an iconic figure with all Liberals. He may have beaten Paul Martin Sr. in the 1968 Leadership Convention — a major disappointment for both father and son — but thereafter he had treated the older man with great respect. So despite the policy disagreements that businessman Paul Martin may have had with him, my association with Trudeau must have been an advantage to me.

So was my work with Brian Mulroney. It may surprise outsiders to learn that Conservatives and Liberals can be friends, but that was the case here. Old Paul Martin had even got to know young Brian Mulroney during his student politics days at St. F.X., and had pulled him aside (one Irish-Canadian talking to another) to wonder aloud what "a good Catholic boy" was doing with the Tories. In the late 1960s (this time as one rising young Montreal business star talking to another), Mulroney advised Martin not to leave Paul Desmarais's Power Corporation, giving him strong advice "to stay put and see what happened." It worked out well, and Martin later hired Mulroney as his labour lawyer.

In his *Memoirs* Mulroney recalled a fishing trip in the late 1970s to Anticosti Island, courtesy of Paul Desmarais: "Paul Martin and I once spent a sunny day there fishing, chatting and speculating about the political future. Paul was then President of CSL (Canadian Shipping Lines) and I was then President of IOC (Iron Ore Company of Canada) and both of us wanted to become prime minister one day, but neither of us was straightforward enough to admit it. We knew our ambition would have strained credulity."

Much later, when Paul Martin had gained a seat in the House, Mulroney's continuing friendship took a tack that was unexpected for a Conservative prime minister dealing with a Liberal Opposition MP. His personal journal for April 17, 1989, reads:

> Paul [Martin] has not done well in his brief time here, in large measure I believe because expectations were so unrealistically high about him. He is a nice, quite gentle individual who may turn out to be a wonderful neighbour but an unsuccessful politician. Perhaps his parliamentary performance will improve and for his sake, I hope so. And I have sent messages to him via Brian Gallery to loosen up in the House; avoid mixing it up with people like Crosbie, who will kill him; and remember that, if he is seeking the Liberal leadership, his enemies are in the Liberal caucus . . .

An entire Ph.D. thesis could be written about this passage. I'll restrict myself to noting that Brian Gallery, the former mayor of Westmount, was a Tory friend and neighbour of the Martins at their farm in Knowlton, in the Eastern Townships, where Paul spent many happy hours driving the tractor and doing weekend jobs for fun — and, no doubt, being a wonderful neighbour.

As for Paul Martin's own memories, in *Hell or High Water: My Life In and Out of Politics* (2008), he records that "Pierre Trudeau treated my father very well after the 1968 convention." He appointed him to the Senate, then when it became clear that the Senate reform that the old man favoured was not on the cards, he sent him to represent Canada in London, a post that he and his wife, Nell, both loved.

John Gray (son of the publisher) wrote a thoughtful biography entitled *Paul Martin: The Power of Ambition*. It appeared in 2003, before Paul rose to the heights his ambition had dictated. Gray calls him "an enigma" suggesting that he was torn between his business-man's financial caution, and the social activism instilled by his father, with whom he talked by phone several times a day.

Paul Martin (Senior) was such a tireless, hand-shaking politician that Gray tells the legendary story of a campaign when he met a line-up of local Liberals early in the day. Seeing a half-remembered face he greeted the man warmly, saying, "Hello, how are you?"

"Good to see you again, Mr. Martin."

"Good to be here. And how's your mother?"

"Actually, she died just before Christmas."

"I'm terribly sorry to hear that. I was always very fond of her."

Unfortunately, the same man was in a later hand-shaking line-up. And the same conversation ensued. Word for word.

In the evening, it happened again. This time, the man allowed his irritation to show. Asked how his mother was, he replied, "Still dead, Mr. Martin."

A word about the formidable Nell, a loving mother who also helped to shape her son's career. As a young political wife in Ottawa she was primed by her anxious husband to make a good impression on his boss, Prime Minister Mackenzie King. Obediently, at their first meeting, as her son's book records, she began according to the pre-pared plan:

> "My husband thinks you're a very great man," she told Mackenzie King as they arrived.
>
> "And what do you think, Mrs. Martin?" Mackenzie King asked.
>
> "I'm going to take some convincing," my mother replied — not exactly the response Dad had coached her to give before they left home.

Amazingly, the next day King dropped by the Martins' apart-ment, and invited Nell to join him on his afternoon stroll.

She was always a political force, and this remained the case, even on her deathbed. When she fell gravely ill, her son had just accepted the post of minister of finance, and had rushed from Ottawa to be with her. As the old lady recovered consciousness, she looked up at the family faces gathered around her bed and said only one word, "Why?" The family explained that her health had taken a bad turn, so they were there to support her as she recovered, and she slipped off to sleep. The book continues:

> She woke up and asked again, "Why?"
>
> I told her, "Mother, we've explained to you. You've been sick and we're all here to make sure you get better." And then she said, "No, no. I don't mean that. I mean, why Finance? Why would you want to be minister of finance?"

Clearly, politics flowed in Paul Martin's veins. Yet he resists the interpretation that he was always bound for a political career. His book states, "From the time my father left politics, my active interest in the Liberal party waned." He concludes, "But if I thought about government at all, it was from the perspective of a businessman."

One of his book's great strengths is that he writes with such infectious excitement about his years as a "corporate fire-fighter" for Power Corporation, dashing to the rescue of failing companies. Even better, we feel the thrill of the boy who loved ships acquiring Canada Steamship Lines, in what was at the time Canada's largest-ever leveraged buyout, then running the growing company for many years.

The thrill continued. In August 2008, a few months after leaving office, he happened to be in Vancouver when he learned that a newly commissioned ship was in the harbour — the *Baldock*, half-owned by CSL. At 10 that night, he and his trusty executive assistant, Jim Pimblett, took a water taxi out into the harbour, "with the glimmering lights of Vancouver around us. The Mounties didn't like it, but I stood outside the cabin of the water taxi on the flat stern section, supporting myself by grasping the metal pole, and took in the sea air. They liked it less when I raced up the *Baldock*'s ladder, maybe four stories in height."

What follows is an exciting tour through the huge ship — well over two football fields in length — including scrambling "over the enormous boilers and the propeller shaft, on catwalks suspended above." And there we get a glimpse not only of the wild Paul Martin, who spent a night in jail after a student altercation with Toronto police, and lost a summer job in Alberta for crashing a company truck on a freelance mission, but, more important, the man of enormous enthusiasm.

But do you remember the fishing with Brian Mulroney story? Paul Martin remembers it differently, in two ways, both revealing. First, he recalls no political conversation, but he does remember that the Anticosti day was so hot that "we both stripped down to what God gave us and plunged into the water to cool off — something that is absolutely forbidden in a salmon pool." (Presumably a salmon-fishing equivalent of the line "I don't care what they do, as long as they don't frighten the horses.") "Then we sunned ourselves on a rock. Someone snapped a picture: two future prime ministers in this exposed state. (Insert your own joke about 'naked ambition' here)."

Yet the subject of his own political ambition gave Paul Martin great trouble. I saw this the first time we met to discuss the book, a breakfast also involving M&S President Doug Pepper and Bill Ross. I suggested that his father's diaries contained the ideal opening line for his own memoirs; discussing his son's political interest in 1977, his father had written in his diary, "He has the bug, I am afraid."

At this, across the table Paul Martin's big body (he's a surprisingly strong man, with a football player's width and depth to his torso) writhed in obvious discomfort. In fact that discomfort was only matched when I told him that Stephen Harper was almost certain to win the next election (which he did, defeating Paul's successor, Stéphane Dion).

As the book took shape, with Paul working with the experienced Ottawa-based political writer Paul Adams, it became clear that he had established a personal narrative that he was a simple businessman who late in his life had sort of backed into politics. This meant, of course, that his father's diary was wrong, and Mulroney's memory was at fault. In fact, the way Paul remembered their conversation was that it happened at a restaurant atop Place Ville Marie, where

> Brian calmly told me of his plans to become Prime Minister one day . . . I remember thinking that he must be smoking something to imagine that a Quebec Tory was going to become Prime Minister any time soon. Nor did it occur to me that our career paths might intersect or even clash. If Brian had asked me that day what my ultimate ambition might be — which he did not — I probably would have replied that I would like to be president of the World Bank or the head of the United Nations environmental program.

As things played out, of course, his successful business career allowed him to leave CSL with the company on an even keel and enter politics as a Liberal MP in 1988, at the age of fifty. Two years later he ran for the party's leadership in a vigorous campaign that left, let's say, "a gulf" between his workers and the victorious Chrétien team. Three years after that, however, he became Chrétien's minister of finance — to his mother's horror, since she knew the post as a career-killer.

It's worth recalling that our financial situation looked terrible at the time. In fact, in January 1993, the *Wall Street Journal* published an editorial announcing that Canada had become "an honorary member of the Third World" because of our crushing debt load. Paul famously promised to fix this "come hell or high water," and set about doing so. How he and his team at Finance turned things around makes a fascinating story.

How he arrived at the precise blow-by-blow account of these years is also fascinating. Knowing that he was at work on his memoirs, the National Archivist, Ian Wilson, arranged for sessions — carefully taped — that were led by Sean Conway, a former politician, now an academic at Queen's. He would assemble small groups of, for example, the top people involved in creating the budget of 1995 inside the department of finance. Sitting with Paul they would compare their memories, arguing and recollecting and correcting until they had all hammered out an agreed version of what had really happened.

This system later came under fire from an Ottawa journalist as a waste of public money. I said then, and say here, that I can think of few more important activities for an institution devoted to preserving our country's history to undertake, and I hope that this effective system — which bequeaths all of the tapes to the National Library — will be repeated for all future prime ministers.

In retrospect, in the lurid light of the Wall Street meltdown of 2008, Paul Martin's years at Finance look very good indeed. His memoirs remind us that he took terrible heat from Canada's banks when he flatly refused to allow any bank mergers. Perhaps the bankers liked the sound of the phrase "too big to fail" that became familiar at the time of big bailouts of banks in other countries after the Crash. And in his championing of the G20, as opposed to the

G8, in international vision he was clearly far ahead of his time.

So what went wrong? What turned the man whom many would hail as the country's best minister of finance into a disappointing prime minister? What occurs to me is the two-word answer . . . Jean Chrétien. First, we should recognize that the long, secret, underground war with the Chrétienites was an amazing success. History affords few examples of a sitting prime minister with a winning record, a comfortable majority in the House, and a good standing in the polls, being forced out by a palace coup from inside his own party. And all without stilettos or machine guns.

Here, an outsider might speculate, perhaps lies an explanation for Paul Martin's discomfort with the word "ambition," applied to his own career. The same outsider might even go on to observe that a team assembled to produce such a successful political assassination might not be the ideal group to go on and run the country.

Then there is the case of what even the most unromantic journalists call "the poisoned chalice." The Quebec sponsorship scandal was a tar baby dumped in his lap by Chrétien on his way out the door, and the tar clung to poor Paul. He was the minister of finance, he was from Quebec, surely he must have known what was going on. Even his eloquent protests that the closed Chrétien Quebec circle would have been more likely to inform "The Little Sisters of the Poor" than their enemies, the Martinites, failed to register widely. To many voters the Liberals were now the party of corruption, end of story.

My friend Eddie Goldenberg would say — hell, did say, in his book — that Martin handled the whole thing badly; he should simply have let the scandal play itself out, with the police arresting the guilty people who made ill-gotten gains, and the Liberal Party and the government moving on. What Martin chose to do was to go on a national "mad as hell" tour, telling all Canadians how outraged he was by what had gone on, and appointing the Gomery Commission to reveal the whole truth. What the Gomery Commission did, of course, was keep the issue on the front pages month after month, reminding Canadians daily of this great Liberal corruption-fest in Quebec.

I think that there may be a reason for the "mad as hell" tour that lies beyond political tactics. Maybe Paul Martin really was mad as hell. Mad that the wily Chrétien had dumped this sticky mess in his lap. Mad that the money had all gone out behind his back, when he was trying to mind the dollars and cents. Mad that the revelations had set the rest of the country against the "corrupt" province of Quebec. And above all mad that he was now stuck trying to defend a Liberal "brand" that had been hopelessly stained by the whole thing. At another level, I'd suggest that maybe Paul Martin, although he was a grown-up well aware that politics can be a rough game, was personally disgusted by the corruption.

In the end — as Eddie Goldenberg would have warned him — the fact that Gomery exonerated him personally from any complicity in the affair simply didn't matter. The Sponsorship Scandal thundercloud hung over his whole term in office. Eventually, with a mysterious assist from the then–RCMP Commissioner Zaccardelli, it burst, and swept him out of office, with most of his ideas still waiting to be enshrined in law.

Ken Dryden is perhaps the best person to demonstrate how frustrating Paul Martin's defeat was — frustrating in that it prevented a major national agreement making it into law. Ken was sworn into the Martin Cabinet as minister for social development in 2004, but he and I go back a long way before that. Like the rest of the country, I used to watch him in his glory days as the Montreal Canadiens' star goalie, in the years when they routinely won the Stanley Cup. I knew that Ken, a Cornell graduate in history who left the Canadiens for a while to complete his law degree at McGill, had a unique set of talents. Some day, I guessed, he might produce a great book from inside the world of hockey at the very top.

I approached him, signed him up, and encouraged him to stick at the project for many years, until in 1983 I was able to publish *The Game*. Trent Frayne, the wise old sportswriter at the *Globe* (who was also married to the wonderful June Callwood), liked Ken's book so much that he described it as "the sports book of the century." How can I argue? It sold accordingly.

Ken and I became close friends as his daughter, Sarah, and my girls, Meg and Katie, played on the same University of Toronto Schools high school field hockey team. Often Ken and I were the only two dads in attendance, punching each other's shoulders in delight as the UTS girls triumphed. Later I teamed Ken up with our friend Roy MacGregor (the man I turned loose on *The Screech Owls* series of hockey books for kids, joking that it would be his pension plan; with over a million copies of the series sold, Roy and Ellen's pension plan is coming along nicely). Together Ken and Roy wrote *Home Game* (1989), a look at hockey's role in Canadian life, based on Ken's TV series with the same name. It sold very well, as you would expect.

Later, I was glad to publish *In School* (1996), Ken's bold idea for a book about what *really* goes on inside our schools each day. I found it hard to believe that he could fold his massive six-foot-four inch frame into a school desk at the back of the room in a way that allowed the teacher and the kids to carry on as if he weren't there. So he arranged for me to come along on a typical day ("No coat or tie, Doug, or they'll think you're a cop"), and I found that, amazingly, being with Ken meant that his magic cloak of invisibility somehow extended over me, too. The only bad moment was when Ken drove me back to the subway, dropping me off at the "Kiss and Ride" section. Not part of the deal, I protested.

We were such good friends that I was able to play a practical joke on him. Our M&S publicist, the lively Kelly Hechler, came into my office one day to say that Preston Manning (then leader of the Reform Party) had just called, to get in touch with (the author and apolitical civilian) Ken Dryden. I felt a shiver of possibility. Had she given the number, and did Ken know that Preston was going to call him? Yes and Yes.

Aha! Most Canadian males of a certain age believe that they can imitate Preston's scratchy, very distinctive voice. This was too good to miss. I dialled Ken's number, muffling my voice slightly with a handkerchief. Ken answered.

"Is that Ken Dryyyden?"

"Yes."

"This is Preston Maaanning. Did you know that I was likely to call?"

Ken, earnestly: "Yes. Yes, I did."

I punched the air. I had him going.

"Well, Mr, Dryyyden — or can I call you Ken? Good, good, please call me Preston. Ken, I've followed your career with interest, and I wanted to call you up and say this." (And now, no doubt, Ken was expecting an invitation to run as a Reform MP.) "What I want to say is . . . why don't you go and just . . ."

And here "Preston" said something very, very rude, meaning that Ken should go away.

I discovered at that moment that it is possible, on the other end of a phone, to hear a jaw drop. Ken had just been sworn at by the saintly Preston Manning, the least foul-mouthed man in Canadian public life, and he was struck dumb.

I resumed the conversation, in my own voice, "Actually, Ken, it's not Preston, it's Doug Gibson, but he will be calling you in due course." I hope that Ken was polite to the real Preston Manning when he called. He took a little time to be polite to me.

When Ken left the world of books to run as an MP, I wished him well, and watched benevolently as he won a seat in the House, and a place in Paul Martin's cabinet. There he performed a miracle. Anyone who remembers Meech Lake knows that for any federal plan to be accepted by every single province is nothing short of miraculous. The odds are heavily against any group of provincial representatives being able to look out of the window and agree as to whether the sun was shining or not. Yet Ken pulled it off with his plan to create a national child-care program.

As Paul's memoirs say: "Ken is quite simply a star, and not only because of his hockey career. His low-key seriousness and obvious goodwill meant that he was extremely effective in building relationships with his provincial counterparts."

Tenaciously and patiently he put together a national daycare strategy, first with Manitoba, "then with the other provinces one by one, until we had a truly national agreement."

Like the Kelowna Accord, which offered a new deal to Canada's aboriginal peoples, whose very disparate leaders all signed on to the accord in good faith, it was one of the Martin Government's great achievements. And, like the Kelowna Accord, it died when the Harper Government took over.

Ken Dryden ran for the party leadership when Paul stepped down. As a friend I attended a couple of his fundraisers where he talked about the child-care agreement that had been trashed. Ken is a thoughtful, soft-spoken, low-key guy, who rarely gets angry (I suspect that there are times when only his wife Lynda and their kids are aware that he is angry). Yet it was striking how passionate he was — in a slow burn sort of way — as he talked about what had been achieved, and then thrown away. We can only imagine how Ken's frustration over just one program must have been multiplied many times for Paul Martin as he looked across the whole range of unfulfilled ideas.

The word "ideas" brings me to an important point, another reason that, I suspect, led to his failure to achieve the results he wanted while in office. Working with him, I found that he was a man of great enthusiasms. No surprise there. I suggest that a large part of his problem as head of government (summed up in the hostile description "Mr. Dithers") was that he was an intellectual.

Let me explain that. He was an intellectual in the sense that he *really* liked ideas. I have worked with bright people of all sorts, often with strings of publications and degrees to their name. But I have rarely encountered anyone who was so genuinely excited by ideas.

Three examples. The national daycare program really started years earlier, in 1996, when a research paper from "the social policy expert Ken Battle at the Caledon Institute" happened to reach Paul's office. The Martin book recalls, "I thought the scheme was ingenious, and I phoned Ken up one Sunday morning to talk about it. We didn't know each other at the time, and he was plainly a little startled at being peppered with questions from the minister of finance . . ." No kidding.

Second, Michael Decter's 2010 memoir, *Tales from the Back Room*, tells of a meeting that Paul, then minister of finance, arranged in order to pick Michael's brains about health care. "I remember it as an unusual experience. Often when someone in political life asks you your opinion after a very short period of time they will tell you their opinion, often at great length. Paul Martin did exactly the opposite. For over two hours at lunch he sought my views, in meticulous detail. I was both intrigued and flattered. Martin proved to be that rare creature, a politician who could really listen."

In a similar vein, Martin cabinet colleague John Godfrey has told me of an incident when he put some thoughts on paper and sent them along to Paul. He received a phone call *on Christmas morning* from Paul, eager to discuss what he had written, tossing around his own ideas.

All of this would have been fine if as head of government Paul had had an experienced team (or maybe a Goldenberg figure) to make sure his trains ran on time, concentrating on this issue, and leaving that one, and that other one, for later attention. I'm sure that his staff tried. It is an ironic theory that this very successful businessman, and the former effective head of an immensely complex finance department, should have failed to achieve as much as he wanted as prime minister, because ideas set him afire with excitement.

The first time I met Paul was at a "Politics and the Pen" dinner in Ottawa. This annual fundraiser for the Writers' Trust, dear to Sheila Martin's heart, features a dinner at the Château Laurier, where members of the public share a convivial table with a politician and a writer. One year I found myself at the central table with Sheila and the prime minister. I was told that I had been selected for the table because an organizer had said, "Oh, Doug can talk with anyone" (which was a compliment that pleased my mother, Jenny, a woman who knows something about talking, and is still notably articulate at ninety-seven). The onstage entertainment after dinner was provided by "Bowser and Blue," and their act consisted largely of doing Paul Martin imitations, as PM the PM talked excitedly about one "priority" after another. All good clean fun. Except it went on and on. This was happening at a time when Paul Martin was being hammered daily in the House, and as the onstage attacks continued, I caught his eye across the table. I tried to convey the message "I know there are lots of things you'd rather be doing in the evening, instead of sitting here in your bow tie, smiling gamely as the folks onstage get into their tenth minute of attacking you." He smiled, and shrugged slightly, inclining his head to one side. What can you do?

He is a nice man. Journalists recall that you could have a real conversation with him, rather than receiving an oration from on high. I'm struck that Mulroney suggested that he might be a good neighbour, but too "gentle" for politics. Certainly any stranger who greets him will find how rewarding an airport corridor encounter with him is likely to be. And he was great, touring the office with me and thanking the M&S staff.

As for his own staff, in his book he makes no secret of his explosive temper, but seemed genuinely surprised when people were unable to shrug it off as just a temporary outburst, over in a moment. His former staff — many of whom were very helpful to me in my task of extracting the final version of the book — are fiercely loyal, always a good sign. And the delightful Sheila is not only the perfect political wife, she is also an admirer of Alice Munro!

As you would expect, he has a good sense of humour, and his funniest stories are often at his own expense. Once Paul accompanied his distinguished father to China, where the interpreter was baffled by the task of introducing two Western dignitaries named Paul Martin. Eventually, in English the father became "Paul Martin, The Great," while our man became "Paul Martin, The Not-So-Great." In the same spirit, the strange sequence of events that led to his being fired or resigning from Chrétien's cabinet is described in a chapter wryly entitled "Getting Quit."

Relations between a ghost writer and the author of record are always confidential, but neither Paul (Martin or Adams) would object to my saying that I sometimes found myself in the role of referee, although problems never reached the level experienced by the stars of the movie *The Ghost Writer*, and nobody was drowned. As for me, my main problem with this nice man was that he could not stop rewriting his book. (Sheila's favourite author, Alice Munro, follows the same practice, but to greater effect.) I would edit what I thought was a final version of a chapter, as agreed by him and Paul Adams, back it would go to him, and then it would come back to me, *largely rewritten*. And so on.

When I remonstrated with him, protesting that he had been spoiled by teams of assistants helping him to make last-minute changes to speeches, a very different matter from rewriting a whole book, he would respond by asking when was the absolute, drop-dead, last date for making any changes if the book was to come out at the promised time. I would hedge, suspecting what was coming. Sure enough, when he got me to name a date, he would say "Impossible!" and we'd argue some more, with me perhaps grudgingly allowing him an extra couple of days.

I notice that in the book's acknowledgements he describes me as "he of the merciless edit, graceful pen, and lack of tolerance for last-minute changes." He is a mischievous fellow. During some of this editorial to-and-fro he began one phone call to me with the grim words "Hello, Mr. Stalin." As you might expect, we had fun together on the promotional trail. When we launched the book at a noisy party at Ottawa's National Arts Centre, it became clear that many of his former staffers were there. When in my speech of welcome I spoke about how his insistence on getting his text exactly right "reflected great credit on him, but was a great trial for me," Martin veterans were loudly amused.

For his part, Paul tore me into little bits. "If Gibson had edited Shakespeare," he declaimed angrily, *"There would be no Shakespeare!"* And so on. He was very good at it, and at the end we agreed that taking our show on the road was a good idea.

A week later, at the Granite Club in Toronto, I scandalized the audience by reminding them of what I called "Canada's Banana Republic Moment." By that I meant the moment in the middle of Paul Martin's last election campaign, when, with the election evenly poised, the police stepped in to tilt the balance. The then-respected Commissioner of the RCMP Guiliano Zaccardelli intervened personally to accuse Liberal Finance Minister, Ralph Goodale of wrongdoing. He did so in what the Kennedy Report into the matter later called "the absence of a rational or justifiable basis for such disclosure." Because, incredibly, Zaccardelli refused to testify (then or since), about this stain on our electoral history, he got away with it — arguably swinging the election, and keeping Paul Martin from achieving his aims as prime minister.

Paul continues, in so-called retirement, to be in demand in the world's capitals as a turn-around specialist for national economies in distress, when he is not working on international causes like the disappearing Congo rainforest. His work on the problems that affect aboriginal youth at home involves a huge investment in time, money, and energy; in the summer of 2010 he was seeking my advice about the textbooks he is creating specially for aboriginal business students.

Later that summer, at my invitation, he came to speak at the annual lakeside Couchiching Conference. The discussion theme that year was whether the Wall Street meltdown of 2008 had been a "Watershed Moment or a Wasted Opportunity," and among the 300 informally dressed ordinary Canadians who enjoy discussing important public issues, Paul was in his element. In an open-neck shirt and light summer slacks, he paced the stage. Speaking without notes, wise-cracking, quoting behind-the-scenes conversations, he explained why the G8 had needed to be expanded to the G20 (really the G19, he noted, but none of the finance ministers or their economists can count), then participated in a panel that developed his themes, and fielded questions from the audience.

It was a masterful performance, revealing a relaxed man who was widely informed, witty, and passionate about the ideas that could lead to solutions for many of the world's problems. When I asked a question about China — quoting the "Paul Martin, The Not-So-Great" story — he took the chance to denounce the horrors of being edited by me, before going on to muse about China's role in the G20.

He was the star of the conference. Dozens of attendees — from young graduate students there on scholarship, to experienced university professors, to engaged senior citizens — were stunned, telling me that they had simply no idea how good he was, and regretting that they had never had the chance to see this Paul Martin when he was prime minister.

He is a very decent man, as even Martha Hall Findlay (bumped by him to make way for the new Liberal "star" Belinda Stronach) is happy to attest. And of course he remains such a devoted family man that even his grumpy publisher had to agree that it was worth holding up the very last photo in the book to allow his latest grandchild to be included in the family grouping.

A final thought: I believe that it's true that Paul Martin was the prime minister we never really got to know. He was teasing me, of course, in his role as non-stop reviser, when he signed my copy of his book with the words, "Doug, There is so much I could add and revise, so much I could say about you. Please give me a chance."

I hope that, to twist the meaning, I have given him a chance here.

# PETER GZOWSKI

Writer, and Voice

He was more — much more — than just a pretty voice. Not that the voice was the traditional FM baritone, the measured voice of the politician or the pitchman. It was too distinctive, too much of what Maritime writer Sheree Fitch called "a stutter stammer" to be a conventional radio voice. But somehow it worked wonderfully well on the radio, and for fifteen years, from 1982 to 1997, for three hours a day on CBC's *Morningside*, it drew the country together as he played the role of what Peter C. Newman has shrewdly called "Canada's Boswell." The warm, rough, unpolished voice with the occasional guffaw gave him the role of uncle to a nation.

If anyone was inclined to doubt the truth of that statement, the reaction to Peter Gzowski's death in January 2002 was proof of his importance as a beloved national figure. On front pages and in news programs people who had known or worked with Peter spoke and wrote about him in his roles as a journalist, radio host, interviewer, author, father, literacy advocate, or chancellor of Trent University. Many of the tributes were notable for their forcefulness and their frankness: "He was a colleague, not a friend," his successor Michael Enright wrote in *Maclean's*, going on to confess, "No him, no me." But the most eloquent tributes of all came pouring in — to the CBC via *Cross Country Checkup*, or the station's website, or in letters to the editor of newspapers across the country — from ordinary people whose lives had been touched by him through the intimacy of radio, and who now missed him. Peter used to be proud of the number of people who listened to him on their tractors, or aboard their fishing boats, or in their kitchens. Now many of these people were signalling back, saying thank you, and doing so with a rare dignity and power.

He was much more than just a voice for two main reasons. First, the voice was attached to an extraordinary, inquiring mind. What listeners heard each morning was a new session in the Education of Peter Gzowski. The compulsive cryptic crossword solver really did want to know what was happening — who was gaining power in Ottawa, what the caplin were doing in Newfoundland, or how the salal berry jam was in B.C. As a result, in the judgement of Dalton Camp, Peter knew more about Canada than anyone in the world. His old friend Robert Fulford called him "the ultimate pan-Canadian figure of his time, at home in Yellowknife, St. John's or Calgary." Of his interviewing style Fulford wrote, "If attentiveness had been an academic subject, Gzowski would have had a Ph.D."

Of course he had not only a capacious mind, but also a very clear one. And it was that clarity that allowed him to take the detours beloved of parodists like Bob Robertson of *Double Exposure* (with "not to mentions" or, "and, I might adds" spiralling endlessly into the ether). At the time of his final *Morningside*, John Allemang in the *Globe and Mail* recalled him "asking questions that seemed to go on forever" — and then — "listening silently for minutes at a time as ordinary Canadians kept a nation spellbound with their words." He knew where his on-air sentence, however complex, was going, and how it was going to end. And he had enough confidence in his skill as an interviewer to know how to keep steering, even as he allowed the answers to dictate the flow and the general direction. His interviews — and he and I spoke more than once of publishing a deconstruction of some of his interviews, with his inner voice keeping up a running sidebar commentary, which would have made a fascinating book — were models of artlessness carried to the level of high art.

Which leads us to the main reason why he was so much more than a voice. He was, first and last, a writer. From his University of Toronto days as an editor at the *Varsity* in the 1950s through his time at *Maclean's*, all the way through his final, brief days as a columnist at the *Globe and Mail* in 2002, he was a writer. While his presence on the radio made him an icon, he liked to say that he was a writer who worked in radio. It was an important distinction. For him the vital skill was not the mastery of the microphone but the writer's craft; he had learned to ask the right questions of the right people, to assimilate the knowledge thus produced, and then to put it into clear, well-ordered prose, getting the story straight. That, to him, was real skill. Fulford, who knew him from his teenage years, when they both worked the night shift on the police beat in Toronto, has written of Peter's dismissal of a young journalist of apparently impressive talents. He would never do really well, Peter said, "because he doesn't know how hard it is." (He was right.) Fulford ended that essay with the thought, "Gzowski knew the difficulty of getting journalism right and remained terrified by the possibility of getting it wrong . . . He was afraid of failing to meet the standards he had set for himself. All his life, he had the courage, and the wisdom, to be scared."

He was born in Toronto in 1934, and at the age of six moved with his divorced and remarried mother to Galt, the Ontario town that is now part of Cambridge. The old mill town was created below the junction of the Speed River with the Grand. Today that grand but not very speedy river curls lazily around the Galt Country Club golf course, where thirteen-year-old Peter Gzowski worked one summer picking up locker room towels and selling illegal beers and cigarettes, and where Louise Brenneman, my remarkable mother-in-law, once got a hole-in-one at the age of seventy-five. Galt, you will gather, is Jane's hometown, and I know it well.

The textile mills beside the Grand drew nineteenth-century immigrants from milling areas in the Scottish Borders (represented by local place names like Dumfries), and it is still a very traditional place. Although she was originally a Toronto girl, Peter's mother ("Mrs. Brown" since her second marriage) had a degree from St. Andrews University in Scotland and put it to good use as the children's librarian in the old Galt Carnegie library, located hard by the distinctive humped bridge downtown. A few blocks uphill to the east — through the handsome stone downtown streets sucked dry by shopping malls in the suburbs — in the official city buildings, Cambridge celebrates its link with Peter Gzowski through a room devoted to him and his books.

In *The Private Voice*, his 1987 memoir, which I published, Peter writes affectionately about his time in Galt, playing in nearby Dickson Park (home of the baseball team the Galt Terriers) and going on to attend historic Galt Collegiate Institute. It all sounds very idyllic, especially the day that he and his pals discovered that an ice storm had left the entire town of 17,000 encased in ice, which allowed them to take their hockey game out of the rink and off — without limits — across the frozen fields. It is a memorable image. But wait.

In 2010 a new book, *Peter Gzowski: A Biography*, appeared. The author, R.B. Fleming, did a remarkable job of researching details of Peter Gzowski's life, and the 500-page book provides interesting information for those seeking a full, detailed account. Yet the very thoroughness of his research has been something of a drawback. When he finds that his hard-won facts contradict Peter's published accounts he takes it very, very seriously. He even quotes — with obvious prim disapproval — Peter's jokey confession that "he never let reality stand in the way of a good story."

In many cases the variations really don't matter: getting wrong the exact dates when his mother was at University in Scotland, ho, hum; at Galt Collegiate Institute, Peter clearly didn't hear William Henry Drummond — dead since 1907 — read his own poems in 1947, a stupid error that should have been caught by his idiot publisher, er, Doug Gibson. And as for Fleming's accusation that Peter simply made up the incident of taking the hockey game exuberantly across the frozen fields, my Galt informants say that in those days there were indeed rinks on the outskirts of the little town where this would have been highly possible. And so on.

But Fleming's basic point is fair. Peter often got the dates, or the facts, wrong, and usually erred on the side of drama and excitement — like, I might add, his hero W.O. Mitchell. Hilariously, Peter once confessed that, posing for a teenaged photo with his Galt football team, he stuck an unnecessary bandaid on his face, to make himself look tougher.

Fleming has done a fine job of untangling the complex lines of Peter's career. How at eleven, he "ran away from home" (or perhaps merely left to visit Toronto, as he often did) and was sent by his Gzowski grandfather to Ridley College, a private boys school in St. Catharines. There he suffered the slow misery of a severe "bleed through your basketball shirt" acne problem, and the sudden trauma of the death of his mother. "Peter," reports Fleming, "claimed that no one had told him of her illness." She was only forty, and her death hit Peter hard. Yet the love of reading that she had instilled in him led him to an interest in writing. From Ridley he went to the University of Toronto in 1952 to study English.

The next few years involved skipping lectures and drinking at his fraternity house or at the King Cole Room on Bloor Street. Much more important, it gave him time to learn the craft of journalism. In term time he worked at the *Varsity*. He also took a summer job at a newspaper in Timmins (it was better than earlier construction jobs in Labrador or Kitimat) and worked nights for the *Toronto Telegram*, until as the editor of the *Varsity* in 1950 he wrote an editorial that criticized the *Telegram*. That ended his job, but caught the attention of the legendary Ralph Allen at *Maclean's*.

After leaving the University of Toronto (without a degree, until the university gave him one in 1996) Peter worked for papers in Moose Jaw and then Chatham before Ralph Allen brought the young prodigy to *Maclean's* in 1958. *Maclean's* sent him and his Prairie bride, Jennie Lissaman, to live in Montreal, where Peter headed the Quebec bureau. Soon, at twenty-eight, he was the youngest-ever managing editor in the history of the venerable magazine.

Fleming has done a wonderful job of showing the wide range of articles Peter wrote during his magazine years, and his output continued long after he left prestigious posts as editor of *Maclean's* and editor of the *Star Weekly*, which was closed down on him after a year. He went through bad career times, even as his marriage to Jennie produced five children, Peter, Alison, Maria, John, and Mick. His kids were used to seeing their father, a traditional sort of dad, arrive at home just in time to peer into the pots to see what his wife was preparing for dinner. Most of Peter's time away from the office was spent with "the guys," playing poker, or bridge, or pool, or hanging out at the Park Plaza Roof cocktail bar, drinking and smoking. "Cigarettes," Robert Fulford noted, were "the emblem of easygoing manhood in his youth." Easy going, indeed.

In 1969 he took a stab at a new medium. He tried his hand at a CBC Radio program called *Radio Free Friday*, which attracted listeners and was noticeably different. In October 1971, with the help of a shrewd producer named Alec Frame (married to my wife's cousin) he created *This Country in the Morning*. And in the three years it ran, it won an ACTRA award for Peter and made him a big name. But what could you do with a radio program to further your wider career?

Enter Mel Hurtig, one of the most interesting Canadians of the century, any century. Mel started life as a bookseller in Edmonton and soon rose to be the president of Canadian Booksellers Association. That was the way it worked for this short, dapper, deeply tanned man. He was such a force of nature — so energetic, with a silver tongue that won him Toastmaster's Awards — that he tended to rise to the top of every organization he ever joined. (Sometimes, admittedly, he short-circuited this process by founding the organization, as he has done with a couple of national political parties.) Eventually, ignoring all advice, Mel decided to put his eternal optimism where it would do most good — as a Canadian book publisher based in Alberta.

Roy MacSkimming in *The Perilous Trade* has given a thrilling account of Mel's roller-coaster ride in the publishing world, a ride that has brought him well-earned fame. His shrewd instinct as a publisher shows in many of the books he chose, not least in the proposition he made in 1972 to Peter Gzowski.

*"But you can't make a book out of a radio program!"* That was the emphatic response that Peter gave to Mel's publishing proposal, one evening in the Park Plaza Hotel. But Mel persisted with the idea, claiming that he had a designer, David Shaw, who would find the perfect way to package what he would call *Peter Gzowski's Book About This Country in the Morning*, so that the book caught the spirit of the show. He had an editor on the scene in Toronto, Susan Kent, and a managing editor back in Edmonton, Jan Walter, who would help Peter pull it all together and make it a huge success.

And so it proved. Mel was right, spectacularly right. The book was a huge success. And the same Peter Gzowski who said so decisively that you couldn't make a book out of a radio program went on to sell many hundreds of thousands of copies of his six books based around his *Morningside* radio program.

Before those days, however, there was the matter of *Peter Gzowski's Spring Tonic*. Buoyed by the success of his first book with Mel, Peter suggested that this book would be a huge success and extracted a large advance from Mel, who was cautious, but agreed to publish it. In the end, the book — hampered perhaps by the fact that a Spring Tonic book logically has to be published in the spring, when book sales are not large — sold very badly. Mel lost money, lost his disappointed author, and lost his managing editor. In working together

Jan Walter and Peter had fallen in love, and she had moved east to Toronto to join him.

And here I must be selfish. I was delighted to be able to hire Jan as an editor at Macmillan. Jan — a lovely, unflappable woman who is gentle in voice and in manner — proved to be a superb editor and publisher, first as my colleague at Macmillan, then at M&S, then as the co-publisher at Macfarlane Walter & Ross.

Yet the break-up of Peter's marriage was hard on everyone, especially when it came to telling the kids. Fleming rightly says, "Peter's writing is at its best in the section of the memoirs that deals with this moment. 'Until I die, I will remember. John, aged twelve, going upstairs to his room, fighting back silent tears.' (Anyone who has had the experience — as Sally and I have — of explaining the break-up of a marriage to their children, will understand.) In fact, the next few years were difficult ones for Peter, after he hosted a late-night TV talk show that became a disastrous, very public failure. After it failed, he drank more than was good for him. It seems clear now that he was also fighting depression. Barbara Frum was a good friend, in this time of need, inviting him to sit in for her at *As It Happens*, which got the voice back on the air.

And then in 1982, came *Morningside*.

But while we let the *Morningside* music theme play in the background, let's stick with Mel Hurtig for now. He became a large part of my life when in 1992 M&S bought Mel's company, and the books, and their authors, that he had published. This brought me in touch with fine authors like Desmond Morton (whose book *A Short History of Canada* is revised every three or four years) and many more.

As a keen birdwatcher I took special interest in *A Bird Finding Guide to Canada* by Cam Findlay. I remember visiting him in Victoria, both of us training our binoculars on the grebes and ducks on the Esquimalt Lagoon, while I worked to persuade him that "updating the book won't really take much of your time, Cam." It worked. And after that, any trip to Victoria involved a birding expedition with Cam. Once, late in the fall, a visit to Goldstream Park had us watching the last survivors of the salmon run, as the exhausted fish slowly heaved themselves the last few yards upstream to spawn. Cam and I were watching a nearby American Dipper (the unique little perching bird that can flit from tree to rock and then plunge under the water for a few seconds before perching on another branch). As we watched, one adventurous Dipper flew *to land on the back of a salmon rolling upstream*, hitched a ride for five seconds, then flew off to perch on a nearby tree.

"Have you ever seen that before?" I asked Cam, the lifelong birder.

"Never," he replied, and we are both glad to be able to tell the tale, quoting a witness, as I do now.

On another visit Cam roped me into banding hummingbirds at dawn in a Victoria garden, catching them in mist nets. Yes, they are just as tiny and weightless in your palm as you would imagine, but that is a tale for another day.

Avie Bennett had been keen to acquire Mel's company, not just to allow me to come to grips with hummingbirds, but because of Mel's greatest achievement, *The Canadian Encyclopedia*. This ten-year project (1975–1985) was in Roy MacSkimming's words "unquestionably a triumph, primarily because of Hurtig's dedication. No other publisher in the country possessed his combination of vision, guts, political savvy, publishing knowledge, marketing skills, financial smarts and personal energy, all needed to implement such a project and surmount the obstacles."

Incredibly, although he had been a Liberal candidate in the province in the 1972 election, Mel was able to persuade the far-sighted Tory Premier of Alberta, Peter Lougheed, to mark the province's seventy-fifth anniversary by making "a gift to Canada" of the Alberta-grown *Encyclopedia*, with the aid of a provincial grant of $4 million. Obviously a project on this scale involved hundreds of workers (even the printing of the three navy-blue volumes required *twenty-seven* different Canadian firms). When he was setting it up, Mel approached me by phone, asking if I would be interested in being general editor. It was an honour to be asked, but I had other exciting fish to fry, as this book indicates. Also, I'm not sure how serious Mel was in his approach, or whether his net was cast really wide. One thing is certain: in James Marsh he got the right man for the job, which has proved to be a lifetime project for my friend.

Mel and Jim have been rightly recognized and honoured by the

Order of Canada and by many other civic and academic bodies, but their real lasting achievement is to be found in the three blue (later expanded to four red) volumes of *The Canadian Encyclopedia* that now adorn so many thousands of Canadian homes. That the second edition, followed by *The Canadian Children's Encyclopedia*, was crippled by quirks of the Canadian book market, and eventually forced Mel to sell his company, is a tragic story well covered by Roy MacSkimming. *The Perilous Trade* is indeed an apt title.

I myself was the publisher of what will surely prove to be the very last printed edition of *The Canadian Encyclopedia*. As MacSkimming put it, in 2000 M&S "published a mammoth unabridged edition in one volume; containing 2,640 pages and over four million words it was the largest single book ever published in Canada." My friend Jim Marsh, of course, was in charge editorially (and he was amused when I had to insert a last-minute biography to prevent a blank page in the middle of the book), and Jim continues his good work in updating the *Encyclopedia* in the electronic forms that have made print versions no longer profitable.

And Mel? After a lively career in bookselling, and an even livelier one in publishing, he became an author. (I am skipping lightly over his other career as a politician.) His autobiography, *At Twilight in the Country* (1996) was a great commercial success and revealed some of the confidence that had marked his career. His other political books all demonstrate his alert, concerned patriotism. We need more Mel Hurtigs — even if no one would call him understated — standing on guard for all of us.

At M&S we published a number of his books, and when I took on the role of editing *The Truth About Canada* in 2008, his former editor, Jonathan Webb, warned me what to expect. According to Jonathan — a superb editor — Mel's general enthusiasm, even reverently expressed admiration, for the vitally useful work of editors, tended to stop abruptly at any actual concrete examples of proposed editorial changes to his own pristine work. I found this to be largely true. . . .

I should explain that I have known Mel for over forty years, having visited him in the room overlooking the first Edmonton bookstore. As a visitor to his magnificent apartment above the Saskatchewan River valley, I have sat on a couch, very still, while his two great

German shepherds, Jasper and Oliver, crouched nearby, looking tense and hungry. Mel, dashing in and out of the room, proudly assured me that they were both very intelligent, and that Oliver, indeed, understood a vocabulary of over 500 words. I tried to find this reassuring as I carefully crossed my legs.

Domestic upheaval led Mel to leave Edmonton (where he was a fixture, and a well-deserved member of the city's Cultural Hall of Fame) and move to Vancouver, where he continues to scan the papers and maintain his contacts in the political world, seeking (and finding) evidence of the corporate sellout of Canadian independence. As he promoted his 2008 book I was sorry to see that, at seventy-six, he had lost some of his vitality and found a nap in my car a necessary prelude to a talk in Burlington. But he is still unsinkable. Some weeks later, reporting on a brilliant success with a speech elsewhere, he challenged me to guess what mark out of ten that superb speech had deserved.

"A ten?" I ventured, knowing my man.

"No. A twelve!" crowed Mel.

Incorrigible.

*Morningside* changed Peter Gzowski's life. And it changed the lives of Canada's writers and their publishers. Because Peter the writer never forgot how hard it was to fill a blank sheet of paper, or a screen, with well-ordered words. As a result he respected the work of other writers, and delighted in celebrating their talents. What he achieved with his one radio program for the authors — and the booksellers and readers — of Canada is almost beyond belief. Long before there was an Oprah there was Peter Gzowski. And long before there was an "Oprah effect," there was "the *Morningside* effect," introduced by words that can still make millions sit up and start to hum. "Good morning, I'm Peter Gzowski, and this is *Morningside*."

"Immeasurable" was the word Jane Urquhart used at the tribute in Convocation Hall to describe the debt that she and the other Canadian writers owed to Peter Gzowski. It may be hard for anyone who was not an adult in Canada in those days to understand just how important that program was to the creation of an audience for our own books and writers. Peter and his brilliant staff actively sought out young and unknown writers — even a young poet named Jane Urquhart — and gave them a public forum. If the interview took flight (as with writers of all sorts they often did), then the phones would start ringing in bookstores across the country. The impact on a book's sales was so immediate and so strong that before the end of the eighties booksellers were pleading with publishers to tell them when an author was going to be on *Morningside*, so that they could order extra copies accordingly. And people in publishing will remember that in the peak years of the program a confirmed interview with Peter Gzowski — or in the case of Alice Munro, a series of interviews — was enough to send publicists whooping down the halls.

Alice Munro has for many years been famously reluctant to undertake publicity tours, and in a position to tell her publisher to abandon any hopes in that direction. But even she was willing to make an exception for Peter Gzowski, and she has given a lovely author's account of an interview with him:

> Having Peter interview you was a lot like learning to swim. He held you up for as long as you needed it, so easily and gracefully and unobtrusively that it almost seemed as if he was learning to swim, too. Then, at some moment, he let you go, let you take your own direction, trusted you to do it right. I think his listeners felt that he trusted them, too. He trusted them to take an adult interest in their country, to wish to be informed and entertained without condescension. And their response showed how their lives were opened and their days warmed by such easy courtesy, such comfortable respect.
>
> I should say, too, that he was a wonderful help to writers. Nobody was ever more effective in getting news of our books out to the people who might like to read them. So I'd say he was a help to readers as well. He was a help to all of us, for a long time.

I first met Peter when he was an aging "boy wonder" in the 1960s, and he struck me then as someone who was working hard at being unimpressed by those around him. But we were moving in the same world and we stayed vaguely in touch. In 1978, during his time as a daily columnist for the *Toronto Star*, for example, he called me up and asked if he could spend an evening canvassing with me for the local municipal elections. Sure enough, we roamed around door-to-door one autumn night, with Peter standing politely in the background while I encouraged the household to vote for my friend William

Kilbourn, and put in a good word for the outsider who was running for mayor, John Sewell.

Peter got his story of a typical canvasser at work, and my involvement in the Sewell Campaign reached the unexpected point that on the day before the vote I found myself addressing the final campaign rally in the St. Lawrence Market North Hall with the words: "And now, the man we've all been waiting for — our candidate, and the next Mayor of the City of Toronto . . . John Sewell!" To everyone's surprise it proved to be true. The outsider made it, and did well at City Hall. Peter did not cover my amazingly successful speech, which clearly turned the tide in John's favour.

Once, during his time with Jan, the Gibson family was invited for a visit to the place at Rockwood, near Guelph. We must have arrived early, for Jan was not around, and our calls of "Anyone at home?" produced no results. Wandering in, we found Peter asleep with his bare feet up in the main room, snoring loudly. What to do?

We tiptoed back out and restaged our arrival in the car, slamming the car doors and shouting cheery comments before banging on the door. It worked. But he really was like a bear with a sore head waking up, and it took a while for him to become a gracious host. And he really did snore to beat the band. He could have snored for Canada.

Peter and I were what you might call working friends. Although I once stayed with him and the admirable Gill Howard (his final life partner, in sickness and in health) at the lovely Sutton house where the backyard merged with a fairway of the Briars golf course (the course his grandfather had played), it was to spend time planning a book. Later, I visited that house on other occasions, around the time of his Red Barn Theatre event and the next day's golfing to raise funds for literacy; they were both events that he loved, surrounded by friends.

Here I must make a confession: although I grew up in an athletic household in Scotland (and my father was the captain of the local golf club, Barassie, on the Ayrshire coast), I became the Most Erratic Golfer in the World. I am the only golfer you will ever meet who *lost a ball approaching the eighteenth green at St. Andrews*. That sacred green, of course, is backed by roads, and buildings, including the big sandstone one that was my residence during my first year at university, and on the right the approach is guarded by parked cars, crowds of pedestrians, shops, and houses. And that was where I sliced my approach shot. Hard. For about ten seconds there was a series of clangs and thuds and jangles, and when I searched for it — afraid of lynching — the ball had simply disappeared. It seemed prudent to abandon the hole. . . .

On occasion, my game achieved respectability. At the Peter Gzowski Invitational Golf Tournament for Literacy (still going strong every summer, having raised over $12 million) at the Briars my game was predictably erratic. There was, however, a short hole where one of the sponsors had donated a new car that would go to anyone who hit a hole in one there, under the eye of a careful watcher. Miraculously, that was the moment my swing came good. As the ball sailed towards the pin, then rolled across the green straight towards the hole I had time to ponder — take the prize, or make the Grand Gesture by transforming it into cash that you donate to the Literacy Fund? But the ball stopped five feet from the hole — a long five feet — and my anguished decision was averted. I still don't know.

In his biography, one of Fleming's two most contentious points concerns golf. He claims that Peter "cheated" at golf (smile when you say that, pardner). Peter, famously, hated to lose at any game, from Monopoly to snooker to bridge, and would go to great lengths to avoid it. But Fleming's golf accusation is not proved in his book. Peter was guilty of bad manners on the occasion in question, and of pushing the envelope, certainly, but not of cheating.

His other very contentious point concerns Peter's supposed ambivalence about homosexuality. Fleming quotes many references to male athletes in his writing, and notes Peter's discomfort with homosexuality, even (unfairly, I think) noting that Peter's name was not among the signers of a pro-gay petition. Fleming may be onto something when he notes Peter's discomfort with the subject of homosexuality, but I think that he underestimates the degree of ignorance of "the love that dared not speak its name" that prevailed in most circles that Peter inhabited in those benighted days.

A story will help to make my point. Around 1970 two of Peter's former colleagues at *Maclean's*, Doug Marshall and Allan Edmonds, were looking for an office for the new magazine, *Books in Canada*, that Doug was co-founding with Val Clery and Jack Jensen. I know this story because (now it can be told!) I was involved as an anonymous essayist, "STET," in the earliest issues.

On this famous occasion Doug Marshall was intent on touring the potential new office premises with the landlord. His colleague Allan Edmonds was at a loose end and asked if he could come along, just to pass the time. Marshall agreed, making it clear that Edmonds had no active role there.

After the landlord had given the tour of the office (around Yonge and Charles Street, as I recall) Marshall agreed to think about the deal, and they parted. Then Marshall shrewdly decided to check on the landlord, the heating, the services, and so on, with another tenant in the building, any random tenant. He and Edmonds found themselves outside the office of the leading homosexual advocacy group in the city, the Toronto Homophile Society. They knocked on the door, and a nice man who introduced himself as George Hislop received them politely.

As Marshall asked him factual questions about the heating and the janitors, Edmonds began to act very strangely, pacing around and snorting. Finally, to Marshall's amazement he burst out, "God, I feel so sorry for you people." This was greeted by stunned silence. But the good-hearted Edmonds was just warming up.

"You must feel so different about your bodies. You must feel so vulnerable."

Marshall was gasping in disbelief. It was getting worse and worse, and Hislop was clearly not impressed.

"And of course," Edmonds blundered on, "so many prominent people in history have been — well, like you, have suffered your disease in secret."

Now Marshall was on the point of manhandling Edmonds out the door, when he went on: "Yes, people like Queen Victoria, and of course the Russian Royal Family."

The penny dropped as these prominent hemophiliacs were mentioned, and Hislop and Marshall went from outrage to helpless laughter. But Edmonds, an experienced journalist at *Maclean's*, had just given an important lesson on just how widespread ignorance of homosexuality and the gay world was in Peter Gzowski's early days.

Since these distant days I have edited books of his such as his autobiography, *The Private Voice* (1988), and am proud that his last book, *A Peter Gzowski Reader*, also bears the Douglas Gibson Books logo.

This is because after many years as a McClelland & Stewart author Peter told me that he'd like to work with me in my editorial imprint. "Ah well," I said, "that really is only open to authors coming from outside M&S. I can't just take over the best authors for myself." He was unimpressed. "What if I stamp my pretty little foot and say that's the way it's going to be?" He won, of course; the stamp of approval, you might say.

I may have counted him as a friend, but Peter was never easy to work with, if "easy" means automatic agreement with the publisher's plans. We sparred over contracts, where I was shocked to discover that he liked to get his own way, and he was a perfectionist over the book's contents. He was, in other words, a pro, and I enjoyed working with him over the years. I was distressed almost beyond speech when I first visited him at the Toronto waterfront apartment he shared with the faithful Gill, and found him with his walker and oxygen tank. Some of my McClelland & Stewart colleagues who had the misfortune to be taking a relaxing cigarette break outside the building that afternoon still recall, no doubt, my explosive return by taxi from seeing Peter laid low by nicotine.

I was less outspoken when on my first phone call after a major operation, I heard him pause and make a tiny sucking noise. "Peter," I said, aghast, "that wasn't what it sounded like? You're not smoking again?" There was nothing to say. His last piece of writing, for the anthology *Addiction*, was entitled "How to Stop Smoking in 50 Years or Less." It was very sad.

My own interviews as a guest on *Morningside* were uniformly sad, dealing with the recent death of authors like Hugh MacLennan or Robertson Davies. (My Vancouver friend Alan Twigg once saw me on TV, and said, "Oh dear, Doug's on the news again — I wonder who has died now.") But I was glad to go through the experience of a Peter Gzowski interview that so many others have described: little eye contact, not much attempt at personal charm, all of the energy going into the questions. He was a keen-eared interviewer, but never a keen-eyed one. At the private funeral at Frontier College, a relative spoke of a moment by the hospital bed near the end when he was drifting in and out of consciousness, and his eyeglasses were put in place. They looked wrong, somehow, and one family member suggested that everyone should fix that by smearing the lenses with their thumbs.

R.B. Fleming's biography shows clearly that Peter was not a saint. Fleming quotes many former friends who talk convincingly about what a fierce competitor he was, and how he could be "brutal" in verbal judgements, and sulk when he lost at games of volleyball (for God's sake) at his Toronto Island summer cottage. In the fundraising book *Remembering Peter Gzowski* that I published in 2002 after his death, his *Morningside* assistant for many years, Shelley Ambrose, affectionately tells of how he tried to dissuade her from taking the job "explaining that he was a difficult person to work with — a perfectionist, a workaholic, a grump — and advised me that I really didn't want this job." Although she took it, and thrived, I have the sense that he was giving her fair warning.

Fleming's book indicates that life at *Morningside* was not always sweetness and light. What, a five-days-a-week three-hour program staffed by bright, competitive people occasionally showing strain? Hard to believe. But I know from my own special friends like Gloria Bishop, Hal Wake, Shelagh Rogers, and Shelley Ambrose — and the many other staffers who contributed so eloquently to the posthumous tribute book — that Peter was for them the life and soul of their program. Hal Wake, in a private letter to Peter in 1997, summed it up. "Everything I know and understand about radio," he began, "I learned from *Morningside*."

Fleming also established beyond doubt that Peter's relations with women were far from perfect. There were, of course, his long, intimate relations with his "three J's": with Jennie, his wife; with Jan Walter; and finally with faithful Gill Howard, his life partner for his last twenty years. Of all people, Mavis Gallant was involved in this final switch in his intimate life. As writer-in-residence at the University of Toronto in 1983–84 she was glad to be asked with her friend Kathleen Davis, wife of Premier Bill Davis, to come with Peter to see the Woodbine Racetrack outside Toronto. (Peter knew of Mavis's enthusiasm for horse racing and light betting on the races.) In Fleming's words, "Gallant noticed that Peter paid a lot of attention to a young woman whom he asked to give Gallant and Davis a tour of the facilities. Gallant wondered about the young woman's

identity. 'Oh,' explained Davis, 'that's Gzowski's new girlfriend.'"
The young woman, of course, was Gill Howard, who handled pub-
licity for the Jockey Club. They had first met when Peter was writing
*An Unbroken Line*, his book about horse racing.

Fleming's book tells an amusing story where simply being under
Mavis Gallant's eye unnerved Peter. In 1997, he and Bonnie Burnard
joined Mavis in Paris to make their decisions as the Giller Prize jury.
Mavis has (as I know) a cool, appraising eye. Suddenly, when the
three judges were chatting over coffee, Peter burst out, "Oh, stop
being Mavis Gallant." She was shocked, and was never clear what he
meant. I think that we can assume that Peter, torn between being a
public figure who wanted privacy, and a private person who enjoyed
publicity, was afraid of Mavis's watchful study, and its potential
appearance in a story some day.

He had reasons to be nervous. Hidden in his past — successfully,
until Fleming the dogged researcher dug it up — was the story of his
affair with his former *Maclean's* colleague Cathy Perkins of Kingston,
who in February 1961 gave birth to Peter's son Robert Lawrence
Perkins. Peter maintained secret contact with her, and with young
Rob ("'You're my father!' exclaimed Rob"), but he never met Rob's
daughter, Caitlan.

In his prime Peter was a big, bulky, shambling man, a bear-walker
you might say. His rumpled appearance (the famous comparison to
"an unmade bed" on bad days was unkind to some beds I have known)
was no surprise to the thousands of loyal fans who lined up to meet
him at book signings, including many for his wildly successful series
of *Morningside Papers*. They were surprised, however, by his shyness,
which was part of the man, and helped account for his failure on live
TV. Yet he willingly undertook these tours because he was a pro who
liked his books to do well, and because he relished witnessing "the
*Morningside* effect" on his own books.

What do these books — and his others, almost all fixtures on the
bestseller lists — tell us about Peter Gzowski the writer? That he
wrote well about his enthusiasms – hockey, or golf, or horse racing,
or journalism, or broadcasting. That he could turn his hand to an
astonishing variety of subjects, from the perils of being dismasted in
mid-Caribbean to the pleasures of family hopscotch. What proved to

be his last book, in his lifetime, *A Peter Gzowski Reader*, demonstrates the range of his skills, as journalist, essayist, narrator, and polemicist for Canada, and shows us he was, always, a writer.

Sadly, what might have been his greatest book will never be written. He was at work in his final years on a book about the North, the last frontier that he knew well and loved with a passion, and he and I often spoke excitedly about its prospects. In the end he lost the race to finish it, and we all lost a potentially great book. At the private family funeral, Susan Aglugark paid an unforgettable Northern tribute to him, her clear voice rising out over the Toronto rooftops as she sang "Amazing Grace" in Inuktitut, magically linking the clouds above with those stretching all the way to the Arctic.

Others have written about the glorious work he did for literacy, raising more than $12 million (and counting, as the tradition goes on) for Frontier College through his golf tournaments. (And his old Frontier College friend John O'Leary remembers other much less glamorous times he spent doing literacy work — in prison, for example, far from the fun of the golf course.) I remember a crowded Saturday meeting at the University of Toronto where student literacy volunteers were gathered from across the country. Did he thank them, and congratulate them? No. He ended his talk with the thought: "Aren't we lucky — *aren't we lucky* — to be able to do important work like this that we love?" I like to think he would have said the same about his own life and work.

# CHAPTER 20

# VAL ROSS

Journalist, Author, and Maker of Rules

The byline was Goderich, Ontario, but the setting of the *Globe and Mail* piece was the neighbouring town of Blyth, where a fundraising dinner was being served to benefit the local theatre. The story began:

"Excuse me, but I hear there's a famous lady writer who lives near here," said the man in the Blyth Hall, summoning an alert-looking, sixtyish waitress to his table. "I hear she sometimes comes to this festival."

The waitress nodded her silver curls.

"Would that by any chance be her?" The man indicated a nearby table. A woman sat alone, artistic and dramatic. Wrapped in patterned shawls, the woman held high a fine head of auburn hair.

"I'm not sure," admitted the waitress. She sized up the woman and then, encouragingly, whispered back, "Yes, I think that might be her."

Alice Munro, who was the silver-haired waitress, gives a guilty laugh when she tells this story.

Val Ross was the author of this famous article, which tells so much about Alice Munro, and about the standard of journalism Val Ross set for herself, reporting on the Canadian cultural scene for *Maclean's* and then the *Globe and Mail*. She looked and wrote like an angel and every sensible publisher spent years trying to get her to write a book. That would, of course, be no problem, slipped in between her time spent raising three children with Morton, kicking people in her karate class, travelling, and leading a life full of friends, and of colleagues who were soon to be friends. How could you resist someone who came up to your desk, bearing sticks of fresh celery and saying, "I've decided that you deserve a celery increase"?

In due course she wrote two excellent books for children. The first was *The Road to There: Mapmakers and Their Stories*, which won the Norma Fleck Award as the best Canadian book of the year for children. The second, *You Can't Read This*, was even more ambitious. In Val's words, "This book is a history of reading. But it is also about people who have been denied the power of reading. It's about lost writing, forbidden books, mistranslations, codes, and vanished libraries. It's about censors, vandals, and spies. It's about people who write in secret. And it's about people who devote their hearts and brains to learning what has been written."

Eventually, I persuaded Val to write a book for adults: it was one of the greatest compliments of my life that she — on first-name terms with every good publisher in the land — chose to publish it with my editorial imprint. The fit was very good. Val's year as a journalism fellow at Massey College had imbued her with the spirit of Massey's founding master, Robertson Davies. Now she had the brilliant idea of producing an "oral biography" of my old friend and author by interviewing people who had known him.

All went well for three years as Val did her research and started the book, and I received pleasing reports of progress. Then came the events that will answer any reader of this book who wonders why a little-published author, with only one adult book — *Robertson Davies: A Portrait in Mosaic* — earned a place here, in this book, alongside authors like Munro, Gallant, MacLeod, and Davies himself.

Read on.

The phone message was recorded early in November: "Doug. It's Val Ross. I have brain cancer and it's been operated on and I'm home and at work on the book. I've almost completed chapter thirty-three and I've roughed out the next two chapters . . ."

And so on, with more book details. It was clear right from the start how Val wanted to play this. Val's Rules.

So I called back and asked about chapter thirty-three, and then talked about how far my editing had gone and what I was finding. And then after ten book-filled minutes I cleared my throat and started: "You'll notice that I haven't said how terrible . . ." And she cut me off, telling me there was no need for any of that. She was a tough Scot, she said, and she was going to get on with finishing the book. Val's Rule Number One: no self-pity.

And so we played by Val's Rules. Our phone calls were always about the book, or about arranging what Val teasingly described as my "house calls." If after the book talk was over, I ventured to ask how she was doing she would say, for example, "Well, I'm not quite in what Bertie Wooster would call 'mid-season form.'" And we'd be off and laughing about Hugh Laurie and his pop-eyed P.G. Wodehouse character, and the subject would be successfully deflected. Val's Rules.

As for the house calls, they were full of work and jokes. We'd sit side by side at the dining room table and do our stuff. Once, just before Christmas 2007, the kids were home and we did our editing together in front of Max and Maddie, both back from university. I'd never edited with an audience before, but there, in that house, it seemed easy and natural and right. Once Val even jokingly complained that she wasn't getting the full authorial treatment: weren't authors and their editors supposed to fight? But we were too busy for any of that, working against a clock that we never acknowledged. Val's Rules.

The house calls revealed physical changes. One day she was wearing a rakish fur hat. "I'm bald," she announced, adding, "balder than you!" This was a detail that I would certainly have edited out.

Then, as her left side seized up, I would sit on her left and turn the pages for her. In the Davies book there are references to his turning the pages for musicians, so even that was fodder for a wry joke. Val's Rules.

I tried to introduce my own rule, which was that as soon as work on the book became too hard for her, I'd take over. "I know what I'm doing," I said. "I've done this before." This was a cue for more jokes from Val, about my boyish inexperience — but she never took me up on the offer.

She saw the book through the proofs stage, approved the cover, and wrote her final acknowledgements just three days before she died.

Following Val's Rules, at McClelland & Stewart we refused to let our grief delay the book, and moved fast to get it out in June. The book was reviewed with admiration and sold well. At the end of 2008 it was selected by the *Globe and Mail* as one of the Year's 100 Best Books. An equally significant tribute came in from the people she had interviewed. When they received their copy of the book, scores of them wrote to me to praise how Val had accurately reflected their words, to say how much they had enjoyed the time spent with her, and to mourn the fact that they could not send their congratulations to her directly.

The February memorial service was held in a packed Massey College, and like the best such "celebrations of a life," it revealed to everyone the wide range of her friendships, and many hidden aspects of Val's life, including this saintly woman's karate skills. Now a discreet plaque in that same common room records the spot where she liked to sit, and talk, or read, or write.

A final thought. When I told Robertson Davies's daughter, Jennifer Surridge, about Val's death, she spoke of the "joy" that working on the book had brought Val in those last few months. I like to think that's true. And I won't forget the "house call" conversation when Val remarked on how many Robertson Davies books had come out since his death. "Yes," I said, carefully, "and books do live on."

The phrase hung in the air between us, and I could see that Val was pleased. But of course she didn't say anything. Val's Rules.

# CHAPTER 21

1931–

# ALICE MUNRO

Not Bad Short Story Writer

When I reach the Pearly Gates, I know that I have the perfect password to get in. Even if St. Peter is at his grumpy, bureaucratic worst — "So what have you ever done in your miserable, selfish life to deserve getting into Heaven?" — I can waltz in simply by saying, "I kept Alice Munro writing short stories."

And he, if his English is any good, will rush to wave me through, maybe even making a saintly exclamation like "Holy smokes, Alice Munro!"

I even have the documents to prove it. When Robert Thacker was hard at work researching his masterful biography entitled *Alice Munro: Writing Her Lives*, (2005, since revised and updated, and published in 2011) he came upon a letter that Alice wrote in March 1986. The situation was this: I had just left Macmillan of Canada to set up Douglas Gibson Books at M&S, and Alice was keen to join me there, with her book *The Progress of Love* that I had signed up for Macmillan. Linda McKnight, the new head of Macmillan, was less keen on this idea. So Alice wrote her the following letter, asking to be set free from her contract, in order to join me:

> Doug first talked to me about publishing with Macmillan in the mid-seventies. I was very discouraged at the time. Ryerson had done nothing to promote or even distribute my first book. McGraw-Hill Ryerson had published the second with expressed reluctance and the third without enthusiasm — merely, I believe, to keep a Canadian fiction writer on their list. Every publisher I had met had assured me that I would have to grow up and write novels before I could be taken seriously as a writer. No one in Canada had shown the least interest in taking on a writer who was going to turn out book after book of short stories. The result of this was that I wasted much time and effort trying to turn myself into a novelist, and had become so depressed that I was unable to write at all. Doug changed that. He was absolutely the first person in Canadian publishing who made me feel that there was no need to apologize for being

a short story writer, and that a book of short stories could be published and promoted as major fiction. This was a fairly revolutionary idea at the time. It was his support that enabled me to go on working, when I had been totally uncertain about my future.

I came to Macmillan because of Doug, and his respect for my work changed me from a minor, "literary" writer who sold poorly into a major writer who sold well. I hope you will understand how I have felt, from that time on, that I owe him a great deal, and I want him to have charge of any book I publish. I am not making a judgement against Macmillan — my relations in the house have always been good — but for Doug Gibson.

In the end, thanks to Avie Bennett's generosity in paying Macmillan a fee to free Alice, it all worked out. In fact it worked out so well that the *Toronto Star* reported that I had "scored a coup by acquiring Canadian publishing rights to the work of Alice Munro from Macmillan." The *Globe and Mail* reported the story, which included the news that Hugh MacLennan and W.O. Mitchell were also coming with me, under the agreeable headline "CanLit Luminaries Stick with Gibson."

It was priceless publicity for my new line. In the next few years, so many Macmillan authors chose to follow me to M&S that Macmillan simply stopped publishing fiction. And *The Progress of Love* sold far better than even our highest hopes had predicted, handsomely recovering our investment.

This is a good place to pay tribute to Avie Bennett, a good friend of Alice, and of mine. It was typical of Avie that he would take the gamble of paying out what I call a large "ransom" to Macmillan (despite which my former employer, sadly, went downhill and disappeared) in order to let Alice's new book start off my new imprint with a bang. He had used that same daring gambler's instinct to make a fortune as a developer, and then, fairly late in his life, after joining the M&S board to help it through bad times, had used it again to buy the company in 1986. He soon lured me there to start my imprint, and from September 1988 until he sold the company in mid-2000, he and I were in and out of each other's office for hours every day, and I got to know him very well.

Michael Levine, the entertainment lawyer, agent, and ubiquitous man-about-town, called us "the Odd Couple," exulting in the
many differences between me, the fancy-pants literary guy, and Avie,
the businessman from the school of hard knocks who, among many
other differences, did not share my aversion to alcohol. Avie used
to complain publicly that I was "stubborn" (a charge I'll fight to my
dying day), and I would roll my eyes at his passion for doing things
differently, for "trying something new." I learned that it was a terrible mistake ever to propose a solution by saying, "Well, here's what
we usually do in publishing. . ." But I also learned that he was such
a bright guy that his new ideas were often good ones, and that they
were motivated by the same love of books — and of doing a good
job for our authors, and selling lots of copies — as my own, more
traditional, plans.

For his dedicated (often very expensive) support of McClelland &
Stewart over the years, Canada's writers — and their readers — owe
him a great deal. His support of many other good causes is impossible to quantify, because he preferred to do so much of his good
work secretly, as an "Anonymous Donor."

Editors, too, are usually fairly anonymous (unless they shamelessly blazon their own imprint all over their books) and it is always
a magical thing for editors to find a book dedicated to them by the
author. That is what happened to me with Alice's very personal 2006
book, *The View from Castle Rock*, which is a fiction collection based
on the history of her own family, the Laidlaws. Her dedication at
the front of the book is pure Alice. "Dedicated to Douglas Gibson,
who has sustained me through many travails, and whose enthusiasm
for this particular book has even sent him prowling through the
graveyard of Ettrick Kirk, probably in the rain" (as I check the exact
wording, I find that Alice has corrected these words in my personal
signed copy, adding "For Doug, who is even more loyal and admirable and funny than this indicates").

Let me explain the Ettrick Kirk reference, by accounting for the
*(rain-free!)* research trip that I took with my wife Jane who is —
almost by definition — a patient woman. She has always cheerfully
accompanied me on the routine social occasions, and even the more
unusual expeditions, that a book publisher's life provides. Yet a raw
winter morning spent poking around unglamorous streets in the east

end of Montreal, following the career of Yves Beauchemin's bold young hero, Charles Thibodeau, once moved her to ask, "Let me get this straight. We're tracing the life — finding the high school, and the church where they buried his mother, and so on — of a *fictional* character?"

It was more a comment than a complaint, you understand, and she listened politely, shivering only slightly, while I explained the need to catch just the right atmosphere on the cover for *Charles the Bold* and the rest of the series, and how vital it is for an editor to fully understand a character's life, blah, blah, blah, blah.

But these things even out. She was much keener when we interrupted a visit to Scotland in order to explore the setting for the first chapters of Alice's then-forthcoming book, *The View from Castle Rock*. We knew that Alice's ancestors, the Laidlaws, came to Canada in 1817 from the Scottish Borders. We had also learned from the first version of the manuscript that the earliest known Laidlaw relative, born around 1700, lived at the very end of the Ettrick Valley, at a farm named Far Hope. We were sure that we could find it.

The Ettrick River flows roughly from west to east into the North Sea about halfway between Edinburgh and the English border. From the town of Peebles we drove south until we met the Ettrick Valley. On the way we passed Tushielaw (Alice, I remembered from the manuscript, on her own exploration had caught a bus from Tushielaw — not a name you forget).

Following the river west we were among wild, lonely, bare hills, sheep country for many generations, ever since the medieval forest that once sheltered William "Braveheart" Wallace's guerillas was felled, leaving no trace but the name "Ettrick Forest." The only place that had even a cluster of houses, and a small grey school, was Ettrick itself. There, in the graveyard by the Kirk, we found the grave of William Laidlaw of Far Hope, locally called "Phaup." The tombstone memorably declares: "Here lyeth William Laidlaw, the far-fam'd Will o' Phaup who for feats of frolic, agility and strength, had no equal in his day."

Beside it lay the grave of the man who wrote the epitaph, Will's grandson, James Hogg, author of *The Private Memoirs and Confessions of a Justified Sinner* (1824), and a great literary figure in his day. I copied the wording down carefully for Alice's book. Inside the spare

Presbyterian church I noted that the first man from the parish to die in the First World War was a Robert Laidlaw, who shared a name — and, no doubt, bloodlines — with Alice's Canadian father.

Jane and I returned to the car and headed west with mounting excitement. Now the Ettrick River was narrowing to the point that we could imagine Will o' Phaup trying one of his legendary leaps (encompassing "frolic, agility and strength") across it. Soon the farms were falling away, the road becoming a track. We parked the car and started to walk in to Potburn, the farm that lies before Far Hope. To our relief, Potburn proved to be deserted, occupied only by sparrows and finches, although the curtains in the windows hinted at recent occupancy. Now the buildings of Far Hope were in plain sight.

"Far Hope" indeed. It was supposedly the highest farm in Scotland, a designation that held no prospect of rich land. Our map told us that the hills that rose right behind the low stone house were the spine of Scotland. Just over their tops the rainwater drained west into the Solway, and the Atlantic, a fact that I was able to pass on to Alice.

The old farm buildings were a surprise and a delight. Usually a visit to a 300-year-old farm site will produce either a heap of rubble showing only bare outlines or, perhaps worse, a working farm, where literary intruders are not routinely welcomed, by man or dog. Miraculously, Far Hope is preserved in something close to its original state, and is unoccupied, yet at the same time open to all comers as a "bothy" (a rough sleeping hostel) on the walking trail known as the Southern Upland Way.

Inside, a literary tourist can pace the rough stone floor, seeing the original kitchen layout around the fireplace, and can easily imagine the old family's straw bedding in place. A stroll around the silent outbuildings reveals where the horse was stabled, and the milk-providing cow. Sheep pens, the farm's raison d'être, are prominent, and the Ettrick provides running water at the door.

Before we left, I wrote in the bothy visitor's book an account of Alice Munro's career, and its links to this small, humble place. I hope that many Canadians familiar with Alice's work, especially *The View from Castle Rock*, will tear themselves away from the fleshpots of Edinburgh and make the pilgrimage to Far Hope.

Failing that, there is another Alice Munro pilgrimage, one much closer to home. Roughly an hour outside Toronto, just north and west of the town of Milton, lies the Boston Church. It is named after Thomas Boston, the minister of, yes, Ettrick Kirk, because so many of his former parishioners chose to come to this area, to settle in this heavily Scottish part of what was then called Canada West. A plaque outside the grey Gothic Revival building notes that the first service was held in 1820, while the handsome building itself was "designed and constructed in 1868 by Charles Blackwood, Thomas Henderson and congregation volunteers from Esquesing's Scotch block." The setting, on a road lined with old maple trees running northwest towards the Halton Hills, is idyllic, with the property itself adorned by maples, cedars, lilacs, and a great weeping willow, with few other buildings in sight. As you approach the church door, turn to the nearest corner on the left, and there you will find the graves devoted to the Laidlaws, Alice's ancestors. Several of these graves have ancient tombstones giving details of the lives of those interred beneath them, including old James Laidlaw Senior, born in Ettrick Forest, Scotland, in 1763, who came to Esquesing in 1817, and died in 1826. And all of this history is to be found, as Alice writes, "almost within sight, and well within sound, of Highway 401 north of Milton, which at that spot may be the busiest road in Canada."

Alice's ancestors moved farther west from here, as pioneers, into the uncleared forest and bush of Southwestern Ontario's Huron County. We get a very clear picture of what life was like for them in Alice's story, "A Wilderness Station," where after a tree-felling accident one character ends up in the Goderich jail. That ancient jail still stands, as a tourist attraction, in the town that anchors the county at the Lake Huron shore. The huge lake has allowed travel industry copywriters to go wild with descriptions of "Ontario's West Coast," complete with dramatic photos of a summer sun sinking into its wide waters. But it is the undramatic landscape stretching east of Goderich — a flat, partly wooded stretch of farming country with no striking natural features — that has become known to numberless readers as "Alice Munro Country."

The word "undramatic" also applies to the history of the area, settled in the nineteenth century by immigrants from Scotland, England, and Ireland, as shown by place names like Dunlop, Clinton, and the ominous Donnybrook. (My old friend Harry J. Boyle grew up near there, admired by young Alice as he walked to work at the Wingham radio station, on his way to a career at the CBC, and to another as the author of many books including *The Luck of the Irish*, and — because he was willing to go along with my mischievous title idea — as the author of record of *The Great Canadian Novel*.) There are other Irish traces in this heavily Scottish area. The nearby community of Dublin has a tiny river running through it. The local blend of sentiment and realism is reflected in the name given to that watercourse, "the Liffey Drain." This is not a land of Great Expectations.

No wars were fought with the Native people who lived here, no great battles with American invaders. Instead it was the scene of countless small heroic family battles, to fell the trees and clear the land, to build a cabin, to get the crops in; in short, to survive. To survive enough winters, in fact, to replace the cabin with a house, and in time to build the little towns with mills, and churches, and schools that dot today's settled landscape. These early struggles are neatly caught, I think, in the C.W. Jefferys drawing of brawny settlers straining to clear away giant tree trunks that I chose to put on the cover of an informative historical novel that I published about these pioneer days. It was called *The MacGregors*, and it was written by Alice's father, Robert Laidlaw.

For today's literary tourist the points of special interest in Huron County are *Clinton*, where Alice now lives, her privacy protected by kindly neighbours (although I, as a privileged visitor, can tell you that this woman who once wrote in A Laundry Room of Her Own, still has no writing room of her own where she can shut her door on a ringing phone, or on the general business of the household, including her husband, Gerry, rummaging around for a snack); *Goderich*, where she prefers to meet visiting journalists, and where the staff at her favourite restaurant on the hexagonal central square are only too happy to tell a visiting publisher, decisively, which potential book cover should be chosen for Alice's next work, and where she is to be met, silver hair blowing in the wind, strolling down by the harbour with Gerry; or *Blyth*, where her father had strong links and she plans to be buried, and where, as Val Ross's perfect story showed, she could be counted on to roll up her sleeves and pitch in as a waitress to help raise funds for the local theatre, where, amazingly, she once played a small part onstage; or the lakeside town of *Bayfield*, where she enjoys the little bookstore, where she once staged a "Long Pen" event to help her friend Margaret Atwood; or, above all, *Wingham*, her birthplace, where the main street is graced by the Alice Munro Literary Garden. In Wingham you will also find a leaflet that will help visitors to follow an Alice Munro walking tour that begins at the house where she grew up. In an ideal world that house will soon be bought by sensible authorities aware that for the next century it can be a well used tourist centre for the many people from around the world who will wish to see "Alice Munro Country" for themselves.

The day in 2002 that the attractive little literary garden was opened in Wingham, Jane and I cut short our honeymoon (are you feeling sorry for her yet?) in order to attend the happy festivities. Speeches were given by old friends like David Staines and Alice's effervescent agent, Ginger Barber, in the grand old Victorian Opera House across Josephine Street from the garden, while Alice, who knew her expected role, smiled serenely beneath a large, flowered hat. It was the only time in my life when I earned a warm round of applause simply by revealing that my middle name is — Maitland! The audience knew that the Maitland River, and its many branches, dominates the Huron County landscape. I knew that not every publisher is lucky enough to have a mother whose uncommon surname was sure to strike Alice as a link with home.

The fine Canadian literary critic Philip Marchand concisely explained the importance of these settings to Alice and her work — and vice versa — in a 2009 review of *Too Much Happiness*:

> If Alice Munro had never existed, part of the soul of Canada would have remained inarticulate, forgotten, submerged. The locus of this Canadian scene rendered so powerfully in her fiction is rural Southwestern Ontario, settled by Scotch Presbyterians, Congregationalists and Methodists from the north of England . . . Everything in her world comes back to that small-town milieu of pokey little stores, dull Sunday-afternoon dinners with aunts and uncles, a mentality made up of respect for hard work, resentment of show-offs and dim memories of Calvinist terrors.

Hmm — resentment of show-offs.

The point of a stroll through these little towns, or a drive along the placid roads dotted with mixed farms (with patches of bush still preserved in the background as a source of firewood or maple syrup) is that what you see around you is so *ordinary*. It's a dull, everyday landscape. And Alice Munro the magician has waved her wand over this undramatic scene, and made it the setting for some of the most astonishing and thrilling short stories ever seen. She has made the lives of people like a chambermaid at the Blue Spruce Inn in Huron County the stuff of world literature. For Alice Munro knows Huron County in her bones. She has been determined to catch it on paper, just as her character Del in *Lives of Girls and Women* hoped: "What I wanted was every last thing, every layer of speech and thought, stroke of light on bark or walls, every smell, pothole, pain, crack, delusion, held still and held together — radiant, everlasting."

Robert Thacker's splendid biography makes it unnecessary for me to run through Alice's life story in any detail, beyond the main points. She was born in the summer of 1931, in Wingham, which was then a town of about 3,000 people. Her father had a failing fox farm on the wrong side of town, and her mother, a former teacher, fell ill early with Parkinson's Disease and died young. Alice was a bright girl who did well in school and went on to the University of Western Ontario, in the conservative, yellow-brick city of London, the regional centre. After two penny-pinching years that saw Alice selling her blood for cash, lack of funds forced her to drop out. But she had met James Armstrong Munro, a fellow student, and soon moved to Vancouver with him as his wife. Jim and she raised three daughters (Sheila, Jenny, and Andrea) there and in Victoria, where the two established a fine bookstore, still going strong.

Sheila Munro's memoir, *Lives of Mothers and Daughters*, tells us a lot about Alice the mother. We know from Robert Thacker's careful account that she started trying her hand as a short story writer in 1953, and after years of contributing stories to little magazines and to the CBC (where a producer named Bob Weaver was her mentor, and her first link with the writing world) she became "an overnight sensation" when her first book, *Dance of the Happy Shades*, came out in 1968 and won the Governor General's Award. The local paper, the Victoria *Times Colonist* (where I once was charmed to see an editor distribute home-laid eggs to colleagues/customers) greeted that book with a headline "Housewife Finds Time to Write Short Stories."

When her marriage broke down, Alice returned home to Southwestern Ontario, where she soon met a contemporary, Gerry Fremlin, who remembered her fondly. They still live together, thirty-five years later, in Clinton, only thirty kilometres away from Wingham. Robert Thacker sees huge significance in the fact that after brief spells in London and Toronto (where at York University she tried her hand at teaching writing, and had the courage to quit when she realized that she was not a good teacher) Alice moved *all the way home*, to Huron County. Certainly, although she has written a number of fine stories set on the West Coast (or in Miles City, Montana, come to think of it), it is Southwestern Ontario that has most reliably inspired her writing.

My own contact with Alice — so generously described by her in the letter I have quoted early in the chapter, a letter I only got to see when I published Robert Thacker's brilliantly researched biography — began with a fan letter from me, followed by a meeting for lunch at the London downtown Holiday Inn. (I recently revisited it on a research trip, and must report that no plaque records our meeting, and even the name of the hotel has changed.) Alice has always been such a beautiful woman that I use the word "courtship" cautiously, but I was certainly courting her professionally, to assure her that she would be comfortable working with me (which took a few meetings), and to promise explicitly that I would never, ever, ask her for a novel.

You know the rest.

Before I came on the scene Alice had brought out *Lives of Girls and Women* (1971), which was unwisely published as a novel. (It's always better to under-claim and try for a Yes-And response, rather than the Yes-But response that the book received from people who liked it, yes, but felt that it wasn't really a novel.) Then came a fine short story collection called — in a typical Munro phrase that fore-tells trouble — *Something I've Been Meaning to Tell You* (1974). I recall an academic conference on Alice's work where I was used by Alice as an observer who could report to her what was being said about her work. I remember her genuine shock and outrage at the waste of an intelligent teacher's time when I reported that one speaker, a well-paid professor, had spent much ingenuity and effort proving that *Something* . . . was really, secretly, a novel!

The very first book we worked on together was *Who Do You Think You Are?* (1978). Usually in those days all Canadian fiction titles had a cover produced by a commercial artist who was instructed to break out a new set of crayons and do a nice picture of the book's most exciting scene. I exaggerate, slightly. It was time, I thought, to change all that for Alice, by seeking out, and paying for, a fine, existing work by a recognized Canadian artist. Our cover, graced by the art of the magic realist Ken Danby, showed a reflective young woman, sitting on a patch of grass, hugging her knees. It went wonderfully well with Alice's stories about a girl growing up, and the double-edged title, *Who Do You Think You Are?*

A note about that title. As I've mentioned, the book's later publishers in the U.S. and the U.K. were alarmed that Malcolm Bradbury had recently used the same title (although book titles are not protected by copyright). So despite the perfect double meaning of the Canadian title, in the other editions the book came out under the feeble name *The Beggar Maid.* Under its proper title it won the Governor General's Award and smashed all existing sales records for a Canadian short story collection. And we never looked back.

The proud roll call of titles continues through the eighties and nineties. *The Moons of Jupiter, The Progress of Love* (the ransomed story collection), *Friend of My Youth, Open Secrets, The Love of a Good Woman.* In the new century the nine- or ten-story collections continued with *Hateship, Friendship, Courtship, Loveship, Marriage,* then *Runaway,* then *The View from Castle Rock,* followed by her 2009 collection, *Too Much Happiness.* My own role in all this was very easy. Basically I was hanging on for the ride, whooping.

I did the odd useful thing, like finding wonderful paintings by people like Alex Colville, Christopher and Mary Pratt, and Paul Peel, to give the books the right, elegant look. I knew that we had succeeded when other Canadian publishers started using Canadian magic realist paintings on their covers, as if waving and shouting, "Hey, this author's kind of like Alice Munro!" without the embarrassing business of having to state the claim openly, in words.

On occasion, I found a good title lurking inside a story. The final story in her most recent book was originally entitled "To the Danish Islands." I suggested to Alice that the main character's dying words,

"Too much happiness," would make a fine title. Then with that installed as the title of the longest story, I suggested that it made an ideal title for the whole book. And so it proved.

And I did try to keep track of all the prizes Alice was winning, all over the world, and the acres of ecstatic reviews that she was receiving. Soon my hardest editorial task was choosing which prizes and which review quotes I should use in my flap copy describing the book. As for my editing, actually working on the stories, that role shrank over the years (from the days, when, as Bob Thacker reminds me, I helpfully cut a long story into two) as Alice became such a popular writer in the *New Yorker* that all of the stories reached me carefully pre-edited. They also were benefitting from the wise editorial attention given by Anne Close, Alice's editor at Knopf in New York.

In fact, often my most useful role was twisting Alice's arm at two stages. First, to get her to agree that, oh all right, we really do have enough stories now to bring out a new collection. (This is a great joke between us, since Alice is famously reluctant to start the publicity windmill yet again. This means that when the issue is whether we should plan to publish a new collection, she has been known to say, "Oh, I guess there's no getting out of it," knowing that the arrival of another new book will complicate her life, even if she does no publicity.)

Then, once we've got the manuscript going through the publishing process, my main arm-twisting role is to stop Alice from trying to rewrite the book, compulsively polishing the proofs as they go to her for what we hope will be purely formal approval. There is a history here, of course. When our first book together, *Who Do You Think You Are?*, was at the printers (carrying along with it our hopes for a successful fall season) I returned home from Saturday shopping to find the phone ringing in the kitchen. It was Alice. Following what she once described as "country manners," she asked how I was, and the family. Then she asked how far advanced her new book was.

"Ah, I've got good news for you there, Alice," I said, "it's at the printers. They start printing on Monday."

"Well," said Alice, "I'd like to change the second half of the book. Is there time to change it all, from the first person to the third person, and add a new story?"

I was speechless. But we arranged that she would come in to the Macmillan office on Monday morning early to discuss it with my bosses while we stopped the printing. The Monday meeting, dammit, ended with everyone agreeing that Doug would read the revised version (including the new story, "Simon's Luck," which Alice felt altered the whole narrative structure) and see if it was such an improvement that it was worth redoing the whole book — and losing weeks, possibly months, of valuable selling time.

We reassembled at 2:00 and I agreed that, yes, Alice was right, and this *was* better, so we should scrap the second half, re-typeset it (including "Simon's Luck") and publish the book later, and damn the torpedoes. As it happened, the printers were so thrilled by this historic high drama that we only lost about ten days of selling time. So it all worked out, and the world got a wonderful, prize-winning book. And Alice, as I had warned her, had to pay the financial penalty for making excessive late changes.

"You made Alice Munro pay a penalty?" scandalized readers may ask. Yes, that was the deal. And I know that Alice expected nothing less, true to her Calvinist Presbyterian background, which does not favour anyone expecting special treatment in this world. I had a flash of similar awareness once when I was visiting Alice in Comox, her B.C. summer home. Our planned dinner was cancelled when Alice had to be taken to the local emergency ward. I tracked her down there, and we chatted as she lay on a bed, awaiting the doctor. When he arrived, I got up from my seat and made to leave. I was just starting to joke with the doctor that I hoped he'd do a good job, since this was a pretty important patient, when I stopped, aware that Alice would not want that. I clapped her on the ankle, and left. Years later, in 2005, when Alice graciously spoke at the Scot of the Year Award ceremony, she complained that I was so physically undemonstrative that she had come that evening in the hope of getting her first hug from me.

When people ask me what Alice Munro is really like, I try to deal with the two halves of the complete Alice. One is the frowning, concerned good citizen, determined to do The Right Thing, and worrying her way towards it. That's the Alice who some years ago quietly put me under pressure to make sure that her next book was printed on recycled environmentally friendly (and more expensive) paper. And this, I should note, was at a time when using recycled paper in books was still rare, and associated with new fringe books by small publishers, not major bestsellers by major writers published by major houses. So her choice had a huge impact.

That's the same Alice who travelled for hours to appear onstage at Massey Hall in Toronto at a rally supporting CBC workers who had been, in effect, locked out. Alice spoke simply and directly about what CBC radio had meant to her as a young girl with ideas growing up in a small town. Then she spoke affectionately about what the support of Robert Weaver, the producer of CBC's *Anthology*, had meant to her in the early, lonely years. Echoes of the ovation she received still ring around the corners of the old hall.

And that, of course, is the same Alice Munro who in 2009 withdrew her new book from the Giller Prize competition, on the grounds that she had won the prize twice already, so she wanted to step aside to make room for a younger writer. This selfless decision — which in the role of selfish, greedy publisher I fought against for weeks, until I saw that Alice's mind was made up — meant that the book lost not only potential prize money, but potential sales and publicity worth hundreds of thousands of dollars. With an earlier book Alice had put herself out of the running for these rewards by agreeing to become a Giller Prize juror that year. "Alice," I said, aghast, "why didn't you ask me about this?"

"Because I knew what you'd say," she replied, and laughed happily.

That's the other side of the complete Alice: she is very funny, and we spend a lot of our time together, on the phone or in person, laughing. I think people catch that when they hear her read her stories, in person or on tape; the stories are much funnier than expected and attract a lot of laughter when she reads them with all the right Huron County emphasis. But Alice in person is also very good company, and it's significant that in the fractious world of Canadian writing she has no enemies. W.P. Kinsella, reviewing *Too Much Happiness* in *BC Bookworld*, described that world as "rife with jealousies, feuds and petty backbiting." Yet he notes that "I have never heard anyone say anything unkind about Alice Munro, personally or professionally. When Alice wins a prize, other writers and critics are not lined up to name ten books that should have won." Even her famous reluctance to tour to promote a new book is based not on a reluctance to meet, and enjoy meeting, new people. On the contrary, it's because her frail health makes travel hard on her, especially when her day involves her in, say, solving the marital problems of the taxi driver who takes her to the radio station.

Our relationship is based on a long-running joke, to see who can "understate" the other, by being more dramatically low key. For example, when she wins another prize, I'll pass on the news as "not bad," and she'll agree, saying, "I suppose it's all right." A wiser head than mine might see this as significant, allowing this woman who grew up from birth believing that "showing off," to use Philip Marchand's phrase, was the ultimate sin ("Who Do You Think You Are?"), to cope with her success. Because, except in the rare case of the writer whose work is torn away from them, and published against their will, writers are indeed in the business of "showing off." They're all saying. "Look at me! Here's what I've written, I think you should pay attention to it!"

I'm the right partner for the low-key game. When Alice won a Giller Prize, I was sitting beside her. When the winner was announced — "ALICE MUNRO!" — there was a blare of triumphant music (possibly the theme from *Rocky*), searchlights caught and held us at the table, and everyone expected the usual Oscar-style ritual of publisher and author and agent hugging and air-kissing interminably for the cameras before the dazed winner ascends the stage. What Alice got from me was "Up you go," and she was on her way to the stage.

A sort of pinnacle of understatement was reached when Alice was nominated for a prize along with several other writers, and told me that she hoped that her friend X would be the one to win. When I heard the results, I phoned her to say that I had good news and bad news. The good news was that her friend X had won the prize. This was greeted with great pleasure on the Clinton end of the line. The bad news was that he had to share the prize . . . with you, Alice.

"Oh well," she said, "if he has to share it with someone, I guess it might as well be me."

It's hard to beat her at this game. She even plays it, for fun, in her stories. In "Fiction," for example, in her 2009 collection, *Too Much Happiness*, the central character is horrified to find that she appears as a manipulative adult in a former pupil's new book: "A collection of stories, not a novel. This in itself is a disappointment. It seems to diminish the book's authority, making the author seem like somebody who is just hanging on to the gates of Literature, rather than safely settled inside."

On the subject of disappointment, I have developed a flourishing career as the man who disappoints audiences by standing in for Alice when she wins awards. This has happened so often that at any event when I hear the words, "Unfortunately, Alice Munro . . ." I start to move towards the stage. It's a terrible thing to see a roomful of heads slump in sorrow, even something approaching disgust, as you approach the microphone. Sometimes it's more personal. Once at a Royal York Hotel event for the nation's booksellers, Stuart McLean, the MC, excitedly announced Alice as the winner. When I emerged out of the bright lights to mount the stage, Stuart said nothing about "my old friend Doug Gibson," although I had provided him with weekly movie reviews for three years on the CBC program, *Sunday Morning*, that he produced. Instead, with obvious dismay, he said, in sinking tones, "Awww . . . it's Doug."

Much more enjoyable are the times when I'm able to see Alice attend to receive an award. The most exciting such event was in 2009 in Dublin (the one with the full-size Liffey) when Alice won the worldwide prize awarded for a body of work, the Man Booker Prize. Since M&S was going through the financial hard times endemic to Canadian publishing, and decided that it could not afford to send me to see Alice win, I transformed myself into a journalist covering the event for the *Globe and Mail*. Typing on my hotel bed, this *Globe* correspondent reported, after a suitable opening:

London's *Observer* believes that, when compared with the Nobel, this prize (presented Thursday for only the third time) "is rapidly becoming the more significant award." And although the thirteen other nominees include Peter Carey, E.L. Doctorow, James Kelman, Maria Vargas Llosa and V.S. Naipaul, there is a general sense of pleasure in the literary world that Alice has received this recognition. James Wood, the Atlantic-spanning critic who writes for the *Guardian* and the *New Yorker*, is wise in the ways of literary juries; at the Griffin Prize in Toronto he quietly expressed his approval of Alice's win. "Sometimes," he said, "they get it right."

Getting it right this year involves choosing the perfect city for a literary prize-giving. As a bookish bastion, Dublin needs no defense . . .

What remains is a matchless literary setting. En route to the opening reception, the dazzled party-goers find themselves lingering over *The Book of Kells*, arguably the Western world's most beautiful illuminated manuscript. It was rescued from the Scottish island of Iona when the Celtic world was both tight-knit and afflicted by Vikings, who had no use for books, unless they wanted to get warm.

Upstairs the 200-strong crowd moves into one of the world's great temples to the book, the Long Room in the Old Library, a jaw dropping sixty-five metres of tall barrel-vaulted glory, all rich brown wood and gilded paint and marble busts and 200,000 ancient books.

At the champagne reception in the library, Alice sits quietly, her silver hair matched by a slim silver gown. Somehow she has mastered the art of shy vivacity, and people enjoy meeting her. Tonight she prefers to reserve her energies until the award ceremony is over.

In truth, I was appalled to find her sitting alone while the party in her honour twittered on around her. Would she like to meet anyone? No, she said, she was just taking it easy, And then, a flash of Huron County. "They might change their mind," she said, darkly.

They did not change their mind, and in accepting the award Alice rose to the occasion. She recalled being seven years old, pacing in her backyard, trying to find a way to make Hans Christian Andersen's story *The Little Mermaid* have a happy ending. She spoke of a writing life since then spent "always fooling around with what you find . . . This is what you want to do with your time — and people give you a prize for it!" Everyone beamed, Canadians most of all.

The *Globe* story ends: "The hours race by until 'Carriages' are due at eleven. Mindful of Cinderella's fate, Alice leaves early. We move out into the eighteenth-century night, reflecting that, as Oscar Wilde might have said, sometimes nice writers do finish first."

"Shy vivacity" is good, I think. Anyone who has seen Alice at a literary party — or even at a book-signing session — will know what I mean. The usual pattern at book signings is for bright, articulate people to spend twenty minutes lining up to meet Alice when she signs their book. I, hovering helpfully, know what happens next. They reach Alice, and their carefully prepared speech becomes "I

just . . . oh, your stories, I mean — it's so wonderful, I really . . ."
And Alice kindly rescues them from more blurting, and the book is
signed, and they float off.

By now, as Bob Thacker's biography shows, Alice's work has been
studied and dissected by hundreds of scholars around the world.
One of the best studies to reach my eyes is the introduction to *Alice
Munro's Selected Stories* by Margaret Atwood. She begins by telling us
flatly that "Alice Munro is among the major writers of English fiction of our time. . . . Among writers themselves, her name is spoken
in hushed tones."

To me, one of her most perceptive points is how often the stories
deal with sex. In Atwood's words, "Pushing the sexual boundaries
is distinctly thrilling for many a Munro woman." As Exhibit A, I
would propose the story "Differently," in which a working mother
accepts a ride home on a motorbike from a dangerously attractive
man, and ends up tussling in the scrubby bushes at the edge of a
Victoria waterfront park. She returns home, telling the babysitter
that she's late because her car wouldn't start. "Her hair was wild, her
lips were swollen, her clothes were full of sand."

One of the things that most fascinates scholars and reviewers
about Alice is how her work keeps changing, so that one of the
hardest sentences for anyone to complete is one that begins, "All
Alice Munro stories . . ." Over the years, Alice's stories have tended
to get longer, and one by one, she has demolished all of the traditional barriers to where the short story supposedly can go.

Think about it. Alice Munro's individual stories may range across
generations and span a century, and they may involve several narra-
tors. These storytellers may be shy teenagers or fierce grandmothers
or any age in between, and they may be men or women. Or the storyteller may be a third-person narrator, more or less omniscient. The
stories may seem to proceed backwards in an artless sort of way that
somehow works. Some readers will laugh out loud at some shaft of
delicious, comic irony, while others will thrill to the sudden, shuddering horrors that are revealed. Some of the incidents clearly spring
from the author's own life, others do not.

The setting will usually be Alice Munro country, or the Canadian
west coast. Then, as if to defy all categories, as if to say, "I'll show

you!," Alice will set a story in Australia, or Scotland, or even in the mountains of Albania almost a century ago. Or she will devote over fifty pages (in *Too Much Happiness*) to the life of a nineteenth-century female Russian mathematical genius.

All this range of material and styles is, of course, populated by characters who become real people, whether they are chambermaids at the Blue Spruce Inn, professors, music teachers, carpenters, librarians, or farmers growing beans in Huron County. No wonder the London *Times* recently reviewed one of her books with the words: "When reading her work it is difficult to remember why the novel was ever invented." The jury for the International Man Booker Prize struck the same note. "She brings as much depth, wisdom and precision to every story as most novelists bring to a lifetime of work."

Comparisons with Chekhov, Flaubert, and other greats of short fiction abound, as reviewers run out of superlatives. It's clear that in the future the single word "Munro" will be used like "Austen" or "Dickens" in literature courses. Some years ago the *Atlantic* magazine's reviewer stated, with a confidence that would impress Saint Peter, "Alice Munro is the living writer most likely to be read in a hundred years' time."

Not bad, eh?

# "What Happens After My Book Is Published?"

In my role as publisher, first at Macmillan of Canada, then at McClelland & Stewart (a period spanning almost precisely twenty-five years) I used to supply this document — headed "AWFUL WARNINGS" — to new authors.

I was pleased to note that the initial reaction was invariably an amused one. About six months later, however, a much more thoughtful letter tended to follow. I should stress that the conditions described here are not restricted to Canada. These warnings were picked up and republished in the U.S., the U.K., and Australia. I like to think that the rest of the world is free of the imperfections mentioned here.

Interestingly, the document fell into the hands of the editors of *Saturday Night* magazine, who published it. This factual working document was published there as "Humour," and was nominated for a National Magazine Award in that category. Fortunately a very witty article in French won the prize, saving me the embarrassment of explaining to the world that this was a realistic piece of advice, not humour.

Now that I have crossed No Man's Land and become an author myself, I hope that what follows will not apply to me, and that my book will prove to be, er, exceptional.

## GENERAL ADVICE

On the day your book is published, the world will roll merrily along, totally oblivious to the new book's existence and totally unaffected by it. This "business as usual" attitude may anger and depress you. Over the next few months, however, you are in for a series of even greater irritations and disappointments. I have listed them for you here, in their main categories: forewarned is forearmed.

## BOOKSTORES

Do not expect to see your book in a bookstore window. This will never happen. Other people will tell you that they have seen it in such-and-such a window, but when you go there you will find the window devoted to a display of skis or tennis rackets, looming over a selection of the appropriate how-to books — or a display of large books on Oriental art that are now on sale. If by some fluke you do find a copy of your book in a window display, it will have toppled over and will be sun-bleached, warped, and topped by dead flies.

You will never find your books in any bookstore. Even stores checked by the publisher's representative earlier that day will mysteriously lose all their copies between his departure and your arrival. Mountains of copies prominently displayed will mysteriously melt away. They will, of course, reappear as soon as you leave. Stock-taking, transferral of stock around the store by the clerks, or large-scale shoplifting by thieves with a conscience — all of these will be used to explain this phenomenon. Such explanations are far-fetched; in fact, it is a physical law of the universe that no bookstore can contain both an author and stock of her books — positives repel.

Never pose as a member of the public asking for a copy of your book in the bookstore. You will be told, first, that you have the title wrong, or the author's name wrong. You will then be told that the book is (a) out of stock; (b) not yet published; (c) long out of print; or (d) disgusting, and not the sort of thing that the store would have on its shelves. If you are unwise enough to ask the clerk how the book is selling, you will be told that there is no demand for it because it is overpriced, in the wrong format, and/or badly written; a rival book on the same subject will then be warmly recommended.

If you ask a bookseller why the book is not in stock, or not selling well, he will blame the publisher.

## FRIENDS

As soon as the book is published, you will find yourself expected to supply a free copy to everyone in the country whom you know by name. This includes everyone in your neighbourhood, every relative with whom you are still on speaking terms, the nice couple you met on holiday three years ago, and the plumber who fixed your sink last winter. You will suffer from the common belief that an author receives at least one thousand free copies of her book, to keep in cartons in her basement or garage or under her bed until she can give them away to all of her deserving friends.

When approached by one of these deserving friends and asked, slyly or openly, for a free copy, angrily blame your tight-fisted publisher for the fact that you have no more free copies to give. (Please feel free to use my name if personal vilification will make your performance more impressive.) Then announce that you happen, by good fortune, to be passing by a bookstore, and offer to lead your friend there so that you can autograph his copy with a message of warm wishes. He will remember a previous appointment, but in time he may be shamed into buying a copy — although only an optimist would regard this as likely.

Your friends will assume that there will be a massive and lavish party to launch the book, to which they will be invited. Blame your publisher for being too stingy to pay for such a party, and assure all of your friends that they would indeed have been invited.

Friends will call you up at 11 p.m. on a Saturday to report that their local store has no stock of your book, and that the clerk at the cash register had never even heard of it. Blame your publisher for this state of affairs, hang up, and console yourself with the thought that a weaker version of the law regarding authors and their books in bookstores applies to authors' friends: an author's friend will *almost* never find a copy of the author's book in any bookstore.

Friends will eagerly supply you with a list of misprints in the book. Accept the list, however questionable, with thanks, and blame the publisher.

Some friends will try to cheer you by announcing that even though the book may not be selling in the bookstores, there is a long waiting list for it at their library. If they blame this waiting list for the fact that they themselves have not yet been able to read your book, refrain from forcing the appropriate number of dollars into their hands and suggesting that they will now be able to buy a copy. This is unprofessional behaviour.

Friends will remember reading, or seeing, or hearing bad reviews of your books. They will be able to recreate these reviews in excruciating detail. Good reviews will, however, be remembered only vaguely, and you will be assured only that the reviewer seemed to like the book all right, for the most part.

## REVIEWS

All reviews of your book will appear either too early or too late. If challenged, the publication in question will blame this state of affairs on your publisher.

Do not, ever, expect to read a review of your book that will strike you as constructive and helpful to you in perfecting your craft as a writer. These reviews do not exist — nor do saintly authors.

You will find that in the print media, reviews fall into six categories:

*good reviews* that consist of the cover copy, slightly rewritten, and that summarize the book fairly accurately and make it sound interesting and worth buying; these reviews are rare.

*good reviews* that are not based on the cover copy but that summarize the book fairly accurately and make it sound interesting and worth buying; these reviews are *very* rare.

*good reviews* that misrepresent the book totally, praising its delicious constant irony when you have carefully kept a serious tone throughout, and so on; such reviews are not as rare as they should be.

*balanced reviews* that find much to praise in the book but work inevitably up to a "however" near the end of the review, designed (in approved Canadian style) to keep the author humble; these reviews make the reviewer feel very judicious, and are the most common of all.

*bad reviews* that make it clear that the reviewer could write a much better book himself; if the reviewer is a reporter on the paper concerned, the review will almost certainly be of this type.

*bad reviews* written by the man known to be your worst enemy in the world; he has been given your book to review because the book editor would like a little blood and guts in his page. The blood and the guts are yours. Here, as in all dealings with reviews and reviewers, neither you nor your mother should become involved in any correspondence without consulting your publisher.

## INTERVIEWS

If you are interviewed about your books for a magazine or newspaper article, do not be surprised if the article concentrates on your interest in growing tomatoes, or on the happy warmth that pervades your household, while completely ignoring your book and your writing; these interviews are intended to add colour to the dull fogies that we all know authors to be.

If you are interviewed on radio or TV, assume that your interviewer has not read your book. Many interviewers in these fields take a perverse pride in having done as little preparation as possible for the interview; a ten-second glance at the book jacket before the interview begins is apparently regarded as sufficient in a field where the badge of true professionalism is the ability to gabble cheerfully and apparently intelligently about subjects of which one is totally ignorant. In these circumstances, your role is to direct the interview. You know what the book is about, the interviewer does not, so you should steer his questions around to what they should be. His only concern is to avoid dead air, so he will have no objections, provided you refrain from showing the audience the alarming depth of his ignorance.

If you are foolish enough to ask (off camera, of course) why the interviewer has not read your book, he will blame the publisher for not sending him a copy. The accusation will be untrue; book publishers, like the weather, exist largely to provide a topic of conversation on which people of all sorts can comfortably agree.

## AUTOGRAPH SESSIONS

Autographing events in bookstores take place only because bookstore managers are incurable optimists. All past experience shows that only people who are famous for not writing books (e.g., sports stars, movie stars, TV stars, axe murderers, former prime ministers, or these people's estranged lovers) attract satisfactory crowds into a bookstore. Yet the chances are that you will be invited to come along to an autographing session at some point in the life of your book.

Always accept such invitations. As you sit there flanked by towers of unsold copies of your book and backed by a blown-up photograph of yourself taken fifteen years ago, you will have a wonderful opportunity to get to know a bookstore manager. He and his staff will look at their watches a lot and mention, by name, several of the customers who had expressed eagerness to come in and meet you, but who obviously have been prevented from doing so because it is so cold/hot/icy/wet/windy/good for gardening after the wet/windy spell. The day of the week will also be blamed, and the time of day (it is extremely impolite for you to ask who decided on the timing of the event) and, above all, the fact that the publisher failed to pull his weight in advertising the event properly. Deflect the conversation from this congenial topic and ask questions that will cast light on the bookstore staff's love and knowledge of books. This may prove to be illuminating. It may also leave the staff with the impression that you are an interested, caring person; to assuage their guilt they will then push your book.

When your time is up, console yourself with the thought that nobody who is not an axe murderer, etc., is ever besieged by lines of smiling book-buyers eager to get the author's signature on their new purchase. In judging autographing sessions, remember Gibson's Golden Rule: selling one book in a half-hour autographing session is average, selling more is a success, selling fewer is a disappointment.

Two further points. Never buy any books in the store in the course of your visit; it may seem a tempting way to pass the empty minutes, but is highly unprofessional. And never agree to participate in a joint autographing session with another author. The phrase "healthy competition" does not apply to such an event.

## READINGS

For similar reasons, beware of giving any public readings in tandem with authors who are practised public performers, old troupers who know how to milk a laugh, have the audience eating out of the palm of their hand, and so on. In these circumstances your only sensible course is to keep your reading brief and audible, and to mention the name of your book loudly at the beginning and end. A dangerous but effective tactic if you have to follow the old trouper is to affect a stutter, bravely overcome. But on no account listen to or compare the applause that greets your reading and his.

Unfortunately, giving a reading on your own is even worse. Here precisely the same factors apply as those affecting bookstore autographing. The chairman of the event will gaze worriedly around the empty hall, naming some of the many people who were eager to come, but prevented by the weather being so hot/cold/icy/windy, etc. After waiting an extra twenty minutes, he will introduce you, getting either the book title or your name wrong (rarely both), then slump into an apparent coma while you read. He will awaken only to thank you briefly, and to explain why he won't be able to give you a ride back as originally planned.

Another Golden Rule: any reading where the audience exceeds the total of the chairman, the publisher's local representative, and the man who has to close the hall *plus one* can be considered a success. Thus all readings, like all autographings, should be gladly accepted as a means of spreading your name around.

Unfortunately, while autographings tend to suffer from an oversupply of copies of your book, copies will rarely be available for sale at your readings, and never at your well-attended readings. Arrangements will have been made for their sale on the spot by a local bookseller, but they will have fallen through. Blame your publisher.

Learn all of the above rules by heart. Please remember that every author always goes through a period of believing that the world is in a conspiracy to prevent her book being talked about and bought. If you remember this, you may save yourself a little heartbreak, but not much. If the agony becomes too much to bear, blame your publisher. The agony will slowly dissolve, and in time you may think about writing another book.

As you can see, it's been a lot of fun. I'm grateful to all of the authors, publishing colleagues, and people in the wider book world who shared my journey over the years, advancing my education as we bumped along together, jumping on or off the bus as it reached their stop.

Shrewd readers — this means you — will notice that this book contains not only condensed biographies of twenty-one noteworthy authors, but also a couple of other lesser themes. The first is my own discovery of the world of books and my education in it, until as the president and publisher of McClelland & Stewart — "the Canadian Publishers" we called ourselves then — I had reached the post-graduate level.

The second is my discovery of Canada. You'll find that this book takes you with me from Harold Horwood's Newfoundland and Labrador all the way to Haida Gwaii, within sight of Alaska, and from the Arctic landscape of James Houston's Cape Dorset far south to Alistair MacLeod's house in Windsor, the scene of the famous "home invasion," where the intruder got away with a priceless manuscript. We go from risking a fight in the mean streets of Saskatoon ("Are these women's boots?") to risking life and limb crossing a traffic-infested street in Montreal with the fearless Pierre Trudeau ("Run!"). I am grateful — in most cases — to the people who showed me so many different aspects of this massive country.

As for the settings of the books described here, they represent dozens of different Canadas: Morley Callaghan's Rosedale; Jack Hodgins' Port Annie, in the wake of a Pacific tsunami; Alan Fry's tepee in the Yukon; Andy Russell's grizzly-rich Rockies; Charles Ritchie's genteel Halifax and Barry Broadfoot's Depression-hit Vancouver; W.O. Mitchell's Prairies; Brian Mulroney's boyhood

Baie Comeau; and the part of Southwestern Ontario now known as Alice Munro Country.

Away from these imagined scenes, the book deals with my vividly remembered physical pleasures: scrambling aboard a Zodiac at Ivujivik, a local story of Henry Hudson ringing in my ears; dumping my kayak in the Tlell River beside James Houston's cottage, or swimming there under Jane's eye; paddling on the Red River in Winnipeg in *Orellana*, the canoe that took Don Starkell all the way to the Amazon; roaming around Lost Mountain Lake with Trevor Herriot, under Saskatchewan skies alive with thousands of southbound snow geese; playing tennis in Hugh MacLennan's North Hatley; and square dancing in Cape Breton with Anita and Alistair MacLeod and their friends.

All great fun (it's surely no accident that the memoir of the great Macmillan of Canada publisher John Gray is entitled *Fun Tomorrow*) and all due to the kindness of my hosts and friends across the country, much too numerous to list. I hope they will be pleased by what they read here.

Some weeks after I finished writing this book, I was invited to give a talk at Toronto's Arts and Letters Club. My choice of title was significant. "Harder Than I Thought: A Publisher Tries to Write a Book." As Christina McCall might have put it, "Lord knows, if any publisher should have been ready for writing a book, it was Doug Gibson." After all, I had edited over a hundred books and published thousands. I had written lots of newspaper articles over the years, and some longer magazine pieces, along with chapters for anthologies. I had written over a hundred weekly movie reviews for CBC Radio and never once missed a deadline. As the ultimate preparation I had edited and published Harry Bruce's delightful book *Page Fright: Foibles and Fetishes of Famous Writers*, which lists, hilariously, the tricks that authors through the ages have adopted simply to keep the words coming.

So in theory I was ready.

Yet to my dismay, the book refused to write itself. Months went by as I sat thinking — or deciding that the leaves outside needed raking, or that the refrigerator required checking. During this time two things happened. My friends in the writing world were — let's say, not unamused — to learn that Gibson, the fierce wielder of deadlines in a previous life, was having trouble writing his book. Much wry pleasure ensued.

The second development, however, was that people rallied round, expressing support at a time when the news that some people really would be keen to read this damned book was very welcome. A visit to the Writers' Union AGM (I am an honorary member, keen to earn *real* membership) showed that I had a supportive peer group, and that — surprise! — only writers really understand what writing a book is like.

During the difficult days of writing, I was encouraged by the kindly interest of relatives, neighbours ("How's the book coming?"), and friends like Alan Twigg, Hal Wake, Sid Marty, Richard Bachmann, Bryan Prince, Ian Elliot, Ernest Hillen, Wayne Grady, Ben McNally, Erna Paris, Andy Schroeder, Charles and Nancy Gordon, Roy MacGregor, Michael Enright, Martin O'Malley, John O'Leary, Bill Harnum and Kathy Lowinger, Bob MacArthur, Richard and Nancy Self, Nancy Naylor and Terry Fallis, Helen Walsh, Gerald Filson, Candy Paltiel, John Pearce, Linwood Barclay, David Carpenter, Keith Spicer, Robert Thacker, beery Nick Pashley, Ken McGoogan, and many others whom I now unintentionally neglect. Above all, I was helped by my young researching and transcribing friend, Nick Bartram. Later, I was greatly assisted by the expert Mark Abley, who commented helpfully on the finished manuscript.

Before I begin a chapter-by-chapter account of the people who helped me in specific areas, I'd like to pay a tribute to Roy MacSkimming, whose book on Canadian publishing in the last fifty years or so is a classic. *The Perilous Trade* is essential reading for anyone who wishes to learn more about the people who work behind the scenes on Canada's books, and who have played a role in making Canada's writers as world-famous as they are today. My own sketches of people like John Gray, Jack McClelland, and Mel Hurtig owe much to Roy's pioneering research and shrewd judgement, and I thank him here for it.

Writing twenty-one chapters about different authors meant that, in a minor way, I researched twenty-one different books. So it makes sense to give specific thanks, chapter by chapter:

*Stephen Leacock*: I thank David Manuel (who hired me into this unusual world, and gave me David Legate's book to edit), and David Legate, Robertson Davies, and Margaret MacMillan, author of the recent perceptive Leacock biography, who gave this chapter a very helpful reading. My thanks also to the *Globe and Mail*, which published my tale of the day I came to Canada, even describing me as a "publishing icon" in the process.

*Hugh MacLennan*: My long-term thanks go to my former in-laws, the Satterthwaite family, and to Sally, who introduced me to North Hatley; to Graham Fraser and Barbara Uteck; and to Hugh's publishers, including Macmillan of Canada, McClelland & Stewart, and the University of Ottawa Press, which published a portion of this essay in their 1994 collection of essays, *Hugh MacLennan*, edited by Frank M. Tierney. Notably, thanks are due to Elspeth Cameron for her biography, *Hugh MacLennan: A Writer's Life* (1981).

*R.D. Symons*: I am grateful to David Carpenter who asked me to contribute an entry on Bob Symons for the fine book he compiled, *A Literary History of Saskatchewan* (Coteau, 2011). A salute also to my friends at the Saskatchewan Writers' Guild, especially my old pal Guy Vanderhaeghe, and to Trevor Herriot, whose birding trip around Regina was so memorable. Even better, his helpful reading of this chapter introduced me to Dr. Stuart Houston, with *his* unforgettable story proving that laughter really can be the best medicine.

*Harold Horwood*: My thanks to Doubleday Canada for allowing me to quote from *Death on the Ice* and *White Eskimo*, and to the magical nature writer Harry Thurston (another Horwood admirer) who helpfully read and commented on this chapter. J.M. Sullivan's *Globe and Mail* obituary was notably helpful. Thanks also go to our Halifax hosts, Silver Donald Cameron and Marjorie Simmons, to Clive Doucet, who helped to make me an enthusiastic Acadian, and to the gallant Russell Jukes, who long ago drove me down to the Annapolis Basin to launch *Dancing on the Shore*, a classic now available through Lesley Choyce's Pottersfield Press.

*Barry Broadfoot*: Allan Fotheringham supplied some fine old *Sun* newsroom stories here, and the chapter was read and helpfully corrected by Vancouver's Alan Twigg, and by my lively historian friend Christopher Moore.

*Morley Callaghan*: Special thanks must go to Morley's younger son, Barry Callaghan, whose book, *Barrelhouse Kings* (1998), perfectly catches his father and that Rosedale house, and who helped me to recall the Dixieland music at Morley's memorable funeral. Thanks go also to the literary critics who are mentioned by name in the course of the essay, and to the *Canadian Author and Bookman*, which once hired me to write a tribute to Morley.

*W.O. Mitchell*: Special thanks here to my Peterborough friends Barb and Orm Mitchell (authors of the classic two-volume biography, *W.O.* and *Mitchell*), who read and corrected this chapter, to my many Calgary friends who loved W.O. and Merna, and to the *Globe and Mail*, who invited me to write W.O.'s obituary.

*Robertson Davies*: Similar thanks go to the *Globe and Mail*, for similar reasons, while special thanks are earned by Jennifer and Brenda Davies, who read this chapter so helpfully, and by John Fraser, the keeper of the Massey College flame. Of course, I owe Val Ross a lot for her richly informative book *Robertson Davies: A Portrait in Mosaic* (2008). As always, like all Davies scholars, I am indebted to the work of the official biographer, Judith Skelton Grant, for her *Robertson Davies: Man of Mystery* (1994).

*Jack Hodgins*: I am grateful to Ray Fazakas for his comprehensive book, *The Donnelly Album*, and to Robin Robertson for amassing the anthology *Mortification*, which contains such unspeakable examples of cruelty to authors. Jack Hodgins' publishers are to be thanked for the quotes given here, as he is for his kindness in checking the text.

*James Houston*: I owe a lot to Matthew Swan of Adventure Canada, whose generous invitation allowed me to see James Houston's Arctic for myself. Through the warm hospitality of James and Alice, I visited and enjoyed their homes in Stonington and in Haida Gwaii, where

Jane and I in due course got to know their friends like Barbara and Noel Wotten, thanks to the remarkable kindness of our Vancouver friends, Richard and Nancy Self. Special gratitude to Alice Houston and to John Houston (the maker of the fine documentary about his father) who both checked the chapter, which was to some extent based on the obituary that I wrote for the *Toronto Star*.

*Charles Ritchie*: My thanks go to the publishers of Charles Ritchie's remarkable diaries, and also of his correspondence with Elizabeth Bowen, *Love's Civil War* (2008), edited by Victoria Glendinning. Silver Donald Cameron helped me track down the Bower in Halifax and the old Ritchie summer base in Chester. Welcome stories were provided by John Fraser, Colin Robertson, Bob Rae, and Roy MacLaren, and less welcome ones about secret revisions by Ramsay Derry.

*Pierre Trudeau*: The *Globe and Mail* ran an early version of this memorial sketch, and it later appeared in Nancy Southam's selection *Pierre*, published in 2005 by McClelland & Stewart. I am grateful for the experience of working with the late Christina McCall and her husband Stephen Clarkson on their fine two-part biography, *Trudeau and Our Times* (1990). After *Young Trudeau* (2006), Max and Monique Nemni's ongoing intellectual biography of Trudeau will see the next volume, *Trudeau Transformed*, published by Douglas Gibson Books at McClelland & Stewart in 2011. He haunts us still.

*Mavis Gallant*: I am grateful to many Montreal-based friends for their help with this chapter, including Margaret Lefebvre and Magda and Bill "City Unique" Weintraub. Special thanks go to Norman and Pat Webster of Montreal and North Hatley, who were notably helpful. I am grateful, also, to many shrewd admirers of Mavis's writing, especially Janice Kulyk Keefer (author of *Reading Mavis Gallant* [1989]) and my versatile friend Linda Leith. I received great help from Timothy Taylor and Lynn Booth, the maker of the fine documentary *Paris Stories* (2006), and am especially grateful that my friend in Nantes, Christine Evain, that fine scholar of Canadian literature, allowed me to quote from her unpublished interviews with Mavis.

*Peter C. Newman*: The world is alive with Peter Newman tales (in his own words, he was "the most cussed and discussed" journalist of his generation) and this chapter is one of many beneficiaries. I thank all those named in the chapter, and those who chose to remain anonymous. Above all, I thank the main source, the indefatigable Peter C. Newman, who has continued to urge me to write this book, despite his awareness that some of its "Hey, Mabel!" moments may not show him in a saintly light. *Here Be Dragons*, indeed.

*Brian Mulroney*: Not all of the sources here are happy to be revealed, but an exception is Arthur Milnes, who worked tirelessly as the researcher on Brian Mulroney's *Memoirs*, and who kindly checked this chapter for me. And I thank Brian Mulroney, now dealing with diabetes, and his supportive family, all of whom I wish well.

*Robert Hunter*: This chapter was generously vetted by Bob's widow, Bobbi Hunter, while Mark Abley made some very useful editorial changes to the sections on my aboriginal contacts. Alan Fry contributed many helpful corrections.

*Alistair MacLeod*: Some of this chapter is based on an essay that I contributed to Guernica Editions' 2001 book *Alistair MacLeod: Essays on His Works* edited by Irene Guilford. I am pleased that Christine Evain allowed me to be present in May 2009, when she interviewed Alistair in a Windsor restaurant for several hours, while Alistair thoughtfully wrestled with her questions. I am equally pleased that in summer 2010, when Jane and I were visiting Cape Breton, Alistair and Anita took us square dancing for an evening, helping to round out my knowledge of Alistair and his world. Generously, Alistair checked this chapter for accuracy, even referring me to his son Daniel for confirmation, which was graciously and promptly supplied.

*Paul Martin*: My thanks here go to Paul Adams, journalist and academic, who worked behind the scenes with Paul Martin on his political memoirs, and took the time to check the accuracy of my recollections. Further thanks go to John Gray, the author whose 2003 biography, *Paul Martin: The Power of Ambition*, provided useful

insights, as well as some classic stories . . . "Still dead, Mr. Martin."
And thanks go to Paul Martin himself, who continues to be available, helping to make the world a little better, whether it's at the
Couchiching Conference, or at international high-finance sessions,
or in chats with aboriginal high-school students.

*Peter Gzowski*: This chapter draws on the *Quill & Quire* article that
I contributed after Peter's death. It was also influenced by R.B.
Fleming's 2010 biography, which I discuss at length in the text. I
thank my Brenneman in-laws for their useful information about life
in Galt when Peter was growing up there. The chapter was kindly
checked by Hal Wake, Peter's old colleague on *Morningside*, and by
Peter's daughter Alison Gzowski.

*Val Ross*: For this chapter I drew heavily from the words spoken at
Val Ross's memorial service at Massey College, and at the bitter-
sweet book launch that summer at the Tom Kierans–Mary Jernigan
home. A shorter version is to be found in the illustrated book in Val's
honour organized by Marcus Gee entitled *In Memory of Val Ross*. I
thank Mort Ritts and the rest of Val's family for their generous help
and understanding throughout.

*Alice Munro*: This chapter draws material from essays I have written
over the years about Alice, notably pieces in the *Globe and Mail* about
a trip Jane and I took to the Scottish Border country in search of the
farm her ancestors left in 1818, and my "Special Correspondent"
account of her Man-Booker Prize win in Dublin in June 2009. I thank
all of the scholars who are quoted in the course of this article, and
above all Robert Thacker, whose masterly biography, *Alice Munro:
Writing Her Lives* (updated, 2011) is essential reading for anyone
who wants to learn about Alice Munro. Finally, I'm grateful to the,
um, fairly good subject of the chapter, who kindly took the time to
read it, and who provided such a generous Introduction to this book.

*Epilogue*: As explained in the text, this jocular guide for authors
was intended to introduce them to a book publishing world where
Murphy's Law reigns unchallenged. It was, however, published as
humour by Robert Fulford's *Saturday Night*, and was nominated for

a National Magazine Award for Humour. As always, I am struck by Robert Fulford's ubiquitous role as an actor in — and shrewd commentator on — the world of Canadian writing.

I have restricted the primary subjects of this book to those authors I worked with *as an editor* (or auxiliary, in the case of Charles Ritchie). In my experience the author-editor relationship is a special one, affording special glimpses of an author at work. Since the editorial role is not a scientific one, but a matter of taste and judgement, no two editors will ever edit a book in exactly the same way. For the same reason, editors always stand to benefit from seeing other editors at work.

Over the years I have learned from working alongside editors such as David Manuel, Jennifer Glossop, Judith Finlayson, Carolyn Smart, Ken McVey, Virgil Duff, Eleanor Sinclair, Pat Kennedy, Dinah Forbes, Jonathan Webb, Alex Schultz, Ellen Seligman (who could certainly write an interesting book some day), Kathleen Richards, Anne Holloway, and Jan Walter and, more recently, among the younger generation, Aruna Dahanayake, Trena White, Elizabeth Kribs, Ainsley Sparkes, and Jenny Bradshaw. Freelance editors I have learned from include Barbara Czarnecki, Wendy Thomas, Heather Sangster, and others who know precisely who they are.

As for this book, it has benefitted from the help of my agent, my former sparring partner Michael Levine; the enthusiasm of my old publishing friend, Jack David of ECW (a man with an enviable collection of publishing memoirs); the shrewd and imaginative copy editing of Jennifer Knoch; and the help of the ECW professionals.

Non-editorial types who have helped me, in theory, to improve over the years include Lynne Schellenberg, the late Gail Stewart, Valerie Jacobs, Nancy Grossman, George Goodwin, Krys Ross, Kong Njo and his legions of clever designers, Scott Richardson (ditto), and at Macmillan in the old days, Rick Miller and his gang. The talent, skill, and care that goes into the tough, penny-pinched world of Canadian books is truly remarkable. I am thrilled that this book has been enriched by the author portraits contributed by the genius of my *Globe and Mail* cartoonist friend, Anthony Jenkins.

It's nice for me to think that this book will occupy the time of sales reps descended from generations of my friends in the business (Don

Sedgwick, Bill Hushion, Jack Jensen, Chris Keen, Nick Hunt, Alan McDougall, Mark Stanton, Pam Robinson, David Drew, Bonnie Harris, Sharon Bodnarchuk, Kerry Longpré, Trish Blaker, Ann Stevens, Peter Waldock, Jim Chalmers, Michael Reynolds, Craig Siddall, Tom Best, and so many more) and that diligent and tireless ECW publicist Simon Ware will be working the phones alongside the ghosts of publicists past. As for my own role in selling the book with personal appearances in friendly bookstores, or at literary festivals, or other events, it's going to be fun.

Finally, I now understand why all of the thousands of "Acknowledgements" that I've published over the years inevitably conclude with a tribute to the "long-suffering" or "endlessly supportive" family. In this case my thanks go to my daughters, Meg and Katie (and Lauren and Lindsay and Alistair), and to Jane. As I worked on the book and she noticed my disturbed sleeping patterns, she tentatively used the word "obsession."

"I think this is the way that books get written," I replied.

She was, as usual, right. But on this occasion I was right, too.

I hope I was right in every detail in the final book. If I wasn't, I am the one to blame — not the publisher.

Douglas Gibson
Toronto, February 2011